P9-DMH-310

WITHDRAWN

WITHDRAWN

EDUCATIONAL PSYCHOLOGY CASES FOR TEACHER DECISION-MAKING

GORDON E. GREENWOOD

H. THOMPSON FILLMER

University of Florida—Gainesville

 Merrill,
an imprint of Prentice Hall

Upper Saddle River, New Jersey   Columbus, Ohio

Library of Congress Cataloging-in-Publication Data
Greenwood, Gordon, E.
    Educational psychology cases for teacher decision-making / by
Gordon E. Greenwood and H. Thompson Fillmer
      p. cm.
    Includes bibliographical references.
    ISBN 0-13-598194-8
    1. Educational psychology—Case studies.   2. Teachers—Decision-making.
    3. Teachers—Training of.   I. Fillmer, H. Thompson.
    II. Title.
    LB1051G745   1999
    370.15—dc21   97-47747
                                            CIP

Cover photo: © Super Stock, Inc.
Editor: Kevin M. Davis
Production Editor: Julie Peters
Design Coordinator: Karrie M. Converse
Cover Designer: Rod Harris
Production Manager: Laura Messerly
Director of Marketing: Kevin Flanagan
Marketing Manager: Suzanne Stanton
Advertising/Marketing Coordinator: Krista Groshong

This book was set in Berkeley by The Clarinda Company and was printed and bound by R. R
Donnelley & Sons Company. The cover was printed by Phoenix Color Corp.

© 1999 by Prentice-Hall, Inc.
Simon & Schuster/A Viacom Company
Upper Saddle River, New Jersey 07458

Printed in the United States of America

10 9 8 7 6 5 4 3 2 1

ISBN: 0-13-598194-8

Prentice-Hall International (UK) Limited, *London*
Prentice-Hall of Australia Pty. Limited, *Sydney*
Prentice-Hall of Canada, Inc., *Toronto*
Prentice-Hall Hispanoamericana, S. A., *Mexico*
Prentice-Hall of India Private Limited, *New Delhi*
Prentice-Hall of Japan, Inc., *Tokyo*
Simon & Schuster Asia Pte. Ltd., *Singapore*
Editora Prentice-Hall do Brasil, Ltda., *Rio de Janeiro*

We wish to dedicate this book to the key people in our lives:

To our wives, Patti Greenwood and Dorothy Fillmer, for their sustaining love and support

To our parents, Annette and Arthur Greenwood and Henry and Vera Fillmer, for their wisdom, caring, and guidance

To our children, Joe, Richard, and Don Greenwood, and Susan Burchfield, Connie Bell, and Tom Fillmer, who give us love as well as hope for the future.

PREFACE

This book is the product of a conversation in 1995 during which Kevin Davis, Senior Editor at Merrill/Prentice Hall, asked me if I was interested in writing a casebook that would parallel the content of educational psychology textbooks published by Merrill, as well as that of other major textbooks in the field. The result was a content analysis of such textbooks, the outcome of which is presented near the end of the Introduction, inside the front cover, and in Appendix A. Later I contacted my good friend and colleague, Dr. Tom Fillmer, with whom I have written a more general casebook for Merrill, *Professional Core Cases for Teacher Decision-Making* (© 1997) and asked him if he would co-author this book.

The cases for this book were drawn primarily from the extensive case material collected from teachers in the field as well as those returning for graduate work since 1970. In addition, we drew cases from our respective teaching careers. I taught middle and high school in Michigan and Indiana for seven years, and Dr. Fillmer taught middle and high school for four years in Ohio and has supervised interns since 1960. We both have been professors in the College of Education at the University of Florida since 1967.

Case material is presented in a variety of formats. For reasons which we enumerate in the Introduction and in Appendix B, we prefer the written dialogue format. Also, all of our cases are left open-ended, problem-centered, and unresolved in order to provoke stimulating discussion, analysis, and decision-making. We agree with a growing number of educators, such as Harry Broudy ("Case studies—Why and how," *Teachers College Record, 91*, 449–459, 1990), who see cases as a means of establishing a professional knowledge base in teacher education. We view cases as application vehicles that serve as a middle step between coursework and actual teaching experience.

Although the cases in this book are intended for use in educational psychology courses, we made no attempt to extract the problem situations presented in the cases from the real world of teaching in order to focus in on context-free psychological issues such as those related to learning, intelligence, or measurement. Education in the public schools occurs in the context of a school, and teachers working in such an environment need to deal with major stakeholders such as administrators, support staff, parents, and other teachers, as well as students. It is too bad that learning in the public schools can't consist of "Mark Hopkins sitting on one end of a log with a student sitting on the other end." Education occurs as a social event in an institution with norms, role-definitions, power alignments, and dysfunctions, just like any other large-scale human endeavor. To portray it otherwise would be unrealistic.

KEY FEATURES

This book contains a number of features that will make it useful to the educational ps chology instructor.

1. Appendix B contains information on how to use cases in the college classroon It is our experience that many college instructors have had little experience using cases and are not sure where to obtain such information.
2. Each case begins with a listing of the psychological theories and sets of princ ples that may be especially useful for analyzing and resolving the case. This may help the instructor select which cases are most relevant to the content being taught.
3. At the end of each case is a series of questions, each of which focuses on the case from the perspective of a different psychological theory or set of princi- ples. These questions will help to stimulate discussion and analysis of the cas
4. Appendix A presents a theory guide that indicates which psychological conte areas, theories, and sets of principles are especially useful in analyzing and resolving the cases.
5. Near the end of each case is some additional material relevant to the case. Th may take the form of a student cumulative record, sample test items, or back ground data on students such as grades, parents' occupations, and so forth. Such information will add further information for case analysis and promote realism.
6. The Contents contains a brief overview of each case. This feature may be of value to the instructor and to students when selecting cases.

ACKNOWLEDGMENTS

The production of a book like this requires the help of many people. The authors wish especially thank Daniel Sanetz and Patti Greenwood for their excellent work in prepari the manuscript. We also thank the many teachers, too numerous to name, who cc tributed case material. Most of the cases in this book are actually composites from seve cases and represent the real-world experiences of more than one teacher. It is our ho that these common problems will serve as realistic application tools for the education future teachers.

Finally, we wish to thank the reviewers of this manuscript: Margaret Anders SUNY, Cortland; Scott W. Brown, University of Connecticut; Peggy Dettmer, Kansas St University; Lee Doebler, University of Montevallo; Gregory Schraw, University Nebraska, Lincoln; and Dale E. Schunk, Purdue University.

Gordon E. Greenwo
H. Thompson Fillm

CONTENTS

PART 1

INTRODUCTION TO EDUCATIONAL PSYCHOLOGY

An educational psychologist is employed as a consultant by a school district to assist in the development of a merit pay plan for teachers. When he meets with the school district planning committee of administrators, teachers, and parents, questions arise regarding the relationship between educational psychology as a science and teaching as an art.

The educational psychologist in Case 1 has been awarded a contract by the school district to develop, implement, and train school personnel in the procedures for evaluating teachers for merit pay purposes. When he meets with the school district development committee, he finds them divided on such issues as the nature and measurement of effective teaching, the value of process-product research methodology, the use of classroom observation procedures, and the strengths and weaknesses of using standardized achievement tests on a pretest-posttest basis as a measure of student learning.

PART 5

MOTIVATION AND CLASSROOM MANAGEMENT

PART 6

ASSESSMENT, EVALUATION, AND TEACHER EFFECTIVENESS

30 Who's the Best?   **288**

A school district selects three teachers to serve on a committee to choose the "Teacher of the Year." The committee finds the decision to be a difficult one as they sort through the survey, classroom observation, and student achievement data that have been assembled for their use.

APPENDICES

NTRODUCTION

EDUCATIONAL PSYCHOLOGY AND TEACHING

What is the science of educational psychology, and how does it relate to the art of teaching? The first chapter of most educational psychology textbooks usually explores the parameters of the field of educational psychology, its history of development, its research methodology, and how its theories, models, and principles are relevant to the educational practitioner. Although a few experts, such as B. F. Skinner, have argued that teaching can be reduced to a technology, the majority seem to agree that teaching fits Gage's (1985) definition of an art as "any process or procedure whose tremendous complexity . . . makes the process in principle one that cannot by reduced to systematic formulas" (p. 4).

One very common explanation of the relationship between educational psychology and teaching is that effective decision-making is the basic skill underlying good teaching and that the research, theories, models, principles, and techniques derived from educational psychology allow teachers to become better decision-makers. Ormrod (1995) points out that "above all, we are *decision-makers:* we must continually choose among many possible strategies for helping students learn, develop, and achieve. In fact, two researchers (Clark & Peterson, 1986) have estimated that teachers must make a non-trivial instructional decision approximately once every two minutes!" (p. 4). Gage and Berliner (1992) add that educational psychology has especially contributed to teacher decision-making in five areas: (1) instructional objectives, (2) student differences, (3) learning and motivation, (4) teaching methods, and (5) evaluation.

How do teachers use such empirically derived knowledge from the field of educational psychology as they make decisions? Eggen and Kauchak (1997) cite an example: "Should teachers wait longer to give students time to think through a question fully, or will long pauses result in choppy lessons that drag? Research doesn't provide a precise answer, so teachers must use their professional judgment and decide how much wait-time to give and how quickly the lesson should be moved along" (p. 13).

CASE STUDIES AND TEACHER EDUCATION

Many programs and techniques have been developed over the years to prepare preserv
and in-service teachers for the real world of teaching. Systematic observation instrumen
microteaching, competency-based programs, parent involvement techniques, and pro
col materials in various forms have all been used, to name a few. In recent years case stu
ies have become increasingly popular as application and discussion vehicles in traini
teachers, and many, if not most, educational psychology textbooks now contain br
cases as a regular feature in each chapter. Additionally, a number of casebooks, such
this one, have been written, and some college instructors build an entire course arou
the use of cases rather than the usual lecture/discussion approach.

What is a case, and what is its role in teacher education? Eggen and Kauchak (199
define cases as "segments or samples of students' and teachers' experiences in the teachir
learning process and other professional events" (p. 11). Cases may take a variety of form
While most are based on actual events, they can vary considerably in length, format, a
the degree to which they are strictly objective reports as opposed to more fictional rep
sentations of reality. They may also differ considerably in focus. Some can focus on an in
vidual student's problem, for example, whereas others might concentrate on a teach
working with an entire class. Although most cases are written, some may be in other form
such as audiovisual, computer software, and demonstrations and role playing.

The case format we have used in this book is the written dialogue format simi
to that used in movie scripts or screenplays. We prefer this format for a number of re
sons. First, such a format is familiar through the influence of TV, movies, and the lik
Second, it is the kind of "reality" that students experience when they observe in schoc
or even see themselves teaching through videotaping such as is done in techniques li
microteaching. Third, the dialogue format more naturally lends itself to activiti
designed to follow up case studies, such as role playing, sociodrama, and the videota
ing of students "acting out" the courses of action they recommend to the teacher in t
case. Fourth, a number of state teacher certification programs involve the direct obse
vation of teacher behavior using observation instruments during the first year of teac
ing. The dialogue format more closely portrays the kind of behavior obsetved. Fifth, t
behavior in the dialogue can be used as "behavioral evidence" by the students to su
port the interpretations made when they analyze a case. What people say and do
more a directly observed behavior than a summary of facts or incidents or a paraphra
ing of events. Finally, since we see the use of case studies as a middle step betwee
coursework and actual teaching experience, the more closely the case format resembl
events actually unfolding in schools, the better. In short, we view them as more reali
tic vehicles for the analysis of behavior and the generation of courses of action in t
real world of teaching.

Whatever form cases take, they may be viewed as application tools that have t
potential of helping preservice and in-service teachers develop and shape their metaco
nitive decision-making abilities. Case studies may be viewed as mediators between trac
tional courses and workshops and actual teaching experience. Broudy (1990) has argue
that the use of cases in teacher education may even help teaching truly become a profe

sion. Noting that "a professional professes a body of concepts that structure its field of practice" (p. 450), he observes that "teacher education has not developed a set of problems that can legitimately claim to be so general and important that all who are qualified to teach and to teach teachers should be familiar with them and their standard interpretations and solutions" (p. 452). He further contends that such a professional core of problems in education should be identified and presented to preservice and in-service teachers in the form of case studies, as has been done in such professions as medicine and law.

The thirty cases presented in this book were selected because they are especially suited to the typical content presented in an introductory educational psychology course. A content analysis of current educational psychology textbooks revealed that most of them cover the following six areas of content: (1) introduction to educational psychology (the nature, history, and methods of educational psychology, as well as its relationship to teaching); (2) child and adolescent development; (3) student diversity; (4) learning and instruction; (5) motivation and classroom management; and (6) assessment, evaluation, and teacher effectiveness.

SAMPLE CASE

The following case is entitled "And If They Don't All Want to Learn?" It was described by the teacher who submitted it as a problem involving the motivation of "disruptive eighth graders from low-income backgrounds in the case of a beginning social studies teacher teaching in an inner-city school." The case will be presented in its entirety, after which strategies for analyzing and resolving the case from an educational psychology perspective will be considered.

Waterford Junior High School is located in a poor, high-crime section of a major metropolitan area in a Midwestern state. Two decades ago, the surrounding neighborhood was made up of small, well-kept homes belonging to middle-income families. Today, the neighborhood reveals the ugly scars of creeping urban blight. A few neat, well-maintained homes remain, but they are outnumbered by those that have fallen into disrepair. Unkept yards, wrecked cars in driveways and on the streets, and spray-painted graffiti on fences are testaments to the decline that has swept over the area.

The school, a three-story warehouse-like structure built at the end of World War II, also shows signs of deterioration and abuse. For years the building's yellow brick walls have been the target of graffiti artists. Nearly a dozen street-level windows are boarded over, an admission by the school's maintenance crew that it can no longer keep up with the destruction of rock-wielding vandals.

Nearly one-quarter of the students who attend Waterford are from families where English is not the primary language, and more than half are from families on some form of public assistance. Rightly or wrongly, Waterford students have a reputation throughout the city for below-average achievement, absenteeism, and chronic misbehavior.

It is 7:45 A.M. on the fourth day of school, and five teachers are seated around a table in the lunchroom having coffee. Sue Adams, a first-year social studies teacher and a recent

graduate of a private liberal arts college in another state, walks up to the table. Willia
Hanover, a mathematics teacher in his fifth year at Waterford, is the first to notice Sue.

William   Morning. *[Standing up and extending his hand to Sue]* You must be the new
      social studies teacher. William Hanover, mathematics.
Sue   *[Shaking his hand]* I'm Sue Adams. You're right, it is social studies. I'm replacing
      Mrs. Watkins.
William   Right, she retired . . . great lady. *[Pointing to the others in the group, who, one*
      one, stand and shake hands with Sue] This is Betty Franklin, English. Mildred
      Hawkins, English. Frank Burns, mathematics. And this fellow on my right is Davi
      Sharp . . . *[with exaggerated respect]* science teacher extraordinaire. *[Everyone in th*
      group laughs.]
Sue   *[To all]* I'm very pleased to meet you. *[She sits down.]*
Frank   So, how'd you end up at Waterford?
Betty   *[Slapping Frank on the shoulder]* That's a terrible way to put it!
Frank   *[Playfully]* Come on, now. Everyone knows Waterford's reputation.
Sue   Well, I just graduated last year, and, believe it or not, I wanted to teach in an urba
      school.
Mildred   I guess you know that Waterford's had its share of problems.
Sue   Well, not really. Is there something I should know?
Mildred   It's just that the school's gotten a lot of bad press in the past.
Betty   Some teachers feel the kids are really hard to handle, but I haven't found them
      be that bad. *[Pausing]* I mean, look at the homes a lot of our kids come from. Som
      of them have gone through things that we couldn't even imagine: parents involved
      in drugs, child abuse, unemployment—
Frank   *[Interrupting]* Right. You name the social problem, you'll find it well represente
      at Waterford.
Sue   *[Uneasily]* Well, just how bad is it? You can teach the kids, can't you?
Betty   *[Laughing]* What a terrible introduction! We've got you all worried. It's not really
      that bad. A lot of the kids really want to learn.
Frank   *[In a serious tone]* Betty's right. Plus, it's hard to generalize. Some teachers have
      problems, others don't have many at all. It's hard to say. . . . Some people just see
      to adjust better than others.
David   You should remember one thing, Sue. If you ever want to talk to someone, we'r
      always here. We may not have any answers, but we're always willing to listen.

Four weeks later, Sue is standing at an overhead projector in front of twenty-eig
eighth graders in her sixth-period social studies class. Her students, thirteen girls and f
teen boys, are seated in five parallel rows. Projected on the screen behind her is a mult
colored outline map of the world.

The students seated near the front of the room appear to be involved in the le
son. They are either looking directly at Sue or writing the names of countries on th
outline map of the world Sue has just passed out. Many of the students seated in th
back half of the room, however, squirm restlessly and exhibit a variety of off-task beha

iors. An African-American girl matter-of-factly braids the hair of the girl who sits in front of her. A redheaded boy seated to the right of her yawns and then places his head on his desk. Two boys look out the window at four youths who are seated on the steps leading into a run-down apartment building across the street. An overweight girl gets up from her desk without permission and walks across the room to deliver a note to a friend.

SUE   OK, class, look at this transparency of the world. *[She steps back a few steps and points to the screen.]* Sheila, sit down right now! I didn't say you could get up. *[Waiting until Sheila takes her seat]* Now, how many people are living right now on the earth? *[Noticing Carla's upraised hand]*

CARLA   One hundred million.

HAROLD   *[Blurting out]* That's crazy! There's a whole lot more people than that!

SUE   *[Sternly]* All right, Harold! That's enough. If you want to say something, raise your hand.

HAROLD   *[Continuing to speak out]* Aw, she's way off!

WANDA   *[Turns in her chair and looks menacingly at Harold]* Well, how many do you think, big head? At least she's got an idea. *[Wanda turns back and smiles at Carla, who is giggling.]*

SUE   OK, Wanda. Settle down.

HAROLD   *[Intimidated by Wanda]* I don't know . . . but there's a lot more than a hundred million.

FREDDIE   *[Yelling out from the back of the room]* Hey, Miss, what's this tape on the floor? *[He points to a circle on the floor made out of masking tape. The circle has a diameter of about eight feet.]*

SUE   That's for an exercise we're going to do a bit later. Don't worry about it. *[Pausing]* Now, Harold is right. There *are* a lot more than one hundred million. In fact, there are more than six billion people in the world. That's six thousand millions.

JUAN   *[With hostility]* How do they know that? You can't count everybody in the world!

RICK   Yeah! Besides, there's people born every day.

SUE   *[With frustration]* Let's calm down! I said there are more than six billion. We don't know how many more, but the number's about six billion. *[She looks directly at Juan and Rick, both of whom have contemptuous looks on their faces.]* Here's another piece of information you probably didn't know. How long will it take for the population of the world to double? *[Calls on Dave, whose hand is raised]*

DAVE   A thousand years?

SUE   Good guess, Dave. Actually, it's much shorter than that. Thirty-eight years. Every thirty-eight years the population of the world doubles.

RICK   *[With disbelief]* Every thirty-eight years?

SUE   That's right. By the time you're about fifty, there will be about twelve billion people in the world. Ah . . . *[She pauses as though deciding what to do next.]* Let's imagine that we were all the people on the earth right now . . . just the twenty-eight people in this room. And let's imagine that the earth was no larger than this room.

HAROLD   *[Spontaneously]* Oh, no, I couldn't get away from that! *[He points to Wanda.]*

WANDA   *[Angrily]* You shut your mouth, boy!

SUE *[Moving toward Harold]* Hey, watch it, you two! *[Harold stares straight ahead.]* So i thirty-eight years we'd have about 56 people in this room. In another thirty-eigh years we'd have about 112 people. After another thirty-eight we'd have about 22 and so on. . . . So what's going to happen eventually?

WILLIE Peoples be fallin' off the earth! *[He laughs heartily. Several other students begin t laugh as well.]*

SUE *[Smiling weakly]* Well, I don't think they'd start falling off of the earth, but it wou get pretty crowded, wouldn't it? *[A few students nod their heads.]* Sue walks back o to the overhead projector and points to the outline map of the world with her pe The silhouette of her pen and hand is projected on the screen.

SUE I hope you've labeled the countries. *[Looking at the back of the room]* Some of you ir the back there haven't done a thing all period. *[The red-haired boy raises his head fro his desk, looks at Sue, then puts his head back down.]* Now, what are the four countries with the largest populations? *[Nobody volunteers an answer.]* All right. Look at this transparency. *[She puts another transparency on the projector. It displays the outlines of four countries.]* Here are the four countries with the largest populations. Do you recognize them? *[She points to one outlined in purple.]* Well, what's this one?

SEVERAL STUDENTS *[In unison]* The United States!

SUE Right.

HEATHER What's that on top of the United States?

FRANK That's Alaska, dummy.

SUE *[Looking sternly at Frank]* Frank! *[Pausing and then pointing to the outline of Alaska]* This is Alaska and—I don't know if you can see them, but what are these tiny do

CAROL *[Loudly from the back of the room]* Hawaii.

SUE Right, the Hawaiian Islands. *[Pointing to the outlines of the other countries]* So, wha are these other countries? *[No response]* All right. This is India. *[She points to the outline of India.]* This is China. And this is Russia. These are the four countries tha have the greatest populations. I want you to remember that, because we'll be hav a quiz tomorrow. *[Several students groan. Sue notices Randy's upraised hand.]* Randy

RANDY I ain't doin' no quiz! You didn't grade the last one right!

SHAWNDA Yeah, Miss Adams, you be givin' us too much work!

SUE *[With frustration]* All right, just quiet down!

SAMMY Yeah, and why'd you tell the counselor I was going to fail social studies?

SUE *[To Sammy]* You don't do your work in class.

SAMMY I do my work at home.

SUE Then why do I have all those zeros in my grade book?

SAMMY I already know this stuff; we had it in elementary school.

RONALD *[Yelling out]* We don't need to learn this stuff! Let's do something interesting.

SEVERAL STUDENTS *[In unison]* Yeah, let's do something else.

SUE *[Trying to keep her composure]* Now everyone, settle down! This is social studies, a we will learn social studies. You need it to get into high school. *[Sue walks over to her desk and picks up a set of photocopied handouts.]*

SUE Since some of you seem to have a problem paying attention today, we'll just spen the rest of the period working on these worksheets. *[Several students groan.]* I'm sorry, but you don't give me any other choice. We can't talk about what's in the book, so you're going to answer some questions about it.

FREDDIE   *[Calling out]* What about the exercise with the circle?

SUE   *[Curtly]* I'm sorry. I've had enough of this foolishness! *[Sue proceeds to give the students at the front of each row enough handouts for the students in that row.]*

SUE   *[As she moves from row to row]* Take one, and pass the rest back.

FREDDIE   Oooohhh, she be angry.

SUE   I want all the questions answered on this worksheet by the end of the period. *[She points to the clock on the wall.]* You'd better get started. You've only got twenty minutes. I don't think anyone can afford another failing grade.

The following morning Sue enters the lunchroom for her usual early-morning cup of coffee and chat with fellow teachers. She wears a haggard expression that her friends are quick to notice.

Frank   Sue, you look beat, and it's not even first period. Are you having a rough time? *[Sue tosses her books and papers on the table and drops into a chair.]*

SUE   *[She sighs.]* It's really getting to me. I don't know if I can go on like this.

BETTY   Did something happen? Do you want to talk about it?

SUE   Oh, I don't know. . . . It just seems to be such a struggle all the time.

MILDRED   What's that saying: nobody ever said teaching was going to be easy?

SUE   *[Continuing]* Mainly it's my sixth-period class. I can deal with the other classes; they're not so bad. But sixth period, they're so hostile. They resist everything!

FRANK   You have a bad class yesterday?

SUE   I'll say! I had this great lesson all planned on world population, and they never even let me really get to it. I ended up giving them a worksheet to do, just to get them to shut up.

DAVID   Sometimes you have to do that. We've all done it. If you don't have order, you can't teach. So you do whatever restores peace. Besides, some classes are just like that.

SUE   I know, but I don't like doing that. I want to teach the kids, but half of them won't let me. *[Pausing]* I don't know . . . am I doing something wrong?

WILLIAM   Come on, Sue, we've all had classes like that. Don't be so hard on yourself. This is the inner city, and the kids just behave differently. You'll get used to it. Just go with the flow. Do what you can.

DAVID   What was your lesson about yesterday?

SUE   Like I said, it was on world population. I had this little exercise all planned. To show the kids that the world's population doubles every thirty-eight years, I made a big circle with masking tape on the floor. I was going to start off by having six kids stand in the circle—you know, for the six billion people on the earth right now. Then in thirty-eight seconds I'd have another six enter the circle. And every thirty-eight seconds I'd double the number of kids in the circle. In no time flat, of course, the circle would be full.

WILLIAM   Sounds like a great way to get them to understand the concept.

SUE   *[With disappointment]* But they were so terrible yesterday! I didn't even start the exercise. I realized they were acting so badly I'd better skip it. Otherwise, I'd have ended up with a riot on my hands!

FRANK It's frustrating to make those plans and then not be able to follow them through.

SUE I also had this neat little lecture all ready on the effects that population growth h. on all kinds of things—food, energy, pollution, housing, jobs . . . all that stuff. E they didn't want to hear it. It's like they either don't want to learn, or they're dari me to try to teach them.

DAVID *[Comfortingly]* Well, maybe they'll be more receptive today.

SUE That's just it. They act like that *all the time!* *[Weakly]* I just don't know how to co with it. How do you put up with that day after day?

Sue Adams' Lesson Plan on World Population Growth

Teacher: Sue Adams   Course: Social Studies 8
Period: Sixth   Date: September 28

Goal: At the end of this lesson, students will understand how people are distributed around the world and some of the implications of continued rapid growth in the world's population.

Specific Objectives:
Students will be able to:

1. Explain why most of the earth's population (two-thirds) lives on only a fraction (8%) of the available land.
2. Identify the four countries that make up half the world's population (China, India, Russia, and the United States).
3. Identify the natural conditions necessary to support large populations.

Materials:

1. Transparencies of world, China, India, Russia, and the United States.
2. Masking tape circle on floor, approximately 8 feet in diameter.
3. Text (Chapter 3).
4. Dittoed worksheets for evaluation.
5. Chalkboard, overhead projector.

Procedure:

1. Introduce lesson by determining population of our city and discussing why population is centered here and not in other parts of the state.
2. Explain conditions necessary to support large numbers of people and why the earth's population is distributed as it is.
3. Identify and locate four countries that account for half of the world's population. (Use transparencies and dittoed outline maps.)
4. Conduct "circle" exercise to demonstrate how world's population is increasing. Discuss activity and effects of increasing world population.
5. Complete population map of the United States.
6. Complete worksheet on Chapter 3 (seatwork).

ANALYZING CASES

Allonache, Bewich, and Ivey (1989), who have conducted workshops on the improvement of decision-making skills, focus on four steps: (1) clearly defining the nature of the problem; (2) generating alternative solutions to the problem; (3) evaluating the positives and negatives of each possible solution; and (4) implementing the solution that is chosen. Step 1, defining the problem, might involve such things as looking at the problem from the point of view of different stakeholders in the situation, such as the teacher, a parent, students, and the principal. It might also mean looking at the problem from the perspective of different theories, models, principles, and values, such as, in the case of educational psychology, different learning theories or classroom management models. Finally, it might also involve examining different kinds of facts or data to help clarify as well as support the perspective taken. For example, one might focus strictly on observed external behavioral events or give equal weight to more internal, self-report type data. In any case, step 1 involves analyzing the case from different perspectives to clarify the nature of the problem.

Step 2 consists of the creative act of generating possible solutions to the problem or problems identified in step 1. This includes projecting what courses of action the teacher might implement to deal with the situation. Step 3 involves the evaluation of the strengths and weaknesses of the courses of action generated in step 2. One aspect of step 3 is forecasting the probable consequence of each course of action. Another aspect would be to consider whether or not a course of action is consistent with or follows from the way the problem is defined in step 1.

For example, suppose a problem identified in step 1 is that a child's shy, withdrawn, and nonparticipatory behavior in the classroom is the result of a negative self-concept stemming from an emotionally abusive home environment. Suppose a step 2 course of action that is proposed involves threatening and, if necessary, punishing the child if he or she doesn't begin to participate more actively in class. From the standpoint of self-concept theory, such an approach is not only unlikely to work but is inconsistent with the application techniques associated with that theory.

Another consideration in evaluating courses of action during step 3 is whether the course of action chosen is practical in terms of the context of the case. Suggesting that the students in a classroom be given an individual intelligence test to assess their intellectual ability is simply impractical considering the cost of such tests and the demands made in terms of time and personnel.

Participants in case studies do not often get to see step 4, the implementation of the courses of action chosen. However, they can increase the likelihood of successful implementation by spelling them out as concretely and specifically as possible. Too often, teachers are given vague suggestions such as individualizing instruction by putting the students in small groups. What are the objectives and teaching strategies involved? How should the groups be formed, and what kinds of evaluation procedures should be used? Suggesting that a teacher use the STAD cooperative learning procedures states a course of action in far more concrete and specific terms.

In putting together all four of the steps discussed above, keep in mind that the framework one uses to define the problem in step 1 is going to affect the choices avail-

able for consideration in the other three steps. In an educational psychology course, t
theories, models, and principles used as frameworks for analyzing a case are likely to
quite different from those used in such courses as teaching methods, school law, or ph
losophy of education, to name a few. Different frameworks lead to different courses
action or application procedures.

We suggest that you follow these steps in conducting a case study in an education
psychology course: First, begin by examining the case in terms of your personal beli
system and use "lay language" to define the problem. Second, analyze the case in terr
of appropriate course content in the form of whatever psychological theories, models,
principles best explain the problem. Third, defend your analysis by citing evidence fro
the case to back up your position. The type of evidence you cite would be dictated by t
theory used. An operant analysis, for example, would require behavioral data-collecti
procedures.

Once you have analyzed the case and defended your analysis, the fourth step is
generate courses of action that are likely to solve the problems identified. In a teach
education program, it makes sense to generate courses of action for the teacher in the ca
to implement. Learning to examine a case from the perspective of parent, principal, ar
students is important, but ultimately preservice and in-service teachers are learning
look at situations in terms of the teacher being the change agent.

The courses of action that you choose for the teacher to implement in order to de
with the problems identified should meet the tests of consistency, operationality, and fe
sibility. Consistency means, for example, that an operant analysis should suggest opera
procedures for the teacher to implement. Operationality means that each course of actio
should be spelled out concretely and specifically. Feasibility means that each course
action should be practical in terms of the context of the case.

The above discussion suggests five criteria for evaluating student efforts at analyzin
and resolving a case: (1) accurately and fully applying a theory, model, or set of principl
in analyzing the case; (2) supporting the analysis objectively and fully with appropriate ev
dence cited from the case; (3) choosing courses of action for the teacher in the case
implement that are consistent with the theory used in the analysis; (4) stating the cours
of action in an operational form so that specific procedures are spelled out; and (5) statir
courses of action that are practical, reasonable, and workable in the context of the case si
uation. (If the student product takes the form of a paper, the instructor may have a sixt
criterion: organizing the paper into a logical and grammatically correct whole.) These c
teria will later be further explained and applied to the sample student paper that follows

The following is an analysis and resolution of the case presented above. It is typic
of work done by students in undergraduate educational psychology courses.

SAMPLE CASE ANALYSIS AND DECISION

Analysis

The case "And If They Don't All Want to Learn?" could be analyzed and resolved from th
perspective of a number of psychological theories: behavior modification, Teacher Effe
tiveness Training (TET), Assertive Discipline, parent involvement techniques, Brune

discovery learning approach, and a number of motivational theories, to name a few. However, the approach chosen is that of Robert Slavin's (1990) cooperative learning model of teaching. According to Slavin, "research clearly shows that academic success is not what gets students accepted by their peers, especially in middle and high schools" (p. 2). He also says that "for most low achievers a competitive situation is a poor motivator" and that "after a while, they learn that academic success is not in their grasp, so they choose other avenues in which they may develop a positive self-image. Many of these avenues lead to antisocial, delinquent behavior" (p. 2). These principles of Slavin seem to fit what is going on in Sue Adams' sixth-period social studies classroom quite well.

Sue is described as a first-year teacher who graduated from a "private liberal arts college in another state" who finds herself teaching in a junior high school "located in a poor, high-crime section of major metropolitan area" in the Midwest. She operates her sixth period class on a competitive basis. For example, the class is divided into winners and losers, apparently as a result of a lack of planning on her part with regard to seating arrangements. A segregation of abilities is apparent:

> The students seated near the front of the room appear to be involved in the lesson. They are either looking directly at Sue or writing the names of the countries on the outline map of the world that Sue has just passed out. Many of the students seated in the back half of the room, however, squirm restlessly and exhibit a variety of off-task behaviors. An African-American girl matter-of-factly braids the hair of the girl who sits in front of her. A redheaded boy seated to the right of her yawns and then places his head on his desk. Two boys look out the window at four youths who are seated on the steps leading into a run-down apartment building across the street. An overweight girl leaves her desk without permission and walks across the room to deliver a note to a friend.

The class is divided into "winners and losers," with the losers at the back and the winners at the front. With her admonishment that "Some of you in the back haven't done a thing all period," Sue shows a negative bias against the students in the back. In an effort to avoid further admonishment and disapproval, these students collectively become non-achievement oriented and withdraw from the class's activity (Johnson & Johnson, 1989, p. 31).

Another indicator of Sue's ineffective use of competition is her use of fear as a motivator. She uses fear to motivate the class collectively, "I don't think anyone can afford another failing grade," and on an individual basis to Sammy, "Then why do I have all these zeros in my grade book?" As tension increases, so does the fear of failure. A classroom environment in which the competition is based on fear and threats creates a tension that makes effective competition difficult, if not impossible.

Sue further emphasizes competition by overgeneralizing the importance of the lesson and by placing too much value on success. She tells the students, "You need it [social studies] to get into high school." Students could infer from her statement that this particular lesson is vital to their success in high school. This would not have been what Sue meant, but she needs to be accountable for a conclusion that students may draw from her quick comment made in frustration. Evidence that she has made winning (success) too important is found in Harold's attack on Carla when she gives an incorrect answer: "That's crazy! There's a whole lot more people than that!" Harold does this to show that even though he does not know the correct answer, he knows more than Ca does. He is focusing on looking better than another student, not on understanding t subject matter.

Finally, and perhaps most significantly, competition is inappropriate when indivi uals lack the social skills and experience necessary to function in a competitive enviro ment. Because Sue's class comes from a neighborhood that is replete with social problen many students may be lacking in cooperative skills that might be present in an econor ically advantaged community. The problems of over-competitiveness in the class may inevitable due to the social problems that often accompany a poverty-stricken inner-c community. The students may simply not know how to get along with each other. Hor ever, Sue must also take some of the responsibility for permitting the negative enviro ment to thrive. She is fanning the flames through not taking steps to stop the misbeha ior. Sue has allowed a ineffective competitive environment to develop, yet she does n have the skills to function in it. Her frustration is evident, but instead of reworking h strategy for the class, she increases the tension in the classroom and creates a cycle th fosters negative competition.

Decision

A competitive situation is one is which "the goals of the separate participants are so link that there is a negative correlation among their goal attainments" (Johnson & Johnsc 1989, p. 4). In order for competition to exist, there must be perceived scarcity. Rewar are given only to those students who attain the highest score or grade. However, "coi petitions can also vary as to how many winners there will be" (p. 4) and "as to the cri ria for selecting a winner" (p. 5); thus the grade (or whatever is needed to achieve wi ning status) depends on the relative performance of the particular contestants or, in t case, students. Finally, "competition requires social comparisons" (p. 5). The students, competitors, receive information on how they performed relative to others, whether th information is desired or not.

Effective competition should be viewed as "first and foremost a cooperative activit (p. 34). In Sue's classroom, however, competition is not based on the children's worki together in groups. In a group, children have the opportunity to gain from each othe varying diversity and perspective. In Sue's classroom, however, the students are sufferi from the negative effects of competition.

Johnson and Johnson (1989) suggest nine basic negative assumptions regardi competition that cooperative learning methods must counter. The first is "negative int dependence" (p. 33), which requires that the participants know that the goal achieveme is restricted and must be won by superior performance. In a cooperative learning sitt tion, this assumption would be countered because the children would work in sm groups and gain from each other's strengths; goal achievement is not restricted. The se ond negative assumption involves "having a clear beginning, a clear ending, clear crite for selecting winners, and a clear set of rules and procedures that control interaction" (33). This element does not foster the appreciation of students' differing abilities. In coc erative learning the students work in diversified groups, so there is not one outstandi student who always receives the rewards.

The third negative assumption of competition is "being able to clearly rank competitors from best to worst" (p. 33). Ranking creates low morale for the slower students, who never win and therefore never receive the reward. Cooperative learning does not use such ranking procedures. The fourth element negative assumption is that "an appropriate task" (p. 33) involves an emphasis on speed in the performance of even very simple tasks. In a cooperative situation, speed is not the main objective; group learning and comprehension are. "Strict control of interaction between competitors" (p. 33) is the fifth negative assumption. This takes away the idea of cooperation because learning is very restricted. Such strict control is not a component of cooperative learning.

The sixth negative assumption of competition is "the ability to audit and monitor progress of competitors in order to engage in social comparison" (p. 33). In cooperative learning, every student—regardless of individual academic achievement—has a chance to be a part of a good team because of his or her effort. The seventh element of negative assumption is "homogeneous matching" (pp. 33–34). Cooperative learning, in essence, is heterogeneous learning, allowing each group of students to be comprised of varying abilities and backgrounds. The eighth negative assumption is that the importance of winning or losing is maximized. With cooperative learning, the individual's winning or losing is not a factor because the group holds responsibility for the outcome. The ninth negative assumption is "competitive skill" (p. 34). The skills include playing fair, being a good winner or loser, enjoying the competition, monitoring the progress of the competition, and not overgeneralizing the results of the competition. Although these are typically used in competitive situations, they can be modified so they can be included in cooperative learning.

In a negative competitive classroom environment, learners are pitted against one another, producing winners and losers. This pattern of winners and losers becomes an academic hierarchy over time and results in negative motivation toward academic tasks, especially cognitively complex ones, among the losers. By contrast, cooperative learning methods group the students heterogeneously into academic teams which are set up, as will be seen, so that each team member can individually contribute to the team effort, regardless of ability level. All competition is between the teams, with team members helping one another (through peer tutoring, for example) so that the team can succeed. Such an approach produces positive rather than negative forms of competition in the classroom.

Four basic forms of cooperative learning have developed from Slavin's (1990) work: Team-Games-Tournaments (TGT), Team-Assisted Individualization (TAI), Cooperative Integrated Reading and Composition (CIRC), and Student Teams—Achievement Divisions (STAD). In all four, students in the classroom are broken up into groups of four, and each group is heterogeneously mixed by ability, sex, and race and changes every grading period. Within each group, students select partners for activities that require pairs. Another commonality among the four approaches is that each follows three criteria for cooperative learning—team reward, individual accountability, and equal opportunity for success—but in different ways. "Team reward" means that a team may earn rewards, such as certificates, if the team achieves a designated criterion of academic success. "Individual accountability" means that the success of the team depends on the individual learning of each team member. "Equal opportunity for success" means that each student contributes

to the team by improving on his or her own past performance. Examples of each of th
follow.

Using TGT, a "lesson" will span three to five days and will involve direct instruct
by the teacher, team work, and learning, followed by a tournament. Members of
group compete against classmates of like ability to gain points for their team. The ir
vidual points are added together to obtain a team total. These team totals are compa
to a standard that is set by the teacher. Any team that passes the set standard receiv
team reward. There are three performance levels: good, great, and super. This form
inappropriate for this particular case study because the classroom is already filled v
too much competition. Sue's classroom needs a break from any form of competiti
effective or ineffective, for the time being. This form may be instituted when she f
confident that the students are prepared to have a little effective competition.

TAI and CIRC were designed to allow individualization of instruction with little
no competition. Tournaments are replaced by weekly quizzes based on each stude
level of ability. In TAI, a student is not allowed to take the weekly quiz unless other te
mates feel the student is ready. In CIRC, a student is not allowed to turn in his or
composition unless the teammates agree that it is ready. Neither of these is appropriate
this case study because TAI was developed for use with math and CIRC was develo
for use with reading and writing.

Probably the best approach for this case study would be STAD. STAD was the
cooperative learning program to be created and is the most widely known because it
be used in any subject and at any grade level. Like TGT, STAD cycles every three to
days with teacher instruction and team work and learning. STAD replaces the TGT to
naments with weekly quizzes. These quizzes provide the element of individual accou
ability required in cooperative learning. Teammates earn points for their team by c
paring their base score (an average of all previous scores) to what they scored on the q
For example (Slavin, 1990, p. 63):

Score	Points Earned
More than 10 points below the base score	0
10 points below to 1 point below the base score	10
Base score to 10 points above the base score	20
More than 10 points above the base score	30
Perfect Paper	30

The average of all team members' scores is compared to the set standard the teacher
developed, usually the following (Slavin, 1990, p. 63):

Criterion (Team Average)	Award
15	Goodteam
20	Greatteam
25	Superteam

Goodteams receive recognition, while Superteams and Greatteams receive certificates
team rewards and privileges. Team privileges might be use of the computer and of s
games as *Where in the World Is Carmen Sandiego?* It is important to note that praise

enthusiasm may be as important as any reward. Rewards and privileges should change frequently.

Sue will discover that by changing her teaching style from ineffective competition to cooperative learning, the students will benefit. One of the benefits documented by Slavin's (1990) research is that the students will receive an increase in self-esteem. Feeling needed by their classmates and seeing an improvement in their schoolwork can significantly increase feelings of self-efficacy. A second benefit of cooperative learning is the development of pro-academic peer norms. If all the students are trying to achieve a common goal, they will naturally want to motivate and help each other succeed, which should result in higher achievement for the entire class.

A more internal locus of control is a third benefit of cooperative learning. When students discover that their own efforts can lead to the success of the team, they come to believe in their ability to contribute academically. The fourth benefit is the increase of on-task behavior. The social nature of cooperative learning fulfills the need to socialize, and at the same time it allows students to continue to work. This eventually leads to students' liking what they are doing. They may come to enjoy working together in groups more than working individually. Liking classmates and feeling liked by others is the fifth benefit. Coming to see each other as working together toward a common goal will allow kids to get to know each other.

Three other benefits of cooperative learning are cooperation, altruism, and the ability to take another's perspective. In cooperative learning there is less emphasis on reaching an individual goal, so students learn that cooperation can lead to rewards for everyone. Students learn that they can reach their common goals by taking the perspective of another and learning from another's viewpoint. Once the students in Sue's class have seen for themselves the benefits of cooperative learning, the class will be much easier for Sue to teach. With cooperative learning, Sue's classroom is likely to become a more pleasant atmosphere for everyone.

References

Johnson, D. W., & Johnson, R. T. (1989). *Cooperation and competition: Theory and research.* Edina, MN: Interaction Book Co.

Slavin, R. E. (1990). *Cooperative learning: Theory, research, and practice.* Upper Saddle River, NJ: Merrill/Prentice Hall.

CRITIQUE OF SAMPLE ANALYSIS AND DECISION

The above analysis and resolution of "And If They Don't All Want to Learn?" is typical of higher-quality work at the undergraduate level in an educational psychology course. Before elaborating on and applying the evaluative criteria mentioned earlier to the student paper, we want to emphasize that this case could have been analyzed and resolved from the perspective of a number of other psychological theories, especially classroom management models. Behavior modification, Assertive Discipline, constructivist cognitive theory, Bruner's discovery learning approach, TET, parent involvement techniques, and

Kounin's principles of classroom management all could have been fruitful perspective: adopt.

This does not mean, however, that all theories and models are equally good for a lyzing cases. In our experience, the more comprehensive and applied a theory is, the e ier it is to use. Analyzing a case in terms of a comprehensive theory that deals with all problems identified in a case is easier than trying to analyze a case with several m theories that may or may not integrate well with one another in terms of assumptic data-collection procedures, and application techniques. Likewise, some theories replete with application procedures, while others are not associated with any clear me ods of application. Operant conditioning theory, for example, is very comprehensive purposes of analysis and has generated a whole host of application procedures. Moti tional theories based on Maslow's need hierarchy are excellent for analysis purposes weak in terms of application procedures. Bloom's Cognitive Taxonomy is somewhat l ited for analysis purposes, focusing primarily on problems dealing with cognitive clas: cation issues. In short, some theories and models are easier to apply to a case beca they are more comprehensive and have generated more application procedures.

The evaluative criteria presented earlier will be used to evaluate the paper. First the problem in the case analyzed fully and accurately from the perspective and using language of the theory applied? Second, is the evidence presented to support the anal cited objectively, and does it cover the major contentions made? Third, are the course action stated for the teacher to implement consistent with the analysis? Fourth, is e course of action stated in operational form (fully spelled out and specific)? And fift each course of action feasible (or practical) in the context of the case? Finally, is the pa well organized and grammatically correct?

With regard to the first criterion, the students have analyzed the case in term: the cooperation versus competition model of Johnson and Johnson from social psycl ogy. The analysis leads effectively into a discussion of Slavin's work on cooperative lea ing methods and a recommendation of one of those methods, thus providing a good f from theory to practice. In other words, the students see the teacher's use of competi structures and procedures in the classroom as the primary problem and advise the teac to institute cooperative learning procedures in the form of STAD to deal with the sit tion. By contrast, an operant analysis might have begun by recording what types behaviors the students are emitting and what reinforcers are maintaining their behav A TET analysis might have started with problem ownership, the types of communicat problems that exist, and the nature of the teacher-student conflict, probably in Metho terms. The point is that a comprehensive statement of the problem must be given t accurately uses the constructs of the theory and states what is happening in the langu of the theory. Note how the students quote from Johnson and Johnson's work and t apply the psychological principles derived from that work. The students address all major facets of the case.

The second criterion regards presenting evidence from the case in as objectiv form as possible to support the analysis. The nature of the evidence cited should be tated by the type of data relevant to the theory used. For example, an operant anal would require baseline data. In this paper, the students quote evidence from the case support each contention in a systematic, point-by-point fashion.

The third criterion pertains to the decision part of the paper. Having argued that competitive classroom procedures are the heart of the problem, the students meet the test of consistency by recommending cooperative learning procedures. Had they recommended that the teacher set up a token economy system instead, that approach would be inconsistent, since such a recommendation would have follow from an operant analysis, not from the analysis used.

As far as the fourth criterion is concerned, the students certainly get down to "brass tacks" by describing how the teacher should go about implementing the STAD method. If they had just recommended that cooperative learning methods be used without indicating that STAD was the appropriate method and then describing how STAD operates, the students would not have met the test of operationality.

Regarding the fifth criterion, the feasibility of the decision, all the STAD procedures recommended seem practical in the context of this case. If the students had suggested giving each student in the case a complex self-esteem inventory, such a recommendation would fall short in terms of feasibility. The main feasibility problem represented by the students' recommendation would probably be that of time—namely, getting the teacher "up to speed" in learning about STAD and how to implement it, as well as the development of the necessary materials and procedures.

In conclusion, the students analyzed the case accurately and fully in terms of a theory, provided evidence objectively and systematically to support or justify the analysis, and recommended a consistent, operational, and feasible set of courses of action for the teacher to implement. Appendix B provides more information on the evaluation of cases.

ORGANIZATION OF CASES

The thirty cases presented in this book focus on six broad areas of educational psychology. These six areas were selected on the basis of a content analysis of major introductory educational psychology textbooks. The cases are divided into six sections as follows:

Section	Case Nos.
1. Introduction to Educational Psychology	1–2
2. Human Development	3–7
3. Cultural Diversity	8–11
4. Learning and Instruction	12–17
5. Motivation and Classroom Management	18–25
6. Assessment, Evaluation, and Teacher Effectiveness	26–30

Following each case, additional material is provided regarding the case, such as a teacher's lesson plan or a portion of a student's cumulative record. At the end of each case, "starter questions" are given that may help stimulate case discussion. Each question focuses on the case from the standpoint of a particular psychological theory or principle.

In Appendix A, a theory guide is provided that matches psychological theories, models, and sets of principles with each case. In other words, these are frameworks from the field of educational psychology that seem especially well suited to analyzing a resolving the cases with which they are matched.

REFERENCES

Allonache, P., Bewich, G., & Ivey, M. (1989). Decision workshops for the improvemen decision-making skills confidence. *Journal of Counseling and Development,* 478–481.

Broudy, H. S. (1990). Case studies—Why and how. *Teachers College Record, 91,* 449–4

Clark, C. M., & Peterson, P. L. (1986). Teachers' thought processes. In M. C. Wittr (Ed.), *Handbook on research on teaching* (3rd ed.). New York: Macmillan.

Eggen, P., & Kauchak, D. (1997). *Educational psychology: Windows on classrooms.* Up Saddle River, NJ: Merrill/Prentice Hall.

Gage, N. (1985). *Hard gains in the soft sciences: The case of pedagogy.* Bloomington, IN: Delta Kappa.

Gage, N., & Berliner, D. C. (1992). *Educational psychology.* Boston: Houghton Mifflin.

Ormrod, J. E. (1995). *Educational psychology: Principles and applications.* Upper Sad River, NJ: Merrill/Prentice Hall.

CIENCE OR ART?

Key Content to Consider for Analyzing This Case:
(1) history of educational psychology; (2) research
methods; (3) teacher effectiveness.

Collinsburg is a medium-sized city of approximately 75,000 located in a Midwestern state. The population served by the Collinsburg School System is approximately 75% white, 20% African-American, and 5% other. Mining, agriculture, and several light industries such as clothes manufacturing comprise the local economy.

Dr. Arthur Haskins is a professor of educational psychology in the College of Education of the largest land-grant, research-oriented university in the state. He sits in the office of Dr. Chester Gunn, the superintendent of schools of the Collinsburg School System. Dr. Gunn's office, which is located in the school board complex in downtown Collinsburg, is large, well lit, and well furnished with artificial plants and wall paintings. Dr. Gunn sits behind his large oak desk while Dr. Haskins sits in a large leather chair facing him.

Dr. Gunn It seems like just yesterday that I was taking your educational psychology course at State, Art. I really got a lot out of that course.

Art I appreciate your telling me that, Chester. That was the beginning graduate-level course, EDP 6225, wasn't it?

Dr. Gunn Yes, I believe it was. I've really used that operant conditioning stuff a lot since entering administration, particularly that idea of contingency management. Those ideas are real basic to good administration. *[Pause]* But I didn't ask you here just to brag on your teaching—I wondered if you'd consider doing some consulting work for us.

Art Sure, what kind?

Dr. Gunn Art, the school board and I want to develop a merit salary system for our school district. I know that a lot of school districts around the country haven't been able to develop one and make it work. But given the current economic and political climate, particularly at the state level, we feel we have to try. *[Pause]* You're the best-qualified person I could think of to head our planning committee. I well remember

your lectures about the research on systematic observation of teacher behavior ar
about the difficulties of measuring good teaching in objective ways. If anybody is
knowledgeable in this area I think it's you, Art.

ART *[Smiling]* Thanks, Chester, but I guess you forgot about the part of the lecture
where I said that we haven't developed valid and reliable procedures for measurii
teachers' effectiveness yet.

DR. GUNN *[Smiling]* Well, all I expect is that you do the best you can. Just get the
planning committee to develop the best evaluation procedures available at the
present time.

ART *[Contemplative]* There are so many unresolved issues, Chester. You have no idea.
[Pause] Who's on the planning committee?

DR. GUNN Oh, it's made up of teachers, administrators, and parents. *[Reflecting]* Let's
see, seventeen altogether, I think, plus you, of course. A school board representa
and member, Mary Lowe, the principals of our two high schools, two middle
school and two elementary principals, two parents elected by our school advisor
committees *[SACs]*, six teachers, two from each of the three grade levels—let's se
that's fifteen. Who else? Oh, yes, of course, I asked Dr. Luke Melvin, head of our
evaluation division, and Dr. Dan Burns, the assistant superintendent for instructi
to serve. You know Luke and Dan, don't you?

ART Yes, I do. Luke got his degree in research methods in our department, and I kne
Dan back when he was a building principal. He was always very helpful to me ai
my doctoral students when we wanted to do research in his school.

DR. GUNN Then you'll do it, Art? Head the planning committee and try to get the be
possible plan out of them to recommend to the school board?

ART I'll give it a shot if you want me to, Chester.

DR. GUNN I do. I think you're the best-qualified person for the job! *[Pause]* Now, let's
talk money. What kind of a consulting fee is it going to take to get you to do this
job for us? *[Smiling mischievously]* Have mercy on us, Art! We're a poor school
district, you know!

It is a Thursday evening at 7:00 two months later. All seventeen members of
committee plus Art sit around a large oval-shaped table in comfortable leather chairs
conference room. Art sits at one end at the head of the table. After conversation expr
ing surprise about who was chosen to serve on the committee, accompanied by so
handshaking, all attention focuses on Art as he begins to speak.

ART I believe everyone is here, so let's begin. I'm Art Haskins from the educational
psychology department of the College of Education at State University. Dr. Gunn
has asked me to chair the important work of this committee. It seems that you a
know one another, except perhaps you might not know Ms. Mary Lowe, the sch
board representative *[Mary smiles and nods her head]*, our two parents, Ms. Jane
Winchester from the Lincoln Elementary School SAC *[also nods and smiles]*, and

Alyssa Baker, representing the Collinsburg High School SAC *[The principal of C.H.S. begins to applaud and shouts "The Cougars are number 1," at which point everyone laughs.]*

ART   Very enthusiastic, Mr. Motto! Mr. Richardson, do you want equal time for the Southside Spartans?

MR. RICHARDSON   No, thanks, Dr. Haskins. Those of us at Collinsburg South have a bit more dignity than our colleagues on the north side of town.

MR. MOTTO   *[Principal of C.H.S.]* That's all they have, Dr. Haskins. You may recall that our football team beat theirs 35–0 last year, and I presume we'll do it again this year! *[Cheers and boos follow as everyone joins in the good-hearted ribbing.]*

ART   We'll let you folks settle that one on the football field. I think we have a big enough challenge right here in constructing a merit pay plan for the school district.

MR. MOTTO   Which brings me to a question, Dr. Haskins. *[Pause]* No disrespect, Dr. Haskins but, well, I don't know about anyone else, but I'm surprised that Chet didn't ask Dr. John Westfall from the educational administration department at State to head this committee. In fact, I could have sworn that that was what he told me at a party he and I attended last week. It seems to me that it would make more sense for somebody like John, who was superintendent of a school system himself before getting his Ph.D., to head up a committee like this than to have someone from psychology.

ART   *[Frowning]* You'd have to ask Chet why he made the decision he did, Mr. Motto.

MR. MOTTO   Please. Call me Harry. Don't misunderstand, Dr. Haskins, I'm sure your credentials are impeccable, but I would think that a job like this would require someone with administrative experience.

MR. RICHARDSON   I usually don't agree with Harry on much of anything, but I think he has a point here, even though he doesn't seem to have had a course in educational psychology.

MR. MOTTO   What do you mean, Barton? I have too.

MR. RICHARDSON   Well, you seem to think that psychology and educational psychology are the same thing. Having had both, I can assure you that they are not.

MR. MOTTO   Is he right? What is he talking about, Dr. Haskins?

MR. RICHARDSON   Psychology is in the College of Arts and Sciences, isn't it, Dr. Haskins? And ed psych is in the College of Education at State. Also, isn't ed psych more applied, and aren't the regular psych professors more interested in theory and research for its own sake? *[A general chorus of disagreement follows.]*

ART   I think you're quite accurate about how things are at State. However, some colleges and universities are organized quite differently from State administratively, and some regular psychology professors are quite applied.

MR. MOTTO   All of which is off target as far as my question is concerned. Aren't educational psychologists primarily researchers? Isn't it true that most of them don't have much background and experience as teachers, much less as administrators?

ART   Some do and some don't, at least as teachers. I had seven years of high school teaching experience before getting my Ph.D.

MR. MOTTO   But no administrative experience?

ART   I was chair of the social studies department at the second high school at which I taught. But no experience as principal or higher.

MR. RICHARDSON   What do educational psychologists do, Dr. Haskins? My youngest s« is thinking about getting his degree in ed psych, and I was wondering what his options are once he gets it.

ART   Please call me Art, Barton. Would the committee consider it a waste of time if I answer Barton's question? Especially since Harry seems concerned about my credentials to head this committee? *[A general chorus of encouragement]*

MR. MOTTO   Now, Art, I wasn't trying to offend you! In all honesty, most of the professors I've met or had a course under at State have had very little real practic: experience as teachers or administrators. They live in a ivory tower, as they say. Y they come in as expert consultants who are going to help us design real-world programs, like this one, that are going to not only affect the lives and incomes of teachers and their families but also the lives of the administrators who have to implement them. I'm just wondering if a Ph.D. in educational psychology qualifi« a person to do a job like that.

MR. RICHARDSON   Harry, why don't you let Dr. Haskins answer my question? *[A gener« chorus of agreement]*

ART   OK. How shall I begin. I guess with my opening lecture for my beginning graduate-level introductory course. Ed psych was pretty much just psychology applied to education until perhaps the 1950s, when many educational psychologists began studying real teachers and real students in real classrooms w systematic observation instruments. This broke them away from the arts and sciences psychologists, as Barton called them, many of whom were generating learning theories by running rats in mazes.

MR. MOTTO   That's what I mean. How unrealistic can you get? How can anyone think rat learning and human learning are comparable? Humans are far more complex than rats.

ART   It's true that few of the learning theories initially generated with rats were carriec the next step and studied in relation to humans. However, have you ever heard c behavior modification, Harry?

MR. MOTTO   Yes, of course. A number of consultants have done workshops over the years with my teachers on classroom discipline using behavior modification.

ART   You're talking about work that began with rats and pigeons done by B. F. Skinne and his operant conditioning colleagues at Harvard. As you know, his work has been very influential in many institutions and programs besides schools. It has certainly affected administrative theory as well.

MR. RICHARDSON   Then most educational psychologists focus on schools and teacher: their research?

ART   It just so happens that my department chair had our graduate coordinator track down some of our former graduate students to see what they're doing now. I hav several copies of the list he made because I intended to pass them out to students in one of my courses tomorrow night. Here. Take one of these, and I'll get the secretary in my office to make up some more copies. *[Pause]* As you can see, our former graduate students have obtained jobs in a variety of settings. I remember reading one study that said that only about half of all Ph.D.'s in ed psych work directly with teachers and schools through teaching and research activities.

MR. MOTTO   OK, so educational psychologists are versatile, but don't most of them focus on research?

ART   I think that's a fair statement. If they aren't doing research they're teaching the results of research in their classes.

MR. MOTTO   OK, now that's my point. They're scientists, right? They use the so-called scientific method to get their answers?

ART   Right.

MR. MOTTO   As far as I'm concerned, teaching is an art, not a science. Teaching can't be reduced to a set of scientifically derived techniques. A good teacher has a certain kind of personality, is interested in the kids, is motivated to learn new teaching methods and—

MR. RICHARDSON   *[Interrupting]* So what's your point, Harry?

MR. MOTTO   That good teachers are artists, not scientists. It's like, say, painters, or poets, or opera singers. You can teach them the usual techniques, but the good ones are more than a bag of tricks. How can a scientist, like an educational psychologist, tell an artist, like a teacher, how good of a job he or she is doing, much less how to do it better? Only another experienced teacher can do that.

MR. RICHARDSON   Harry has a point there, Art. In what areas has ed psych helped teachers?

ART   Many argue that ed psych has helped teachers more in the decision-making area than any other.

MR. RICHARDSON   What do you mean?

ART   An excellent question, Bart. It might get us on to our purpose of developing evaluation procedures for measuring teacher merit. *[Pause]* One way of looking at the job of the teacher is that it involves three phases: pre-instructional, instructional, and post-instructional. The pre-instructional phase involves the teacher planning what he wants to teach, how he wants to teach it, and how he wants to take student differences into consideration. Of course, the instructional phase involves how the teacher interacts with the students in the execution of the plans. Especially how the teacher makes moment-to-moment decisions as he is in the act of teaching.

MR. RICHARDSON   The post-instructional phase would be the teacher evaluating how well he has done and how much his students have learned, I would guess.

MR. MOTTO   If you're talking about using that view of teaching as a model for evaluating teaching, it's pretty limited, isn't it?

ART   What do you mean?

MR. MOTTO   I mean being able to make good decisions only relates to the intellectual part of a teacher. What about the teacher's personality, the teacher's knowledge of techniques and how to use them, the teacher's creativity, and so forth? Teachers are more than a brain.

ART   Our problem as a committee is to come up with reasonably objective procedures for measuring effective teaching. The idea of seeing the teacher as a decision-make is based on the notion that the really effective teacher not only knows teaching strategies and skills but is a master decision-maker when it comes to choosing which one to use at the right time. For example, it's one thing to know how to ask an open-ended question. It's another to know when to ask such a question. That involves decision-making—and some experts say that teachers make an important instructional decision about every two minutes when they're teaching.

MR. MOTTO   That still seems too intellectual a view of teaching. What about teacher enthusiasm? What about a teacher showing that she cares? What about how creative she is in choosing teaching methods and making instructional materials. Your decision-making model doesn't have any heart or desire in it as far as I'm concerned. Besides, how does all this relate to educational psychology?

ART   The argument goes that educational psychology can provide a scientific base of knowledge that the teacher can draw from in making more effective decisions.

MR. MOTTO   How convenient! So this decision-making model of teaching is the one th you propose we should use to develop our evaluation procedures?

ART   [With controlled anger] That's up to this committee. It seems like your real question Harry, is whether or not I'm the best person to head this committee—perhaps whether any educational psychologist is qualified to head it. You seem to be sayin that this committee should be composed solely of experienced teachers and heade by someone with an educational administration background like Dr. Westfall—an excellent man, by the way. If that is this committee's view, then I'll simply tell Dr. Gunn that I don't have the confidence of the committee and therefore won't be ab to serve as chair and consultant. What is your desire, folks?

DR. MELVIN   Harry, if you and Barton will let me get a word in edgewise, I'd like to say something.

MR. MOTTO   Be my guest, Luke. Help us out of this situation—please!

DR. MELVIN   Harry, what you don't seem to realize is that we have to select or develop measurement and evaluation procedures regardless of what model of teacher effectiveness we decide to use. Dr. Haskins is an expert in that area, and what he doesn't know I'm sure he can find out from some of his colleagues in his department. I know that to be true because I obtained my doctorate from his department. [Pause] Another thing you don't seem to know is that a lot of the research that has been done on teacher effectiveness has been done by educationa psychologists. In fact, and I'm sure that Dr. Westfall would agree with this if he were here, a lot of the research in the area of educational administration has been done by educational psychologists working with people like Dr. Westfall. Educational psychologists have developed a lot of the relevant theory and measurement procedures that we need to do our job. Having had Dr. Haskins' graduate ed psych survey course, I can assure you that he knows that literature!

Dr. Burns   And I can assure you that Dr. Haskins is familiar with the real world of teaching, Harry. I can assure you that he and his graduate students were constantly in and out of the classrooms of Collinsburg High School collecting data when I had your job!

Ms. Lowe   I'd like to add that I also think Dr. Haskins is more than qualified to serve as chair and consultant for this committee. After all, Dr. Haskins teaches classes at the university as well as doing research and writing. He is an experienced teacher.

Mr. Motto   OK, people! I hear you. I apologize for questioning your credentials, Art. I have no doubt that you're excellent at what you do. But I still think that your educational psychology focus is too narrow to provide us with procedures for evaluating good teaching, especially if that teacher-as-decision-maker business is an example. Teaching is too complex of an art to be reduced to that. Perhaps we need people from some other fields to serve on this committee or at least consult with us. [Pause] Dr. Haskins, has educational psychology developed any other models or methods to evaluate good teaching? Aren't there other disciplines, scientific or applied, that we should consult as well?

FIGURE 2   Dr. Haskins' Handout on Employment for Educational Psychologists

I. With a masters or specialist degree
  A. Junior or community college teaching
  B. School districts (e.g., evaluation division or grants)
  C. Private research agencies
  D. Health and rehabilitative services agencies (e.g., cottage training instructors in institutions for mentally retarded or trainers in sex offender or drug abuse programs)
  E. Government agencies: local, state, and national (e.g., data collector for state department of education)
  F. Corporations and private sector (e.g., television, publishing, in-house training)

II. With a Ph.D. or Ed.D. degree
  Above employment plus:

  A. College teaching and research
  B. Medical and dental schools (e.g., faculty evaluation and development)
  C. College or university office of instructional resources (e.g., instructional materials development, personnel counseling and evaluation, clinical and counseling psychology)
  D. Prison instruction and counseling
  E. Sports and recreation research and counseling

QUESTIONS

1. What is educational psychology? How does it differ from other branches of p: chology? How does it differ from educational sociology, educational philosophy, and e« cational administration? What kinds of activities do educational psychologists engage a

2. What does Harry mean when he says that educational psychology is a science a teaching is an art? What relationships exist between educational psychology and teachi:

3. What is a science, and what is the scientific method? What scientific methods educational psychologists use? On what kinds of topics or issues do educational psycl ogists conduct research?

4. What did Art mean when he conceptualized teaching as a decision-making ac ity? Is Harry right in viewing this model of teaching as too narrow? What other com: nents of teaching should be considered?

5. What is a merit pay program for teachers? Are there successful merit pay p: grams in the United States? What are the components of such programs?

6. Has Dr. Gunn assembled the right people for a committee to develop a merit plan? What kinds of people should be on such a committee? Should teachers be in majority? Should students be on the committee? Should corporate executives serve on committee? Was Art a good choice to head the committee?

7. Why is Harry objecting to Art's chairing the committee? What kind of qualit does he want in the committee chair? Is he correct in his assumptions?

8. At what level of Maslow's need hierarchy do Harry and Art seem to be prima: operating? Why do you think so? What is the most effective way to relate to a per: operating at that need level?

9. Describe the three phases of teaching (pre-instructional, instructional, and p« instructional). What research has been done on them? Can they serve as a model for e: uating teacher effectiveness?

10. Is Luke Melvin right when he says that educational psychologists have done a: of research on teacher effectiveness? What research has been done, and has it led to development of valid and reliable methods of evaluating teacher effectiveness?

11. Does Ms. Lowe make a valid point in saying that Art is an experienced teacher teaching at the college level comparable to teaching in grades K–12?

12. How should Art respond to Harry's questions about other models and meth: developed by educational psychologists? About whether experts from other fields, sc: tific or applied, should be working with the committee?

QUALITY CONTROL

Key Content to Consider for Analyzing This Case:
(1) research methods; (2) measurement and evaluation (standardized tests, formative vs. summative evaluation, observation schedules); (3) teacher effectiveness (process-product research).

Collinsburg is a medium-sized city of approximately 75,000 located in a Midwestern state. The population served by the Collinsburg School System is approximately 75% white, 20% African-American, and 5% other. Mining, agriculture, and several light industries such as clothes manufacturing comprise the local economy.

Dr. Arthur Haskins is a professor of educational psychology in the College of Education of the largest land-grant, research-oriented university in the state. He sits in the office of Dr. Chester Gunn, the superintendent of schools of the Collinsburg School System. Dr. Gunn's office, which is located in the school board complex in downtown Collinsburg, is large, well lit, and well furnished with artificial plants and wall paintings. Dr. Gunn sits behind his large oak desk while Dr. Haskins sits in a large leather chair facing him.

DR. GUNN *[Frowning]* Art, I heard about Harry Motto giving you a hard time about whether or not an educational psychologist should be the one to head up and act as consultant to our merit pay committee. I don't know what's wrong with Harry! Sometimes I think that his promotion to principal at C.H.S. has gone to his head. He was clearly out of line to treat you that way, and I told him so.

ART *[Smiling]* I think Harry really believes that educational psychologists are ivory tower researchers who are out of touch with the real world of teaching. Although the whole situation made me angry at the time, I've gotten over it, and I'm sure I can work with Harry and the rest of the committee.

DR. GUNN I'm really pleased to hear that, Art! Where is the committee at this point?

ART I've got all seventeen committee members working in four subcommittees. Luke Melvin *[evaluation specialist]* is heading a subcommittee to examine the literature on teacher effectiveness. Luke and I talk just about every day. Dan Burns *[assistant superintendent for instruction]* and his subcommittee are getting together the literature on merit pay programs around the country.

DR. GUNN   And what committee is Harry Motto heading? If I know you, you put him in charge of one!

ART   *[Laughing]* You know me well, Chester! Harry's subcommittee's job is to collect information from teachers, parents, and students. Barton Richardson's *[principal of Collinsburg South High School]* committee is collecting information from the school board, school administration, and the teachers union leadership.

DR. GUNN   That sounds like you've covered all your bases, Art. *[Pause]* What about community people, business leaders, and the like?

ART   Harry's committee is supposed to consult with that group as part of what they do.

DR. GUNN   When do you meet again?

ART   On Thursday the fifteenth, a little over a month from now.

DR. GUNN   Sounds good! Let me know if I can support your work in any way. What you're doing is very important to all of us.

It is more than a month later on a Thursday evening at 7:00. The eighteen members of the Merit Pay Plan Committee sit around a large, oval-shaped table in a conference room. Art sits at the head of the table and presides over the meeting. The other members of the committee are Harry Motto, principal of Collinsburg High School and Barton Richardson, principal of Collinsburg South High School; Mary Lowe, school board member; Dr. Luke Melvin, head of the evaluation and research division of the local school system; Dr. Dan Burns, assistant superintendent of instruction; Jan Winchester, Lincoln Elementary SAC member; Alyssa Baker, Collinsburg H.S. SAC member; four other principals (two from middle schools, two from elementary schools); and six teachers (two each from the elementary, middle school, and secondary levels).

ART   We have a lot to do, so let's get down to work. *[Looking at Luke]* Luke, your committee has been pulling together the teacher effectiveness literature. Do you have a report for us?

DR. MELVIN   We aren't finished by any means, but I can go over what we've found so far.

ART   Excellent! Please proceed.

DR. MELVIN   Some of this gets a bit complicated, so don't hesitate to ask questions as we go along. *[Pause]* I guess we should begin with the process-product literature, where educational researchers, many of whom were educational psychologists like Art, used observation schedules to observe teachers and students interacting in the classroom and correlated that data with various measures of student achievement. Since the observational instruments were used to collect data on the instructional process and the student achievement data were considered the outcome or product of the process, it's generally called process-product in the literature.

MR. MOTTO   Isn't the process part what principals have been doing for a long time when they observe in the classroom and rate the teacher's performance?

DR. MELVIN   Not really. Principals usually use rating scales chosen by the school district not the more complicated systematic observation schedules used by the researchers. For example, the researchers might record certain numbers every three seconds that would describe what was going on in the classroom. The researchers were concerned with measurement issues such as scoring reliability and various kinds of validity. The rating scales adopted by school districts usually contain items agreed to by various committees and are not so concerned with validity and reliability issues. The items chosen are usually not selected on an explicit theoretical or empirical basis.

Mr. Motto   *[Smiling]* My, how you research types throw around technical jargon! What do you mean by an explicit theoretical or empirical basis?

Dr. Melvin   By a theoretical basis I mean generating the items from a theory of teaching that is rather clearly spelled out, like that of Dewey, Skinner, or Bloom. By an empirical basis I mean doing what one researcher did by having his grad students place tape recorders in classrooms and then generate items that would describe or code what was going on in the tapes.

Mr. Motto   Don't the committees have a theory of teaching in mind when they choose items for a rating scale to be used for observation?

Dr. Melvin   Not in my experience. If a theory exists, it's not clearly stated. For example, someone will say that the teacher should be organized. Another will say that the teacher should know her subject matter, while another will say that the teacher should be enthusiastic and that her students should be paying attention and actively involved in what's going on in the classroom. The rating scale used is either a camel created by a committee or one adopted from another school district and modified a bit.

Mr. Richardson   So how did this process-product research come out, Luke? Did it tell us which teacher behaviors are best?

Dr. Melvin   You've got to remember now that all this research, years of it, is correlational, not experimental in nature. They were running correlations between categories of teacher behavior and different measures of pupil achievement.

Mr. Motto   For Pete's sake, Art, what is he saying?

Art   Luke is saying that the data revealed relationships between variables but that you can't draw cause-and-effect conclusions from them.

Mr. Motto   OK, I understand enough about research to grasp what you're saying: they couldn't put them all in a laboratory and control all the variables that could affect the learning of the students. I also know something about correlations. What kind of correlations did they get when they did this process-product research?

Dr. Melvin   Most of the statistically significant correlations were in the .20, .30 range. Significant, but not large, depending on your point of view.

Mr. Motto   *[Intently]* What I hear you saying is that these high-powered researchers did years of this kind of research at the taxpayers' expense and ended up finding a bunch of weak correlations for their efforts.

Dr. Melvin   Well, not exactly, Harry. You see, some of the studies were better done than others and had very large sample sizes—

Mr. Motto   *[Interrupting]* Give me the bottom line, Luke. Can these researchers tell us what teacher behaviors are the good or effective ones and which ones aren't?

Dr. Melvin   In a word, no.

Mr. Motto   *[Angrily]* No offense, Luke, but researchers sometimes make me mad. They're the big experts who get big grants to do studies and come up with nothing.

How can you say that the fancy observation schedules they developed are any better than a lot of the classroom rating scales now in use in a number of school districts around the state?

ART   Luke, I don't want you to think I'm cutting you off, but why don't we move on to Harry's committee at this point. His committee's job was to collect information from teachers, parents, and students, as well as various community leaders such as businessmen. Is that right, Harry?

MR. MOTTO   Yes, it is.

ART   Perhaps then you could go on and tell us what you found when you interviewed these people. We can always come back to the research literature.

MR. MOTTO   I'll attempt to summarize what various people representing all the educational stakeholders that Art mentioned had to say. First, there seemed to be general agreement that most people are able to identify who the good and poor teachers are in a school. Students tell their parents or siblings who to take and not to take. The problem is how to objectify this subjective information. Perhaps you research types could help us develop instruments that we could use to identify our best and worst teachers by surveying parents, students, administrators, and teachers

DR. MELVIN   You might be able to cut the extremes off from the middle, Harry, but that won't help you with your measurement of teachers who aren't at the extremes.

Mr. Motto   *[Frowning]* Don't you professors do something like that at the college level, Art? I remember doing student ratings on my professors' teaching when I was a student at State.

ART   That's true, although the validity and reliability of such measures are often questioned. But we don't generally do student ratings of teachers in K–12. The question is whether or not students are capable of judging whether teaching is good or bad.

MR. MOTTO   Well, let me just throw that out as an idea then and let it go at that. I strongly feel that we should consider surveying the major stakeholders. However, an idea that everyone seemed to agree on is that of measuring how much a student learns from a teacher.

DR. MELVIN   And how would you do that, Harry?

MR. MOTTO   Simple. Pretest the students at the beginning of the school year, and posttest them with the same or parallel test at the end of the school year. After all, isn't student learning what education is all about?

DR. MELVIN   Your committee isn't the first one to suggest such a plan. What test or tests would you use?

MR. MOTTO   I don't know. That's not my expertise. I'll leave that up to you researchers. suppose standardized tests would have to be used.

ART   There are a number of problems in trying to measure pupil learning. One is that most standardized tests don't go beyond the first three levels of Bloom's Cognitive Taxonomy. We are constantly saying in education how much we regret that American students aren't exposed to higher-order thinking or to the kinds of cognitive processes represented at the three higher levels of Bloom's taxonomy.

MS. WINCHESTER   And problem-solving. I was watching a show on TV the other day about how American children are behind Japanese children in problem-solving skill

ART   Also, Harry, what about classes in art, music, shop, physical education, and the like?

Mr. Motto   OK, so regular achievement tests won't do the job in all classes or measure all the different kinds of learning we want to measure. Aren't there people around who know about other kinds of tests we could use?

ART   Frankly, I don't know of any. But even if we fixed that problem, how would you deal with the problem of student diversity?

Mr. Motto   What do you mean?

ART   How would you collect your pre-post achievement data to take student differences into consideration? You have students from different races, SES *[socioeconomic status]* backgrounds, ethnic groups, reading abilities, and so forth. How are you going to compare the growth of students in an advanced-placement English class with one that not only contains average-ability students but also has mainstreamed kids with disabilities? It would be like comparing a football coach with highly skilled and highly recruited players with one who has low-ability players. You'd be stacking the deck against some teachers.

Mr. Motto   *[Frowning]* I see what you mean. But isn't there some way to statistically take those differences into consideration?

Dr. Melvin   Not that I know of. The home environment these kids come from helps produce differences that you can't remove, no matter what you do statistically.

Mr. Motto   What do you mean?

Dr. Melvin   I mean that the parents of kids who are high achievers in school have different values, are more involved with the school, and push their children for good grades. If you're going to evaluate me as a teacher, give me some of those students from strong middle-class backgrounds to teach. The pressure to achieve will come from home as well as from the teacher at school.

Mr. Motto   *[In exasperation]* Surely you experts can come up with some way of measuring student learning! If you can't, then how is education ever going to be accountable to the public?

ART   Did your committee come up with any other ideas, Harry?

Mr. Motto   Yes, one of our curriculum specialists brought me a copy of an observation schedule used by a school district in another state that has a merit pay plan. I wrote to them and they sent me information on what they do that really impressed me. *[Passes out copies of the observation schedule]*

Dr. Burns   This is the Jackson School District observation schedule, Harry. That is the kind of thing that my committee is supposed to look into. They sent us their material as well.

Mr. Motto   *[With exaggeration and insincerity]* I'm really sorry, Dan, if we crossed the boundary and got into your territory. But here is a plan that really works. It was designed by both their administration and the teachers union.

ART   Why don't you go on and tell us about it. We'll let Dan chip in when you're finished.

Mr. Motto   Well, to begin with they just added a merit step to their salary schedule.

ART   Their salary schedule is a step schedule based on years of teaching experience and amount of education, like the one here at Collinsburg?

FIGURE 3 Teacher Observation Schedule Proposed by Harry Motto

Teacher Evaluation Report
Jackson School District

Teacher's name: _____   School: _____
Evaluator: _____   Date: _____
Grade: _____   Time of observation: _____ _____
                                                          began   ended
                                      Conference time: _____ _____
                                                          began   ended

RANKINGS: Outstanding: Performance reflects exceptional qualities
                               of teaching and class management
              Satisfactory: Exhibits expected and desired
                               professional behavior.
              Unsatisfactory: Exhibits weak performance and/or
                               teaching deficiencies

Mark *X* below the appropriate ranking: Outstanding (O), Satisfactory (S), or Unsatisfactory (U), after each item:

	O	S	U
I. TEACHING PROCEDURES _____			
A. Evidence of organization and planning _____			
B. Knowledge of subject matter _____			
C. Individualization of instruction _____			
D. Variety of teaching strategies _____			
E. Effective use of wait-time _____			
F. Encourages good work-study habits _____			
G. Appropriate practice/review procedures _____			
H. Evaluates learners effectively _____			
I. Effective use of class time _____			
II. CLASSROOM MANAGEMENT _____			
A. Effective classroom management _____			
B. Attractive physical setting _____			
C. Effective interaction with pupils _____			
D. Maintenance of appropriate records _____			
E. Positive classroom climate _____			
F. Appropriate use of group work _____			
G. Effective monitoring of pupils _____			
H. Is reasonable, fair and impartial _____			
I. Keeps pupils on task _____			
III. PROFESSIONAL CHARACTERISTICS _____			
A. Accepts responsibilities _____			
B. Encouranges self-disipline _____			
C. Continual self assessment _____			
D. Keeps abreast of new ideas _____			
E. Professional appearance _____			
F. Develops rapport with pupils _____			
G. Keeps parents informed _____			
H. Follows school district policies _____			
I. Poised and self-assured _____			

MR. MOTTO   Right. All they did was add a merit step. Of course you could add as many merit steps as you want, but they only added one.

MR. RICHARDSON   So how do they decide whether or not a teacher gets the merit step?

MR. MOTTO   I was coming to that. It's simple and elegant at the same time. Each teacher must be observed at least four times over the school year if he voluntarily decides to go for merit that year. And curriculum specialists gather the observation data, so you have a person outside the school collecting the data. The instrument covers most of the important things, as you can see, and is easy to use. You just rate the teacher as outstanding, satisfactory, or unsatisfactory in each category. They set a cutoff score to determine whether you get merit or not. *[Pause]* I was thinking, folks, if we used something like this, couldn't we adapt it in some way to send it out to the various stakeholders as well? Maybe we could develop a student rating schedule along these same lines, and a survey instrument to send out to parents and other teachers.

DR. MELVIN   What about validity and reliability, Harry? Do we know that the items on the instrument really measure good teaching? Would two different raters observing a teacher at the same time agree on their ratings?

ART   Bill Jensen, is there something you want to add as a classroom teacher? You look like you want to say something.

BILL   *[Secondary teacher]* Yes. It so happens that I have a cousin who teaches in the Jackson School District. He tells me that their teachers union was forced to help develop those merit pay procedures, and especially this rating scale, and that a lot of them resent it. He says that a sizable block of teachers there who are active in the union refuse to participate in their merit plan. They say that it only pits teachers against one another and overlooks the fact that all their teachers do a good job.

MR. MOTTO   *[Laughing]* All of them? That sounds like a bunch of physicians talking.

BILL   If they're not doing a good job then they should be fired.

MR. MOTTO   That's not so easy to do, Bill, if they have tenure. But if we have some hard data like this to work from, perhaps it could even be used to get rid of some incompetent teachers who hide behind tenure. *[Pause]* So, what I'm recommending—OK, I guess what my entire committee is recommending—is the Jackson plan, locally adapted, of course. I know it would take some work and Luke, you could do validity and reliability studies on it to your heart's content. The only other suggestion I'd make would be to go Jackson one better and find some way to measure student learning and take that data into consideration along with the observed teacher ratings in deciding whether to award merit or not. What do you think, folks? Shall we do it, or does one of you have a better idea?

QUESTIONS

1. What is the distinction between experimental and correlational research that Luke Melvin mentions? Why is most research on teacher effectiveness correlational in nature? What are the limitations of such research?

2. Who are the "stakeholders" in the field of education that Harry Motto keeps refer ring to? How much influence should such stakeholders have in influencing school poli cies and practice? Should they be surveyed as one source of data for teacher evaluatio purposes?

3. What does Luke Melvin mean when he tells Harry Motto that surveys of stake holders "might be able to cut the extremes off from the middle" but that they wouldn help with the measurement of teachers who are in the middle? Would such survey dat be subjective or objective in nature? What do objective and subjective measurement mea in the context of teacher evaluation?

4. What motivational patterns are portrayed by Harry Motto? For example, from th standpoint of Maslow's need hierarchy, at what need level does Harry seem to be prima ily operating? How would such information help Art in dealing with Harry?

5. Luke Melvin refers to the "process-product" research. Describe that research liter ature. Do you agree with Luke's interpretation of that literature and Harry's criticism of i implications? What are the applications of this research to teacher evaluation?

6. Do you agree with the arguments against evaluating teaching through the use achievement tests given on a pretest-posttest basis as measures of student learning? Wh or why not? What are the best such tests available, and what aspects of student learnin do they measure? How strongly do such variables as the student's home environmel affect student achievement?

7. How valid and reliable are observation rating scales of the type Harry Motto wan to use? How are they different from systematic observation systems used in proces product research? How often should a teacher be observed using such a rating scale, ar who should do the observing?

8. Describe the teacher effectiveness research mentioned by Art and Luke. Does th literature suggest valid and reliable methods of evaluating teaching?

9. What are formative and summative evaluations? Which is more important whe it comes to evaluating effective teaching? Can both formative and summative evaluatic be used, or does the use of one preclude the use of the other?

10. Describe the merit pay program literature that Dan Burns and his committee a pulling together. What are the most successful programs and evaluation procedures th have been developed so far?

11. What role has educational psychology played in doing research on or developi programs and procedures for evaluating and improving teaching effectiveness? What ro might educational psychologists play in this regard in the future?

12. Should the improvement of teaching and the evaluation of teaching go hand-i hand? Why do they not do so? What are the best teacher improvement or instructior development programs that have been developed so far?

13. Do you agree with Art's explanation that the role of educational psychology is make teachers better decision-makers? How would teacher effectiveness be evaluat from this perspective?

14. Should the committee accept the plan presented by Harry Motto? Why or wl not? If not, what plan should be adopted instead?

ᴛᴏ ᴿᴇᴛᴀɪɴ ᴏʀ ᴺᴏᴛ ᴛᴏ ᴿᴇᴛᴀɪɴ

Key Content to Consider for Analyzing This Case:
(1) physical development; (2) social development;
(3) language development; (4) cognitive development.

Nell Johnson is in her fifth year of teaching first grade. However, she is completing her first year of teaching at Van Buren Elementary, since she and her husband, Steve, moved last fall to the large urban area in the Southeast where Van Buren is located. The school serves a primarily lower-middle-class attendance area consisting of an approximately 75% white, 20% African-American, and 5% Hispanic population.

Tyrone Baker is African-American and has been principal of Van Buren Elementary for sixteen years. Having put a note in Nell's mailbox that he needed to see her, he invites Nell into his office with a smile, offers her a seat, and closes the door for privacy.

Mr. Baker Nell, have you had a good year so far?

Nell I've had a very good year so far, Tyrone. Are you going to spoil it for me?

Mr. Baker *[Laughing]* No, Nell. Not at all. I have nothing but good things to say about your teaching. All the teachers I've talked to, including the other two first-grade teachers, feel the same way.

Nell Well, then, I guess I'm a bit curious about why you wanted to see me.

Mr. Baker It's about one of your students, Juan Rodriguez. I see that he's on your promotion list.

Nell Yes, I recommended that all my first graders be promoted. I didn't see any reason why Juan shouldn't be promoted, too. I know he isn't into the reading primer yet, but frankly I feel that it does more harm than good to retain students.

Mr. Baker I'm surprised, Nell. Are you saying that you believe in social promotion and are against retaining students under any circumstances?

Nell Well, no, I guess not. Probably there are circumstances that justify retention, but I guess I'd have to be convinced that it would do the child more good than harm. It certainly doesn't seem to me that it would help Juan to be retained. He's such a small, thin child who constantly needs prodding and reassurance. I really think it would crush him to make him repeat first grade.

MR. BAKER   Yes, I was watching him out on the playground the other day trying to play
   with the other kids. He's the smallest boy in your class, isn't he?

NELL   Yes, I guess he is.

MR. BAKER   I noticed how poorly coordinated he is when the other boys would let him
   play ball with them. And that wasn't often.

NELL   What do you mean?

MR. BAKER   I mean that he doesn't seem to have any close friends. The other boys seem
   to tolerate him at best, and he seemed to play alone a lot.

NELL   Yes, I guess I've noticed that in class somewhat, too. Juan cries easily and
   sometimes engages in baby talk. I guess that doesn't endear him to most of the
   boys.

MR. BAKER   Exactly! I guess we could say that Juan is somewhat emotionally and
   physically immature.

NELL   That may be true. But how is it going to help him by retaining him? He might get
   bigger physically in a year, but how is retention going to help his emotional
   development? You know how cruel children can be to one another! Can't you
   imagine the kinds of things they're going to say to poor Juan when they find out he
   was retained?

MR. BAKER   I can't deny that point! It's bound to affect his self-concept some, but how
   much I'm not certain. But we've got to look at all the factors involved in deciding
   whether to promote him or not. How would you assess him academically?

NELL   Well, I'm sure that you know that Juan comes from a large family—I believe he
   has five or six brothers and sisters—and English is his second language. I spoke to
   his mother on the phone one day and I had a difficult time understanding her. It
   embarrassed me to constantly ask her to repeat things.

MR. BAKER   Juan has a real reading problem, doesn't he?

NELL   Yes. He's such a sweet, cooperative child and he tries very hard. He finished the
   second preprimer and will probably finish the third. But he won't get to the primer
   by the end of school. If his second-grade teacher, someone like Mimi Sims, could
   start him in the reading primer, he would be so much better off! If he repeats first
   grade he'll be bored during readiness activities and may fall behind again! It seems
   such a waste! He knows what sounds are about, and he's ready to read.

MR. BAKER   But we've got to face the fact that he's way behind academically now, Nell,
   and I'm afraid he'll be hopelessly lost in the second grade, even if I put him in
   Mimi's class. He won't be able to keep up, and he'd take up so much of her time
   that it wouldn't be fair to the other students.

NELL   Then you've made your mind up to retain him?!

MR. BAKER   No, Nell, I haven't. I want us to look at the big picture and try to decide as
   objectively as we can on what the best thing would be for us to do. [Pause] Nell, are
   you crying?! I'm sorry if I said anything to upset you!

NELL   You didn't, Tyrone. It's just that this whole conversation reminds me of Randy
   Duncan, a boy I decided to retain during my second year of teaching. A decision I
   came to regret!

MR. BAKER   This was when you were teaching in Illinois?

NELL   Yes. The school district had a policy of retaining first graders who couldn't read. Randy was big for his age and came from a family of repeaters. Some of his older brothers and sisters had repeated grades. This was one of those small towns in southern Illinois, and you know what it's like growing up in a place like that!

MR. BAKER   Yes, as a matter of fact I do. Not in Illinois but in Alabama. So what happened?

NELL   Randy was slow academically even though I gave him lots of extra help. I tried to call his parents and sent letters asking them for a conference, but they just never responded. It was almost as if they expected Randy to fail and thought nothing of it!

MR. BAKER   What finally happened?

NELL   My principal looked at Randy's work and test scores and told me to retain him, so I did. I sort of lost track of Randy until the end of the next school year when I talked to Meg Ryan, a friend of mine who taught Randy when he repeated first grade. She told me how Randy stuck out like a sore thumb and how the other children said things like, "There goes that stupid Randy Duncan! He flunked first grade!!!" Meg said that Randy developed into a full-blown behavior problem and was constantly getting into fights with the other children. It just broke my heart when I remembered how cooperative and helpful he was in my class. I may have ruined Randy's life, Tyrone! That's why I think retention can destroy children's lives!

MR. BAKER   [Sympathetic but businesslike] Nell, I understand how you feel. And maybe Randy should have been promoted. But maybe there are situations where retention can actually help a child, and that's what we've got to decide about Juan. Randy was physically big and Juan is small, for one thing. And I guarantee you that we'll get his parents involved. Also, I don't think he comes from a family of repeaters, and this sure isn't small-town southern Illinois! Tell you what, let's turn all this over in our minds and continue our discussion this Friday after school.

NELL   OK. And I'll bring some information with me that I compile on all my students, mostly from their cumulative records.

MR. BAKER   Great! Have Mary [the school secretary] make copies for me of anything you have.

It is Friday after school four days later. Nell and Tyrone meet in the principal's office with the door closed.

MR. BAKER   Mary gave me copies of the information you compiled on Juan, but I've been so busy that I really haven't had a chance to go over it. Let's see here [looks at papers], he seems to have been absent when we gave the Metropolitan Readiness Test. But he did take the Peabody Picture Vocabulary Test, and he also took the California Test of Mental Maturity and scored in the average range, although he scored higher on the non-language part than he did on the language part. That would suggest reading problems, wouldn't it?

NELL   Yes, I guess it would.

MR. BAKER   His parents' names are Maria and Raul. He's a janitor at the Ames Corporation and she's a checker at a supermarket. You said that you talked to them.

NELL   I talked to the mother, but not about retaining Juan.

MR. BAKER   Oh, yes, and you said that you had a hard time understanding her.

NELL   Yes, that's right.

MR. BAKER   Nell, let me call them and talk to them. I'll tell them that we're trying to d
what's best for Juan and wonder how they would feel about him repeating first
grade. In the meantime I want you to do something.

NELL   What's that?

MR. BAKER   Talk to Juan. Ask how he would feel if he had a chance to start over again
the first grade with new students. Find out a bit more about his brothers and
sisters. How they might react if he was retained. Let's meet Wednesday after schoc
and make a final decision. OK?

It is Wednesday after school, and Nell and Tyrone meet in Tyrone's office with t
door closed to make their final decision about promoting or retaining Juan.

MR. BAKER   Were you able to talk to Juan, Nell?

NELL   Yes. But it was very difficult. I thought we were both going to break down and c
He's such a sweet, shy child and those big brown eyes remind me of Bambi in the
movie.

MR. BAKER   Oh my! Then he felt bad about the idea of being retained?

NELL   He wants to go to the second grade with his classmates.

MR. BAKER   What about his brothers and sisters?

NELL   He said that none of them had ever been retained. He said they might make fun
him for a while.

MR. BAKER   [Thoughtfully] I see.

NELL   Did you call his parents?

MR. BAKER   Yes, I did, and it was like you said, difficult to understand their broken
English. I talked to both of them at different times. The mother, Maria, seemed to
understand the situation and said that she thought we should do what we think is
best for Juan. But the father, Raul, was somewhat upset. He said that he doesn't
want his children to fail and felt very strongly that we should promote him and gi
Juan special attention in the second grade to get him up to speed.

NELL   So where does that leave us, Tyrone?

MR. BAKER   Nell, where it leaves us is that in my best professional judgment it would b
best if you retained Juan. This is the time to do it, in the first grade. If he were in
the fourth or fifth grade I'd say go ahead and pass him. But retaining him now wil
allow him to develop both physically and academically and catch up with his
classmates. I'll see that he gets into Mimi Sims' class. I'll explain it to Juan's father
and deal with him. [Pause] So what do you think, Nell?

FIGURE 4   Student Information Sheet for Juan Rodriguez, Complied by Ms. Johnson

Pupil: Juan Rodriguez
Birthdate: 12/15/92
Age: 6

Metropolitan Readiness Test: Absent
Peabody Picture Vocabulary: Scored in the very low, normal range
California Test of Mental Maturity: Language IQ: 93
                                        Non-Language IQ: 107

ACADEMIC RECORD

| | Grading Periods | | | |
	1	2	3	4
Language Arts	U	U	N	
Spelling	U	U	U	
Math	S	S	S	
Science	N	N	S	
Social Studies	N	N	N	

(Grading scale: E = excellent; S = satisfactory; N = needs improvement; U = unsatisfactory)

Parents conference notes:
Talked to Mrs. Rodriguez (Maria) on 10/17/98. She's a checker at Food Giant supermaket, and her husband (Raul) is a custodian at the Ames Corporation. She said that Juan has five brothers and three sisters from her first marriage, and that she is two months pregnant. She said that she didn't graduate from high school but that her husband did. She doesn't seem greatly interested in Juan's schooling.

Comments:
Grading period 1—Juan is a shy, immature child who is very small physically. He cries easily and engages in baby talk sometimes.

Grading period 2—Juan is a sweet, cooperative child who just can't read English. I thought he might have a learning disability, but he scored low normal on the Peabody.

Grading period 3—Cooperative, immature, still some baby talk, not good at sounds. However, he is making some progress. He has finished the second preprimer and will probably finish the third before school ends. But he won't get to the primer this school year.

QUESTIONS

1. What kinds of evidence should be considered in making promotion/reten decisions? What kinds of decision-making models exist in the literature?

2. What does the research on promotion and retention say about their effects on dent learning and emotional and social development?

3. What impact should Juan's home environment have on the retention decis How much weight should Nell place on the father's attitude and that of Juan's siblings example?

4. How much weight should be placed on Juan's emotional immaturity, such as crying easily and his baby talk? How much weight should be placed on physical fact such as his being the smallest boy in the room and his lack of coordination?

5. How much consideration should be given to a child's age, grade level, and ger in making a promotion/retention decision? Would the situation be different if Juan v in the third or fourth grade?

6. What is "social promotion"? How strong is the research support for such a pol

7. How many times does it make sense to retain a child during the child's acade career? What are the negative effects of retention on a child's self-concept, social inte tions in class, sense of efficacy, and locus of control (or attributions)? How do these re to school achievement?

8. In making a promotion/retention decision, how much relative weight should placed on child factors (e.g., physical size, psychosocial maturity, neurological matu self-concept, independent functioning, and basic skill competency) as opposed to far factors (e.g., parent attitudes, sibling attitudes, bilingualism, and racial/ethnic differenc and school factors (e.g., school and teacher attitudes, availability of personnel resources to help, and school system attitudes)?

9. From the viewpoint of social expectancy theory (self-fulfilling prophecy resear and that of labeling and stereotyping in social psychology, how might retention af Juan?

10. From an operant conditioning framework, retention may result in punishing behavior of a six-year-old boy. What relationships exist between punishment and lea ing? What is "stimulus generalization" due to punishment, and how might it affect Ju behavior?

11. Should school districts set standards to guide promotion/retention decisions should such decisions be made on a case-by-case basis by the teacher and princi involved? For example, what are the consequences of a policy like that of the school trict in which Nell had worked before, which required that first graders not be promc if they can't read at the end of the school year?

12. What response should Nell make regarding Mr. Baker's decision to retain Ju Why? Should Juan be promoted, or should he be retained? What weight should be gi his physical, language, and cognitive factors in making the decision?

C A S E 4

⟨S⟩PLITTING THE DIFFERENCES

Key Content to Consider for Analyzing This Case:
(1) cognitive development; (2) cognitive style (field
dependence/independence); (3) measurement and
evaluation; (4) motivation (mastery vs. performance
goal orientation, attribution theory, sense of efficacy);
(5) competition vs. cooperation.

Wilson Middle School is located in a large urban area in the Southwestern part of the United States. Its attendance area serves a population that is approximately 55% white, 25% Hispanic, and 20% African-American.

Tony Green, who is a graduate of a teachers college in the Midwest, is in his second year of teaching experience, all at Wilson. It is the first class meeting of his third-period Math 8 class. All thirty-one students look at Tony as he begins class.

TONY   *[Smiling]* As you all know, this is Math 8. I assume you're all in the right place, or did some of you think this was algebra or plane geometry? *[Students laugh.]* Not quite ready for algebra yet, I gather! *[More laughter]* OK, well, let me assure you that the material you'll be learning in this class will be useful to you in life—everyday stuff. We'll be learning about proportions, percents, ratios, decimals, fractions, positive and negative numbers, square roots, and a lot of other important stuff. This is everyday stuff to businessmen, cooks, mechanics, bankers, bookkeepers, and people from every kind of job you can think of. We're going to take it slow in here, make sure everybody has a chance to learn the material, and I think we're going to have some fun in the process. Yes, what's your name?

RAE ANN   Rae Ann Sullivan. How are we going to be graded in here, Mr. Green?

TONY   Good question, Rae Ann. I was just coming to that. Each Monday I'll introduce a new math concept. We'll begin with proportions this week, for example. I'll explain the concept and give you plenty of examples. It will be real important for you to pay attention when I do that. Then you'll do the assignments in the workbook that goes with your textbook and then turn them in to me for scoring. Each Thursday I'll give you a final test over the material. Then the next Monday we'll start the cycle all over again. Yes, what's your name?

JUAN   Juan, Juan Sanchez. What do we do on Friday, then, if we take the big test on Thursday?

TONY   [Smiling] I'm glad you asked, Juan. Do you all know Mr. Garcia, the teacher wh chair of the mathematics department? [Many nod their heads affirmatively.] Yes, good! Well, I've talked Mr. Garcia into letting us go to his math lab each Friday. [Some students voice surprise and excitement.]

JUAN   You mean we don't have to come to class on Friday?

TONY   Here's the deal. If you do your assignments successfully and hand them in on time, and if you make a passing grade on the Thursday test, then you get to go to the math lab on Friday. And Mr. Garcia has all kinds of interesting stuff in there! H has math games, math puzzles, filmstrips, records, tapes, computers, and all kind of stuff. If there's something relating to math that you're interested in but can't fin there, Mr. Garcia has extra money and can make it available if it isn't too expensiv He'll be there to help you if you have questions, and I hope to be there at least par of the time too.

JUAN   What happens if you don't pass the test or turn your assignments in?

TONY   Please raise your hand instead of just speaking out, Juan, if you please. [Brief pause] As thoroughly as we're going to go over everything, Juan, I don't see any reason why everyone can't go. But people who don't do their work are going to have to stay right here in the room and do it while everyone else goes to the math lab. [Several students groan and protest.] That means I have to stay here and work with you and retest you, so I don't get to go myself. [With emphasis] That would make me very unhappy, and don't forget who gives out the grades around here! Keep me happy, people! [Students laugh.] [Pause] If you don't do your work on Fridays, then I'm going to send home a message [holds up blank form] explaining this to your parents, which your parents must sign. If you don't return them to me on Monday all signed and dated in proper order, then I'm personally going to call them and talk the matter over with them. [Several students groan and protest.] [Paus Now, let's begin by my calling the roll. Please raise your hand as I call your name s I can begin putting names and faces together.

Two months later, Tony sits in the classroom of Ramon Garcia, chair of the ma department, who has ten years of teaching experience. The school day is over and t classroom is empty except for the two of them.

TONY   Ramon, I'm really getting frustrated and anxious about my third-period Math 8 class.

RAMON   What's the difficulty, Tony?

TONY   It's a little hard to know where to begin, but the class seems to be divided into two groups: students who are bright and students who are slow.

RAMON   Do you mean that in an intelligence sense?

TONY   No, not so much IQ, although I suppose IQ might be related. But I'm talking about math abilities. Some of the kids seem to grasp the math concepts very quickly, while others are very slow catching on.

RAMON   How are the groups divided? Along sex or ethnic or racial lines?

TONY   No, I guess it's more along intelligence lines.

RAMON   I was wondering if there were more girls in the slow group, since a lot of them have math anxiety.

TONY   No, not at all. The girls are fairly evenly represented in both groups. Rae Ann Sullivan definitely has math anxiety, though.

RAMON   How's that?

TONY   I had a conference with her the other day at which I was trying to praise her for her good work. She told me in no uncertain terms that she just wasn't good at math. She said her mother hadn't been good at math either, so she was sure it runs in the family. When I pointed out to her that she had scored in the 80s on her last two tests, she just chalked the whole thing up to good luck. She said she really didn't understand how to do the problems but just guessed at the answers and got them right.

RAMON   [Laughing] Yes, I've heard that before from students. I wonder if they think good luck runs in the family too!

TONY   [Laughing] Yeah, right! But I sometimes wonder how the slow students do get the answers. They just seem to guess at the answers or use trial and error. They are poor analyzers and undisciplined in the way they approach problems.

RAMON   You have some troublemakers in there?

TONY   No, no real discipline problems. They are just unsystematic in the way that they approach math problems. Some of them just can't see the trees because of the forest. They just can't break a problem down into its parts.

RAMON   What do you mean?

TONY   Well, like the other day. I drew two circles on the blackboard, representing pies. I explained that one was an apple pie and the other a cherry pie. I divided the apple pie into six slices and the cherry pie into five. I then took two slices out of each pie and asked them which pie had the most pie remaining, and that if I put the two slices of the cherry pie into the apple pie and vice versa, would I have the same amount of pie that I started out with? That problem really blew the minds of some of the slow students. Juan Sanchez said that you couldn't mix cherry and apple pie together like that. Rae Ann Sullivan said that you'd have the same amount of pie that you started out with since you still had all the pieces. All you've done is move the cherry slices into the apple pie and vice versa. When I asked her if it made any difference that I had divided one pie into five slices and the other into six, she said it didn't matter since both pies were the same size to begin with.

RAMON   I see what you mean. Did any of the kids understand the problem?

TONY   Oh, yes. My bright kids, like John Bailey, quickly converted the fractions to 30ths and pronounced that two slices of the cherry pie were 12/30 of the pie, while two slices of the apple were 10/30 and therefore more would be left of the apple pie and that while the two slices of the apple pie would fit into the cherry pie, the two slices of the cherry pie would be too big for the apple pie.

RAMON   How did the slower kids react when they heard John's explanation?

TONY   In a word, they just didn't get it. I explained and reexplained the whole thing several times, and finally, the next day, they began to get it.

RAMON   How did the bright kids react to that?

TONY   At first they smirked and made wisecracks and rolled their eyes at one another, but by the second day they were just plain bored and exasperated.

Some of them laid their heads down on their desks and slept. Others read books or whispered.

RAMON   So you're just not able to get some of your students to learn the material? That confuses me because it seems like your whole class comes to the math lab on Friday.

TONY   No, practically all of them learn the material eventually. But, Ramon, it's like pulling teeth! I have to go over the stuff again and again until they get it!

RAMON   But they do get it?

TONY   Right, but we're moving very slowly and the bright kids are bored out of their skulls. The tortoises plod along very slowly while the hares want to rush on up ahead and explore new territory. The bright kids want new stuff, while the slow kids want to keep going over the old material to make sure they understand it and, I suppose, to enjoy what little success they get. I suppose, too, that the slow kids also want to make sure they get to go to math lab every Friday. So, we're way behind where we should be. I guess I've really been teaching to the slow kids, hoping that the bright kids will be patient. But the natives are really getting restles

RAMON   What do you mean?

TONY   Mr. Harris [building principal] called me in yesterday to tell me that the parents o three of my bright kids have called him about how I'm holding their kids back. I don't blame them. They know their kids have to take the PSAT next year, and they want them to be ready.

RAMON   So what did Mark [building principal] tell you to do?

TONY   [Smiling] Why, to get in here and see you as quick as I can! He said you'd tell me what to do.

RAMON   [Laughing] I guess that's one way to solve a problem. Mark uses that one a lot! [Pause] Well, Tony, your situation isn't a new one. Many teachers in a situation like yours have wondered whether they should teach to the slow students, the fast students, or somewhere in the middle.

TONY   What's the answer, Ramon? I don't remember anyone discussing what to do in a situation like this when I was at Teachers College.

RAMON   Most teachers have dealt with situations like yours by putting the students into slow and fast groups and working with them separately. The faster students shoul either be allowed to move ahead at a faster pace or work with enrichment materia that go beyond what the slower kids are working on in class. Your job will be to figure how to explain all this to them and to budget your time as equally as possib between the two groups. In a way it's like planning for, teaching, and evaluating two different classes that happen to be meeting in the same room at the same tim

TONY   Boy, that's going to be a challenge, not to mention time-consuming.

RAMON   Yes, but look at it this way, Tony. Teachers have been doing this since the days of the old one-room schoolhouse. Some of them had several grades in one room.

TONY   That's true, isn't it? Ramon, that's what I'll do! I'll figure out some way to group them and work with the groups separately. I'll use different grading standards to determine whether they get to go to math lab or not. I'm not real sure how to do that, but I'll try to figure out a way!

RAMON Grading differentially has been an issue from the beginning of tracking or grouping students by ability levels. Some have solved it by saying a B in a higher-ability group is equivalent to an A in a lower-ability group, for example. Just work on it. I'm sure you'll develop a grading system suitable for your situation.

TONY Many thanks, Ramon. Now I know why Mr. Harris sent me to see you!

It is third period on a Monday morning one month later. Tony has reorganized his class of thirty-one students into five groups: two "fast" groups (groups 1 and 2) with seven students in each, two "slow" groups (groups 4 and 5), with seven in one and six in the other, and one "middle" group (group 3) of four students.

TONY OK folks, there's the bell! Let's all settle down! *[Pause]* It's Monday, and you know what that means. We're starting a new math concept. This week we're going to work on positive and negative numbers. The idea of a negative number is difficult for some people to understand, but I'm going to explain it real clearly and give you lots of examples. Please move into your groups now. *[Students move their chairs into five groups arranged in circles.]* Now let me give each group your weekly assignment sheets. Would one person from each group come up here and get the assignment sheets for your group? *[Hands sheets out as students come up to desk.]* *[Pause]* OK, settle down now so I can give each group its assignment. *[Pause]* OK, first I want to make a few general remarks about the nature of positive and negative numbers that you all need to listen carefully to and take notes on. Then groups 1 and 2 can go ahead and begin working on your assignment sheets. Yes, Jamal?

JAMAL I think you gave us the wrong assignment sheets! This stuff is hard! This can't be ours!

TONY *[Walking over to Jamal and looking at sheet]* Yes, you're right, Jamal. This is group 1's assignment sheet. John, let me see the sheets that I gave you for group 1. *[John brings his copy up to Tony and Tony examines it.]* Yes, I'm sorry. Would groups 1 and 4 exchange assignment sheets, please? *[Students stand up and exchange papers.]* Yes, John.

JOHN Mr. Green, how come groups 4 and 5 get to do that easy stuff and we have to work twice as hard for the same grade?! That's not fair!

TONY Now, John, don't you remember us talking about this when I set the groups up? You have students operating at different levels academically just like you do in sports. Not everybody gets to play on the first-team varsity squad. However, that doesn't mean that everybody shouldn't have the chance to play on some team at some level.

JOHN So we're the varsity in here? *[One student in group 1 begins to chant "We're number one, we're number one!"]* Right. Well, we may be number one, but those other groups get just as good a grade for doing their easy stuff as we do our hard stuff, and that isn't fair! *[Other students in groups 1 and 2 shout agreement.]*

JUAN So what does that make us, chopped liver?! I hate math, and this stuff is hard for me!

RAE ANN Yes, some of us can't do this easier work, much less that hard stuff! So does that make us bad people or something? We're good at other things, though, like English. I love English! *[Some students voice agreement.]*

JOHN *[Mocking Rae Ann]* I just love English! *[Several group 1 and group 2 students laugh*

TONY *[Angrily and loudly]* Stop it people, right now! *[Students all stop talking.]* This has gone far enough! Why can't you people treat one another with a little respect! *[Pause]* Now look, guys, not all people are the same. Some are good at math, som are good at English, and some are good at sports, but I don't know of anybody who's good at everything. Even the best math student in here might be a poor basketball player. Why can't we just accept one another's strengths and weakness since we all have them? *[Pause]* I know that the work some groups are doing in here is more advanced than that of other groups. I explained that to you a month ago when we formed the groups. Yes, John?

JOHN But can't we get extra credit for doing harder work, Mr. Green?

TONY I considered doing that when I formed the groups and decided against it. It seemed undemocratic somehow. However, maybe I should rethink it. Perhaps a for more difficult work should be considered equivalent to an A for doing less difficult work, for example.

RAE ANN But that wouldn't be fair, Mr. Green! We'd never get as good a grade as peo in groups 1 and 2!

JOHN It's because we're better in math than you are, Rae Ann! If you can do the same stuff we do, you can get an A too!

TONY *[Angrily]* John and Rae Ann—not one more word! Don't anyone speak out without raising your hand again! *[Several hands go up.]* No, I'm not recognizing a of you right now! We're all too upset to talk this through rationally. Let me think of this over, and we'll discuss it another day in a calmer and more organized manner. *[Pause]* Now, take out your notebooks and write down what I'm about t explain to you about positive and negative numbers. *[Several students groan.]*

It is two weeks later on Friday afternoon after school. Tony and Ramon Garcia in chairs talking to one another in Ramon's classroom.

TONY Ramon, organizing my third-period class into ability groups seemed to be working. I had developed three different levels of materials, and everything seem to be going along just fine. Then a couple of weeks ago all heck broke loose.

RAMON What happened?

TONY Well, it all started when I accidentally passed out the assignment sheets on positive and negative numbers to the wrong groups. The students got upset whe they compared the differences in the difficulty level of the work they're doing. Some of the brighter kids complained about getting the same grades as the slow students even though they have to work harder. When I talked about grading th work of the groups differentially, like a B in an advanced group being equivalent an A in a slow group, then the slower students complained that that wouldn't be fair because they're working as hard as they can at their level.

RAMON Well, surely you can get them to brainstorm a bit about what grading proced would be fair to all and work out some kind of win-win solution. Getting them calm down and look at what's fair for everybody is the key. Maybe you could tu into a kind of game or challenge. Kids love solving puzzles.

TONY   Yeah, maybe. But things have just gotten worse since that day. The bright and slow kids are constantly teasing, taunting, and backstabbing one another. It has solidified into a hostile rivalry between groups. I've noticed that the bickering has spilled out into their interactions outside the classroom, even during the breaks between classes. They yell obscenities at one another in class until I step in like a referee and blow my whistle for them to stop. I'm not sure I could get them to brainstorm in a rational way.

RAMON   That does sound bad, Tony!

TONY   Yeah, and to make it worse, Mark Harris called me into his office to tell me that three of my parents are complaining about the discipline problems in my class. They say I can't control the class and their kids' learning is suffering. They're afraid they won't be ready to take the PSAT.

RAMON   Have you lost control of the class, Tony?

TONY   No, of course not! Well, I don't think so anyhow! I can still calm the kids down and make them quiet down and get to work. They are angry with one another, not me. *[Pause]* But there's another problem that goes beyond the control issue that keeps nagging at me.

RAMON   And what's that?

TONY   The differences between the groups is getting bigger and bigger. The slow groups just keep falling further behind. After school I work with as many of them as I can, but it doesn't seem to make a dent. Those kids aren't going to be ready for the PSAT or algebra or anything else! And with the classroom atmosphere being what it is, I just have no hope they'll ever catch up to where they should be. I'm at my wit's end, Ramon. Can you think of anything at all that I can try?

FIGURE 5 Student Information Assembled by Tony Green on His Third-Period Math 8 Class

NAME	GROUP NO.	GRADING PERIOD GRADES 1	2	METRO ACH. TEST, MATH SUBSCALE[1]	I.Q.[2]	ELIGIBLE FOR SCHOOL LUNCH
1. Adams, Jennifer	1	B	A	7	110	No
2. Anderson, Willie	3	C	C	5	98	Yes
3. Bailey, John	1	A	A	8	133	No
4. Butler, Latesha	4	D	C	3	92	Yes
5. Carter, Billy	2	B	B	7	115	No
6. Conner, Wayne	2	C	C+	7	128	No
7. Ferguson, Scott	1	B	A	7	131	No
8. Gil, Maria	2	C+	B	7	116	No
9. Gonzalez, Donna	5	D	D	2	88	Yes
10. Greene, Laura	1	B	B	6	111	No
11. Harris, Mark	2	B+	B	6	117	No
12. Hernandez, Rita	5	D	C	3	103	Yes
13. Herrera, Gerardo	5	D	F	1	83	Yes
14. Jackson, David	1	A	A	9	142	No
15. Johnson, Tyrone	4	D	D+	2	88	Yes
16. King, Jerome	3	D+	C	5	97	Yes
17. Landry, Greg	1	B+	A	8	131	No
18. Lewis, Jamal	4	D+	C	3	101	Yes
19. Martin, Debra	2	A	B	7	127	No
20. Martinez, Luis	5	D	D+	3	98	Yes
21. Miller, Tekha	4	D+	C	4	103	Yes
22. Mitchell, Cynthia	4	C	B	5	105	No
23. Murphy, Iris	2	C	B	6	111	No
24. Ramos, Hosea	3	C	C+	5	108	Yes
25. Samuelson, Sarah	1	B	B	7	118	No
26. Sanchez, Juan	4	D	C	3	107	Yes
27. Sullivan, Rae Ann	4	C	C	4	109	No
28. Valdez, Julio	3	C	C	5	105	Yes
29. Washington, Cassandra	5	D	D	2	91	Yes
30. White, Dannette	5	C	C+	5	104	Yes
31. Young, Karen	5	C+	B	5	109	No

[1]Metropolitan Achievement Test, Advanced, math subscale in stanines, given in grade 7.
[2]Total IQ Score on California Test of Mental Maturity, intermediate level, given in grade 7.

QUESTIONS

1. What is a discipline problem? What models of classroom management might Tony consider using with his class? For example, how useful would Teacher Effectiveness Training, Assertive Discipline, or behavior modification be in this situation?

2. How could Tony have handled the assignment sheet mixup more effectively? What were the underlying causes of the students' reactions in that situation?

3. How effective is ability grouping in education, especially at the eighth-grade level? What kinds of ability differences existed between the "bright" and "slow" students in Tony's class? To what extent are the differences due to intelligence? Cognitive style? Underachievement?

4. How good a job did Tony do in grouping his students? What other types of grouping procedures could he have used? What are enrichment materials, and does their use make sense in this case?

5. What kind of evaluation procedures should Tony have used? Does it make sense to "grade differentially" (i.e., a B in the "fast" group is equivalent to an A in the "slow" group)?

6. Tony decided to "teach to the slow group" at first and then tried grouping. What other curriculum and instruction procedures might he have used to take individual differences into consideration? For example, could he have used individual contracting plans, in which each student could move at his or her own pace?

7. Do time limit pressures (e.g., finishing by the end of the semester or being ready to take a standardized test the next year) prevent students from learning at their own pace? What role do politics and money play in limiting "moving at own pace" options in education?

8. What role is competition among students playing in this case? Would you recommend that Tony implement a cooperative learning model in this situation?

9. What are the causes of math anxiety, especially among female students? What role does it play in this case?

10. Tony's use of the math lab on Fridays could be viewed as a contingency management technique. How effectively did Tony use it? Would you recommend that he not use it at all or use it differently?

11. At what level of Maslow's need hierarchy do Tony, Juan, Rae Ann, and John seem to be primarily operating? How does this help explain their behavior?

12. What role is self-fulfilling prophecy playing in this case? For example, what expectations has Tony developed regarding his "bright" and "slow" students? What beliefs do they seem to have developed?

13. To what extent should teachers like Tony concern themselves with preparing their students to take a standardized test like the PSAT? What are the issues and dangers involved?

14. How has the home environments that the students come from affected their classroom behavior? What kinds of pressures are the parents putting on Tony and the students? What parent involvement techniques can be used to help deal with such pressures?

15. What cognitive style differences exist among Tony's students? For example, field dependence/independence problems exist in the cases of Rae Ann and Juan? Wh can teachers do about such problems?

16. What differences in motivational patterns exist among Tony's students? For exa ple, do differences exist in terms of mastery versus performance learning orientatior Internal versus external locus of control or attributions? High versus low sense of ma efficacy?

17. What should Tony do next? Should he continue his groups as they now exi Change his evaluation procedures? Attempt to communicate with and involve the p ents?

ᴀITING THE Hook

Key Content to Consider for Analyzing This Case:
(1) constructivism; (2) cognitive development (Piaget);
(3) information processing theory; (4) motivation
(mastery vs. performance goal orientation, sense of
efficacy, underachievement); (5) self-concept; (6) social
development; (7) home environment (including
parenting styles).

Wilson Middle School is located in a large urban area in the Southwestern part of the United States. Its attendance area serves a population that is approximately 55% white, 25% Hispanic, and 20% African-American.

Tony Green, who is a graduate of a teachers college in the Midwest, is in his second year of teaching experience, all at Wilson. It is three and a half months into the first semester and it is almost the end of third period on a Thursday morning. Tony has just asked the thirty-one students in his Math 8 class to turn in their weekly tests on positive and negative numbers.

TONY   OK, gang, pass 'em up to the front row and then down to Rae Ann. Rae Ann, will you collect them for me? *[Rae Ann smiles and nods her head affirmatively.]*
Wayne, I need to talk to you for just a minute when the bell rings.

WAYNE   OK. I have study hall next period anyhow.

TONY   And it's my planning period. I'll give you a note to take to your study hall teacher if you're late. *[Bell rings.]* See you all in math lab tomorrow, I hope! *[Holds test papers up high as he speaks. Several students laugh.]* Pull a chair up to my desk, Wayne, so we can talk. *[All other students leave the room.]*

WAYNE   *[Pulling a chair up to teacher's desk]* What did you want to talk to me about, Mr. Green?

TONY   Your grades, Wayne. *[Pulls out Wayne's test paper and grades it as they talk]* Wayne, I was talking to several of your teachers about you the other day in the teachers' lounge. We were all in agreement that you're a very bright guy, but your grades don't seem to show it.

WAYNE   I do OK. I'm getting C's in most of my classes, and that's average. That suits me just fine.

TONY   You're right on target, Wayne. I just graded your test and you got a C.

WAYNE   See! That's just fine. I get to go to math lab tomorrow just like the other guys.

Tony That's true, Wayne. You would even have gotten to go if you had made a D, bu
why do you set such low standard for yourself when you have such potential?

Wayne I'm not that good at math, Mr. Green.

Tony Not that good, or is it that you just don't want to work that hard? I have no do
that you could be making A's in here if you set your mind to it.

Wayne I study the stuff hard enough. Math isn't exactly easy for me.

Tony That's what I wanted to find out from you. Is it that the material is hard for you
or do you only put out enough effort to make C's?

Wayne No, math isn't exactly easy. Take negative numbers. I may have passed the tes
but the idea of not only not having anything left but going into the hole by so
much still confuses me. Like if I go fishing and catch five fish and the game ward
comes along and says that the five fish that I caught are illegal and that I not onl
have to give those five fish back but also five others that I haven't caught yet—yo
know that example you gave in class—well, I guess it's OK and I understand tha
example OK. It's just when you start giving us numbers by themselves that I get
confused. When you take the examples away and I have to work with the numb
by themselves, that not only confuses me but bores me, Mr. Green. I'm an action
person, not an Einstein.

Tony Is that why you've been turning in some of your assignments but not others? Y
like the concrete examples but not abstract numbers?

Wayne I don't know what you call it, but those assignments with just numbers both
me and I guess bore me too much to try to figure them out. Some of the earlier s
I could think out how they apply to fishing, but it gets hard with some things lik
negative numbers.

Tony Why fishing?

Wayne Just because I go fishing all the time. That's my favorite thing to do. Dad and
go out about every weekend to one of the four or five lakes we fish.

Tony That's great, Wayne! I used to do a little fishing myself when I was a kid. But y
say you go with your dad? That's great!

Wayne Yeah. Dad works in an office all week and we like to get out together as often
we can. He finally bought an eighteen-foot aluminum boat and put a fifty-horse
Mercury engine on it, so we can move right along! The boat's real stable, too. You
can stand almost anywhere in it and cast a line without feeling like you're losing
your balance!

Tony It sounds like you're quite a fisherman, Wayne. What does your dad do?

Wayne He's an accountant. Has his own business downtown.

Tony Is that what you want to do when you graduate?

Wayne I don't know. I haven't given it much thought. I don't think I want to go to
college, though, not unless they'd let me major in fishing! [Both Wayne and Tony
laugh.]

Tony Well, I don't know, I'm sure there must be a lot of careers you could explore th
involve fishing and the sea. Have you done any saltwater fishing?

Wayne [Eagerly] No, but Dad and I have been planning to! Dad says we need to go
down to the Florida Keys during his next vacation and rent a boat and go after
those big marlins! Do you have any idea how big those marlins get, Mr. Green?

TONY   Yes, I've seen pictures on TV. But what else do you like to do besides fish, Wayne?

WAYNE   Oh, not much. I'm not interested in much of anything else.

TONY   What about sports?

WAYNE   Dad thought I should try out for the basketball team. I wasn't much good.

TONY   What do you like to do with your friends?

WAYNE   I don't hang with the guys much. Sometimes John Bailey and I go to the mall and mess around a while, but I mostly just like to stay home and read.

TONY   Oh. What do you like to read?

WAYNE   Mostly just books and magazines about fishing. Dad's bought me subscriptions to practically all the good magazines, and that one bookstore in the mall gets a lot of good books on fishing. Dad lets me charge all the books I want. He says books are one thing you shouldn't be cheap about.

TONY   I couldn't agree with your dad more! *[Pause]* Well, Wayne, this has been very interesting getting to know you a little better and to find out that you're such a fisherman and all. But I'm still convinced that you can make better grades than you are making, and I want to work with you more on helping you understand abstract numbers better. Will you work with me?

WAYNE   Sure, Mr. Green. Anything you want. Just let me know what you want me to do.

TONY   OK, Wayne. Let me get a little more information and we'll set something up. Here, let me write you a study hall pass since the bell has already rung.

As soon as Wayne exited from the room, Tony walked down the hall to the counselors' office and walked up to the open door of the office of Kimberly Crandall, who is looking down at some forms she is filling out.

TONY   Hello, Kim.

KIM   *[Startled and looking up]* What!? Oh, hello, Tony!

TONY   *[Smiling]* Sorry to startle you. Do you have a minute?

KIM   *[Putting up the forms and a pen]* Sure. Come on in. *[Motions to a wooden chair]* These forms will keep. What's up?

TONY   I wonder if you can tell me who's Wayne Conner's counselor. I'd like to look at his folder.

KIM   You've come to the right person. I was making some entries in some of the folders yesterday, and Wayne's was one of them. *[Pulls a folder out of a large stack of folders and hands it to Tony]* As a matter of fact, I talked to Tony's mother on the phone last week about where he ought to go to high school.

TONY   Oh, really?! What was her concern?

KIM   You'll see my note in the folder. Basically, I think she's a bit concerned about Wayne and just wanted to talk to me about it. In a nutshell, I think she believes that Wayne is an underachiever, and both she and her husband feel that he's college material and are disappointed that his grades are so, well, average.

TONY   That's really interesting. I just came from a conference with Wayne where he and I discussed these same issues. I got the feeling that Wayne is perfectly content to make C's and has no real ambitions to attend college. All he really seems to be interested in is fishing.

KIM   Yes. Marie, that's Wayne's mother, said that Wayne and his father go fishing together all the time. You'll note from the folder that Wayne is their only child, an they may be a bit overprotective. Marie was describing Wayne's room at home, an it sounds like he has everything money can buy.

TONY   He doesn't seem to have many friends his own age, though. Sounds like his dad his best friend.

KIM   I hear that sometimes happens with only children.

TONY   His dad's an accountant or something? [Looks at the folder] Oh, yes, here it is. Hi dad's a CPA and his mother is an elementary teacher. Now, this is interesting: he was tested last year, and his IQ is 128. I thought he was bright! And he's at the seventh stanine on the math portion of the Metropolitan Achievement Test. I compiled this information on all my third-period students over a month ago in order to assign them to groups and had forgotten about it! Well, this just reinforce my belief that Wayne should be doing a whole lot better than he is in my class!

KIM   And not just in math, I might add. He's pretty much a C student in all his classes. Do you think it's a lack of motivation, Tony?

TONY   I'm not sure. Partly, I guess. But he also seems to have a problem with abstrac material, at least in math. In my class he only does the assignments that interest him. But the only ones that interest him seem to be those dealing with concrete material or else material he can relate to fishing examples. I don't know how his algebra teacher is going to get him interested in algebra when he takes it next year!

KIM   Let me know if I can help in any way, Tony.

TONY   Thanks, Kim. This helps a lot.

It is late on a Friday afternoon about two weeks later. School has ended, and m of the students have already left the building. Tony has arranged a conference w Wayne's parents, Wayland and Marie Conner. They sit in movable desks in Tony's cla room facing one another.

TONY   I really appreciate you two taking the time to come in and meet with me. I've been wanting to talk with you about Wayne.

MARIE   [With concern] And we have really wanted to talk to someone here, Mr. Green. Wayne has told us that you've tried to help him.

TONY   I think what it comes down to, Mr. and Mrs. Conner, is that Wayne isn't workir up to his potential. I've talked to a number of his other teachers and to his counselor, Ms. Crandall, and I've gone over his cumulative record with his test scores and all. All the information seems to point to Wayne being what we call an underachiever. He seems to be willing to settle for C's when he could be making A in his classes, including mine.

WAYLAND   I think you've sized Wayne up rather accurately, Mr. Green. He does just enough work to get by with C's but just isn't interested enough in his schoolwork put forth the effort to make A's. I go over this with him just about every time he brings home a report card. *[Pause]* You know, Mr. Green, I'm a CPA and have a rather well-established and profitable business. We just hired another young man yesterday who is fresh out of college who reminds me a lot of Wayne. Wayne could fit right in and take over my firm when I retire if he wanted to. The opportunity is there for the taking. But when I talk to him about it, he just says he isn't sure whether he'd like being a CPA or not. When I ask him what he'd like to do if he could do anything he wanted to, he just says he isn't sure. It seems like fishing is the only thing that really interests him. *[Smiling]* He doesn't even seem to have really discovered girls yet.

MARIE   We have talked to him about his grades and his future a lot, Mr. Green. But he's our only child, you know, and all we really want is for him to be happy. We don't want to put too much pressure on him. After all, he's only thirteen, and sometimes I think that's too young for anyone to be making decisions about what they want to do with the rest of their lives. We're disappointed that he isn't making better grades, but we hope he'll improve as he gets older and matures a bit. If he doesn't, then maybe he can go to a community college later on and take some courses in things that interest him. *[Pause]* I know Wayland wants him to eventually step into his firm and take it over, but that may not be what Wayne wants to do or would be good at. Wayne has to find himself first before he makes big decisions about his life. He's still really just a little boy in many ways.

WAYLAND   *[With annoyance]* Yes, all that may be true, Marie. But when I was thirteen I at least had a desire to make something of myself and had a little ambition. Wayne doesn't seem to have any drive at all. And what worries me most is that he's such a loner. He doesn't seem to have people skills. You've got to learn to relate to other people if you're going to be a success in life.

MARIE   *[Animated]* Wayland, you have to learn to look at the good side of things more! Wayne has a wonderful relationship with you, and he is a good boy. I'm glad he's not into that adolescent drug and party scene. I'm real glad we don't have the kinds of problems with Wayne that the Masons have with their son.

TONY   One of my concerns as Wayne's math teacher is that he seems to have trouble learning abstract concepts. If he can't relate what he's learning back to concrete examples, he has real difficulties. The only way he could deal with negative numbers, for example, was to relate them to catching fish. This concerns me because he's going to have to grasp abstract concepts when he takes algebra next year.

WAYLAND   *[Frowning]* See! That's what I mean, Marie! Wayne's not dumb! He just doesn't try to use his brain! *[Smiling]* No offense, Mr. Green, but I think he's got his teachers fooled into believing he can't think in abstract terms. He sure doesn't have any trouble figuring out abstract issues when it comes to fishing! *[Eagerly]* He's really quite an expert when it comes to fishing, you know. He can tell you all about the habits of various fish, the effects of lake temperatures on the eating habits of the fish, what lure to use under what circumstances, and you ought to see him cast! He can put it anywhere he wants it! It's amazing. *[Pause]* No, Mr. Green, I think he just doesn't *want* to think abstractly about certain subjects.

TONY   [Frowning] You may be right, Mr. Conner. It may be more of a motivation problem than an abstract thinking problem. All I can say is, if it's true, he sure had me fooled!

WAYLAND   [Smiling] Believe me, he's no dummy, Mr. Green! Well, Marie and I do appreciate all that you're trying to do for Wayne. If he could just get into his schoolwork the way he's into fishing, he would end up as valedictorian when he graduates. But I guess he's got to decide that his schoolwork is important to him. Well, thanks again, Mr. Green, and if there's anything we can do to help, please le us know.

MARIE   [Smiling] Yes, thanks so much, Mr. Green. I want you to know that we do talk him about his schoolwork at home, but Wayland is right. Wayne is evasive and doesn't want to talk about it. [Pause] But I don't know about the abstract thinking thing you were talking about. I've noticed that several times when I've sent him to the store for me, he has trouble with simple things like making change and figurin out how much things cost in his head. If he and I shop together at the supermark I always get one of those shopping carts with a calculator on it so Wayne won't ge confused.

WAYLAND   [Interrupting] He just doesn't pay attention, Marie! Believe me, if he wanted to, he'd become an expert in no time.

MARIE   But like the other day when you and Wayne were making that new lure.

WAYLAND   You mean the yellowjacket?

MARIE   Yes, the black and yellow one. Wayne couldn't follow what you were telling hir until you drew it up on a piece of paper. Then he put it together without any problem.

WAYLAND   [Reflecting] Yes, that's true. But didn't you have to take a picture of the haird that you wanted to your beautician the other day so she could get it the way you wanted it? It's the same thing.

MARIE   [Puzzled] Well, maybe you're right. I don't know. [Pause] Well, thanks again, M Green. We appreciate your helping Wayne.

TONY   And thank you both for taking the time to come in and talk. Let's keep in touch I'm sure the three of us can figure out ways to help a bright guy like Wayne do better in school.

It is the following Monday afternoon after school has ended. Tony sits in the cla room of Ramon Garcia, chair of the math department. They sit in chairs facing c another.

TONY   Ramon, I need to ask your advice about one of the students in my Math 8 class

RAMON   Your third-period class?

TONY   [Smiling] Yes. How did you guess? I seem to have more trouble with that class than all my others, don't I?

RAMON   Who's the student?

TONY   Wayne Conner. He's a classic underachiever. He has an IQ of 128 and works ju hard enough in his classes to make C's. His dad's a CPA and his mom's an elementary teacher. We had a conference about Wayne last Friday. The picture th

FIGURE 6   Portion of Wayne Conner's Cumulative Record

WILSON MIDDLE SCHOOL
Cumulative Record

Name: Conner, Wayne Lynne   Home Telephone: 313-318-1423
Address: 6023 Robin Lane Rd.   General Health: Good
Father: Wayland D. Conner   Occupation: CPA
Mother: Marie R. Conner   Occupation: Elementary Teacher
Siblings: None   Handicaps: None
Former Schools: Blaine Elementary   Date of Birth: 11/13/86
Date Entered Wilson: 8/30/98   Age: 13 years

TEST RECORD

Intelligence Tests	IQ	Date	Grade
Otis-Lennon Mental Ability			
Elementary I	121	9/1/94	3
Intermediate	128	9/5/98	7

Achievement Tests

Metropolitan Advanced	Math	Basics Total	Complete Total
(in stanines)	7	7	7

ACADEMIC RECORD

Grades 1–6 (year averages)	1	2	3	4	5	6
Language Arts	A	A	B	B	C	C
Reading	A	A	B	B	B	B
Writing	A	A	B	C	C	C
Spelling	A	A	B	C	C	C
Social Studies	A	A	B	C	C	B
Arithmetic	A	A	B	C	C	C
Science and Health		A	B	C	C	C
Music	A	A	A	A	A	A
Citizenship	A	A	A	A	A	A

Grade 7 (year average)

English	C
Geography	C
Arithmetic	C
Phys. Ed.	C
Science	C
Exploratory	C
Per./Social Dev.	C

emerges is a thirteen-year-old kid who is a loner and spends all of his time with his father fishing. Wayne's a real expert on fishing. His mother seems a bit overprotective but cares a lot about Wayne. I think Wayne's father believes that Wayne's just unmotivated about schoolwork and could do better if he really tried.

RAMON   And what do you think?

TONY   I don't know, Ramon. Something tells me that it's more than just motivation. I think Wayne may have some difficulty in the area of abstract thinking. He has to relate abstract concepts to concrete examples, usually fishing, before he can understand them. His dad thinks this is just a game that Wayne plays with his teachers to avoid working too hard. His mother isn't so sure and says that she's noticed some abstract thinking problems at home. *[Pause]* I guess that my instinct tell me that Wayne's father is wrong and that Wayne's abstract thinking problem real.

RAMON   This is a difficult and unusual situation, Tony. Did you look up his records or talk to his counselor to get additional information on this?

TONY   Yes, I did. And guess what! He's at the seventh stanine on the math subtest of the Metropolitan. I almost forgot that bit of information. Maybe his dad is right after all

RAMON   Maybe. Maybe not. What's your next step, Tony? Or is that why you came to me?

TONY   *[Smiling]* That's why I came to see you, Ramon. We're starting square roots this week. How would you go about teaching square roots to a student who is an expert on fishing but who may have an abstract thinking problem? Are there some tests can take that would help me figure out how to help him?

QUESTIONS

1. What is an underachiever? To what extent is an IQ score a good predictor of student ability or potential? Is Wayne an underachiever?

2. Is Wayne's problem motivational or cognitive, or both? What type of motivation or cognitive problem does Wayne have? What can be done about such problems?

3. Describe teacher expectancy theory. Is there a self-fulfilling prophecy at work in Wayne's case? What expectations or beliefs seem to be influencing Wayne's behavior?

4. How would you describe Wayne's home environment and his relationship with his parents and his peers? Are Wayne's parents overprotective? How would Erikson's theory of personality development explain the development and effects of parental overprotectiveness?

5. From Baumrind's perspective, what parenting style do Wayne's parents exhibit: authoritarian, authoritative, or permissive? How does such a parenting style relate to school achievement?

6. Wayne is an only child. What types of personality development and achievement patterns are associated with being an only child? Does Wayne's behavior fit the pattern?

7. What are concrete and abstract learning? Given that Wayne is thirteen years old does he seem to exhibit problems in making the transition to formal operations (from standpoint of Piaget's theory of cognitive development)?

8. From the standpoint of constructivism, does Wayne seem to be "in the zone" with regard to learning Math 8 concepts such as negative numbers? What type of learning scaffolds would be helpful to a student like Wayne?

9. From the motivational perspective of Ames' mastery learning versus performance learning, does Wayne seem to be more oriented toward mastery or toward performance in his schoolwork? In the area of fishing? How can Tony take advantage of this information?

10. At what level of Maslow's need hierarchy does Wayne seem to be primarily operating? At what level are Wayne's parents primarily operating? How can Tony use this information?

11. From a social development frame of reference, is Wayne's mother correct in her belief that society puts too much pressure on students to make early career choices? Should such choices be made at the middle school level? What pressure is being put on Wayne, and how is he responding to it? What can Tony do?

12. Should Tony refer Wayne to a school psychologist for further testing—for example, to shed more light on the issue of abstract versus concrete thinking? What kinds of tests would be valid and reliable for that purpose?

13. How well did Tony conduct his conference with the Conners? Is there anything you would have done differently?

14. What advice should Ramon give Tony about teaching his unit on square roots so as to involve Wayne? Can Wayne's interest in fishing be utilized in some way? How can Wayne's abstract thinking skills be developed?

CASE **6**

THROUGH THICK AND THIN

Key Content to Consider for Analyzing This Case:
(1) social development (especially socialization, self-concept); (2) physical development (especially anorex[ia]/bulimia); (3) child abuse.

Spangler Junior High encompasses grades 7–9 and is located in a city of appro[xi]mately 60,000 people in the Midwest. Its attendance area is approximately 7[9%] non-Hispanic white, 20% African-American, and 1% other.

Terri Taggert has seven years of teaching experience, the last five of which ha[ve] been at Spangler teaching social studies. It is approximately one month into the [fall] semester, and Terri stands in the parking lot next to her car talking to her friend and c[ol]league Gloria Simmons, who teaches English. It is approximately thirty minutes bef[ore] first period begins. As Terri and Gloria talk, they look toward the school. They b[oth] watch two girls walking together. One is rather small, extremely thin, and somew[hat] slump-shouldered. The other is blonde, very physically attractive, and walks like a fa[sh]ion model.

GLORIA   There go the Bobbsey twins! I swear, Terri, those two are always together! They're inseparable!

TERRI   I'd say that "the odd couple" would be a more apt description.

GLORIA   What do you mean? The blonde is Allison Rhine. She's in my fourth-period class. Who's the brunette she's always with?

TERRI   That's Sherry Sinders. They're both in my American history class. But such a contrast! Allison is good looking, popular, outgoing, and athletic. I think she's [a] cheerleader. Sherry is so thin and frail and shy and retiring! I swear, Gloria, I just can't get Sherry to talk in class. But then Allison talks enough for both of them, and sometimes in class she even answers questions I ask Sherry.

GLORIA   Those kinds of relationships always make you wonder, don't they? Obviously[,] poor Sherry leans on Allison for support all the time, but why does Allison provi[de] it? And I wonder what poor Sherry's story is. Why is she so thin and so sad all th[e] time? And as pretty as Allison is, she's bound to get into a serious relationship so[on] and then what will happen to poor Sherry?!

TERRI   Gloria, you are something! I think you're just a romantic! You've got their whole
relationship plotted and ending in a tragedy!

GLORIA   *[Smiling]* Well, Terri, what do you expect from an English major?

TERRI   *[Laughing]* I don't know, but I think we'd better get to our rooms and do
something useful instead of standing out here like two old gossips!

GLORIA   *[Laughing]* You're just a spoilsport! OK, let's go in and go to work!

It is fifth period the same day. Terri is leading a discussion on colonial America. A
group of six students—including Allison, who served as group chair, and Sherry—has
special responsibility for the material being discussed, since they had to prepare a report
on problems of the time in the form of a newspaper reporting key events in modern
terms. Terri is determined to get Sherry to participate in the discussion.

TERRI   *[Holding up the newspaper that the group has prepared in front of the class]* So, your
lead story is about the Molasses Act of 1733: *[Reads headline aloud]* "Parliament
Angers Colonists With Sugar and Molasses Tax." A bit long for a headline, but very
accurate and complete. Now, please explain what was going on here, group. What's
the background?

ALLISON   Well, the British Parliament had already made the colonists mad because they
told them that they had to sell any tobacco they grew to England. The colonists
thought they should be able to sell it to whoever they wanted to.

TERRI   Sherry, what countries besides England did the colonists especially want to sell
tobacco to?

SHERRY   *[Looks down at floor]* I don't know.

TERRI   *[Speaking softly]* Sherry, didn't you help prepare the group's report? *[Sherry nods
her head yes.]*

ALLISON   Oh, yes, Ms. Taggert! She helped a lot! She just has a little trouble speaking in
front of a lot of people.

TERRI   *[Smiling]* Is that true, Sherry? *[Sherry nods her head affirmatively.]* Well, believe it
or not, I used to have that trouble too. I would get scared when I had to get up and
give a speech in a public speaking course that I took in college. But, as you can see,
I got over it. *[Pause]* Before I forget it, could I see you for a minute after school,
Allison? I need to ask you about something. *[Allison nods her head affirmatively.]*

School has ended, and about five minutes after the last bell, Allison shows up in
Terri's classroom. Terri, sitting behind her desk grading papers, looks up at Allison,
smiles, and motions for her to have a seat in front of her desk.

TERRI   Thanks for coming, Allison. I won't keep you long.

ALLISON   *[Frowning]* Did I do something wrong, Ms. Taggert!

TERRI   Oh, no, Allison! I just wanted to talk to you about your friend Sherry. *[Pause]*
Allison, I'm a little worried about her. To begin with, she seems so serious and frail,
like she has the weight of the world on her shoulders. And she just won't

participate in class. Why is she so shy, Allison? As her teacher, I just want to understand her better.

ALLISON   I don't know, Ms. Taggert. She's just real shy around people. She doesn't even talk much when we're with the guys.

TERRI   Doesn't talk much even when she's with her friends?

ALLISON   Yes, well, you see, *[pause]* can I tell you some things just between us?

TERRI   Yes, of course!

ALLISON   Well, hardly anyone knows this, but Sherry has a real hard life!

TERRI   What do you mean, Allison?

ALLISON   Well, her mother is real hard on her. You see, her parents were divorced when she was five, and it's just her and her mother. It's real bad for her at home. Her mother's always yelling at her and making her do stuff. She won't let her have any friends except me, I guess. For some reason her mother likes me.

TERRI   *[In a serious tone]* Allison, I worry about Sherry being so thin and frail. Doesn't she eat enough!

ALLISON   *[Confidentially]* Ms. Taggert, please don't tell anyone this—

TERRI   Sure, Allison. I'll keep our conversation confidential unless you're about to tell me that Sherry's doing something illegal like drugs of some kind.

ALLISON   No! Nothing like that! It's just that Sherry has—well, a weight and eating problem.

TERRI   *[With surprise]* Allison, are you telling me she's anorexic? *[Allison begins to tear up and nods her head.]* Is she getting help?!

ALLISON   She's been to the doctor, and he told her mother that Sherry needed to be put in a program. But Sherry's mother says they don't have the money for that and blames Sherry for being stubborn. She says Sherry doesn't eat just to hurt her, and she's always after Sherry to eat. *[Starts crying]* Sometimes after Sherry's mother makes her eat, it makes Sherry sick and she vomits it all up! I've seen her do it lot of times.

TERRI   Doesn't Sherry see that she's just skin and bones? Doesn't she see that being that thin isn't pretty? Surely she wants to be pretty like you.

ALLISON   I really don't think she cares anymore! I sometimes think she's just starving herself to death!

TERRI   *[Sighing]* This is terrible, Allison. I'm not sure what to do to help. Let me think about all this.

ALLISON   Sherry would just die if she found out I told someone about all this! She'd never trust me again!

TERRI   Don't worry, Allison. I'll keep all this confidential.

The next day, Terri goes to the office of Sherry's guidance counselor, Charles Bow den, and asks to see Sherry's cumulative record. Charles hands the folder to Terri and invites her to sit down.

TERRI   *[Looking up from the folder]* Charles, I'm concerned about Sherry Sinders, and I'm not sure what to do to help her.

CHARLES   Academically, or personally?

TERRI   She's extremely shy in class and won't participate in class discussions, but her grades are OK, mostly C's and a few B's I see. Her IQ is 111. I'd say her problems are more personal than academic.

CHARLES   Have you ever talked to her mother?

TERRI   No, why?

CHARLES   I have on several occasions. She reminds me of a female Hitler.

TERRI   *[Laughing]* That bad, huh?

CHARLES   Absolutely. If I had a mother like that I think I'd starve myself to death, too, just like Sherry is.

TERRI   *[Nonplussed]* What are you saying, Charles?

CHARLES   That's she's a walking case of anorexia nervosa if I ever saw one!

TERRI   That's what I think, too, Charles, but I didn't know anyone else knew. What can we do?

CHARLES   The girl obviously needs help. She needs to get counseling and be in a special program, but her mother would never agree to that even if it was free. I know how she thinks—she honestly believes that Sherry is just a willful child.

TERRI   Have you talked to her about this?

CHARLES   No, but I have talked to her about a number of other things. She's just plain uncooperative.

TERRI   Do you plan to call her?

CHARLES   About Sherry's anorexia? It would be a waste of time, and, unlike poor Sherry, I don't have to take that woman's punishment.

TERRI   *[With determination]* Then if nobody else is going to try to help Sherry, do you mind if I try?!

CHARLES   *[Grimacing]* Be my guest! But don't say I didn't warn you!

Three days later, Terri is anticipating a conference with Sarah Sinders, Sherry's mother, in her classroom after school is out. Terri had to set the conference for 5:30 P.M. to accommodate Sarah's work schedule. When Terri phoned to set up the conference, Sarah was rather cold and suspicious in response to Terri's explanation that the conference was about Sherry's work in school, but she agreed to come "if it's all that important that I have to traipse down to school right after getting off work."

When Sarah arrives, exactly on time, Terri is somewhat surprised at her appearance. Sarah stands five feet, nine inches tall and is rather heavyset, with broad shoulders and close-cropped brunette hair. Her facial features somewhat remind Terri of an English bulldog.

TERRI   *[Nervously but friendly]* Hello, Ms. Sinders, I'm Terri Taggert, Sherry's teacher. *[Shakes Sarah's hand]* I so much appreciate your taking the time to come talk to me.

SARAH   *[Suspiciously]* Well, I hope this is important! I'd really like to be home relaxing now after the day I've had!

TERRI   Oh. Where do you work, Ms. Sinders?

SARAH   At an attorney's office. I'm the executive secretary there. They do accident cases, and there sure are a lot of them right now! Now, what's up? What's Sherry done now!?

TERRI   She's done nothing wrong, and she's not in any kind of trouble. It's her grades that I'm concerned about, and I wanted to talk to you to see if you could give me any insights that could help me work with her more effectively.

SARAH   *[Puzzled]* Well, I know her grades aren't what they should be, but don't think fo a minute that I don't get on her about them! She does her homework first thing when she comes home from school. When she's done with that she does her chore around the house. Only when she's done with all that can she watch certain TV programs. And some nights there's no TV at all because Sherry can be a bit on the lazy side if you don't keep after her. *[Pause]* I've long suspected that some of Sherry's teachers let her play around a bit too much and that's why her grades aren what they ought to be. But it sure isn't because I don't make her do her schoolwor at home!

TERRI   *[Tentatively]* It certainly sounds like you're strict at home, Mrs. Sinders, it's just that—

SARAH   *[Interrupting]* Well, what's the problem then! What did you want to talk to me about?!

TERRI   *[Hesitantly]* Well, Mrs. Sinders, Sherry is so shy in class. I've tried very hard to ge her to participate in class discussions, but she always shakes her head or says she doesn't know the answer when she really does. I guess it makes her look like she hasn't studied.

SARAH   Well, then, let me make a suggestion, Ms. Taggert!

TERRI   Please do.

SARAH   Set her down and give her a good talking to. Explain to her what you want and tell her that you're not going to settle for anything less. She can be a very stubborn child, and you have to let her know that you aren't going to settle for any nonsense She'll participate when you make it clear to her that she has to.

TERRI   But she seems like she's such a frail, delicate child that making such demands on her might make her extremely anxious and maybe even result in unhealthy stress reactions. She seems so thin and extremely underweight that I wonder if somethin isn't wrong with her, Ms. Sinders. Physically, I mean.

SARAH   *[Belligerently]* Oh, I see! You heard that anorexia stuff from some of the people around here! Well, let me tell you like I told them! Her doctor has given her a clea bill of health, and he's been her doctor since she was born. She doesn't eat like she should, but that's her choice. Whether she's just mad at me because I make her toe the line or whether she wants to be thin like the other girls, I don't know. But I do know that she can be very stubborn when she wants to, and that's a good example of it. Lord, Twiggy must have made a million dollars back when she was a fashion model, and nobody worried about her being anorexic! *[Chuckling]* Sometimes I wish I could control my weight the way Sherry does.

TERRI   But Ms. Sinders, a number of people here at school who are respected professionals are concerned about Sherry. They think—

SARAH   *[Interrupting angrily]* OK, look! I came down here because you said you wanted to talk about Sherry's grades, but now I see that you've been listening to some of the other people around here! *[Stands up to leave]* I don't have time for this! I've been over this ground before, and for your information, Ms. Taggert, I am a good

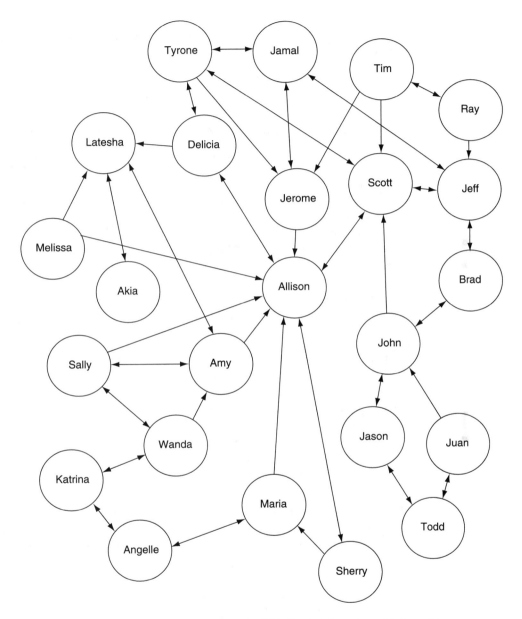

FIGURE 7 A sociogram of Terri Taggert's Fifth-Period American History Class. Students Were Asked With Whom They Would Most Like to Work on a Small-Group Class Project.

parent and Sherry is going to turn out just fine! My suggestion to you is for you t
tend to teaching your classes and let me parent my child! Now, please don't cont
me again unless it's a real emergency! Good-bye! *[Walks out]*

It is one week later. Allison asked Terri during class if she could talk to her a
school, and Terri agreed. All the other students have left the building, and Allison sit
a desk in the front of the classroom talking to Terri, who sits behind her desk.

ALLISON   Ms. Taggert, I know that you wanted to help Sherry when you met her moth
but it's just made things worse for her. Her mother accused her of getting you to
talk to her and telling lies. Sherry is afraid to tell you and asked me if I would. Sh
asks you to please not try to talk to her mother again. It just doesn't help. The
woman just won't listen to anyone. But she wants you to know that she appreciat
your caring for her.

TERRI   You are such a good friend, Allison! I think it's wonderful that a person like you
who has their life together as well as you do is such a good friend to poor little
Sherry!

ALLISON   *[Tearing up]* Oh, Ms. Taggert, I'm not so perfect! My life's not so great either.

TERRI   *[Concerned]* Allison, I'm sorry! Did I say something to upset you! I didn't intend

ALLISON   *[Crying]* No, it's just that everybody thinks my life's so good, but it's not!

TERRI   What's the matter, Allison? I won't tell anyone. You know that I kept what you
told me about Sherry confidential. What is it?

ALLISON   Sherry's not the only one who has an eating problem. I have a terrible time
keeping control, and sometimes I go crazy and just eat everything in sight! Then
have to go to the bathroom and get rid of it before I get fat! It's awful! What am I
going to do, Ms. Taggert?!

TERRI   Oh, lord, Allison! I don't know! I don't know what I'm supposed to do!

QUESTIONS

1. What are bulimia and anorexia nervosa? What are their causes and most effective
treatments? What signs or symptoms may indicate that a student has a problem in that
area? What role should the classroom teacher play?

2. What is child abuse, and what forms does it take? Is Sherry an abused child? Wha
is the teacher's role in the identification and referral process?

3. How effectively did Terri handle her conference with Sarah Sinders? What should
she have done differently?

4. At what level of Maslow's need hierarchy are Sherry and Sarah primarily operating
How could Terri use this information?

5. From the perspective of self-concept theory, how would Sherry evaluate her sel
worth in the following areas: (1) scholastic competence; (2) social acceptance; (3)
behavioral conduct; (4) physical appearance. How is the self-concept formed, and
under what conditions does it change? How can Terri use this information?

6. How can Sherry's and Allison's behaviors be explained from the standpoint of observational learning? Who are the effective models in their lives? In what areas would their sense of self-efficacy be high or low? How could Terri use this information?

7. Why is Sherry so isolated socially, with only Allison as a close friend? What is a sociogram, and what does the sociogram that Terri did (see figure on page 65) tell you about Sherry's and Allison's social positions in the class? Does the sociogram indicate that Sherry is an social isolate and Allison a social star? How can Terri use such information?

8. What are self-regulation methods, and how effective are they in working with anorexic and bulimic girls? Would such methods be helpful in the cases of Sherry and Allison?

9. Is Sherry emotionally handicapped in the sense of evidencing severe withdrawal? Does she evidence a "consistent and persistent" pattern of withdrawal? Who should determine this, and how? What role should Terri play?

10. As far as Sherry is concerned, would it be helpful for Terri to use cooperative learning methods in running her class? Would such procedures help "draw Sherry out" socially? Would this strategy help Sherry in the long run?

11. What is stress, and how is it related to anxiety and fear? Can anorexia nervosa be a coping response to stress? What are the sources of stress in Sherry's life, and how can Terri use this information?

12. What would you advise Terri to do about Sherry and Allison? What are Terri's responsibilities and limitations in the "information and referral agent" aspect of her role as a teacher?

CASE 7

HONESTY OR MATURITY?

Key Content to Consider for Analyzing This Case:
(1) moral development; (2) observational learning;
(3) parent involvement.

Lakewood Elementary is a new school with an excellent physical plant and abundant facilities that are only two years old. It is located in an upper-middle-class suburb of approximately 60,000 people on the West Coast of the United States. Its attendance district is approximately 80% white, 15% African-American, 3% Hispanic, and 2% Asian-American.

Akia Brown is an African-American teacher with five years of teaching experience, the last two years at Lakewood. She is currently teaching a third-grade class with twenty-four students, evenly divided between boys and girls.

It is early in the school year, and Akia has introduced her students to the multiplication tables, twos through nines. She has put the multiplication tables in large block symbols on a large piece of white construction which she has placed on an easel in front of the class. As she talks she uses a wooden pointer to point to the particular item she is talking about.

AKIA Now children, there are a lot of ways to learn the multiplication tables. You can learn them by using them over and over again, or you can learn them by thinking of a picture of something that goes with each number. But no matter how you do it, you've got to practice. Yes, Sarah?

SARAH What do you mean pictures?

AKIA That's a good question, Sarah. I was just coming to that. In a class I took as a college student a long time ago, I learned a system of using pictures in your mind as a way of remembering things. *[Goes to the blackboard, picks up chalk, and writes the numbers from 2 to 9 in a vertical column]* Now here's the pictures of things I think of when I see each number. I want you to close your eyes and imagine that you see two pennies. Can you all see two pennies? Who doesn't see two pennies in their mind? *[No hands go up.]* Now, those two pennies form a group of two. We could use real pennies, but we won't always have real pennies with us, so it's better to use your imagination. Yes, Brad?

BRAD   Is one penny a group?

AKIA   That's a very good question, Brad, and I promise that I'll answer it later. But ones and zeros are a little more difficult, so I want to do them after we learn twos through nines first. Now look at the chart *[points to 2 × 1 = with the wooden pointer]*. Think of the 2 as the number in a group, like in this case two pennies. Think of the 1 as the number of groups. So class, if you have a group of two pennies and only one such group, that means 2 × 1 = what?

CLASS   *[In unison]* Two!

AKIA   Right! Who doesn't understand? Roger, you're frowning.

ROGER   Well, I was thinking that one penny would be a group of one and 1 × 1 would be the same as one group of one penny. But then 1 × 0 would be one group of one penny times no groups. I don't get it. *[With sudden insight]* Oh, I get it! No groups of even one penny so 1 × 0 = 0!

BRAD   *[Without raising his hand]* Wait a minute! What did he say?

AKIA   Yes, that's very good, Roger. But how many of you understand what Roger just said? *[Six hands go up, one hesitantly.]* Well, we'll come back to the ones and zeros like I promised. But for now close your eyes again, class, and imagine a group of two pennies again. *[All students close their eyes.]* Now imagine two groups of two pennies. How many do you have?

CLASS   Four!

AKIA   So, *[using wooden pointer]* 2 × 2 = 4. Right?

CLASS   Right!

AKIA   Yes, Annmarie?

ANNMARIE   I understand it all right. When you multiply, it's the number of times that you increase the groups. But I just tried to imagine nine groups of nine pennies and I couldn't hold them still in my mind so I can count them. I keep losing track. How am I going to remember all those pennies?!

AKIA   *[Smiling]* I was just trying to explain to you what you're doing when you multiply. There's only one way to remember them, though. You've got to memorize them and practice repeating them often. When you get stuck, though, you can always figure it out using the method I just taught you. *[Passes out papers.]* Now, everybody take one of these. We call this a pretest. See how many of the multiplication tables you can do now on your own. Do your own work and keep your eyes off other people's papers. Now start.

As all the students get down to work, Akia begins to do her own work but looks at what the students are doing from time to time. One time when she looks up she notices that Brad is looking at Roger's paper. She quickly looks back down at her work so Brad won't know that she has seen him. She covertly watches Brad's copying of Roger's answers from time to time.

AKIA   OK, children, turn in your papers. *[Collects papers as they are passed in]* By the way, Brad, I need to see you for just a minute when school's out. So don't run away without seeing me. OK?

BRAD   OK.

The school day has ended, and Brad remains after school to talk to Ms. Brown. A
sits behind her desk, and Brad sits in a chair in front of the desk. Akia pulls out Br
and Roger's papers and lays them side by side so she can compare the answers.

AKIA   Brad, I watched you when you were doing your multiplication tables and saw y
        copying Roger's answers.
BRAD   *[Angrily]* I did not! I looked over toward Roger's paper, but I didn't copy his
        answers.
AKIA   There's no need to lie to me, Brad. I watched you do it for some time. Also, here
        your two papers. Every answer is exactly the same. I'm really disappointed in you
        Brad! Don't you know better? You never learn anything when you copy someone
        else's work except how to cheat.
BRAD   *[Contritely]* I'm sorry! I just wanted to get a good grade! I didn't know how to d
        them!
AKIA   Brad, you can't pretend that you know the multiplication tables by copying
        someone else's answers. Even if I hadn't caught you, you still wouldn't be able to
        them on the next test unless you cheated again.
BRAD   *[Looking down at the floor]* I know.
AKIA   Have you cheated in here before, Brad!?
BRAD   *[Sternly]* No! And I won't do it again.
AKIA   I hope not, Brad. Next time I'm going to have to talk to your parents about
        OK?
BRAD   *[Dejectedly]* OK.

It is two weeks later. Akia has asked her class to bring in either a picture or act
figure of their favorite cartoon or television character for a sharing and writing assi
ment. Brad has brought in the blue Power Ranger to share with the class. He conclu
his explanation of the history and powers of the superhero and goes back to his se
Roger is called on next. He goes to the front of the class and takes an action figure ou
a box he is carrying.

ROGER   *[Holding action figure up high for everyone to see after placing the box on Akia's
        desk]* I'll bet everybody knows this one. He's called Wolverine and he's one of th
        X-Men.
BRAD   *[Without raising his hand]* Cool! He's really big! Where did you get him?
ROGER   My dad got him for me on his last trip to New York. You can't get them here. I
        looked. *[Pause]* Now watch this. *[Roger pushes a button on the action figure's back an
        "claws" pop out, then retract from the action figure's hand. Several boys, including Brad
        shout exclamations of wonder and disbelief.]*
AKIA   That's really interesting, Roger. What does Wolverine use the claws for? *[Several
        boys, including Brad, shout out that Wolverine uses them to fight the bad guys with.]* O
        well, now will you be able to write me a paper about Wolverine and the X-Men a
        explain how they fight against the bad guys?
ROGER   Oh, yeah! That's one of my favorite things! I really like this assignment!

AKIA   OK, Roger, we're about out of time. Why don't you put Wolverine back in the
        box, and you can tell us more about him later.
ROGER   OK. *[Puts action figure back in the box and leaves it on the teacher's desk]*

It is later that same day, and Akia is listening to the students take turns reading.
Brad has just finished.

AKIA   OK. Annmarie, it's your turn next. Yes, Brad?
BRAD   I have to go to the bathroom real bad! I can't wait!
AKIA   OK, Brad. Go ahead and come right back. *[Pause]* Go ahead, Annmarie.

Akia listens to Annmarie read, but some intuition tells her to watch Brad out of
the corner of one eye without turning her head. As Brad walks by her desk on the way
to the bathroom, Akia sees him quickly pick up the box with Roger's action figure in it
and put it under his shirt. He continues on into the bathroom. Akia continues with the
reading.

There are ten minutes left in the school day, and Akia tells the students to pick
everything up, clean up the room, and get ready to go home. There is considerable hus-
tle and bustle as students move around the classroom. Roger walks over to Akia.

ROGER   Ms. Brown, I can't find my Wolverine! It was on your desk.
AKIA   *[Loudly]* Has anyone seen Roger's action figure that was in a box on my desk?
        [Students shake their heads or say "no" quietly.] Would Brad, Jeremy, and Annmarie
        please help Roger look? Look everywhere and see if you can find it. Roger doesn't
        want to lose what belongs to him! Now look hard!

After five minutes, the three students and Roger come over to Akia and tell her that
they couldn't find the action figure.

AKIA   OK. Thanks for looking, children. *[Turns to Roger]* Roger, I'm sorry this happened
        but I'll bet that your action figure shows up. *[Pats him]* Don't worry about it now.
        [Children begin to move away from her to go their desks.] Brad, I need to see you for a
        minute after class is dismissed. Please don't leave.

All the students have left except Brad. Akia motions for Brad to sit in a desk at the
front of the classroom, and she sits on top of her desk looking down at him.

AKIA   *[In a serious tone]* Brad, where's Roger's action figure?
BRAD   *[Looking down]* I don't know! We couldn't find it! We looked all over!
AKIA   Brad, I deliberately gave you a chance to return it. Now you're lying on top of
        stealing it. I saw you take it off my desk and stick it under your shirt on the way to
        the bathroom. Now, you get Roger's action figure right now or we're going down to
        the principal's office and call your parents right now!

Brad *[Tearing up]* Oh, OK. *[Leaves the classroom and returns in a couple of minutes with box containing the action figure. He hands it to Akia, who lays it down on the desk. Bra sits back down at the desk and hangs his head.]*

Akia *[Quietly]* Brad, why did you steal this from Roger?

Brad *[Crying]* I don't know! I just wanted it real bad! I knew that I'd never find one t good!

Akia Brad, do you think you can go through life stealing whatever you want? Don't y know what happens to people who live that way?!

Brad Yes, I know it's wrong. I would have given it back to him after I played with it f a while.

Akia Maybe you would and maybe you wouldn't. But let me ask you this. Suppose th the action figure you took belonged to you and you brought it in to share with th class and another student stole it from you. How would you feel?

Brad Bad.

Akia That's called the Golden Rule, Brad. Do unto others as you would have them do unto you. Have you ever heard of it?

Brad Yes.

Akia But you don't think these things through before you do them, do you?

Brad No.

Akia Brad, I'm worried about you. As far as I'm concerned, you're on probation. The very next time I catch you stealing or cheating or lying in my classroom I'm going to involve the principal and your parents. Do you understand me?

Brad Yes. I'm sorry. I promise I won't do it again. *[Wipes a tear from one eye]*

Akia OK, Brad. This is your last chance. Go on home.

It is one month later, and the school day has just ended. All the students exce Annmarie have left the room. Akia sits at her desk, and Annmarie walks over to t to her.

Akia Annmarie, don't you have to catch your bus?

Annmarie Yes, but there's something important I have to tell you, Ms. Brown.

Akia Oh! What is it?

Annmarie Well, you know when they called you down to the office today?

Akia Yes, what about it?

Annmarie Well, I saw Brad go up to your desk and take your purse out of the drawer. He took some money. I told him to put it back, but he wouldn't.

Akia *[Shocked]* What! Are you sure? *[She opens the drawer, opens up her purse, takes out her billfold, and sees that the five-dollar bill, the only paper money she had, is missing.]* Oh, my lord! He took my five-dollar bill. *[Calms down]* Thank you so much for telling me, Annmarie. It shows that you are honest and have a lot of courage.

Annmarie My mother says that you're supposed to tell when you see something bad.

Akia Your mother is so right, Annmarie. Now please, let me handle this. Don't talk about this with the other children.

Annmarie OK, I won't. Can I tell my mother?

AKIA   That would be OK, but tell her I want to handle this my own way and that I'd appreciate it if she kept it to herself. And thanks again so much!

ANNMARIE   OK. Good-bye, Ms. Brown.

The next morning, Akia sends Brad to the principal's office with a note in a sealed envelope for the principal. When the principal talks to Brad, he denies taking the money and the principal calls Brad's mother, has her take Brad home for a couple of days, and schedules a conference for the next day after school. However, the principal is called to an "emergency meeting" downtown and suggests that Akia go ahead and meet with Brad's parents, Charles and Gloria Downing, in Akia's classroom after school. Before the conference, Akia has a chance to look at Brad's cumulative record and notices that his father is an attorney and his mother is a high school social studies teacher. He also has a sister who is two years younger than him. The parents seem very friendly and concerned as they sit in movable desks facing Akia, who also sits in a desk.

GLORIA   We were very surprised—I guess shocked might be more accurate—when Ms. Martin [the principal] called us and told us that she thought it best for Brad to stay home until we had all talked about this. What's this about Brad stealing from your purse, Ms. Brown? We just can't believe he'd do something like that. We give him a good allowance. Why would he need to steal money? Did you actually see him take it out of your purse?

AKIA   I'm afraid that this isn't the first situation that has come up, Ms. Downing. [At this point Akia reiterates the details about Brad's cheating on the test, stealing the action figure from Roger, and taking the money from her purse.] And in all these cases he tried to lie his way out of the situation until he was confronted with the facts. Perhaps I should have contacted you earlier about these things, but I kept trying to give Brad another chance. But this time I knew that I had to do something.

CHARLES   [Smiling reassuringly] And we're really glad you did, Ms. Brown! What a stupid way for Brad to behave. We give him a more than generous allowance, and you should see his room! He has everything a child his age could want. Why he feels a need to go around stealing toys and money is beyond me! Really stupid! And his copying the other kid's answers! Now that really bothers me! I have no doubt that Brad has what it takes to get a college scholarship and get accepted to law school one day. A bright kid like Brad should have other students copying answers from him!

AKIA   Well, Mr. Downing, I don't think any student should cheat, or steal for that matter!

CHARLES   Oh, of course. I was just making a point. I'm really disappointed in Brad and he's going to catch it at home, I can guarantee you!

AKIA   My concern is that Brad is at a formative age and seems to value lying, cheating, and stealing as acceptable ways of getting along in the world.

GLORIA   Yes, I know what you mean. I see the results of that in some of the adolescents I teach in high school. I think a lot of it goes back to changes in our society since the 1950s. The emphasis on competition and getting your own way by walking over other people that starts with our politicians and state and federal government has

FIGURE 8   Portion of Cumulative Record for Brad Downing

LAKEWOOD ELEMENTARY SCHOOL
Cumulative Record

Name: Downing, Bradley Omar   Home Telephone: 408-472-1411
Address: 3221 Elm Road   General Health: Excellent
Father: Downing, Charles B.   Occupation: Attorney-at-Law
Mother: Downing, Gloria A.   Occupation: Secondary Teacher
Siblings: Downing, Elizabeth, Age 6 Handicaps: None
Former Schools: None   Date of Birth: 03/13/91
Date Entered Lakewood: 8/30/96

TEST RECORD

Intelligence Tests	CA	MA	IQ	Date	Grade
California Test of Mental Maturity				5/14/97	1
Language	6–9	7–6	111		
Non-Language	6–9	7–10	116		

ACADEMIC RECORD

Grades 1–6 (year averages)	1	2	3	4	5	6
English						
Reading	3	3				
Writing	3	3				
Spelling	3	3				
Social Studies						
Arithmetic	3	3				
Science and Health						
Music	3	3				
Citizenship	2	1				

KEY:

1. Child is working below grade level
2. Child is working below grade level, but is making progress
3. Child is working at grade level
4. Child is doing excellent work at grade level
5. Child is working above grade level

filtered down even to the children in our elementary schools. Get your own way at any cost!

CHARLES   Unfortunately, that's the way world is now. *[Reaches for his wallet and takes out a twenty-dollar bill]* Ms. Brown we're really sorry that Brad stole the five dollars out of your purse, and we insist on reimbursing you with some extra for damages. *[Hands the money to Akia]* Brad never does these kinds of things at home, and I can't understand why he does them at school. I guarantee you that we'll get to the bottom of it before we're through. *[Pause]* I hope that as Brad's teacher you'll be able to put his immature and thoughtless behavior in perspective. I'm sure he's going through a phase, and I'm certain that we'll all be glad when he gets through it. *[Extends his hand to shake Akia's hand and stands up, following which Gloria does likewise]* Thanks so much for talking with us and for helping Brad.

GLORIA   Yes. Thank you, Ms. Brown, and don't hesitate to let us know if he does anything further. We need to nip this thing in the bud right now!

AKIA   *[Also stands up]* Yes, well. OK, Mr. and Mrs. Downing, and thanks for coming. I'm sure we'll be talking to one another again.

It is the next day after school, and Akia sits in the office of the building principal, Celia Martin.

CELIA   Well, tell me, Akia, how'd your conference with the Downings go yesterday?

AKIA   My impression was that they weren't all that concerned. They took a sort of "kids will be kids" position and that Brad is going through a phase he'll hopefully outgrow. Can you believe that Mr. Downing gave me a twenty-dollar bill to make up for a five that Brad stole from my purse?! They say they're going to give Brad a good talking to at home. Apparently Brad's behavior makes no sense to them since he has about anything money can buy at home.

CELIA   Yes, he's an attorney isn't he? And she's a teacher at Lincoln High. So you don't agree with their analysis or approach to handling Brad?

AKIA   Of course not! The problem is going to get worse unless somebody does something! I'm not sure I handled the conference with the Downings well. I wish you could have been there, Celia. But Brad will be back in my class tomorrow. What am I going to do with him? How can I get his parents involved?

QUESTIONS

1. At which of Kohlberg's stages of moral development does Brad seem to be operating? What moral education methods seem to work best with children at that stage? How effective are they?

2. At which of Erikson's stages of personality development does Brad seem to have unresolved crises? What therapy techniques work best in such cases?

3. From the standpoint of Ames, does Brad have a mastery or performance goal orientation toward learning? How does such an orientation develop, and what can be done to help children move toward a mastery orientation?

4. From an observational learning perspective, what kinds of behaviors are modeled by Brad's parents? What can a classroom teacher do to change a child's behavior that stems from patterns of modeling and imitation that originate in the home?

5. In terms of cooperation versus competition, what kind of classroom environment has Akia established in her classroom? Would the establishment of cooperative learning teaching methods in her classroom help in Brad's case?

6. From a cognitive learning perspective, how effective is Akia's "imaging technique" in getting her students to learn the multiplication tables? What method would have bee more effective?

7. How effective was Akia's conference with the Downings? What should she have done differently?

8. At what stage of Maslow's need hierarchy does Brad seem to be primarily operatir How can Akia use this information?

9. What methods(s) of classroom management would be most useful to Akia in this situation? What are the relative merits of Reality Therapy, Teacher Effectiveness Training and behavior modification in this situation?

10. Akia and the Downings discuss values during their conference. What values has Brad acquired, and how? What methods of values clarification and change exist that might be helpful to Akia in working with Brad and his parents?

11. What parent involvement techniques might Akia consider using in this situatior How effective are such techniques?

12. What advice should Celia give Akia about working with Brad when he returns? About working with Brad's parents?

'OTPOURRI

Key Content to Consider for Analyzing This Case:
(1) cultural diversity; (2) intelligence; (3) cognitive style (field dependence/independence); (4) exceptionalities; (5) Bloom's Cognitive Taxonomy.

Notth Middle School is twenty-five years old and is located in a low socioeconomic neighborhood that is many years older than the school. The community in which the school is located is part of a large metropolitan area in the eastern United States. The student population is approximately 70% white, 20% African-American, 7% Hispanic, and 3% Asian-American.

Abe Goodman, who is twenty-three years old, is beginning his first year at North as an eighth-grade American history teacher. Last year Abe taught eighth grade in a small rural middle school in the southern part of the state, near the prestigious private university from which he graduated with a B.S. in education, with a major in social studies.

It is the sixth period of the first day of school, and the American history students are entering the classroom. There is much talking, pushing, and laughing, but the pupils quickly find seats. Abe notices immediately that there is a wide diversity of pupils in the class, and that they have segregated themselves into ethnic groups. As Abe makes eye contact with pupils who are talking, they continue to talk. It is not until he taps a paperweight on his desk that the pupils gradually quiet down and give him their attention.

ABE   *[Smiling]* Welcome to American history class. As you've probably noticed, I'm a new teacher here. Last year I taught in Bowen Middle School in the southern part of the state.

ELIJAH   *[Speaking out]* Man, what kinda name is dat fo' a school?

ABE   It's the last name of a man. Frank Bowen was the superintendent of schools for many years and a leader in that community. Everybody liked him and appreciated what he did both for the schools and the community. The school was built shortly after he died, so the people in town agreed that they should name the school in his honor. The full name of the school is the Frank E. Bowen Middle School.

ELIJAH   That's cool! I'd like a school named after me. *[Much laughter and derision from the class]*

ABE   *[Holding up his hand for silence]* What's your name?

ELIJAH   Elijah.

ABE   Elijah what?

ELIJAH   Elijah Duwaine Jackson. *[More laughter from the class. Some pupils say "Wow, Duwaine," "What a classy name for such an unclassy guy," etc.]*

ABE   *[Holding up his hand for quiet]* That sounds pretty good to me—Elijah Duwaine Jackson Middle School. *[More laughter and derision from the class. Abe quiets the laughter and speaks seriously.]* Maybe someday you'll have a school or some other public building named after you, Elijah. If you work hard in your community, an people appreciate what you do, it can really happen. *[While some of his friends poi at Elijah and jeer, he sits quietly as if he is pondering this possibility.]* It could happen anyone else in this class, too—if you help people in your community. That's how people get buildings, roads, parks, libraries, and other public properties named after them. As we study American history in this class we'll learn about many people who've become famous because they helped other people. These are nam that you and I know even though the people have been dead for hundreds of yea *[A girl near the front raises her hand. Abe looks her way.]* What's your name?

ANGELA   I am Angela Aguila, and I know people like you talk about. Like Thomas Jefferson, and Ben Franklin, and J.C. Penney—people like that. *[Some pupils laug*

ABE   That's great, Angela! Those are people who are part of our history. In this class w learn about people who helped to develop our country.

MOSES   You ain't gonna make us memorize lots of names and dates, are you? I hate th I just can't remember names and dates. *[Several other pupils support Moses, saying "Right on," "Ya," "That's right," etc.]*

ABE   Well, I'll want you to know some of the people who were famous for certain accomplishments. For instance, you probably know the name of the sailor who's given credit for discovering America, don't you?

MOSES   *[Exuberantly]* Right on! That would be Columbus!

ABE   *[Smiling]* That would be the right answer.

JANET   What other kinds of assignments will we have?

ABE   Basically, I'd like you to know about the discovery and settlement of our country winning our independence from England through a revolution, establishing our own government, the westward movement, the Civil War, Reconstruction, the Industrial Revolution, and the westward expansion.

IONA   *[Sounding discouraged]* That sounds like a lot of work. *[Other pupils agree.]*

ABE   But remember, we're talking about a year's work. And I plan to have you do mos of that work in groups. Each group will research a different part of the topic and report on it.

BARBARA   I hate doing reports. I always read everything we're supposed to read, and then I can't figure out what to put in the report.

ABE   Well, don't become discouraged just yet. I can show you how to outline your reports so that you'll know what information you should include. *[The bell rings.* OK. Class is over. I'll see you tomorrow. *[Pupils leave. Many of them complain to ea other about the proposed class assignments.]*

The following Wednesday, Abe is in the guidance office recording information from the cumulative records of the pupils in his sixth-period American history class. Sherry Matson, the guidance counselor, is working at her desk.

SHERRY   Are you finding everything you need, Abe?

ABE   I'm not finding what I wanted to find, but I'm finding what I need.

SHERRY   What did you want to find?

ABE   I wanted to find that the children in my sixth-period class were all like the children from Lake Woebegone—cooperative, attractive, and all above average in intelligence. Alas! That isn't what I found.

SHERRY   Why doesn't that surprise me?

ABE   I guess it's because you've been here longer than I have. [Handing Sherry the paper on which he's been writing] Here's the information I took from the folders of my pupils. [Holding the sheet so that they can both see it]

SHERRY   [After perusing the list of names] Yes, I know all these pupils. And, indeed, some of them are quite challenging. And what a range of abilities you have—from Mose Gully to Chan Yin!

ABE   And the sad part is that Mose seems to try as hard as anyone else in the class. But, unfortunately, he doesn't seem to have enough background information to carry it off.

SHERRY   Yes, I know about the home situation. The father left the family years ago. The mother seems to be gone most of the time. Mose has both an older and younger sister, and the three of them survive the best way they can. None of them do well in school, but, to their credit, they've managed to stay out of serious trouble.

ABE   I don't know other members of the family, but I like Mose. He really tries hard, but he has trouble learning. Then he becomes frustrated and disruptive. I need to find a way to keep him occupied.

SHERRY   [Looking at the list] I see that Kevin Felton and Connie Petty are both in that class. They're probably difficult to deal with also. You probably already know that Kevin Felton's been diagnosed as socially maladjusted and Connie Petty as having attention deficit hyperactivity disorder.

ABE   I wasn't informed of this, but they've demonstrated their disabilities. Kevin wanders around like a lost soul, and Connie's usually out of her seat wandering around the room at least half the period. I walk her back to her seat and sit her down, but she's up again before I can get back to the front of the room. Knowing that they have disabilities will help me to be more patient with them. [Begins to walk toward the door] And thanks for making your records available to me. I'm going to use the information to form heterogeneous groups.

SHERRY   [Walking beside him] You're welcome. I've enjoyed talking with you. If there's anything else I can do to help, let me know.

During his planning period the following day, Abe went to the teachers' lounge and found two other teachers there, Mary Johnson and Don Bradbury, both of whom teach English.

ABE   [Feigning surprise] There must be something special happening in the lounge tod

MARY   Yes, we heard you were planning to grace us with your presence during your f
period. To what can we attribute this honor?

ABE   Ordinarily I come here regularly on my free period, but I've been busy trying to
figure out how to deal with my sixth-period American history class.

DON   What's so special about that particular class?

ABE   They're a wild and crazy bunch of eighth graders with a wide range of intellectu
and cultural diversity, and many of them don't want to do any work at school, it
seems. Other than that, they're fine.

MARY   When you get a combination like that, it usually complicates your life. Have y
come up with any creative ways of dealing with them?

ABE   I'm working on one. Yesterday I went to the guidance office, and Sherry let me
collect information about my pupils from their folders. Having seen how diverse
they really are, I've decided that the best way to work with them would be to div
them systematically into heterogeneous groups and have the groups work togeth
on projects.

DON   How did you decide to divide them up?

ABE   I thought about that a lot while I was reviewing their records, so when I went
home yesterday I got some index cards and wrote down each pupil's name, ethn
background, IQ score, social studies score and total score on the Metropolitan
Achievement Test, whether the pupil qualifies for free lunch, and whether he or
prefers to work alone or in a group.

MARY   [Enthusiastically] Wow! I'm really impressed. I can hardly wait to see how you
used all that information! I divided my pupils into groups, but I used only their
reading level.

ABE   Well, it really helped to have the information on cards because I decided that it
would be manageable to have six groups of six pupils each. I began by identifyir
the six brightest pupils. I put one in each group. Then I found the six poorest
pupils and put one in each group. Next, based on the remainder of the informat
on the cards, I added the other four pupils so that the groups would be fairly mi
in terms of ability, SES [socioeconomic status], work preference, and racial or ethn
group.

DON   I'm impressed too. How long did it take you to assign pupils to the six groups?

ABE   It really took me longer than I anticipated. I started as soon as I got home from
school. Then I ate dinner. After dinner, I went through the piles several more tir
and rearranged them. Then, I took some time to consider several types of
assignments. After that, I went through the cards one more time and made a few
changes. By then it was almost bedtime. I spent more than five hours in all. But
really consider that to be time well spent.

MARY   Now that you've arranged the class into heterogeneous groups, what kinds of
assignments are you going to give them?

ABE   [Hesitating] I'm not really sure. In fact, I was planning to ask you what kinds of
assignments you gave to the pupils you grouped by reading levels.

MARY   Well, I grouped my pupils by reading levels, because in my class we read
literature. I found that their reading levels ranged from grade two through grade

nine, with more than half of them below sixth grade. You'll probably find the same situation in your class.

ABE   I imagine I will. But how did you use this information to make class assignments?

MARY   That's the beauty of reading-level grouping. After I assigned them to groups by their reading levels, I was able to let them choose their own books to read. Our library has a great collection of trade books, and Susan, our librarian, has them grouped by levels of reading difficulty. You might consider allowing your pupils to read trade books in history instead of the textbooks. That way, Susan could help them select books on their own reading level.

ABE   [Apologetically] I'm embarrassed to have to ask this, but what are trade books?

MARY   [Smiling] Well, we English types know what trade books are because they make life easier for us and our pupils. Trade books are literary selections not written primarily for instructional purposes. I'm sure there must be thousands of trade books that would be appropriate for teaching history. What are you teaching now?

ABE   The discovery of America.

MARY   Wow! There must be zillions of trade books you could use for that—biographies of Christopher Columbus, Amerigo Vespucci, Queen Isabella, Indian chiefs, books about ships, explorers, and stories of the various Indian tribes that were living in America then. [Pauses] See, I just thought of these books instantly, without half trying. I'm sure that with your knowledge of history, you could find enough trade books to teach your entire course. They're written on all levels of difficulty and are really interesting for kids.

ABE   Trade books sound interesting. There's no question that my pupils would have an easier time reading them than they're having with the text we're using now. [A bell rings signaling the end of the period.] Thanks to both of you for the great suggestions!

Several days later, the pupils in Abe's sixth-period class enter the room, sit with the other members of their group, and begin to work on reports that they have negotiated with Abe. Each group had chosen a major topic related to the discovery of America. Each major topic was divided into six subtopics. Each group member was responsible for a report and presentation on the topic he or she had chosen.

ABE   I'm really proud of this class. You're becoming good workers already. I'm sure your reports will be excellent. Today I'll visit each group and see how the research on your topics is coming. If you have questions, ask me while I'm with your group. [He walks over toward the closest group. Just then there is a loud noise followed by shouting.]

EDWARD   [Loudly] Connie, what's wrong with you! That globe'll break if you drop it on the floor!

CONNIE   [On the verge of tears] I was just looking at it.

EDWARD   I'm using that globe for my report! You don't need to be messing with it!

CONNIE   [Shouting] I said I'm sorry! I didn't mean to drop it. [Begins to cry]

EDWARD   So what! Just leave my stuff alone. [Connie returns to her seat and continues to sob.]

ABE   *[Walks to Connie's chair]* You're all right, Connie. Ed was just upset that you dropped the globe that he needs to write his report.

CONNIE   *[Sobbing almost out of control]* Everybody's so mean to me. I didn't mean to do anything wrong. I'm just so upset. I need to go to the office.

ABE   Why do you need to go to the office?

CONNIE   My mother gave Ritalin tablets to the principal so that his secretary can give me one when I need it. *[Sobbing]* I need one now, I'm so upset.

ABE   I don't know anything about this arrangement, Connie. You just sit here until you feel better. Then join your group and work on your report. I'll walk with you to the office as soon as class is over and find out about these arrangements you mentioned.

CONNIE   *[Sobbing again]* But I'm telling the truth. My mother came in this afternoon and made the arrangements.

ABE   I believe you, Connie, but I don't know anything about these arrangements. As soon as I find out what they are, I'll be happy to let you go. *[Connie continues to cry. Abe walks back to the group he was approaching before the fall of the world. He stops beside Barbara.]* Wow, Barbara! You really have a pile of information there. Are you planning to go on a cruise?

BARBARA   *[Smiling]* No, these travel brochures are for my report on the differences between the lives of Columbus' sailors and the lives of sailors today. I went to the Star Travel Agency and found all these brochures on some of their cruises. They give good information on the size and equipment of their cruising ships.

ABE   That's a great idea, Barbara. Do you have the same type of information on Columbus' ships?

BARBARA   Yes, I found a book in the library that described them.

ABE   Terrific! So now all you need to do is write a report comparing life aboard one of Columbus' ships with life on a modern ship.

BARBARA   *[With resignation]* I just can't do it. I have all the information about the ships, but it doesn't tell anything about the lives of the sailors. I haven't been able to find any books that tell about sailors' lives.

ABE   But Barbara, you have all the information you need right here to compare the sailors' lives. Make a list of some of the things today's sailors can do because they have electricity, motors, navigational equipment, and radios that Columbus' sailors didn't have. Just use your own ideas.

BARBARA   I just can't make things up out of my mind. I need information that I can see.

ABE   Let's think about this for a minute. Did the early sailors have air-conditioning?

BARBARA   No.

ABE   Then how would that make their life different from today's sailors?

BARBARA   I don't know. I can't think that way.

ABE   Well, what does air-conditioning do?

BARBARA   *[On the verge of tears]* I don't know. I just don't know! Don't ask me all those questions. I can't work this way. You expect me to figure out all these things by myself, and I can't. Teachers are supposed to tell us what we need to know and then test us on it to see if we learned it. *[Puts her head face down on the desk and covers it with her arms. Abe stands by her desk for a while, but she won't look up, so he moves on to Aaron's desk.]* Aaron, you're writing on the Indian tribes who lived in eastern America around the time of Columbus, aren't you?

AARON   *[Pointing to a pile of trade books on his desk]* Yes, I found all these books on these five different tribes. I read them and learned a lot about how Indians live, but I'm really having trouble writing a report that tells the differences between the tribes. I just get all mixed up when I try to separate them from each other.

CONNIE   *[Stamping her foot and screaming loudly]* Kevin! Let me alone! Go away! You're bothering me!

KEVIN   *[Getting out of his seat and confronting Connie]* Shut up and go back to your seat, stupid! You're a real nerd! You walk up and down the aisle poking me with your finger while I'm trying to work. Then you scream bloody murder when I tell you to stop! *[Turning to Abe]* Mr. Goodman, can't you do something about this pest?

ABE   *[Sternly]* Both of you—calm down. Connie, what are you doing on this side of the room? Your desk is way over there. *[Connie hangs her head and remains silent.]* Kevin! Why do you have to yell out and disturb everybody in the class?

KEVIN   *[Yelling]* I get tired of her bothering me when I'm trying to work!

ABE   Connie, I want you to move your desk to the front of the room next to my desk. I don't want to see you up walking around unless you raise your hand and get permission from me. Do you understand me?

CONNIE   *[Shouting]* It's your fault! You wouldn't let me get my pill!

ABE   *[Slowly and sternly]* We're going to talk about your pills after class! Now do as I asked! *[Turning to Kevin]* Kevin, go back to your seat and continue your work. Connie won't bother you anymore. *[At this point the bell rings and Abe gratefully dismisses the class.]*

During his free period the following day, Abe enters the office of Mark Reid, the curriculum supervisor.

ABE   *[Extends his hand]* Mark, I'm Abe Goodman, the new eighth-grade teacher. I appreciate your seeing me so quickly. As I told you when I called yesterday, I'm looking for some suggestions that'll help me be more effective with my sixth-period American history class. A number of teachers have recommended you highly and suggested that I talk with you.

MARK   Well, I'm pleased that some of our faculty think I'm doing my job well. How can I help you?

ABE   My sixth-period American history class is extremely diverse. They're generally pretty well behaved, but some of them just seem to be unable to learn the material. For instance, one of the girls did research on the differences between Columbus' three ships and modern-day ocean liners. She'd written several pages of statistics, but she was unable to use them to write a comparison between the old and new ships. Another pupil had a similar problem. He found quite a bit of information on various Indian tribes. He's very well informed on the common characteristics of those tribes, but he isn't able to tell how they differ. He just couldn't see the forest for the trees.

MARK   I guess all classes have pupils who are better analyzers than others and respond better to certain approaches to teaching, such as problem-solving, drill, individual reading, group reading, or lecture.

ABE   Yes, but in my class this is a major problem.

MARK   I see. Have you considered using grouping procedures for dealing with your students' analyzing differences?

ABE   Well, I recently divided them into heterogeneous groups, hoping that the good pupils would help some of the poorer ones. But most of the poorer pupils have such poor backgrounds that they seem to be beyond help. Other pupils prefer to work independently.

MARK   Have you considered homogeneous grouping—putting the analyzers and non-analyzers in different groups? Or perhaps put the non-analyzers together and wor with the analyzers on an independent study basis, since they're often more self-directing. The non-analyzers often need more structure and support, in my experience.

ABE   No, I really didn't consider grouping the students that way. I guess I've got a bias when it comes to homogeneous grouping. Somehow that approach seems undemocratic. Maybe I'm wrong, but it seems to me that part of our job as teache is to help kids from varying backgrounds and ability levels learn to get along and work with one another. Somehow homogeneous grouping doesn't seem compatil with that goal.

MARK   I understand your position, Abe, and I respect it. Perhaps we should consider then how to make your heterogeneous grouping approach work more effectively.

ABE   I don't want you to think that none of my groups are working. Some of them wo quite well.

MARK   Can you put your finger on what makes your good groups work well?

ABE   Now that I think about it, in the good groups the stronger students help the weaker ones. I don't know, maybe it's the analyzers helping the non-analyzers. Al thanks to Mary Johnson, I learned about trade books, which helped me meet the various reading needs of some of my weaker students.

MARK   Well, it sounds like you're experimenting with several approaches to teaching. But with regard to pupils helping other pupils, sometimes that helps the good pupils as well as the slow ones.

ABE   Perhaps some of my groups aren't working because of other differences in the cl; besides the analyzer/non-analyzer one we've talked about.

MARK   Oh? Such as?

ABE   There are so many differences that I don't know where to begin! I've gathered so information on my students' differences from their cumulative records. I used th information to group them. [Hands sheet to Mark] Besides racial and ethnic differences, I have IQ differences plus I have two exceptional students, Connie Petty and Kevin Felton. You'll also notice differences in work preferences, which got from a questionnaire I gave them.

MARK   Do your analyzers prefer to work independently and your non-analyzers in groups?

ABE   Yes, that's the general pattern.

MARK   Tell me about your exceptional students. What kinds of disabilities do they have?

ABE   Connie Petty is ADHD, and the other day she announced that her mother had made arrangements with the principal to allow her to take a Ritalin pill twice a day when she or I decide that she needs one. But I hadn't even been consulted. I checked with the front office after class and, indeed, this is the case. I'd already recognized that Connie has trouble sustaining her attention. In fact, I just moved her seat close to my desk, away from other pupils, this morning.

MARK   And the other student? I believe you said his name is Kevin?

ABE   Yes, Kevin Felton. He's diagnosed as socially maladjusted. When he's annoyed he goes out of control, and this happens several times a day.

MARK   Let me ask you this, Abe: are Connie and Kevin in the groups that you are having trouble with?

ABE   Oh, yes. They had a big blowup in class the other day. But like I've been saying, they aren't the only ones having trouble in my sixth-period class. *[Pause]* What do you think, Mark? Do you think I should change my grouping procedures, or even get rid of them? But what can I do to deal with so many differences in one class?

FIGURE 9 Information Collected by Mr. Goodman's on His Sixth-Period History Students

NAME AND ETHNIC ORIGIN[1]	IQ[2]	TOTAL SCORE[3]	SOC. ST. SUBTEST[3]	ELIGIBLE FOR FREE LUNCH	WORK PREFERENCE[4]
1. Adams, Anthony (W)	110	5	5	No	I
2. Aguila, Angela (H)	90	3	3	Yes	G
3. Brown, Lamar (AA)	90	3	2	Yes	G
4. Edwards, Elaine (AA)	95	4	4	Yes	G
5. Castillo, Maria (H)	90	3	4	Yes	G
6. Collins, Horace (AA)	80	2	1	Yes	G
7. Davis, Terry (W)	96	3	4	No	G
8. Edmonds, Edward (W)	84	3	3	No	I
9. Epling, Sally (W)	102	4	4	No	I
10. Espinoza, Edwardo (H)	96	3	1	Yes	G
11. Evans, Christina (W)	105	5	5	No	I
12. Felton, Kevin (W)	95	3	3	Yes	I
13. Griffith, Lawanda (AA)	88	2	1	Yes	G
14. Gulley, Moses (AA)	80	2	1	Yes	G
15. Ho, Wan (A)	110	5	5	No	I
16. Jackson, Elijah (A)	100	2	1	Yes	G
17. Jarvis, Robert (AA)	95	3	3	Yes	G
18. Johnson, Sarah (W)	103	4	4	No	I
19. Kane, Charles (W)	100	4	3	No	I
20. Lake, Sharon (W)	97	3	3	Yes	I
21. Matthews, Elaine (W)	101	4	4	No	I
22. Nazario, Merida (H)	96	3	2	Yes	G
23. Nero, Charles (AA)	96	3	2	No	G
24. Norton, Pearl (AA)	98	4	4	No	G
25. Owens, Janet (W)	106	5	5	Yes	I
26. Patrick, Natasha (AA)	94	3	2	Yes	G
27. Petty, Constance (W)	98	3	2	Yes	I
28. Rozelle, Patricia (W)	102	3	3	No	G
29. Samuels, Barbara (W)	89	2	1	Yes	G
30. Thompson, Martha (W)	107	5	5	No	I
31. Vaughn, Paula (W)	89	2	1	No	G
32. Velasques, Iona (H)	85	2	1	Yes	I
33. Williams, Victoria (W)	109	5	5	No	I
34. Wilson, Aaron (AA)	105	5	2	Yes	G
35. Yin, Chan (A)	115	5	6	No	I
36. Zimmer, Karl (A)	102	4	4	No	G

[1]W = Non-Hispanic white; H = Hispanic; AA = African-American; A = Asian-American
[2]IQ = Total IQ on California Test of Mental Maturity
[3]Total and Social Studies subtest stanine scores, Metropolitan Achievement Test
[4]I = Individual work preference; G = Group work preference

QUESTIONS

1. What is diversity in the field of education? What kinds of diversity are portrayed in this case? What kinds of diversity exist in this situation that Abe recognizes, and what kinds did he not recognize?

2. What are ethnic differences, and how do they differ from racial differences? What kinds of ethnic differences exist among students in this case? Do students prefer to work with students from the same or a similar ethnic background? Why? What is the best way for teachers to deal with biases toward certain ethnic groups?

3. What are racial differences, and which ones are portrayed in this case? What teaching methods work best with students from different racial backgrounds? How can teachers cope with racial biases?

4. Two of Abe's students have trouble seeing the "forest for the trees." What are field dependence and field independence in the cognitive style literature? Do field dependent/independent students prefer to work independently or in groups with structure?

5. Two of Abe's students have disabilities. What kinds of disabilities do they have, and what is the most effective way to work with these students? How well did Abe handle them? What effect is Ritalin supposed to have on persons with ADHD? How effective are such drugs?

6. Abe tries to deal with his class by setting up heterogeneous groups based on information that he obtained from his students and from their cumulative records. Is this the best way to group these students in this situation? What would be a better way?

7. Cooperative learning methods are popular today as a way of working with students in groups and of reducing competition in the classroom. Would cooperative groups have been a better approach for Abe to have used? Would he have grouped the students differently to form cooperative groups? How would he have grouped them? What are the strengths and weaknesses of cooperative learning?

8. How effective are Abe's classroom management procedures? What classroom management models might be most effective in this situation? Why? For example, would Teacher Effectiveness Training have been a good classroom management model to use in this situation?

9. In terms of teacher expectancy or self-fulfilling prophecy theory, does Abe evidence any biases toward any of his students? What are the best ways to deal with such biases?

10. How would you describe Abe's view of the nature of learning? Would a cognitive or behavioral model best fit his learning orientation? What model of learning would you advise Abe to consider applying in this situation?

11. What is Bloom's Cognitive Taxonomy? At which of Bloom's levels are Abe's students able to work? At which levels are Barbara and Aaron not able to operate? How can a teacher help students move to higher levels of thinking?

12. What advice should Mark give Abe? What teaching methods might work in this situation? What should Abe do differently?

C A S E **9**

THE COMPUTER GENERATION

Key Content to Consider for Analyzing This Case:
(1) generational (cohort) differences; (2) gender differences; (3) teacher training in computer technolog(4) learning theory (operant, observational);
(5) motivation (attribution theory, Maslow's need hierarchy).

gnes Fouts has taught sixth grade at Smithfield Middle School since the scho opened twenty years ago. She is forty-four years old and prides herself both being a good disciplinarian and on her ability to teach her students the ba skills.

Smithfield Middle School is located in the upper Midwest, and the city of Smit field has a population of approximately 50,000. It serves approximately 700 pupils grades 6 through 8. The school population is approximately 70% white, 27% Africa American, 2% Hispanic, and 1% Asian-American. Most students are from middle-cla and upper-middle-class homes.

It is the first day of the pre-school workshops, and many of the Smithfield teache are very excited. The auditorium is filled with new computers which will be placed in the sixth-grade classrooms this year. A computer technician has been conducting a wor shop to show teachers how to boot up the computers, use the function keys, and becon familiar with the various types of software programs. After the workshop ends, teach are invited to go to the other end of the auditorium and enjoy some refreshments. Agr and another sixth-grade teacher, Grace Fisher, have chosen soft drinks and small bags potato chips and taken them to a nearby table.

GRACE   *[Enthusiastically]* Isn't this just great! The administration's been promising us computers for years. Now we have them! I think it's exciting, don't you?

AGNES   *[With reservations]* I'm not sure. I've always avoided computers because I'm terrified of them. I became so upset as I spent the whole day worrying about havi a room full of computers that I don't even remember how to work the function keys.

GRACE   *[Reassuring]* Oh, don't worry about that, Agnes. After you've worked with the computer for a few days, you'll pick it right up. And, if you don't, there'll be pup in your class who have computers at home and know all about them.

AGNES   Well, I feel rather uneasy about that, too. It doesn't seem to me that sixth graders should have to instruct their teachers on equipment that's being used in the classroom. I don't like to have activities in my class that the pupils know more about than I do. Besides that, I worry that they'll spend valuable classroom time playing games and doing other non-educational activities on their computers when they could be reading books, using reference materials, making maps, and working on other more educational projects.

GRACE   It's interesting that you feel that way, Agnes. Many times I've given assignments that the students know more about than I do. They think it's neat that they're helping the teacher learn, and I think it's neat that my pupils can teach me something.

AGNES   *[Shakes her head vigorously from side to side—says with feeling]* Oh, no! I'd be very uncomfortable in a situation like that! I just feel more secure when I'm teaching materials that I thoroughly understand. I guess I'm old-fashioned, but I'm really embarrassed when students have to "help me out."

GRACE   *[Looking at her watch]* Well, I have to run now. I hope that when your class begins to use the computers you'll feel comfortable with them and become a computer buff.

AGNES   *[Unenthusiastically]* Well, maybe I will, but I doubt it. *[Pauses and then becomes more animated]* Thank you for asking me to sit with you. I enjoyed it, and I'll see you next week when school starts.

The following Monday morning, Agnes is having a get-acquainted session with her pupils. She is sharing with them the types of assignments some of her other sixth-grade classes have enjoyed doing. Mike raises his hand, and Agnes calls on him.

MIKE   There's a sixth-grade class in Casper, Wyoming, that's building a log cabin that's just like the log cabins built by the first settlers in Wyoming. It's a part of their social studies class.

AGNES   That's very interesting, Mike. Do you have a friend in Wyoming who's involved in this project?

MIKE   Oh, no, I was online on my home computer and found this information on that class's homepage.

LOUISE   *[Blurts out]* My dad has America Online on his computer, and it's really neat. Last year I learned that I could type in "Homework" and find references to help me with whatever assignment I was working on. It's really cool. *[Several other pupils speak out to say that they have America Online and that they call up interesting files on it.]*

BARRY   I'd really like to learn how to get information from AOL too, Ms. Fouts. Are you going to let us do that in here?

AGNES   Not right now, Barry. Maybe after I see how well you learn the library skills, we can play some with the computers. We have a really good school library here at Smithfield, and I think it's important for students in middle school to learn to use the reference system to find books in the library. We can practice using the card catalog, learn how the books are arranged on the shelves, and find information from the various types of books in the reference section. Those skills are just as important as computer skills. In fact, I've made arrangements for us to tour the library next Monday with Ms. Renner.

The following Monday, Agnes is reviewing for the class the various competen· she wants them to acquire when they visit the library that morning. She reiterates that is planning to have them learn the library skills that she enumerated the previous we·

AGNES   I'm excited about our visit to the library this morning. The things you'll learn there will be useful to you all the rest of your lives.

BARRY   Ms. Fouts, I don't understand why we have to go to the library when we coulc stay right here in our classroom and learn all those library skills on our compute· I can't wait to get on the computer and start going somewhere! Can't we just figu· out how to search for the library materials from here?

CHARLIE   Yes, Ms. Fouts. If you would tell us what you'd like for us to find in the encyclopedia, then we could bring the encyclopedia up on our computers and p· out a report. Then you could check to see whether we did it right.

MIKE   *[Speaking out]* And if you ask us to find something that's not in our library, we c· call up another source on the Web that'll give us the answers.

AGNES   I don't understand why eleven- and twelve-year-old girls and boys think that so important to sit at your desks so much. I've become really concerned about h· inactive children in our country have become during the past several years. Mor· than half of our pupils are overweight. And I've read several studies that tell us t· children in every other industrialized nation in the world are in much better physical condition than children in our country.

VIKKI   Well, at least we're better than they are in athletics. We won most of the medal· the Olympics.

AGNES   Yes, that's right. Our athletes are better than their athletes. *[Pupils cheer—Agn· holds up her hand for silence.]* But unfortunately, our young people generally, including those your age, are in the worst physical condition of all the children i· the world's industrialized nations.

VIKKI   *[Shocked]* But I don't understand. We have to go to physical education, and we· have city sports programs for kids all over town. What do the kids in other countries do that we don't do?

AGNES   Well, for one thing, they walk a lot. Very few families have more than one car· and some families don't own a car. And those who do have cars don't drive them· nearly as much as we drive ours, because gasoline costs more than twice as muc· most other countries as it does here.

MARVIN   Do they have school buses in those countries?

AGNES   No, they don't. And they don't have school lunches and interscholastic athlet· either. We're the only industrialized nation that transports pupils to school and feeds them while they're there. *[Students look at each other in disbelief.]*

CHARLIE   Then how do those students get to be in such good shape?

AGNES   Good question, Charlie. They do have physical education at school, but it
            doesn't involve team sports. They have calisthenics, gymnastics, fencing, and other
            individual sports that help them stay in good physical condition.
CHARLIE   But don't they have any team sports?
AGNES   Yes, but team sports are usually sponsored by community organizations and
            businesses, not schools.
CHARLIE   Wow! That's really different, isn't it?
AGNES   [Smiling] Yes, Charlie. It's really different. [Looking at her watch] But we'll have to
            continue this discussion another time. We began discussing that topic because of
            my concern that you students seem to want to sit so much. But now you'll have an
            opportunity to have some exercise because we're going to walk to the library. I told
            Ms. Renner that we'd be at the library in about five minutes, so we'd better leave
            now. [The pupils put away their books and prepare to go to the library, many of them
            reluctantly.]

It is one month later, and Agnes has become aware of the fact that the vast majority of students in her class are cooperative and well behaved. They also do good work academically. She has been quite pleased with their progress and has decided to reward them
by allowing them to do more work on the computers.

Unfortunately, one of the students, Barry, frustrated by not getting to use the new
computers, hung around the classroom after school and tampered with several of the
computers by changing the margins, line spacing, type size, and justification on the software programs. Since no one had used the computers, only the guilty party knew that
they had been altered.

AGNES   I'm really proud of this class because you've done such good work during
            the past few weeks. To reward you I'm going to allow you to do some work
            on your computers today. [Class members cheer.] Now, I know there are many
            different activities we could choose to do on the computers, so why don't you
            computer users make some suggestions. Then we can select the ideas that sound
            best.
VIKKI   My friend Marianne in Ms. Fisher's class said that they're playing educational
            games that teach about history, problem-solving, science, and things like that.
            That'd be fun to do.
JERRY   I don't know how to type very good, and I'd like to work with a computer
            program that teaches typing. I want to go to college, and I know you have to type
            when you go there.
AGNES   Yes, this would be a good time for you to learn to type. In our society today
            students need to know how to type. Otherwise, you have to pay typists to type all
            your papers. [Louise waves her hand in the air.] Louise?
LOUISE   Like I said before, my dad has America Online on his computer. Is our school
            on it? Why don't we look at the directory on our computers and see if AOL is
            there? Then maybe we could pick what programs we'd like to work with. We don't
            all have to work on the same program at the same time, do we? Let's turn on our

computers and find out what we've got. Maybe Jerry can find a program to help him learn to type. Let's do that.

JERRY   Killer! I need to type better!

AGNES   I agree. Thank you for your suggestion, Louise. Let's turn on the computers and see what's on them. *[Students quickly figure out how to turn on the computer and monit*

MIKE   *[Speaking out]* OK. The screen that's up now shows what programs are already c our hard drives. Jerry, I don't see a typing program. Maybe we can find one and install it on the hard drive.

ABE   *[Shouting]* Hey! The letters on my screen are great big. Does anybody else have great big letters on their screen?

EBONY   No, but my letters are really tiny, and they aren't straight. How come our computers are so different, Ms. Fouts?

AGNES   *[Very concerned]* Why, I have no idea! How many of you have computers that aren't acting right?

CHARLIE   Well, there are at least three or four spaces between each line of print that I type. And the ends of my lines aren't straight. The only other time I typed on a computer, both the left and right margins were straight. My left is straight, but th right one is all jagged.

MARVIN   *[Laughing]* Look at mine! All my sentences begin at the middle of the page. A each line has a number in front of it! This is really weird. My computer's out of control. It needs help.

AGNES   *[Obviously shaken]* What can we do? I can't imagine what's happened to our computers. We haven't even used them. Do you think they're all broken?

MIKE   *[Calmly]* They're not broken, Ms. Fouts. I think somebody's been messing arou with them. Do you want me to see if I can fix them?

AGNES   *[Feeling quite helpless and trapped in an impossible situation, she pauses for quite a while, then responds very reluctantly.]* Thank you, Mike. It's kind of you to voluntee to do that. All right, class. Take out the books you're reading for your book repor and we'll have a free reading period.

MIKE   *[Moving from computer to computer and entering a variety of commands from the keyboard of each computer, he finishes his work in about fifteen minutes.]* Ms. Fouts, I' got all the computers formatted the same way. Someone had changed the format settings of all those machines so that they were are all formatted differently. That' why the spacing, print, margins, justification, and other settings were different fr machine to machine.

AGNES   *[Embarrassed]* Thank you for straightening out the computers for us, Mike. H did you know how to do whatever you did?

MIKE   *[Pleased]* There's a function key labeled "Format" on every computer. I just pusl that key, and that brought up the format window on the monitor. That let me see how each computer was formatted. Then I selected a format and entered it on all the computers. My dad taught me how to use the format codes on our computer home. It would only take me a minute to teach the class how to format their computers, and I'd be happy to do it right now if you want me to.

AGNES   *[Feeling very defensive and mumbling aloud]* Format key. Format key. We had a workshop the day before school began, and the computer technician showed us how to use those function keys. But I didn't bother to look at the computer screens today to see what was the matter with them. Had I done so, I'd probably have realized that the format settings were different.

MIKE *[Diplomatically]* That's OK, Ms. Fouts. I'm sure you'd have noticed right away what was wrong with them if you'd had a chance to look at the function keys. Besides, a lot of the teachers here let the students who have computers at home work with those who don't know about computers yet. If you want me to, I'll show the class how to use the function keys.

AGNES *[After a long pause, she forces a smile.]* Thank you, Mike. It's kind of you to do that for us.

By the second week of February the students had been given several opportunities to use their computers to work on the programs of their choice. There had been no class projects involving the use of the computer.

AGNES Can anyone tell me what holiday we celebrate next week?

ABE *[Speaking out]* Valentine's Day.

AGNES That's right, Abe.

EBONY Can we give each other valentines in class, Ms. Fouts? We did that in Ms. Graham's class last year, and it was lots of fun.

AGNES Yes, that's what I had in mind, Ebony. But I was in a card store last night and I looked at the valentines for sale there. They were really expensive. Then, I thought it might be fun to bring in art paper, pictures from magazines, glue, sparkle, and doilies and make our own valentines. It would be fun, save us all money, and would also be a good art lesson.

MARGE *[Excited]* That sounds like fun. What day are we going to start doing it?

AGNES Well, Valentine's Day is a week from Friday. Perhaps we could begin next Monday. Meanwhile, you could be deciding who will receive your valentines, how many you'll need, the kinds of cards you'd like to make, and what kinds of materials you'd like to use to make them. I'll also collect some colored craft paper, paints, crayons, paste, and other things we might use on our valentines.

MIKE We have a graphics program on our computers, Ms. Fouts. We could probably make some really neat valentines on our computers, and we wouldn't have to bother collecting all those materials you were talking about. We could just look at the materials on the computer, choose the ones we want to use, arrange them the way we want them arranged, and then print them on the printer. That way we'd each use different materials and have our own special valentine.

AGNES *[Feeling defensive]* I know we could do that, Mike, but I want to have the making of valentines as an art project. I want us to improve our drawing, painting, creating, designing, and all the skills and activities associated with art. Printing pictures already on a computer program would produce valentines, but it won't help you develop the skills that I want you to learn.

LOUISE But picking the pictures and decorations that fit in with the type of valentine you're trying to make can help you learn about design, color, patterns, and things like that.

AGNES   Oh, I agree that you would learn certain skills by using the computer to make
your valentines, but for this particular unit, I want you to learn the skills that I've
already mentioned. Maybe some other time you can use some of the art on the
computer program.

BARRY   Couldn't we do both? Those who want to use the computer could, and those w
want to use other supplies could do that. Some could probably do both. That way,
we'd all learn more. *[Class members agree, saying "Yes," "Killer," "Let's do that," etc.]*

AGNES   *[Seeing the logic to the argument]* All right, you've convinced me. Go ahead and
begin on the computers now. But I want you all to bring supplies for making
valentines by hand tomorrow. For now, you can use the computers. *[Students
immediately begin to work with computers.]*

MARION   *[Waving her hand]* Ms. Fouts, my computer seems to be stuck. I can't make it
do anything.

AGNES   *[Goes to computer and presses various keys. Nothing happens.]* I can't imagine wha
the trouble is. It just won't do anything.

MIKE   May I look at it? *[Approaches the computer and pushes the control, alternate, and
delete keys simultaneously, rebooting the computer]*

AGNES   *[Embarrassed]* Thank you, Mike.

The following Monday, Agnes is eating in the school cafeteria. Her friend Gra
approaches her table.

GRACE   Hi, Agnes. May I join you?

AGNES   *[Enthusiastically]* Of course, Grace, I haven't had an opportunity to talk with yo
for quite a while. How's your class this year?

GRACE   *[Smiling]* It's great. I'm having more fun this year than I've ever had before. I
guess it's because of the computers. My kids are wild about them. And, I must
admit, I enjoy them too. How's your class going? You seem to have a lot of nice ki
this year.

AGNES   Oh, I do! These students are probably the nicest I've ever had! *[Sadly]* But,
unfortunately, I'm not really having a very good year. But it's my own fault.

GRACE   I'm confused. If your kids are the best you've ever had, how could your year be
bad? What do you mean it's your fault?

AGNES   Remember when we had the pre-school workshop on computers and I told yo
I probably wouldn't be able to learn how to operate them?

GRACE   Yes, I do remember that.

AGNES   Well, I've just been miserable. I think the times have just passed me by! Every
time I let the kids use the computer in class, something happens that makes me
demonstrate my ignorance. I'm sure they think I'm just a relic.

GRACE   *[Somewhat taken aback]* I'm sure that's not the case, Agnes. You've always been
one of the students' favorite teachers. And I know that many parents ask Ms.
Martin to assign their child to your class.

AGNES   Well, they probably won't do that anymore since we've moved into the comput
age. I'm sure some of them tell their parents how dumb I am about computers. I'v

just humiliated myself time and time again. In fact, every time I give a computer assignment I do something stupid. I made a fool of myself by not remembering a thing about the format key. One of the students had to take over the class and fix our computers.

GRACE   Oh, I'll bet the pupils didn't think a thing about that. They realize that people of our generation didn't grow up with computers. I mess up on the computer all the time, and every day I learn something new from one of the kids.

AGNES   I guess my problem is that I don't like computers. I don't want to learn to use them. I guess the younger generation's just passed me by. But I worry about them because they're so inactive. They seem not to want to get any exercise. I've read that more than half of them are overweight. And instead of getting exercise they sit at their desks and get library information on their computers instead of walking down the hall to the library. They don't seem interested in learning research skills in the library. They don't read real books if they can read something on their computer. They don't write on paper. They type on their computers. I'll bet that all of them suffer from that "carpal tunnel syndrome" by the time they're thirty!

GRACE   But Agnes, there are always things that change from generation to generation. That doesn't mean that the older generation is bad or stupid. It's just that technology becomes more efficient as the successive generations develop. And the younger generations always uses new technology more than the older generations do. It's just natural. You're still an excellent teacher. You not only teach them what you know, but you make it possible for them to branch out on their own and learn new skills.

AGNES   You're a wonderful friend, Grace, and a great teacher. But I'm really convinced that time's passed me by. I'm seriously considering retiring from teaching at the end of this year. I think I'm in the same position as the manufacturer of buggy whips after the automobile became popular.

GRACE   [Concerned] It upsets me to see you so discouraged, Agnes. I think you're a wonderful teacher and a great role model. It seems to me that what's upsetting you most are your feelings of insecurity in using the computer. And you can do something about that. All you need to do is call the computer technician who gave the workshop we attended. He's employed by the school district, and his job is to help teachers use computers in their classes. If you call and tell him you need help, he'll come here and tutor you until you know all the things you need to know about the computer.

AGNES   You're a nice person and a good friend, Grace. But I really think I'm just too old to learn everything I'd need to know to use the computer in my teaching. I seriously question whether I'm willing to put forth all the time and effort needed to become competent in using the computer, because I don't think I'm capable of changing my teaching strategies so drastically. I just don't think lessons would really help me. From the way things have been going this year, I wonder whether anything will help.

FIGURE 10   Schedule for Pre-school Computer Workshop at Smithfield Middle Schoo

---

WORKSHOP SCHEDULE

8:30–9:00	Coffee and rolls
9:00–10:15	How Computers Can Help You in Your Classroom:
	1. Individualize instruction and assessment
	2. Connect home, school, and community
	3. Provide unlimited resources
	4. Expand and extend learning
10:15–10:30	Break
10:30–12:00	Resources the Computer Can Provide for You:
	1. Teachers share resources they have found to be effective
	2. Workshop instructor discusses the unlimited resources available through numerous networks upon request
12:15–1:30	Lunch
1:30–2:45	How Your Computer Works:
	1. Practice using function keys
	2. Creating, printing, and saving files
	3. Practicing commands
2:45–3:00	Break
3:00–3:30	Resources Available Through the School District:
	1. Workshop instructor distributes lists of resources
	2. Resource solicited from workshop participants
	3. Question and Answer Period
	4. Adjournment

QUESTIONS

1. How do generational (cohort) differences develop with regard to such technolog
cal advances such as computers? Is there a critical period for adapting to computer
What role, if any, does intelligence play?

2. Are there gender differences in adapting to computers? If so, will such differenc
disappear as future generations adapt to computers?

3. Is the use of computers in classrooms part of the program for training teacher
Should it be? If so, in what form?

4. At what level of Maslow's need hierarchy is Agnes primarily operating? What abo
Grace? How can Agnes deal with her need deficiencies?

5. From an observational learning perspective, how might Agnes have developed suc
a low sense of efficacy regarding computers? What programs and procedures have bee
developed to help change sense of efficacy?

6. Analyze Agnes' behavior from an operant conditioning perspective. What type
behavior is she emitting with regard to the use of computers? Why? How might pro
grammed instruction procedures be used to help shape her behavior toward increase
effective use of computers?

7. Does attitude change precede or follow behavioral change? What are the most effective methods of creating attitude change, say toward the use of computers? For example, what self-regulation methods or cognitive behavior modification procedures might work?

8. How does the literature on risk-taking and fear of failure help explain behavior like that of Agnes? How can fear of risk-taking and failure be changed?

9. From a Piagetian viewpoint, how would you explain Agnes' attitudes toward new learning? How would Piaget's adaptation construct of assimilation and accommodation explain her behavior, especially her reluctance to learn?

10. What kind of workshop on the use of computers would be most helpful to a teacher like Agnes? What should be included in such a workshop to help allay fears and encourage self-motivated exploration?

11. What are internal and external attributions? What attributions does Agnes have about computers? Under what conditions can attributions change? What are attribution training programs?

12. What resources are available to teachers like Agnes? Where can she turn for help?

CASE 10

DOUBLE TROUBLE

Key Content to Consider for Analyzing This Case:
(1) exceptionalities (especially ADHD, behavior disorders); (2) behavior modification; (3) observation[a] learning; (4) classroom management.

Martha Thompson is a twenty-seven-year-old African-American who joined t[ ] faculty of Jackson Elementary School as a fourth-grade teacher upon gradu[a]ing from college one year ago. Jackson Elementary is located in an old secti[ ] of a large metropolitan city in the Southeastern United States. The school has a stude[ ] population of approximately 900 pupils and has four sections at each grade level fr[o] K–6. This population represents an equal mix of low-SES residents and upper-SES fam[ ]lies who have restored large old homes located in the district served by the school.

Martha married her college sweetheart during her final year of college. He works [ ] an accounting firm on the same side of town as the school. The Thompsons reside in[ ] large old home which they bought last year with the intention of gradually restoring [ ] while they live in it.

It is Monday morning of the second week of school. Martha's twenty-four fourt[h] grade students are reading independently from the trade books they have selected fr[o] the classroom library. There is a knock on the door. As Martha walks toward the do[or] Art Hagstrom, a special education teacher, opens it and smiles. He has two boys wi[th] him.

ART   Good morning, Ms. Thompson. Nice to see you again.
MARTHA   Hi, Mr. Hagstrom. To what do I owe this pleasant surprise? And who are the [ ] young men accompanying you?
ART   *[Nodding toward one of the boys]* This young man's Bill Matz, and *[nodding toward th[e] other boy]* this young man's Evan Carter.
MARTHA   *[Smiling]* Hello, Bill. Hello, Evan. Why don't you boys take a seat? *[She looks towards Art for an explanation as the boys move away.]*
ART   If you remember, during the pre-school workshops three weeks ago, Ms. Jamison *[principal]* told us that our school district's making an effort this year to mainstream[ ] more special needs pupils out of separate special education classes and into regula[r] classes.

MARTHA   Yes, I remember that. I assumed that this was to be done the first day of class.

ART   *[Apologetically]* Well, we tried to place the students before school started, but the criteria for placement are pretty complicated, and we just finished making the assignments last week.

MARTHA   *[Smiling at the boys, who are seated]* And Bill and Evan are going to be in my class.

ART   Yes. They'll be in your class all year.

MARTHA   *[Walking over and shaking each boy's hand]* Bill. Evan. Welcome to my class. *[Pointing to different seats]* Bill, this can be your seat. Evan, that can be your seat. *[Evan flops down in his seat with great fanfare.]* Is there anything else you can tell me while you're here, Art? I'd like to get these boys started on some reading.

EVAN   *[Shouting loudly]* Oh, no! I hate reading!

ART   *[Ignoring Evan]* No, it looks to me like you're doing fine. I'll come to your room to help you work with these boys. We can set up a regular schedule after they get settled.

MARTHA   That's good. I'll probably need some help because I haven't had much instruction on working with special education students.

ART   *[Reassuring her]* I'm sure you'll do fine. I'll be in touch real soon. *[Leaves the room]*

MARTHA   Now, class. Each of you has a book to read that you selected from our classroom library last week. I want you to get out that book and read it now. *[To Bill and Evan]* Come with me to the bookshelves, and we'll find you books to read.

BILL   That's OK. I don't want a book. I don't like to read. I can't read very good.

EVAN   Me neither.

MARTHA   You don't need to worry about that in this class. I've arranged all the books on these shelves from easy to hard. *[Pointing to the K–3 bookshelf]* These are the easiest books on the bottom shelf. The hardest are on the top shelf. The others are in between. Pick your books from this shelf here *[points to the K–3 bookshelf]*. These are fairly easy books you can start with. Then you'll find out whether you can read harder ones. Take a few minutes to find a book you want, then show it to me. *[Walks to the center of the room to see that everyone is reading. After a few minutes, Evan leaves the book corner and walks toward Martha.]*

EVAN   Ms. Thompson, I'm not gonna read a book. I don't like to read, and I can't do it very well. Can't I do something else besides reading? I'm a good drawer. Could I draw instead of reading?

MARTHA   *[Enthusiastically]* That's great that you can draw, Evan. I like to have somebody who can draw in my class, and you'll be able to get grades sometimes for drawing. But, you'll also have to read. That's one of the main things people learn in school— to learn to read. Maybe you can draw scenes from stories you read.

EVAN   *[Just about to cry]* But I can't read. I get upset when I try to read.

MARTHA   *[Enthusiastically]* I know what you can do, Evan. Find a book on this shelf *[pointing]* that has an interesting cover. Then you can draw the scene that's on the cover. After that, maybe I can help you read the book.

BILL   *[Interrupting]* Ms. Thompson. Here's a book I'm going to read. *[Evan takes a book off the shelf and walks back to his seat.]*

MARTHA   *[Reading the title of Bill's book]* Daddy Is a Monster . . . Sometimes. That's a neat title. Why'd you pick this book?

BILL   I don't know. It just sounded good. I looked at a couple of pages in it, and I can read them.

MARTHA   *[Handing the book back to Bill]* Great! It sounds interesting. I hope you like it.
[Bill takes the book and walks back toward his seat. On the way he hits Malcolm hard on the back of the head with the book.]

MALCOLM   *[Jumping out of his chair and knocking it over]* Hey, why'd you hit me! I didn't do anything to you!

BILL   *[Shoving Malcolm down over his upturned chair]* Because I don't like the way you look! You look like a wimp!

MALCOLM   *[Scrambling to get up off the floor]* What's the matter with you? You're crazy!

BILL   *[Shoving him over the chair again before he can regain his footing]* Who're you calling crazy? Not me! Nobody calls me bad names! *[Malcolm falls hard again.]*

MARTHA   *[Rushing over to the boys, Martha grabs Bill and pushes him toward his chair.]*
[Crossly] Go sit down this instant! *[She helps Malcolm get untangled from his desk.]* A you all right, Malcolm?

MALCOLM   *[Rubbing his elbow]* I skinned this elbow when I fell, but I'm all right, I guess

MARTHA   That's good. I'm glad you're not hurt seriously, but I'm not sure what happene between you two.

MALCOLM   I didn't do nothing! That new guy's really a creep!

At the end of the following school day, Martha goes to see Art Hagstrom in the sp cial education office. Since she had made an appointment the previous day, he is expec ing her. The door is open when she arrives. Art sees her approaching and motions her come in.

ART   I'm glad you called about Bill and Evan. I wanted to talk with you at length before I put them in your class, but, as I told you, the placements for the mainstreamed students were made the same morning I brought them to your class.

MARTHA   *[Sighing]* Well, the two of them together are really challenging. They take mor of my time than all the other pupils in the class put together. The two days he's been in my class, Bill's started three fights. He seems unable to relate either to adults or age mates. On Monday he was all over the classroom annoying other students. He got into three fights. Today he sat and stared at the wall all day and totally ignored the other students and me.

ART   *[Smiling]* I was afraid of that. He's been diagnosed as having a behavior disorder.

MARTHA   *[Exaggerated]* Well! Great! But I'm not really interested in what they've labeled him. I want to know what I can do to help him learn something!

ART   I know, and I intend to help you to teach him. But first, tell me about Evan.

MARTHA   Evan worries me more than Bill does. He's so disorganized he can't do anything. He forgets what the assignment is, even before he begins. He doesn't listen well. He can't concentrate. He can't even copy information accurately. He jus seems like a zero personality. He can't stay on task or sit still for thirty seconds. He constantly out of his seat disturbing other students or messing around with objects in the room.

ART   Evan's been diagnosed as having attention deficit hyperactivity disorder, better
        known as ADHD. As you know, such disorders can't be corrected easily or quickly,
        but there are some things we can use to help these students learn to take some
        responsibility for their actions.

MARTHA [Relieved] That's welcome news. I've never had any courses in special
        education. I don't feel confident in working with these two students.

ART   [Smiling] From the little I've observed in your class, you seem to be quite sensitive
        to the needs of all your students. That's half the battle. When I brought Bill and
        Evan to your class, I told you that I'd help you work with them. I have free time
        from 9:00 to 10:00 on Monday, Wednesday, and Friday. Would it be OK if I come
        to your class at those times to help with Bill and Evan?

MARTHA [Delighted] Would it! You've made my whole day! As you work with them,
        maybe you could make specific suggestions to me on how to change their behavior.

ART   I'm sure we'll find something that works if we try enough different strategies.
        They've had a lot of success using behavior modification with behavior disorders,
        and drugs like Ritalin can help with ADHD students.

MARTHA I've tried to work on classroom management this past week. I had the class
        establish behavior guidelines and penalties for violating them. They're working well
        for everyone but Bill and Evan.

ART   That's good. That way Bill and Evan won't feel discriminated against if we enforce
        those rules. Evan's records indicate that his doctor prescribed Ritalin for him. Has
        he gone to the school nurse to take it?

MARTHA He has some, but he often forgets to take it and, frankly, I've forgotten to
        remind him.

ART   Well, let's make out a schedule and post it to make sure he takes it at regular
        intervals. That'll probably help him control his outbursts.

MARTHA That's a good idea. Well, I'll look for you tomorrow morning, then?

ART   Yes, I'll be there around 9:00 as usual.

MARTHA I'll see you then, Art.

The following morning Art comes to Martha's class a little before 9:00. She suggests
that he might like to help Evan read a story. Art finds that although Evan can say most of
the words, he can't follow the meanings of the sentences. The more Evan reads, the more
frustrated he becomes. He loses his place in the story, mispronounces words, and can't
remember what happened earlier in the story.

The other students are working quietly in groups on social studies units. Martha is
moving among the groups to help them as needed. Suddenly the hum of conversation
among the students working on their projects is shattered by a loud exclamation.

JACK   [Jumping from his chair after Bill jabbed him with a pin] Damn you, Bill! You're really
        a jerk! [He grabs a handful of Bill's hair and pulls him out of his chair onto the floor.]

BILL   [Screaming at the top of his lungs] Let go of my hair, Jack-Ass! Let go of me or I'll kill
        you. [He throws his weight against Jack and drives him against the wall. He repeatedly
        lunges into Jack with his shoulder.]

ART   [*Jumps out of his chair and runs toward Bill and Jack*] Bill! Stop that immediately!
MARTHA   [*Running toward the struggling boys*] Boys! Stop that! Take your seats
        immediately!

        Martha and Art reach the boys at the same time and manage to separate the
Martha takes Jack to his seat, and Art escorts Bill to the principal's office.

___

        That same day, immediately after the students are dismissed, Art sticks his head in
Martha's classroom.

ART   Anybody home?
MARTHA   [*Coming out from beside the bookshelves*] Yes, I'm straightening out the books.
        How're you doing?
ART   I came to see if you had time to talk about the fiasco this afternoon and to see wh
        we could do to avoid future problems of that type.
MARTHA   Sure. I've been thinking about that incident ever since it happened. I think
        Bill's a dangerous person, and I'm worried about what he could do in my class.
ART   I agree. And that's one of the reasons why I'm here. The other reason is that I have
        some information about Bill that I haven't shared with you yet.
MARTHA   I'm certainly interested in learning all I can about Bill. Tell me what you know
ART   Well, I think that Bill may come by his abusive tendencies naturally.
MARTHA   Why do you say that?
ART   Well, one day last year after classes were over, I left the building and saw Bill on
        the basketball court shooting balls with two or three other guys. Then I saw a man
        that I later found out was Bill's father striding quite purposefully across the field. I
        walked to the basketball court, grabbed Bill by the shoulders, and shouted at him
        at the top of his voice that Bill was supposed to be waiting in the parking lot. He
        shook Bill pretty hard, and then literally threw him toward the parking lot. Bill
        almost fell to the ground. Bill's father then unlocked the car door on the passenger
        side, opened it, grabbed Bill's arm, and shoved him roughly across the seat. He the
        went to the driver's side, started the motor, and burned rubber for about thirty
        yards as he squealed out of the parking lot.
MARTHA   Sounds as if I'm dealing with a "like father, like son" situation. Maybe Bill's
        selection of the book *Daddy Is a Monster . . . Sometimes* wasn't just a coincidence.
ART   I'd say based on what I saw that's definitely the case.
MARTHA   Then I guess I'd better forget my plans to call his father. He probably wouldn
        be willing or able to offer me much support with Bill. I think we're better off
        making our own plans.
ART   I think so, too. And I think it's important for us to consider using a behavior
        modification procedure like time-out with Bill the minute he begins to get out of
        control.
MARTHA   That's fine with me! We just can't have him disrupting the entire class every
        day and give him an opportunity to seriously injure one of the other students.
        What kind of time-out procedure do you have in mind? How do you use time-out
        I've never tried it.

ART   Well, I checked with Ms. Jamison, and she told me that the small room adjoining her office is vacant all day and that we can use it as a time-out room. I could take Bill there, and he would be monitored while he's there by the principal and the secretaries.

MARTHA   *[Excited]* That's perfect! Let's do that! How long will he stay there?

ART   Let's start with fifteen minutes. We can lengthen it, if necessary.

MARTHA   I'm glad we're going to help Bill develop some self-control. Let's begin the time-out as soon as you come in on Friday. We'll need to explain it all to Bill first.

ART   That's fine with me. *[Enthusiastically]* Friday's the day!

Before the pupils arrive on Friday, Martha arranges the chairs in circles for the groups and lays out their project materials. She notices that Bill has taken some notes relating to a group project. She puts Evan's book on his desk.

When Art arrives a little before 9:00, the groups are busy at work. Bill is taking notes from a reference book. Evan is at his desk with his book open, looking around.

ART   *[Smiling, nods toward Martha and sits down beside Evan]* Good morning, Evan. How're you coming with your book?

EVAN   Not too good. I have trouble reading it.

ART   Do you like the book so far?

EVAN   Yes, I like it, but I just can't stay in the right place.

ART   How would it be if I'd read the book to you for a while.

EVAN   *[Smiles] [Enthusiastically]* I'd like that!

ART   Good. Here we go. *[Begins to read with much expression]*

As Martha circulates from one group to another, she is pleased at how well the class is going. Then she remembers that she hasn't told Bill about the time-out procedure. She looks in his direction and sees that he is not working on his assignment, but is staring into space. So she walks over toward him.

MARTHA   *[Softly]* Bill, I need to talk to you about something. *[Pauses]* Bill, you've gotten into a lot of fights lately, and that has to stop. The next time that happens, I'm going to say "time out" to you and you'll need to leave the room with Mr. Hagstrom for fifteen minutes. He'll tell you when you can come back to class. Do you understand?

BILL   I guess so. Can I go out in the hall and get a drink?

MARTHA   Yes, that'll be all right. But come right back. *[Martha circulates from group to group answering questions and observing their progress.]*

Art stops reading and gives the book to Evan to read aloud. As he is listening to Evan try to figure out the pronunciation of words in the story, he looks out the window at the playground equipment. He catches sight of Bill furtively coming out a door and immediately going around a corner of the building. He immediately tells Evan to read silently, gets up, and walks over to Martha.

ART   I just saw Bill leave the building. I'm going out to get him.

MARTHA *[Angrily]* It's my fault. I guess I felt sorry for him when I told him about time-out and let him go. I'm sorry.

ART *[Reassuringly]* Don't take the blame for a student who deliberately breaks rules. Don't worry. I'll get him back.

Art walks quickly out of the building in the direction he saw Bill take. As he roun the building, he sees Bill walking quickly down the street away from the school buildir Since Art is behind Bill, he can run toward him without Bill's seeing him. He con within reach of Bill before Bill is aware of his being there.

ART *[Taking Bill firmly by the arm]* You need to come back to class with me, Bill. Walki away from school is considered truancy. You don't want go be truant. That's breaking the law.

BILL *[Jerking his arm away from Art]* Lemme go! Keep your hands offa' me, man!

ART *[Taking a firmer grip on Bill's arm and pushing him forcefully toward the school]* I'm taking you back to your class right now!

BILL *[Runs forward, then twists quickly and breaks Art's grip]* Leave me alone! Let me go! *[He runs away from Art.]*

ART *[Catches up with Bill and grabs him]* You're coming with me!

BILL *[Spins around and hits Art hard on the jaw]* I'm not going back to school! Leave me alone!

ART *[Hurt and infuriated, he grabs Bill around the neck from behind with his left arm and twists Bill's right arm up behind his back with his right arm]* Now you've done it! I'm tired of being gentle with you now. *[Shoves him forward]* Now march back to the school and be quick about it!

BILL *[Walking ahead of Art reluctantly]* What are you going to do to me when we get back?

ART I don't know yet. But whatever it is, you won't like it! I could have you arrested f assault.

BILL *[Quite upset]* You won't do that, will you?

ART Probably not, but it might be good for you. It would teach you to respect other people's rights.

BILL If I promise not to run away, will you let me walk by myself into the school?

ART Are you embarrassed to have me hold onto you when we enter the building?

BILL Yeah, everyone would make fun of me.

ART *[Smiling]* Yea, that'd be bad. OK, it's a deal. *[Art releases his hold on Bill. They walk into the classroom together.]*

After classes are dismissed the following Monday afternoon, Martha and Art m with Carolyn Nevin, a school psychologist, in her office.

MARTHA Thanks for seeing us on such short notice, Carolyn. We need some help dealing with the two special ed students in our class.

CAROLYN *[Smiling]* That's why I'm here. The two students we're talking about are Bill Matz and Evan Carter, right? *[Hands both teachers a sheet of paper]* I've been lookir at their IEPs *[individualized education programs]*, and I've prepared a handout on their disabilities that I hope will be helpful.

MARTHA   Good. Well, we've had them in class for a week now, and, frankly, we don't know what to do with them. Everything we've tried has failed. Art and I spend 90% of our time working with those two, and we've been unsuccessful most of the time.

CAROLYN   Describe "unsuccessful" for me.

ART   The most notable "unsuccessful" for me was getting hit by Bill on Friday afternoon. I chased him down when he was trying to run away from school.

CAROLYN   *[Sympathetically]* Yes, I'd call that unsuccessful.

MARTHA   Neither of these boys is learning a thing. Bill physically abuses other students regularly, and Evan's like a loose cannon rambling around the classroom unable to attend to anything for more than five minutes or so. And that's with one-to-one tutoring. We were going to try time-out with Bill, but we never had the chance before he ran away.

ART   What we're saying is that we really need help. We need help in controlling the boys. We need to figure out how to help them get themselves under control and how to help them learn. We also want to turn the classroom back into a good learning environment for the other children in the class.

MARTHA   I think Art said it well. Can you help us, Carolyn?

FIGURE 11   Handout Prepared by Carolyn Nevin, School Psychologist, on Behavior Disorders and ADHD

BEHAVIOR DISORDERS

Symptoms of pupils who are diagnosed as having behavior disorders:

1. inability to learn that cannot be explained by intellectual or health problems
2. poor relationships with others
3. extreme reactions to ordinary events
4. moodiness or depression
5. fear or physical problems related to school difficulties

Recommended teacher strategies for working with pupils who have behavior disorders:

1. explain to pupils how they cause negative reactions from classmates
2. assure pupils that others have similar problems
3. model appropriate responses to frustrating situations
4. praise desirable behavior when it occurs
5. clearly state expectations
6. realize that improvement is a long-term project

ATTENTION DEFICIT HYPERACTIVITY DISORDERS (ADHD)

Symptoms of pupils diagnosed with ADHD:

1. excessive general activity (haphazard climbing, crawling, or running)
2. difficulty in sustaining attention, remaining seated, being attentive
3. forgetful
4. impulsive; talks excessively, intrudes on others, and engages in dangerous activities such as dashing into the street without looking

Recommended treatment of pupils diagnosed with ADHD:
   The use of stimulant drugs such as Dexadrine and Ritalin has been found in some experiments to be twice as effective for treating pupils diagnosed with ADHD as behavior modification strategies.

QUESTIONS

1. How have the Education for All Handicapped Children Act (P.L. 94–142) and the Individuals with Disabilities Education Act (IDEA) changed special education? What kinds of disabilities, ages, and types of diagnoses do these laws address? What educational treatments do they prescribe? How was special education conducted in the public schools prior to the passage of these laws?

2. What is a behavior disorder, and what forms can behavior disorders take? What are the signs and symptoms? What treatments are most effective with a behavior disorder like Bill's? How effective is behavior modification?

3. What is ADHD, and how does it differ from ADD? What are the signs and symptoms of ADHD? How well do drugs like Ritalin work with a student like Evan? How well does behavior modification work?

4. What is an IEP? Is such a program being followed by Art in working with Bill and Evan? Who designs an IEP? Who is responsible for its implementation?

5. Bill and Evan have been mainstreamed into Martha's class. How is mainstreaming supposed to work? What does the research say about the effectiveness of mainstreaming in terms of its effect on regular students as well as on the mainstreamed students? What attitudes do teachers, administrators, and parents have toward mainstreaming?

6. What are school psychologists, and what role do they play in special education? How does a school psychologist differ from a school guidance counselor or an educational psychologist?

7. What relationship should exist between the regular classroom teacher and the special education teacher? Who makes decisions regarding student learning and grades? What problems sometimes develop in the relationship between the regular teacher and the special education teacher?

8. Examine the relationship between Bill and his father from an observational learning perspective. Can children learn aggressive behavior from their parents? What can the teacher do in such cases?

9. Martha seems to have developed a classroom management procedure that worked with her regular students. What classroom management model would you recommend in her new situation?

10. Cooperative learning methods have been found to work well in some mainstreaming situations. Would you recommend them in this case? If so, which cooperative learning program?

11. Art suggests that behavior modification procedures have been found to work well with students like Bill and Evan. What is behavior modification, and which techniques would be helpful in this case? Art says he should observe Bill and Evan. What kinds of observation procedures are used in behavior modification?

12. Art and Martha decide to use a behavior modification technique called time-out with Bill. What is time-out, and how is it supposed to work? What mistakes do Art and Martha make in their attempts to use time-out? For example, what are Differential Reinforcement of Other Behavior (DRO) and Differential Reinforcement of Low Rates of Responding (DRL), and how are they supposed to be used in conjunction with time-out?

13. What advice should Carolyn give to Art and Martha? Outline the mistakes they have made, and make suggestions for changes in the case of each mistake.

C A S E **11**

MY BROTHER'S KEEPER

Key Content to Consider for Analyzing This Case:
(1) exceptionalities; (2) giftedness; (3) parent
involvement; (4) motivation (Maslow's need-hierarchy)

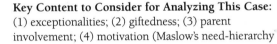

Garfield High School is located in a Midwestern state west of the Mississippi Riv
in the city of Fairview, which has a population of approximately 90,000 with
its city limits. The attendance area of G.H.S. is approximately 60% non-Hispar
white, 35% African-American, 4% Hispanic, and 1% other. While Fairview has its sha
of industry, agriculture still dominates the local economy. The value system of the are
"leading citizens" might be described as strongly conservative.

The principal of G.H.S., Niles Quinlan, has developed an unusually strong scho
advisory committee (SAC), which advises him on decisions such as those relating to bu
get, curriculum, and rezoning. The committee meets monthly or on special call. Havi
built such a strong SAC, Niles realizes he has to think twice before going against
"advice." The current SAC consists of twenty-five members: fifteen parents, five studen
two teachers, one custodial staff representative, and two at-large community represen
tives.

Niles sits at his desk in his office talking to Wayne Matson, president of the SA
Bob Guinagh, a teacher in the gifted program; and Margaret Swaybe, a special educati
teacher. They all sit in chairs in front of Niles' desk. It is early in November of a ne
school year, and they are meeting to discuss the upcoming monthly SAC meeting.

NILES   Folks, I want to be fully prepared for the next SAC meeting, and Wayne, I
especially want you to be ready to handle anything that might come up.

WAYNE   Why, Niles? What's happened?

NILES   You wouldn't believe the phone calls I've had from irate parents about the defea
of the property tax increase referendum at the election and the school board's
subsequent decision to make cuts in our programs for gifted and talented childre
Of all the programs to cut! But the board wouldn't listen, and now that they've
taken a position they won't back down.

WAYNE   They're trying to punish the public for voting against the tax increase by cuttin
programs they value, aren't they?

NILES   That's the way I see it, Wayne. I'm just surprised they didn't cut football or basketball, or even band.

BOB   *[Laughing]* They wouldn't dare do that! They'd get impeached! *[Everyone laughs.]*

WAYNE   So, Niles, you think they're going to be at the SAC meeting arguing against the cuts? Why?

NILES   The school board wouldn't listen, so they're turning to the SAC. I'd say that they hope the SAC has some influence with the board. *[Pause]* However, the reason I wanted to talk to all three of you is that this thing has taken an ugly turn that I want us to be prepared for.

MARGARET   Us?! Bob and I aren't members of the SAC. Do you want us to attend the next meeting?

NILES   Yes, I do, Margaret. And I think you and your special ed colleagues may want to turn out in force when you hear what some of the parents of the gifted students are proposing.

MARGARET   What's that?

NILES   That the money cut from the gifted programs be restored by taking it from the handicapped students' programs.

MARGARET   *[Angrily]* What?! They can't do that! Don't they know that those programs are protected by law?!

NILES   *[Smiling]* Of course, they do. Their argument is that the federal government will restore whatever is cut out of the handicapped programs' budgets. Naive, aren't they?

MARGARET   Niles, didn't you tell them that they can't do that?!

NILES   Of course. But do you think they listened? One of their ringleaders is Dave Oakmont.

WAYNE   The attorney?

NILES   The very one.

BOB   Oh, brother! His son Tommy is in my third-period class! Oh, my!

NILES   Yes, well, now you see why we have to be prepared. Margaret and Bob, your jobs are to inform the troops and get them to the meeting. Wayne, if you ever followed Roberts' Rules of Order, you'd better follow them at this meeting. Oh, and here's a handout that I intend to give out at the meeting. *[Gives each one a copy]* If you think anything should be changed or added, let me know right now. My intention is to give them some information on the laws mandating both the handicapped and gifted programs. *[All three read the handout quietly.]*

It is Wednesday evening at 7:30 one week later, the regular monthly meeting of the SAC. Anticipating a large turnout, Niles has moved the meeting to the school auditorium rather than its usual meeting place, the school library. Approximately one hundred people show up for the meeting, including the twenty-five regular members of the SAC. Niles notices a local newspaper reporter in the audience.

Niles has the regular SAC members sit up on the elevated stage in metal folding chairs while nonmembers are asked to sit in the fixed but more comfortable seats below the stage. Niles has placed a wooden lectern in the middle of the stage so that he, the

SAC president, and any other speaker can address the entire gathering through a micro phone.

NILES   *[Speaking into the microphone]* I want to welcome everyone to our regular month meeting of the Garfield High School School Advisory Committee. My, what a nice turnout! I wish we had this kind of attendance at every meeting! *[Polite laughter follows from the audience.]* At this time I'll turn the meeting over to the president o our SAC, Mr. Wayne Matson. *[Polite applause, during which Wayne steps up to the lectern and Niles sits down]*

WAYNE   *[With slight nervousness]* I wish to add my appreciation to that of Mr. Quinlan fo your attendance at our meeting tonight. We will follow our usual order of business tonight by first asking for the secretary's and treasurer's reports, then moving to old business and new business in that order. *[A half dozen people in the audience groan quietly when they hear that announcement.]* So, I'm going to ask our secretary, Ms. Anne Riley, to begin by reading the minutes of our last meeting.

It is forty-five minutes later. The reports of the secretary and treasurer have be presented, discussed, and approved as read. All old business has likewise been discuss and appropriate action taken or delayed. Wayne then announced that the "floor is n open for new business" and that the first item was the program cuts that were necess due to the defeat of the tax increase proposition at the last election. He said that he wo "turn the floor over to the building principal, Mr. Niles Quinlan" so he could "give eve one the necessary background information on the issue." After that he would "open floor for discussion," first hearing from regular voting SAC members on all sides of issue and then from "others attending the meeting."

NILES   *[Standing at the lectern]* I'm really pleased to see this fine turnout at our SAC meeting. I know from talking to many of you that you're upset about the schoo board's intention to cut programs for gifted and talented students as a way of dealing with the recent defeat of the tax referendum. *[Pause]* As you know, we have two kinds of programs for the exceptional students in our school district: those for handicapped students, and those for gifted students. I have prepared handout that I hope clarifies the legal basis for and the nature of the students i those programs. *[Wayne passes out Niles' handout.]* Let me emphasize one point before we begin our discussion about what programs should and should not be cut. *[With emphasis]* Ladies and gentlemen, I can't emphasize enough that programs for handicapped students are mandated by federal law. We must offe these programs. They cannot be eliminated from our program to save money. *[Several hands go up from the audience.]* OK, I'm going to turn things back over Wayne, and I assure you that all of you who have questions will have an opportunity to ask them.

WAYNE   Niles, why don't you move your chair over here next to the lectern, since you going to have to talk a lot. *[The audience laughs, and Niles smiles and moves his cha Now, let's begin with questions from the SAC members. *[One hand goes up.]* Yes, Rita?

RITA   Yes, I'm Rita Malloy and I've heard a rumor that some people here tonight want to cut funds from the handicapped students' programs instead of the gifted programs. I think that's terrible! What kind of person would want to do that?! Those poor children need all the help we can give them! *[Pause]* Now, don't misunderstand me. I think the gifted children need special programs too. But if you have to make a choice, those children are smart and are able to survive quite well whether they are in special classes or not. That's all I wanted to say.

WAYNE   Ms. Mosier.

MS. MOSIER   My daughter Sarah is a senior and is a gifted student. Now, I don't intend to demean any of our fine teachers of gifted students here at Garfield, but she keeps me up-to-date on the kinds of things they do in the gifted classes, and a lot of it just seems like a waste of time! They seem to spend a lot of time doing things like meditating, some kind of talking called brainstorming, and just generally messing around in what they call exploratory activities like painting. Sarah and I have had a number of arguments about whether she should stay in the gifted classes or if she'd be better off in regular classes. Frankly, if I'd had my way, she would have taken regular classes. *[Smiling]* But parents don't always win these arguments. *[Laughter from the audience]* I say cut the gifted program! I agree with Rita!

WAYNE   Does any other SAC member want to make a statement or ask a question? Does anyone want to take the other side? *[No response]* Well, then, I'll open it up to the general audience. Yes, Mr. Oakmont.

MR. OAKMONT   Thank you, Mr. Matson. I'd like to begin by asking Mr. Quinlan a question. Mr. Quinlan, you indicated in your opening remarks that the programs for handicapped students must be legally provided as required by federal law. But does that mean that financial cuts cannot be made in the programs? Can't the handicapped programs be cut back to a required minimum level of operation?

NILES   Yes, that's true, Mr. Oakmont, although if you did that it would damage the program's delivery of services considerably.

MR. OAKMONT   Thank you, Mr. Quinlan. And might I add that nobody here would want to make those cuts, much less try to totally eliminate our programs for handicapped students. But on the other hand, is it wise to eliminate our programs for gifted students? I think that doing that would be equally bad. *[Pause]* Ms. Mosier has indicated in her remarks that she hasn't exactly been impressed with what goes on in her daughter's gifted classes. My experience has been the opposite. My son, Thomas, has also been in gifted classes. *[Looks at Bob Guinagh]* As a matter of fact, he is currently in Mr. Guinagh's class and, like Ms. Mosier's daughter Sarah, he loves it! I can't tell you how much he's grown as a result of his experiences there! He's explored areas like art and sculpturing that he knew little about but became utterly fascinated with! Some of the class discussions got him so agitated that he brought them home, and he and I would discuss issues into the wee hours of the morning! My experience of gifted education is quite different from that of Ms. Mosier. *[Pause]* Mr. Quinlan, could I ask you another question?

NILES   Yes, of course.

MR. OAKMONT   I understand that there has been a lot of research on mainstreaming, which seems to be the very heart of the programs for handicapped students. Is th true, and are you familiar with it?

NILES   Yes, I attended a workshop just before school started during which Dr. Milligan from the university discussed the research on the effectiveness of mainstreaming.

MR. OAKMONT   And what was Dr. Milligan's conclusion about whether mainstreaming had a positive impact on the achievement of the handicapped students mainstreamed into regular classes?

NILES   He said that the research generally found that it doesn't improve the achieveme of the handicapped students. But he also said that it didn't have a negative effect the achievement of the regular students.

MR. OAKMONT   And what about other kinds of research? For example, does it help improve handicapped students' self-concepts to be put in with regular students, does it improve the attitudes of the regular students toward being more accepting of handicapped students, since they are around them daily?

NILES   I think he concluded that the results of studies done on those kinds of things were mixed. Some found positive results and some found negative results. I do remember him saying that it depended on the type of disability and the type of teaching method used by the teacher. Regular student attitudes improve more toward students with physical types of disabilities than toward those with mental disabilities. He also said that cooperative learning types of teaching methods seer to be the best as far as attitudinal changes are concerned.

MR. OAKMONT   So, if I follow you correctly, a recognized expert from the university found that mainstreaming has no impact on student achievement and obtained mixed results at best as far as attitudinal studies are concerned. Is that correct?

NILES   Yes, although, as I said, he did suggest that attitudinal studies did indicate that some disabilities were being helped and that certain teaching methods seemed to hold great promise.

MR. OAKMONT   OK, but even so, you've got to admit that the research on handicappe programs doesn't exactly indicate that they are an unqualified success that we should keep pouring public tax money into. Gifted programs may have their problems, but so do handicapped programs. There is at least as much justificatio for cutting handicapped programs as there is for cutting programs for the gifted. And, Mr. President, if I could have the floor for just a moment longer, I'd like to make one more point.

WAYNE   Please proceed.

MR. OAKMONT   Ladies and gentlemen, what I'd like to say is this. Our gifted childr are indeed, as Mr. Quinlan writes in his handout, a "national resource," and i our job to "help these students develop their talents." These young men and women are the cream of the crop. The best our society has to offer. The futur leaders of our society. How can we consider for one minute cutting programs that will help them reach their potential?! [Pause] I want to add that I don't favor eliminating the programs for our handicapped students. I just want to p them back to the minimums in order to save our programs for the gifted. Bu having said that, let me tell you how I really feel. No matter whether you look at insects, higher animals, primitive humans, or civilized mankind, that society thrives that allows its best and fittest members to thrive and rise to positions of leadership and productivity. The weakest members should cared for, but not at the expense of the fittest members. Any society that allows the weakest to survive at the expense of the fittest is doomed in the long run. Therefore, I rest my case, Mr. President: don't cut the programs for the gifted! Pare back the handicapped programs to the bare required minimums first before making any cuts in the gifted programs. *[Sits down amidst cheers, boos, shouts, and applause]*

WAYNE   *[Shouting over the din]* Ladies and gentlemen, please! *[They calm down slowly.]* At this time I want to ask Mr. Bob Guinagh, one of our teachers of the gifted, and Ms. Margaret Swaybe, one of our special education teachers, if they would like to comment. *[Margaret shakes her head "no."]* Mr. Guinagh?

BOB   I guess what bothers me about this whole situation is that we are put in a position where we have to pit two fine programs against one another. We need both groups of students. *[Applause]* Having said that, I guess I'm willing to leave the budget cutting decisions to Mr. Quinlan. However, I do have some suggestions about the gifted programs. When most of us think about working with gifted children we immediately think of working with them in special separate classes that we refer to as advanced-placement classes. As valuable as I think such classes are, there are other ways of working with gifted students that may be more cost-effective. Those other ways are called acceleration and enrichment. Acceleration means moving the student through the program at a faster-than-normal rate. Some of you might have been double-promoted when you were elementary students or were in early college entrance programs when you were juniors and seniors in high school. *[Several parents smile and nod their heads affirmatively.]* Enrichment involves putting gifted students in regular classes but allowing them to work on special advanced learning materials that go beyond what the regular students in the class are doing. While some argue that this is a more democratic way of working with gifted students, it does require extra work from the classroom teacher. But then I guess that's true of any kind of mainstreamed student. Anyhow, I throw out for your consideration the idea of moving more in the direction of acceleration and perhaps enrichment if they are indeed more cost-effective. Thank you. *[Applause]*

WAYNE   Who else would like to speak on this issue? Mr. Oakmont, you wish to add more?

MR. OAKMONT   Not really, Mr. President. But I would like to ask you and Mr. Quinlan if you're willing to conduct a "straw vote" of those present to see how the majority of us feel about what should be cut? Of course, such a straw vote is in no way binding on Mr. Quinlan, who has to make the final decision, but it might give him some guidance as to our feelings. If you agree, I suggest that such a straw vote be done by secret ballot so no one will feel undue pressure in making their decision.

NILES   I think a better idea, Dave, would be to send a ballot out to all of our parents rather than assume that tonight's gathering of parents reflects the opinions of all of our parents.

MR. OAKMONT   That makes perfectly good sense to me, Niles. Let me withdraw my suggestion then.

WAYNE   OK, then. We'll send a ballot out to all our parents and ask them to vote on this issue. It should be understood, however, that such a ballot is advisory and that Mr. Quinlan will make the final decision about what budget cuts will be made. *[Pause]* OK. Unless someone else feels a need to voice something regardin this issue *[a pause of five seconds with no response from the audience]*, then let's mo on to the next item of business. *[All parents leave except those who are members of the SAC.]*

It is one month later. Once again Niles sits behind his desk in his office with t door closed meeting with Bob Guinagh, Margaret Swaybe, and Wayne Matson, who sit hardbacked wooden chairs in front of his desk.

NILES   Since you three met with me to plan strategy before the SAC meeting, I wanted you to be present to witness the results of our parent survey. My secretary, Margar Landsford, and I have tallied up the ballots, and when we're finished talking I wa you three to recount the ballots as witnesses.

WAYNE   What were the results?

NILES   Believe it or not, 88% of the parents returned ballots. I'm told by our evaluatior and research people that that's an unbelievably high return rate. About 59% vote to cut the handicapped program back as far as possible rather than cut gifted programs. *[Margaret groans.]* I've been told that Mr. Oakmont's arguments impressed them and that his faction organized an effective telephone campaign tc get parents to vote their way.

MARGARET   The other faction did the same thing, but not as effectively, I guess.

BOB   I brought this issue up in my gifted classes, and the student's conducted a straw vote there. You may be interested to know that 68 out of 101 gifted students favored making cuts in the gifted programs. Just the opposite of the parents.

NILES   I might add that over a hundred parents added comments to their ballots to the effect that if the cuts are made in the gifted programs, they plan to pull their children out of Garfield High and send them to private schools. I think I see the fine hand of Mr. Oakmont in the way parents worded their statements. They wer too much alike to be spontaneous.

WAYNE   Oakmont is impressive. He certainly did his homework. I think I'd consider hiring him as a lawyer if I was in legal trouble.

NILES   Yes, he is impressive. But this is a school, not a courtroom. We have to do wha best for our students and program within legal constraints.

WAYNE   And do what's best for the parents as well?

NILES   Of course. What's best for all the stakeholders: the students, the parents, the teachers, the school system, and the community. *[Smiling]* Did I leave anyone o

BOB   The taxpayers? *[All laugh.]* Seriously, Niles, I'm sure glad I'm not in your shoes. Even though the straw vote is only advisory, it may seriously cost you if you deci to go against the vote. Still, is 59% that big of a message?

WAYNE   So, Niles, don't keep us in suspense. What have you decided?

MARGARET   Yes, are you going to be your brother's keeper and decide in favor of the handicapped programs or not?

FIGURE 12   Memorandum to School Advisory Committee Members on Programs for Exceptional Students

---

MEMORANDUM

FROM: Niles Quinlan, Principal
TO: Members of School Advisory Committee
RE: Information regarding programs for exceptional students

Both handicapped and gifted students are considered exceptional students. However, the programs we have developed here at Garfield High School are governed by different laws. Perhaps the following information will be helpful.

1. Handicapped students are defined and programs appropriate for their education specified by two laws: (1) the Education for All Handicapped Children Act (Public Law 94-142) of 1975, and (2) the Individuals with Disabilities Education Act of (IDEA) of 1990. P.L. 94-142 guarantees to all children with disabilities a free and appropriate public education. It outlines extensive procedures to make sure that exceptional students aged 3–18 are granted due process with regard to identification, placement, and educational services received. This law applies to disabilities including hearing and sight impairments, physical impairments and crippling disorders, speech defects, mental retardation, emotional disturbances, social maladjustment, and learning disabilities of an academic nature. This law must be followed by every teacher and school in the nation. IDEA extended P.L. 94-142 to students with disabilities up to the age of 21. IDEA also changed the terminology from "handicapped students" to "students with disabilities."

2. Gifted and talented students were legally recognized by the Jacob K. Javits Gifted and Talented Students Act of 1988. This law asserts that such students are a national resource and that elementary and secondary schools need to develop programs to help these students develop their talents responsibly. The U.S. Office of Education in 1978 defined "gifted and talented" as follows: " 'gifted and talented' means children and whenever applicable, youth who are identified at the preschool, elementary, or secondary level as possessing demonstrated or potential abilities that give evidence of high performance responsibility in areas such as intellectual, creative, specific academic, or leadership ability, or in the performing and visual arts and who by reason thereof require services or activities not ordinarily provided by the school."

QUESTIONS

1. What are exceptional children? How do they differ from disadvantaged children? How do special education programs differ from compensatory education programs?

2. What are gifted and talented students? Do they differ from or include creative students? What types of programs have been developed for working with such students,

and which ones are the most effective?

3. Weigh the relative merits of acceleration, enrichment, and special classes methods of working with gifted students. What does the research show on effectiveness of each procedure?

4. Involving parents as decision-makers through such vehicles as the school advise committee or PTA has been mandated by law in some states and is common in feder. funded programs. What are the strengths and weaknesses of such parent involveme What does research indicate about the relationship of such parent involvement to stud achievement?

5. Niles refers to stakeholders that are served by the school. Who are the stakehold in this instance? Which stakeholders is it most important to serve?

6. What programs did P.L.94-142 and IDEA put in place for students with disabili with regard to diagnosis, program individualization, parent involvement, regu classroom teacher involvement, and follow-up and evaluation? How effective are su programs?

7. Mr. Oakmont seems to suggest that the mainstreaming of students with disabili into regular classrooms doesn't have research support. Is this true?

8. How effective are programs for gifted students? What research support exists their effectiveness?

9. How far back can financial support for handicapped programs be cut? What wo a minimal program consist of? How far back can gifted programs be cut?

10. Niles suggests that cooperative learning types of teaching methods may hav positive impact on affective variables such as self-concept and social acceptance. Is t assertion borne out by the research literature? What are the strengths and weaknesse: cooperative learning methods?

11. From what level of Maslow's need hierarchy does Niles seem to be prima operating? Mr. Oakmont? How would such information be helpful in dealing with eacl

12. What decision should Niles make, and why? What might the consequences b he votes against the majority view? Should Niles be the one to make this decision, should he involve the superintendent of schools in a matter involving his schc programs?

REMEMBERING STUFF

Key Content to Consider for Analyzing This Case:
(1) information processing theory; (2) constructivism;
(3) Bloom's Cognitive Taxonomy; (4) meaningful verbal
learning (Ausubel); (5) transfer of learning;
(6) measurement and evaluation (objective vs. essay
tests, norm- vs. criterion-referenced evaluation).

Wiley Senior High School is located in a middle-sized city in the Midwest. Its physical plant is of the red brick, cement block variety of World War II vintage, but is quite well groomed and maintained. Its student body is approximately 75% white, 20% African-American, and 5% other in grades 10–12. Approximately 70% of Wiley's graduates enter college.

Jack Shaw is a graduate of the College of Education at a nearby Big Ten school and is beginning his first year of teaching social studies. His wife, Arlene, is a beginning elementary teacher in a nearby school system. They have one child, Brad, who is four years old.

It is the week before school begins during teacher preplanning, and Jack sits in the classroom of Donna Landry, the chair of the social studies department at Wiley and a veteran of twenty-four years' teaching experience. They sit in chairs at one side of the classroom facing one another as they go over Jack's teaching assignment for the year in their first one-on-one conference.

DONNA   As you can see, Jack, Mr. Nesbitt *[building principal]* has given you a fairly light load: three sections of world history and two of U.S. history. Only two preparations.

JACK   Yes, I really appreciate that. And I love to teach history. But you know that my real loves are psychology and sociology. Do you think I'll ever get to teach those courses, Donna?

DONNA   *[Smiling]* Maybe someday, Jack. You know very well that those courses are my favorites. I love working with advanced-placement seniors in elective courses like those two. However, I just might retire one day and maybe you'll inherit them. But as the new kid on the block, you have put your time in by teaching the basic, required courses first.

JACK   *[Smiling]* I know, Donna. I'm just putting my bid in so maybe somebody will consider me when the time comes.

DONNA   Mr. Nesbitt and I have already discussed that possibility for the future.

Jack That's all I can ask! And I really do appreciate the teaching load that you two hav given me.

Donna Good. Now, do you have any problems or questions about teaching your classe:

Jack Yes, I do. In my coursework at the university, I became intrigued with discovery learning methods. I was wondering if I could use them in teaching my history courses.

Donna Tell me more about that, Jack. You know that we have a strong college prep emphasis here at Wiley, so everyone expects our kids to do well on the SAT. The parents want their kids to get scholarships to help with the terrible cost of sendin them to college. The more National Merit Finalists we produce, the better. I think parents all pretty much feel that way.

Jack So what does that mean as far as teaching methods are concerned?

Donna It means that you need to emphasize the content that will help them score hig on the test, and that you need to give objective tests similar to those they'll be taking. What did you want to do?

Jack Well, I read and hear about how the U.S. is behind in teaching our students to engage in higher-order thinking and develop their problem-solving skills. I want them to do more than just memorize important dates, battles, people, and events history. I want them to analyze events and determine causes and patterns, and be able to evaluate what happened and relate it to today's events.

Donna There's nothing in the world wrong with that, Jack. But just don't do those things at the expense of the basics. There's nothing wrong with asking students tc do lower-order thinking as well. Too many elementary students don't know their ABC's or the multiplication tables. Why, I was at the supermarket the other day ai the computers were down. The poor little cashier didn't know how to make char and count it out to me. Just don't neglect basic learning, Jack, because parents aren going to thank you if their child doesn't do well on the SAT. That's the bottom lin

Jack Thanks, Donna, that helps. One more question. Can I use the contract method grading, or does everyone grade on the curve?

Donna Most grade on the curve using the 95 to 100 is an A standard printed on th report cards. I don't know of any teacher using the contract method. *[Pause]* I think that if I were you I'd emphasize the norm-referenced type of grading procedures my first year of teaching, and I'd be sure that my big tests—the unit exams, for example—were objective in format. Try that for a while, Jack, and maybe later, when you have tenure, you can experiment with some other thing:

Jack OK. Thanks, Donna. I'm sure that's good advice.

It is third period of the first day of classes, and Jack meets with the thirty-six juni in his U.S. history class. The students take notes as Jack outlines his course expectati(and evaluation procedures.

Jack What it comes down to, guys, is that I'll give you a weekly quiz, usually on Fridays, and a unit exam. These tests will be objective in format, although every now and then I'll throw in an essay question to make you think. I know that you and your parents want you to do well on the SAT when you take it this school year, and I plan to do my part in helping to prepare you to take it.

In addition to the tests, I expect you to keep a notebook which will be turned in at the end of each unit. The notebook must include, for each chapter covered, first, history makers, that is, what each does and why it's important; second, definitions of key terms like *circumnavigation* and *Amerind* in the first chapter; third, the ten most important events; and fourth, the marked and labeled map locations of key places and events. Needless to say, I expect you to attend class and participate in class discussions. I see that you're already pretty good note takers for those times when I lecture.

One other thing I need to mention is that I think that seeing relationships between historical events and current events is important. Therefore, I'm going to give you the opportunity to turn in current events reports in a format that I'll give you in a minute, and I expect you to put the newspaper or magazine article that you use on the bulletin board in the back of the room for everyone to see. You can turn in up to two such reports for each unit. This might help you if you're on the borderline between two grades. Yes—Rachael, isn't it?

RACHAEL   Yes, Mr. Shaw. How will you grade the notebooks and current events reports?

JACK   Very subjectively, I'm afraid. I guess comprehensiveness and accuracy will be the two most important criteria I'll use. Yes, Manuel?

MANUEL   What kinds of objective tests will you give, and how will you grade them?

JACK   Oh, the usual. A lot of multiple choice along with some matching and fill-in-the-blank. Like I said, maybe an essay question from time to time. Probably no true-false since they're not very good kinds of items. All the weekly quizzes will be multiple choice. *[Pauses]* The unit tests will probably be worth 100 points. I'd say that the weekly quizzes will be 5 to 10 points each. Juan?

JUAN   How will you grade the essay questions, and how much weight will you give things?

JACK   I know of only two ways to grade essay questions: compare them to a model answer, or read all the papers and put them in piles from best to worst. I suppose I'll do both. *[Pause]* As far as weighting is concerned, the unit exams and weekly quizzes will be one-half of your grade, the notebook about one-fourth, and the current events reports and attendance and participation about one-eighth each. Something like that. Rachael?

RACHAEL   These chapters are so big, and they have a lot of maps and tables. Do you expect us to know all this stuff?

JACK   Anything is fair game, Rachael. If it's in the book or we talk about it in class, it's fair game! *[Several students groan.]* Yes, Rachael?

RACHAEL   Mr. Shaw, I just don't see how you can expect us to remember all this stuff!

JACK   *[Smiling]* Well, Rachael, you're right. It is a lot of material per unit. But you guys are Wiley students, right?! *[With animation]* I'll bet the students at a certain high school across town couldn't handle half that much material on tests any more than they can beat us at football or basketball! *[A few students shout agreement.]* After all, what's the best high school in the whole state, both athletically and academically?! *[All the students except Rachael shout "Wiley!"]*

It is Monday of the fifth week of classes, and Jack returns the first unit exam, whi he gave the previous Friday at the end of a unit entitled "How Our Country Was Disco ered and Settled." He passes out both the test booklet and the answer sheet and instru the students that he wants both returned to him by the end of the period.

JACK　As you can see from the distribution of grades that I've put on the board, we did do especially well on this test. Out of 100 possible points, the highest score was 8 and the lowest score was 8. The average score was 59.2. Not a very high average even if I use 90 to 100 as an A instead of 95 to 100. What I'm going to do is adju the scale by adding 8 points onto everyone's score. *[A few students voice their approval.]* That only raises the average score to 67.2 though. If we use the school standard of 70 to 76 being a D, then the average person in here failed the test. Ev if we set 60 as the minimum passing score, that makes the average score a D. Not very good no matter how you cut it. Yes, Rachael?

RACHAEL　Mr. Shaw, I think this test was unfair! I don't think I've ever taken a more difficult test! *[A general chorus of student agreement]*

JACK　What is it about the test that makes it so difficult, Rachael? Or do you think it w the way that you studied for it?

RACHAEL　I studied real hard for this test, Mr. Shaw! There was just too much stuff to remember! This is the lowest grade I've gotten in any of my classes since I came here!

JACK　*[Smiling]* OK, calm down, Rachael. I don't think getting the top grade in the clas is too bad—and, don't forget, I'm raising it to a 95 when I add points on.

RACHAEL　Yes, but that's still right on the borderline!

JACK　Well, Rachael, maybe it would be good for all of us to talk about how you studie for this test. It might help others in the class, since we're going to have other test: like this one.

RACHAEL　Well, I just read the book and underlined all the important people, dates, treaties, battles, and names of things—especially the things we talk about in class also take notes about what we talk about in class. Then the night before the test I go back over everything again and again so I'll remember it.

JACK　That sounds good to me, Rachael. So look at the thirteen items you missed on t test. Why didn't you remember them?

RACHAEL　Well, take number 3 in the matching. I knew it was either Magellan or Balb who was the first to sail around the world, but when you said he was Portuguese that confused me. I thought that Magellan was Spanish and that he died before th voyage ended. So I figured that you were being tricky and chose Balboa.

JACK　I wasn't trying to trick you, Rachael. I think that what we have here is a good student reading too much into a test item. Magellan was Portuguese but he was sailing for Spain. Also, if you look at the item carefully, you'll notice that it says t Magellan's ship, the *Vittoria,* not Magellan himself, was the first to circumnavigat the globe.

RACHAEL　*[Reflectively]* Oh. I see. I don't think I knew too much, Mr. Shaw, I just didn pick up some of those details. That's what I mean, Mr. Shaw, there's just too man things to remember. It's like going into a cafeteria to eat.

Jack   What do you mean?

Rachael   Well, like you have to make all those choices. First comes the salads, then the desserts, then the meats, then the vegetables—

Jack   Yes, yes. So how does that relate to the test?

Rachael   Well, you've got all these different things to remember in four different chapters and they don't have much to do with each other. Like what does the Pope's Line of Demarcation in the first chapter have to do with the Mayflower Compact in the third chapter or the Molasses Act of 1733 or the Peace of Paris in the fourth chapter? It's like you have to take these unrelated pieces of information and keep going over each one separately until you remember it.

Jack   How did you remember the Molasses Act of 1733, for example?

Rachael   Well, I remembered that my grandfather was born in 1933, so I just had to substitute the 7 for the 9. Also, I tried to memorize that the British put a tax on sugar and molasses that the colonists hated and wouldn't pay the tax on. I guess that might have caused them to be independent from England.

Jack   Good point! It did just that!

Rachael   Well, sometimes I can take a lot of things that I have to remember and make a word from the first letters of the first word of each and remember them that way.

Jack   You mean make an acronym?

Rachael   I guess so. But I just couldn't do that with most of the stuff in these four chapters. There's just too much!

Jack   OK. I hear you, Rachael. How would you make the test better if you could?

Rachael   I'd ask essay questions. If you'd ask why the explorers from the different countries wanted to risk their lives and sail around the world, and who some of them were and what they did, I could have done a much better job than I did on this test.

Jack   Why is that?

Rachael   Well, I understand the ideas from the first two chapters because I've seen a lot of movies like that. I understand what the explorers wanted to do and why they wanted to do it. And then it's real easy to remember the names and countries, and maybe even sometimes the dates when the people did the exploring. It just all seems to hang together somehow, like writing a screenplay for a movie. But this test gets down to nitty-gritty little details that don't seem to have much to do with each other. These sure don't tell a story. *[Pause]* See, I can even understand the Pilgrims, and Puritans, and Roger Williams.

Jack   What do you mean?

Rachael   I mean why they wanted to go to a new world so they could be free to practice their religion their own way. I mean they were different and all, with the Puritans wanting everybody to do it their way, while Roger Williams would like people do their own thing. But—

Jack   You're right on target, Rachael, but didn't you miss the second completion item about Roger Williams?

Rachael   Yes, I guess I just couldn't associate him with Rhode Island. All I could remember was Connecticut. Weren't they like Rhode Island?

JACK   Yes, in the sense that you didn't have to belong to a particular church in order t
       vote. But that was Thomas Hooker, not Roger Williams.

RACHAEL   [Reflectively] Oh, yes. That's right.

JACK   The bottom line here is that I could have asked essay-type questions, but I kno
       you're going to have to learn to deal with objective-type items, especially multip
       choice, when you take the SAT. As you know, our students have done very well i
       that regard in the past, and I suspect that's because they've had to cut their teeth
       tough tests like this one in their classes. But I promise you that I'm going to give
       this whole matter more thought. And thank you, Rachael, for sharing your
       thoughts on the matter with the class.

It is the beginning of the second grading period, and Jack is sitting in the classro
of his friend Will Nelson, a fellow social studies teacher with five years of experience, a
school has ended. They sit in two movable chairs facing one another in front of Will's d

WILL   You need my advice about what, Jack?

JACK   I'm not sure how to explain it. I've tried to take to heart what Donna told me abo
       preparing my kids to take the SAT, but I'm not sure whether I'm helping them or r
       [Pause] I've tried to stick to objective tests and teach the material by telling them v
       important people, places, dates, and events to zero in on and why they're importa
       I make each student keep a notebook on these things and give them credit for doi
       current events reports relating the things they're studying to current events.

WILL   Sounds good to me. What's the problem?

JACK   The test scores are awful. Even those of good students like Rachael Young. I ha
       to add points onto practically every test.

WILL   So what do you think is going wrong?

JACK   The only thing that I can think of is that the subject matter is just not being
       presented in a meaningful, motivating way so that it sticks with the kids. I had t
       big discussion about our tests in class one day, and they—maybe I should say
       Rachael, since she did most of the talking—said that the material is just too
       piecemeal and doesn't hang together.

WILL   I had Rachael in world history last year. She's a character, isn't she? The though
       getting anything less than an A kills her.

JACK   Yeah, well, she made me really look at what I'm doing. I just don't know how to fix

WILL   Are you giving them too much material to learn?

JACK   Four chapters per unit. My unit exams are 100 items.

WILL   That sounds reasonable.

JACK   Rachael said I should give essay tests more. And from what she's saying, I shou
       somehow present the information in a more organized fashion so it hangs togetl
       better.

WILL   Why don't you try that, Jack? To heck with the SAT. I get tired of hearing abou
       around here. Sometimes I think we let the "tail wag the dog" in our teaching. I
       don't think that test scores should be the be-all and end-all of education. Try
       something different, Jack!

It is Monday of the next week of classes, and Jack begins the third period with his U.S. history class.

JACK   I want you to know that I've really listened to some of the things that you've told me about our tests in here. For one thing, I heard you saying that you had to memorize too many unrelated facts. When I realized that as your teacher I still couldn't remember all your names after all this time, I had to admit that you have a good point. [Pause] So, how are we going to change things? First, I'm going to make essay questions a bigger part of our tests. These questions will make you organize and analyze the information better. Second, I'm going to give more weight to your current events reports. These reports help you make connections between the material we're studying and what's going on today. Third, and perhaps most important, I'm going to introduce each unit differently. I'm going to put you in small groups of four to six students and have you identify the major themes and ideas running through all the chapters in a unit. That way I think you'll get the big picture better before you start learning the people, places, and things associated with each theme. I think it'll help you organize the information better. What do you think? [General chorus of approval, including Rachael] OK, then, shall we begin our new unit entitled "How the Sections of Our Country Began to Strive for Their Special Interests"? Let's begin by breaking down into small groups.

It is three weeks later, and Jack enters Donna Landry's classroom twenty minutes after the end of the last period. Donna sits behind her desk and motions for Jack to take a seat next to her desk.

JACK   I got your note that you wanted to see me, Donna.

DONNA   Yes, thanks for coming in. Jack, since this is your first year of teaching I want to make sure that you get off to a good start. I hear from the grapevine that you've changed your testing procedures. I hear that you changed to essay tests.

JACK   That isn't quite true, Donna. I give both objective and essay questions on my tests.

DONNA   How much would you say is essay?

JACK   About half and half. You see, Donna, I realized that I was presenting the subject matter in a piecemeal fashion that didn't hang together for the kids and that I was testing for isolated facts. So I went in and talked to Will Nelson about it and, well, he was very helpful and as a result of his encouragement I changed the way I presented the material and began to give more essay questions. The students seem to understand the material better that way and are doing much better on the tests.

DONNA   [Frowning] Why did you take your problems to Will, Jack? Why didn't you come see me?

JACK   [Hesitantly] Well, Will is a friend of mine and I happened to need to talk to him about another matter anyhow and I had this on my mind a lot and—

DONNA   [Seriously] Jack, come to me with these problems. Will may be your friend, but he isn't necessarily a good model to follow when it comes to teaching. He's somewhat of a rebel and sometimes, according to Mr. Nesbitt, he borders on

FIGURE 13   A Sample of Items From Jack Shaw's First Unit Exam in His Third-Period U.S. History Class

I. MATCHING

Directions: Match the last names of the people listed in the right-hand column with the important roles that they played in the discovery and settlement of our country. Write the letter identifying the person's name in the blank to the left of the role played. Some people's names will not be used.

____ 1. Claimed the northeastern coast of North America for England around 1497.

____ 2. A merchant of Florence and navigator after whose first name "America" was named.

____ 3. A Portuguese navigator whose ship *Vittoria* was the first to circumnavigate the globe.

____ 4. First of the Spanish conquistadores to set foot within the present boundaries of the United States.

____ 5. Founder of the English colony of Georgia.

____ 6. British commander who defeated the French at Quebec.

A. Vespucci
B. Balboa
C. Cabot
D. de Leon
E. Magellan
F. Columbus
G. Drake
H. Oglethorpe
I. Franklin
J. Wolfe

II. MULTIPLE CHOICE

Directions: For each question select the one best answer and write the letter preceding your choice in the blank to the left of the question.

____ 1. Which of the following is *not* one of the terms of the Peace of Paris in 1763? A) France ceded Canada to England. B) England gave France Guadeloupe, Martinique, and some small West Indies islands. C) Spain gave all her claims west of the Mississippi to England. D) England restored Havana and Manila to Spain, but kept all of Florida.

____ 2. In which of the following groups of colonies was the Anglican Church most dominant? A) The Northern Colonies (New England). B) The Middle Colonies. C) The Southern Colonies (south of Mason-Dixon Line). D) The Western Colonies (west of the Mississippi River).

____ 3. Which colony was founded by the Puritans in 1628 and insisted that only members of the Puritan church be admitted as "freemen" to participate in the government? A) Massachusetts Bay Colony. B) Plymouth Colony. C) Maryland Colony. D) Colony of Rhode Island.

____ 4. When the Pope drew the Line of Demarcation in 1493, he assigned all new lands to be discovered one hundred leagues *west* of the Cape Verde Islands to what countries? A) England. B) France. C) Spain. D) Portugal.

____ 5. In 1620 the Pilgrim Fathers signed a document agreeing to self-government, the first such agreement in U.S. history. What was the name of this document? A) Peace of Paris. B) Mayflower Compact. C) New Virginia Charter. D) Albany Plan of Union.

contine

III. COMPLETION

Directions: Fill in the blank by writing in the correct term, name, or words as required.

____ 1. The _____ case in 1734 raised the issue of whether the press should or should not be free to condemn the acts of public officials.

____ 2. The _____ colony was founded by Roger Williams to foster religious freedom and was the first colony in which church and state were separated.

____ 3. What was the name of Sir Francis Drake's ship in which he became the first Englishman to sail around the world from 1577–1580?
_____

____ 4. Ponce de Leon's reason for sailing to what is now Florida in 1513 was that he wanted to search for the _____.

____ 5. By 1760 the population of the English colonies had grown to how many people? _____

uncooperative and insubordinate. His students don't do especially well on the SAT, Jack, and I'm afraid that's where you might be heading too.

JACK   *[Nonplussed]* Donna, I just want to be the best teacher that I can! My students just seemed to have a hard time memorizing isolated facts, and I was just trying to improve their learning.

DONNA   *[Smiling]* I know that, Jack, and you're going to be an excellent teacher. But learning can't always be sugarcoated, and these kids of ours simply have to learn that you have to work hard to become a success in life. And at this point in their lives, the SAT is the measure of their success. One of your parents, Manuel Herrera's father, called up Mr. Nesbitt and asked why you aren't giving tests like the SAT. Mr. Nesbitt asked me to call Manuel's father, so that's why I put a note in your mailbox to see me.

JACK   *[Frustrated]* I hear you loud and clear, Donna. I should go back to objective testing. But Donna, I know that my students are having trouble remembering the material, and I'm not much better—I haven't even learned all the students' names yet! What can I do to help them learn the material better?

QUESTIONS

1. What are Jack's instructional objectives? At what levels of Bloom's Cognitive Taxonomy does Jack seem to be focusing his teaching and testing procedures? What levels should he be aiming for in a U.S. history course?

2. What are the different types of objective and essay test items? What are the advantages and disadvantages of each? Which seem most appropriate for Jack's situation? How could Jack have used item analysis on his objective test items?

3. What kinds of test items are on the SAT? Should teachers adapt their teaching an testing procedures so as to "teach to the test"? What levels of Bloom's Cogniti Taxonomy does the SAT measure? Is there a danger of "minimums becoming maximum and the "tail wagging the dog," as Will suggests?

4. What is meaningfulness? How can content, such as history, be presented so that is meaningful to the students? What are advance organizers, schemata, concept learnir and paired associate learning, and how might Jack apply some of these constructs to h teaching?

5. What are organization, rehearsal, and elaboration? How could they apply to th case?

6. What are mnemonic devices? Could the use of such devices help in this case? they were used, would the learning be meaningful?

7. Is there a difference between memorizing facts and learning principles? Which retained longer, facts or principles? Why? Which should Jack focus on, and why?

8. What are sensory register, short-term memory, and long-term memory? How these constructs from information processing theory apply to this case? How can Jac take advantage of them in his teaching?

9. Is Jack's use of current events reports a good idea? Would such reports enhan transfer of learning? Would they serve as motivators? How so?

10. What are cognitive or metacognitive strategies? How would they apply to th case? How would they relate to student studying and test taking?

11. What is constructivism, and how would a constructivist analyze this case? Ho might Jack take advantage of such constructs as scaffolding and the zone of proxim development?

12. Donna encourages Jack to use norm-referenced evaluation procedures. What a they, and how do they differ from criterion-referenced procedures? Which makes t most sense in this situation?

13. Jack says that he favors the discovery learning method of teaching and t contract method of grading. What are they, what are their strengths and weaknesses, an do they make sense in this situation?

14. Given the employment context in which Jack finds himself as a first-year teache what do you think he should do regarding how the material is presented and what kin of tests he gives? If you were advising Jack, what course of action would you recommen that he take to deal with this situation? Why?

LEARNING THE LINES

Key Content to Consider for Analyzing This Case:
(1) information processing theory; (2) operant
conditioning; (3) meaningful verbal learning (Ausubel).

Amy Pace and Tracy Kirk are English teachers at Smithfield Consolidated High School, which is located in the city of Smithfield, a Midwestern city with a population of 20,000. Located in the center of hundreds of acres of farms and villages, Smithfield is both the supply center for the farmers and the cultural center for all the residents in the surrounding countryside. Area pupils are bused to the high school, which has an enrollment of approximately 2,500 pupils made up of approximately 89% white, 10% African-American, and 1% other.

Amy is twenty-two years old and graduated with a B.Ed. from the local state teachers college at the end of the spring semester. In the summer she married her college boyfriend, Carl, and they both moved to a farmhouse on seventy acres owned by Carl's family, which they gave to the newlyweds as a wedding present. Immediately upon their move to Smithfield, Amy was offered and accepted a position as teacher of English at Smithfield High School.

Tracy was born and reared in Smithfield and graduated from the same college as Amy fifteen years ago. Like Amy, she returned to Smithfield after her graduation. When the consolidated high school was built, Tracy obtained a position as English teacher, and she has taught there continuously ever since. Because Tracy and her husband, a local merchant, knew Carl and Carl's family, they worked hard to make Amy and Carl feel welcome in both the school and the community.

The week prior to the beginning of classes, the faculty and staff had a three-day workshop. During this workshop, Amy and Tracy sat together. Tracy took every opportunity to introduce Amy to the other teachers. On the last day of the workshop, Frank Carr, the principal, asked Amy and Tracy if they would meet with him in his office after the workshop ended. They agreed to do so and had reached the office just as Frank arrived.

FRANK Thank you both for meeting with me on such short notice. But there's a matter I need to discuss with you as early in the school year as possible.

127

TRACY   *[Smiling]* And I bet I can guess what it is.

FRANK   OK. Guess.

TRACY   I'll bet you want to talk with us about producing the first senior play that Smithfield Consolidated High School has ever had.

FRANK   Bingo! I guess the same parents who talked with me have been talking with you also. *[Looking to Amy]* Not only is our school an educational center for the entire area, it's also a cultural center.

TRACY   That's true. Even our friends who have no children look forward to attending a the school events.

FRANK   Which leads me to the reason I asked you to meet with me this afternoon. Sinc we've been able to employ Amy, we're now in a position to produce a senior play this year. And I'd like you two to be in charge of it.

TRACY   What play would you like us to produce?

FRANK   Since you're both English teachers, I'll leave that up to you. I'm sure there are plays that are typically selected by English teachers to be produced by high school students.

AMY   Yes, there are. I saved my college textbook from my "Teaching English in the High School" course. It has a list of such plays for students to produce.

TRACY   Good. We can go through them and select one. *[Turning to Frank]* I have a question about practicing. Since most of our students are bused to school, we wor be able to practice after school. Will it be OK to practice in our classes?

FRANK   It seems to me that the production of a play's certainly an appropriate topic to study in an English class. And I know that both of you have a senior class during the second and third periods. I don't know why you couldn't combine classes for play practice. In fact, one of you could take a group to the auditorium when it's fre while the other works with groups making scenes, costumes, and so on. But you can work those things out as you see fit. But be assured that I consider the play an appropriate assignment for students in an English class.

AMY   I like that idea. It'll certainly encourage more students to participate.

FRANK   I'd really prefer to have all the students participate. There are certainly enough jobs in play production to involve lots of students. You've got scenery, costumes, stagehands, prompters, and gofers, as well as actors.

TRACY   Do you know yet when the play will be presented?

FRANK   I've checked the school calendar and talked with parent groups in the various communities whose pupils attend S.C.H.S. about preferable times. We want to present the play late in the school year for many reasons. It would give you more time to prepare for the presentation. The play will be our biggest project of the yea so it will help us end the academic year on a high note. And it will leave school personnel, parents, and students with a good feeling about S.C.H.S. The dates that seem to be the best for all the groups I talked with are Wednesday through Saturday, May 14–17. The consensus was that it should begin at 7:00 each evenin; Parents liked the idea of having a Saturday matinee at 2:00.

TRACY   That sounds great! It'll give us plenty of time to teach a comprehensive unit on drama as well as prepare for the presentation of a play.

AMY   Yes, and as you say, it'll be a great culminating academic experience for our seniors.

FRANK   And it will also be an effective public relations effort for our high school. *[Pauses and smiles]* That is, of course, if the play is well done. So, at this point, I'll let you two begin whatever you need to do to get this project under way.

After leaving Frank's office, Tracy and Amy go to Amy's classroom to talk more about their new assignment.

TRACY   Obviously, one of the first things we should do is to decide what play we'll present.

AMY   During the meeting I mentioned that I have a book that lists plays suitable for high school pupils to perform. I just remembered that I enrolled in a drama class, and the theater professor was really interested in drama productions in high school. I think I'll call him and see if he'd recommend some plays.

TRACY   *[Enthusiastically]* Oh, that's really a good idea. I'd feel more comfortable choosing a play that someone with experience in high school productions recommended.

AMY   OK. I'll call him this week. I'm sure he'd still remember me. I was in his class my senior year.

TRACY   We have a lot of decisions to make very soon, such as how do we recruit students to be in the play? How many do we need? How will we match students with parts that are appropriate for them?

AMY   That's right! And we'll have to talk about how we can select students who are able to learn long parts and act well. And also how often we'll rehearse.

TRACY   Well, let's do what we can do now. You call your professor and read your book on plays. Then after we clear everything with Frank, we'll meet again and get down to serious business.

The following Monday, Amy and Tracy arrive in the parking lot at the same time. They talk as they walk together to the school building.

AMY   I talked with Professor Arnold Saturday afternoon. He told me that in the fifteen years he'd been working with interns in high school, he's found that *Macbeth* is definitely the classical play most commonly performed in high schools.

TRACY   That's good news. If other high schools can do it, so can we. But I wish we had information on how to go about preparing the students.

AMY   Me, too. I had a college class on teaching English in high school, but I don't recall that we even discussed anything about how to teach pupils to present a play.

TRACY   I'm sure I didn't study anything like that in college either. Now I'm sorry I didn't try out for a play somewhere along the line. Then I would've learned at least one approach to directing a play.

AMY   *[With concern]* I'm not even sure how to select the main characters. Students in these roles have a lot of memorizing to do and a lot of stage directions to remember.

TRACY   That's right. I'm also concerned about how we should assign roles. I know pupils who would be terrific as lead actors, and I know others who would be awful. Is it appropriate for us just to assign major roles to pupils we know can handle them? I read *Macbeth* again after we began talking about it. It seems to me that there are

only seven major characters: Macbeth, Lady Macbeth, King Duncan, Banquo
Macduff, Malcolm, Ross, and Lennox. The rest are gentlemen, officers, soldiers,
murderers, attendants, messengers, witches, and ghosts. I think it would be OK t
encourage some of our best students to sign up for the major roles. If we have
several people sign up for one role, we can have an audition and select the one w
think would do the best job.

AMY   That sounds good to me. Then we could list each of the minor acting roles along
with support roles like stagehands, ushers, costumers, set designers, makeup
specialists, light operators, prompters, and so forth. I'll bet we can find a job in th
play for every senior.

TRACY   *[Enthusiastically]* I really like that idea! That would make it truly a class play! L
you have time to meet after the last class today and organize these lists?

AMY   Yes. I think we're on a roll now! I want to keep it moving. We can probably deci
which students we should encourage to sign up for the major roles, as well as list
all the support jobs and how many students we need for each of them. Then we
could prepare the sign-up sheets for each of our classes, post them tomorrow, and
have our actors and crew identified by the middle of the week.

TRACY   That's fine with me—the sooner the better. I'll see you in my room after the las
class.

By midweek all the pupils in the four senior English classes had signed up for
least one job connected to the play. Kathy and Amy had invited students they thoug
would be able to play the leading roles to sign up for particular parts. By Thursday aft
noon they had auditioned all the applicants who had applied for major roles and int
viewed and/or auditioned those who had applied for supporting roles in the play.

On Monday morning at 9:00 both Kathy and Amy were in their classrooms d
tributing a paper to each student which explained that student's role in the senior play

TRACY   Congratulations. Each of you will have an important role in the first senior-clas
play ever to be presented by S.C.H.S. Of course, I'm sure that you all want it to be
first-class production so you can set an example for all successive classes to strive
match. The papers I'm distributing to you indicate what role you have in our play
You could have signed up for either an acting or a support role. All of you were
given the type of role you requested. All students in senior English classes will ha
some role to play in producing the play. Ms. Pace is handing out the parts and job
to her students also.

MARK   When we practice the play, will we all be able to practice together?

TRACY   This class and Ms. Pace's second-period class and both of the third-period class
will be able to practice together whenever Ms. Pace and I think we should. It will
be more difficult for the second- and third-period classes to practice at the same
time because there are other classes involved. But we'll make arrangements for all
the cast and support workers to rehearse at the same time when we get closer to
showtime. But for now, you actors, especially the leads, need to begin memorizing
your lines immediately because many of you have large parts to learn.

BETH   I've never had to memorize long parts before. What's the best way to memorize lines?

JAY   I was just about to ask the same thing. There must be a best way to do that.

TRACY   Probably the most efficient way is to copy all your speaking parts in the order that they appear in the play. Then start with the first few lines of the first part. Read them over and over again until you can say them from memory. Then, go on to the next few lines. Keep that up until you've memorized the whole thing. You should also identify cues that will help you know when to come in.

JAY   *[Speaking out]* Wow! That sounds like it'll take a long time!

TRACY   Well, it might if you have a really long part. But it's the most logical and direct way to learn your parts. Start at the very beginning, and move right through until you come to the end. Practice makes perfect!

Amy has also assigned acting and support roles to her students. They begin to ask questions about how to learn their lines.

PAM   *[After raising her hand and being recognized]* Ms. Pace, I really have a long part. I don't know how to memorize such a long part. Can you give me some suggestions on how to do it?

AMY   That's really an important question, Pam. And I'm sure that there are other students here who have the same concern. *[Many other pupils nod their heads.]* I think the best method is to actually try to become the character. Read through the entire play and see what your character does and says. Get a feeling for the type of person your character is. How does your character interact with other characters? How does your character respond to certain things? What is your character's role in the story? Where does your part fit into the plot of the story? *[Tim raises his hand.]* Tim?

TIM   How does doing that stuff help us remember our lines?

AMY   Well, when you know all about the character you're playing and how he fits into the overall play, you have a good idea of his thoughts, ideas, and generally how he'd respond to different situations. So, even though you may not be able to recite the part exactly, you'll be able to respond generally the way your character would respond. *[To the class]* So your assignment for tomorrow is to read the entire play and become acquainted with all the characters in the play. Begin to practice thinking and acting like your character. Then return to the beginning of the play and reread the seven scenes of Act I very carefully. We'll discuss that act in class.

After school, Amy goes to Tracy's room to see how her class responded to their assignments of roles for the play. Tracy was still in her room.

AMY   *[Walking into the room]* Hi. I'm glad you're still here.

TRACY   *[Startled]* Oh! *[Pauses]* Amy, I'm glad you came over. How'd your assignments go?

AMY   Well, the students with large parts seemed to be overwhelmed at the prospect of memorizing so much material.

TRACY   *[Smiling]* That's exactly what happened in my class.

AMY   My kids were so excited when we were talking about the play last week that I was really excited, too. But now that they're worried about learning their parts, I'm worried too.

TRACY   Me too. One of the students asked me if I could tell him a way to memorize his part.

AMY   *[Excited]* That happened in my class, too! What did you tell him?

TRACY   Well, I told him to copy all his character's speaking parts. Then begin to read th first few lines over and over until he had them memorized. Then go on to the next few, and so on. And to pay attention to cues on where to come in.

AMY   *[Upset]* Oh, gosh! I told them just the opposite. I told them to read the whole thing and see how their part fits in. I also told them to learn how the character thinks, responds to things, and to essentially try to become the character.

TRACY   Isn't that called the holistic approach, or something like that?

AMY   Yes. I think so. I remember one of my professors talking about it in an educationa psychology class. He said it was a good approach to remembering material. In fact, here's an old handout he gave us in the class. It gives some reasons why children forget things and what to do about it. I thought it might be useful sometime, so I saved it. *[Hands Tracey a paper entitled "Why People Forget"]*

TRACY   *[Studies the paper]* Well, these suggestions look pretty straightforward. And it doesn't make sense at all to have half of our actors using one approach and the other half using a different one. I'd like to have them use the approach you described, but I don't think I know it well enough to teach them how to use it.

AMY   Well, I have two suggestions. I could teach you the approach and you could teach your class. Or I could teach it to your class. But I'd rather teach it to you because you need to know it to be sure that your students are using it appropriately. Do you have to be home before 5:30?

TRACY   No. Carl doesn't get home until almost 6:00, and we're going out to dinner at 7:00.

AMY   Good. *[Pointing to a chair at a table]* Sit right down here. We're going to plan how we'll teach these pupils to remember their lines.

Two weeks later, all four senior English classes are in the auditorium having thei first all-cast practice. They plan to start at the beginning and go through the entire pla Amy and Tracy have asked them to try to speak their parts from memory as much as pos sible. The stage crew will learn what needs to be done in the various acts of the play. Th first scene is over. The sound crew did well with the lightning and thunder. The thre witches knew their parts.

TRACY   *[Loudly]* That's a good Scene One, people! Now let's get ready for Scene Two. Duncan, Malcolm, Donalbain, Lennox, Sergeant, Ross, and Attendants. Enter stage left. Sergeant, crawl in from stage left. OK. Begin. *[Silence]* Duncan, speak up.

DUNCAN "What bloody man is that? He can report, as seemeth by his pliget, of the revolt of the newest state."

TRACY   Duncan, that word is "plight," not "pliget." And speak your lines as if you've seen a wounded and bloody man, not as if you're talking about the weather. OK, Malcolm.

MALCOLM   "This is the sergeant who, like a good and hardy soldier, fought 'gainst my captivity. Hail, brave friend! Say to the kind the knowledge of the broil as thou didst leave it."

SERGEANT   *[Word by word]* "Dubful, it stood. As . . ." *[Pause]*

MALCOLM   That's "doubtful," Matt. "Doubtful it stood as two spent swimmers, that do cling together and choke their art."

SERGEANT   *[Angrily]* C'mon, Tom. That's my part, not yours.

TOM   It doesn't sound like it's yours. Matt, you don't even know it.

MATT   I just haven't had time to study it yet.

TOM   Well, why don't you? It's not that big of a part. We were supposed to have our parts in the first act learned by today. If you're not willing to learn your part, let somebody else do it. You're going to screw up and spoil it for everybody!

TRACY   Tom's right, Matt. If you're willing to learn your part, that's fine. But if you don't have the time, or if you just don't want to, now's the time to tell us so that we can get somebody else to do it.

MATT   *[Upset]* I'm going to learn it! I'll have the whole part learned by our next rehearsal.

TRACY   That's great. We want you to be in the play. But we also want the play to be a really good play.

In the back of the auditorium, Amy is working with the students who are in Scene Three.

AMY   *[Looking at the witches]* You witches did a good job in Scene One. You look ready to go back on in Scene Three. Good. *[Loudly]* Macbeth, Banquo, Ross, Angus! Where are you? *[The four boys come backstage from the seating area.]* Good! Do all of you know your parts? *[Silence]* Oh, no. Don't tell me you haven't learned your lines yet!

MACBETH   I've worked hard on mine, Ms. Pace. But it's a long part and I haven't got it memorized yet. Can you help me learn to memorize? I think I have one of the parts learned, and then the next time I try to say it, I've forgotten it. *[The other actors all speak out at once to say that they're having problems, too.]*

AMY   Yes, I can help you all. In our next class, I'll teach you some principles of remembering information. Then we'll apply them to our parts.

Throughout the practice, some of the students knew not only their own parts, but several other parts as well. But a substantial number of the students did not know their parts, when they were supposed to speak, or the appropriate inflection.

After school was dismissed, Tracy came to Amy's room and slumped down in a seat as if she were exhausted.

TRACY   What a day! I'm really depressed.

AMY   Let me guess. You're worried about the play.

TRACY   Yes! I don't think that the students will be ready to perform it in May.

[*Discouraged*] We're liable to become the laughing stock of the school!

AMY   Don't give up yet. This was just our first practice. We have six months to get ready for the presentation. I'll admit that I was discouraged this morning. And I think we're definitely going to have to make some changes if the play is to be a success.

TRACY   I agree. But one of the biggest problems is going to be getting the kids to learn their lines and when to come in. Frankly, Amy, I know we talked about that and you showed me that paper from your class, but what are you going to tell the kids

FIGURE 14   Handout on Forgetting From Educational Psychology Class

WHY PEOPLE FORGET

1. **Failure to recall:** Not enough associations with information to help them retrieve the information.

   Example: Rod cannot recall the name of a minor character of a story but can recognize it on a multiple-choice test.

   Solution: Help Rod relate the name to the character's actions that are familiar to Rod.

2. **Partial recall:** Can remember parts of information, but fills in the remainder based on what seems to be logical.

   Example: Martha remembers some of the character's lines verbatim but ad-libs other lines.

   Solution: Be certain that Martha identifies and learns the exact words of the speaker.

3. **Confusion:** Associations in long-term memory related to similar items interfere with each other.

   Example: Sam recites lines from a play he learned last year instead of similar ones from the play he is learning.

   Solution: Help Sam understand how the character's comments are related to the flow of action in the play he is learning.

4. **Disuse:** Information cannot be recalled because it has not been used regularly.

   Example: Maria is unable to remember her lines because she has not practiced them enough to overlearn them.

   Solution: Review information daily until it is memorized accurately.

5. **Failure to process:** Information was never adequately stored in long-term memory.

   Example: Lois cannot remember her lines because she hasn't learned the play well enough to know what happens next or where her part fits in.

   Solution: Make sure that Lois knows both the context and where her lines fit in.

who still haven't learned their lines? What's the best way to memorize stuff like Shakespeare?

QUESTIONS

1. Examine this case from the standpoint of the three-component information processing model. How can information be moved into long-term memory? What happens when information doesn't register on the sensory register component or is quickly lost from short-term memory? How does this relate to the students' learning their lines?

2. What is forgetting? How does the retrieval theory of forgetting differ from other views, such as interference, disuse, or reconstruction error?

3. What is meaningfulness? What makes the material meaningful in some plays but not others? How can the material in a play of Shakespeare be made more meaningful to today's students?

4. What is organization, and how does it relate to meaningfulness? What is a learning hierarchy, and how can the hierarchial arrangement of information be applied to learning a play?

5. What is elaboration in cognitive learning? What elaboration devices might high school students use to learn a play?

6. What is rehearsal in cognitive learning? How can rehearsal be used to learn a play? How is rehearsal related to meaningfulness?

7. What is overlearning, and how is it related to rehearsal? How much overlearning is desirable in learning a play?

8. What are mnemonic devices? How do the keyword method, the peg word method, and the method of loci relate to meaningfulness? What, if any, mnemonic devices would be useful in learning a play like *Macbeth*?

9. What are advance organizers? How could Amy and Tracy use them to help their students learn the play?

10. What is the whole-part method of cognitive learning? Should students try to get the gestalt (or "big picture") first, then go to acts and scenes before attempting to memorize their lines? Or should the students learn line-by-line and gradually come to understand the entire play in a step-by-step fashion?

11. What advice would you give the two teachers with regard to helping their students learn their lines? What should they do next?

CASE **14**

MAKING CONNECTIONS

Key Content to Consider for Analyzing This Case:
(1) transfer of learning; (2) information processing
theory; (3) meaningful verbal learning (Ausubel);
(4) motivation (mastery vs. performance goal
orientations); (5) Bloom's Cognitive Taxonomy;
(6) measurement and evaluation (standardized tests,
types of test items).

Fred Myers is twenty-five years old and has taught high school social studies
another state for two years. He is applying for a social studies teaching position
Central High School, which is located in a city of approximately 100,000 in
Midwestern state west of the Mississippi River. Central's physical plant is old but w
maintained. Its student body is approximately 80% white, 19% African-American, a
1% other.

Fred has been sent to the school by the personnel department of the school syste
to be interviewed by the building principal, Alma Messick. Alma sits behind her de
while Fred sits in a chair to her right. The office door is closed.

ALMA   I notice from your application *[looking at paper in her hand]* that you mainly
taught history in your first job.

FRED   Yes, that's right. As a new teacher I was assigned required courses. *[Eyes light up]*
One of these days, though, I really want to teach psychology and sociology. They
are my favorite courses.

ALMA   *[Smiling]* I'm sure that's possible. Mr. Tucker, the department chair, has taught
those courses for years, but I hear him talking about retirement more and more.
We'll see what happens. Do you think you'd enjoy teaching civics or economics?

FRED   I can certainly teach them, but to tell you the truth, I'd rather teach history. I lov
history. It's just that world and U.S. history are required courses and, well, I'd like
shot at teaching seniors in an elective course like psychology.

ALMA   Well, we'll keep that in mind, Fred, and see what we can do. However, this year
you'll be teaching three sections of world history and two of U.S. history. Instead o
a sixth class, I'm going to give you a study hall, the third period. You'll need to
assist Mr. Tucker with the Tri Torch Club as well. Their big project is building a
float for the Merchants' Christmas parade. Eventually, when John retires you shou
be ready to take over the club's leadership.

FRED   *[Frowning]* I see.

ALMA   Any questions, Fred?

FRED   Not really. Well, I guess I'm wondering about evaluation procedures a bit. But maybe I should talk to Mr. Tucker about that.

ALMA   John isn't around this week. I think he has a cold. But I'm sure he'd emphasize getting our students ready for taking the SAT.

FRED   So most of the teachers give objective-type tests?

ALMA   Yes, and emphasize content mastery, not playing around. We're very proud of the high percentage of Central students who are National Merit Finalists and go on to college with scholarships.

FRED   I'm aware of that. That's one reason I wanted to teach at Central.

ALMA   *[Smiling]* Good! I think you're going to fit in around here just fine, Fred. *[Standing up]* Let me know if I can help you in any way.

It is the first day of classes of the new school year. The bell has rung to begin the fifth period. Fred smiles at the thirty-four sophomores sitting in movable chairs in this world history class as he stands at the lectern in front of the room. The classroom is adorned with the usual maps, globes, and bulletin boards typical of a social studies classroom.

FRED   As most of you probably know, I'm Mr. Myers *[writes last name on blackboard]* and this is world history. Does everyone have a copy of the text that we'll be using? *[Holds up his copy of the textbook for the students to see]* Anyone not have the right book? *[No hands go up.]* Good. To tell you the truth, students, this is not the text I would have chosen. I would prefer a text that begins with the present and moves backwards. I think that approach allows students to make the connections easier between the past and the present. Instead, we'll begin with prehistory and move forward to the present. Those times are so different from ours that it's more difficult to make the connections between what happened then and today's current events. Yes—Marie, isn't it?

MARIE   Yes, Marie Rawlings. How will we be graded in here, Mr. Myers?

FRED   *[Smiling]* I was just coming to that, Marie. Thank you. *[Pause]* I know that a lot of you are good students and that you and your parents are concerned about the SAT and your getting a college scholarship. So our unit tests and quizzes will mostly be objective-type tests. You do need to know how to write the King's English, however, so we'll have projects with each unit. They will involve short papers or reports which you can do individually or by working with a small group of up to four students. That will be your choice. Yes, Marie?

MARIE   What kind of projects?

FRED   That will vary according to the unit, of course, but take our first unit on prehistory. There are a lot of interesting topics or problems that you could prepare a report on, like whether we evolved from a so-called "missing link" in the theory of evolution, or how prehistoric man learned to use fire, or how tribes developed and carried on warfare among themselves. These reports don't need to be long, but they should be well researched and well written. I think they have a written section on the SAT these days. *[Pause]* Then there's current events. I'm going to ask you to bring in articles that you find in newspapers and magazines that relate to topics we're studying. I think it's important for us to make connections between historical events and what's going on today. Yes, Bart?

BART   What do you mean? Like we find articles where archeologists have found some new mummy or something?

FRED   Well, yes, that would be great when we study ancient Egypt, but I mean anything that shows relationships between what's going on today and the lessons of history.

BART   Well, like what?

FRED   Well, Bart, have you even thought about what prehistoric man and modern-day man have in common? It's easy to think of all the differences between then and now, but what things do we have in common with our ancestors?

BART   I don't know. I really can't think of any. I mean, they didn't have telephones or cars or computers or even TV back then. They just lived in caves and hunted wild animals and, I don't know, I guess they fought other tribes. I can't see how they're like us at all.

FRED   OK. So many things have changed since then, and I expect that people in the twenty-third century might look back on us and say that they have nothing in common with us since things have changed so much.

BART   Right. And I'll bet they won't want to study history either. They'll just want to do things that are important then.

FRED   But think about some of the things that you said about prehistoric man, and I'm sure you took most of them from movies you've seen instead of from reading our text.

BART   [Smiling] Right. You got me.

FRED   You said that they lived in homes in the form of caves, that hunting was their major job, and that they fought wars against other tribes. Don't we live in homes, go to work, and fight wars too?

BART   [Puzzled] Well yeah, right. But we don't live in caves, and we have nations instead of tribes, and their wars were nothing compared to ours.

FRED   OK, but do you suppose they learned anything when they did those things? Take wars, for example. Granted warfare has changed since then. Heck, we can blow up a whole building with one missile now and they fought with clubs, rocks, and spears. But let me ask you this, Bart. Even though they used those kinds of weapons, don't you suppose they had to have courage to go into battle, just like now?

BART   Yeah, I suppose so.

FRED   Do you suppose they learned lessons about the importance of training soldiers so they could win, and learned discipline so they could function as a unit and not turn tail and run in confusion? Do you think they learned some things that others built on and learned from the mistakes that were made?

BART   Yeah, I guess.

FRED   History has a way of repeating itself if it isn't studied. For example, we got to the final four in the state basketball tournament last year, didn't we?

BART   Yeah.

FRED   And we should have beat the team we played in the semifinals, shouldn't we?

BART   [Loudly] Yeah! [Several other students voice agreement.]

FRED   But we made a big mistake at the end of the game with the score tied, didn't we? What was it?

BART   One of our players got a rebound and called time-out with five seconds left. We had used up all our time-outs, so they called a technical foul on us and we lost the game.

FRED   Now, do you think Coach Evans will remember that game even though it's ancient history now and make sure that his players don't make that mistake again?

BART   Well, yeah, but—

FRED   But what?

BART   Well, cavemen didn't even play basketball.

FRED   Oh, boy! [Looks at his watch] Well, the bell's about to ring, so let me leave you with something to think about. A famous man once said that we need to study history so that we won't get traveling so fast that we fail to look back and make sure that we're traveling forward. When you look back on some of the mistakes that mankind has made, like enslaving people, killing people in unnecessary wars, and allowing dictators to rise to power and ruin people's lives, you'll realize that we have to study what happened and how so that we can profit from our mistakes and prevent those things from happening again. [Bell rings.] OK. See you guys tomorrow.

It is five weeks later. Fred is returning the first of two unit tests, this one on ancient Greece. His plan is to complete Unit Two by beginning the material on ancient Rome and give the second unit test over that material. The test over ancient Greece was worth 100 points and was composed of multiple-choice, matching, true-false, and short-answer completion-type questions. Fred decided that the A's should begin at 90, the B's at 80, the C's at 70, and so forth. The average score was 68.4. Out of thirty-four students, there were two A's, two B+'s, four B's, four C+'s, four C's, eight D+'s, five D's, and five F's.

After telling the students how disappointed he is in the test results, he reads the correct answers to each question and has the students double-check his grading. He then goes over several questions that students had trouble with and explains the rationale for the correct answer.

FRED   Alright, people. I'd like an explanation. Why did you do so poorly on this test? Didn't you study? Marie?

MARIE   I studied hard for this, Mr. Myers, and I still didn't get an A! This test was hard. There was just too much material! Too much stuff to memorize! Too much of it is too much alike.

FRED   Well like what?

MARIE   Well like those two sculptors, Phidias and Praxiteles. They are too much alike. I couldn't remember which one carved that statue in the Parthenon. And Socrates, Plato, and Aristotle. I knew that one of them said to "Know Thyself," but I guessed the wrong one. And all those battles. I knew all the names, but how am I supposed to remember which battle was the final one at which the Persians were defeated? Plataea, Thermopylae, and Marathon all look alike to me. I know they're all important battles but I didn't know which was the most important.

FRED   Well, I guess I really don't understand what you're saying, Marie. They all look quite different to me. How did you study for this test?

MARIE   I underlined all the things you said were important and then went back over them before the test.

FRED   Take those four battles. Open up your book to page 70. *[Pause]* Do you have *Plataea* underlined?

MARIE   Yes.

FRED   Did you just underline the word *Plataea,* or did you also underline the part that says, "In 479 B.C. the forces of the allied city-states under a Spartan king dealt the Persians their final defeat at Plataea. The Persians left Greece and did not return."

MARIE   No, I just underlined the name of the battle.

FRED   See, there's your problem. You needed to underline the whole thing so that the name of the battle gets associated in your mind with the fact that it was the final defeat for the Persians. But you were only four points from an A, Marie. You can make up for it on the test on Rome. *[Pause]* Anybody else? Yes, Bart?

BART   I agree with Marie. All this junk is too much alike.

FRED   And how did you study for the test, Bart?

BART   I don't know. I read the stuff and went back over it.

FRED   Did you underline like Marie, or do you outline the material or put it on index cards?

BART   *[Angrily]* No, I just read it. That was bad enough. I had a hard time reading it all again just before the test.

FRED   Why?

BART   Who cares about this junk?! I don't care what happened to some Greek guys two thousand years ago. What's this stuff got to do with today? When I graduate from high school, I'm going to go to the Ford Mechanics School in Michigan like my brother did. How's this stuff going to help me? My brother's making big money as mechanic and wants to open his own shop in a few years and says he'll hire me. He's doing just fine and he sure couldn't tell you or even care about what battle th Greeks beat the Persians. The only reason I have to learn this stuff is to make a passing grade in here so I can get a high school diploma. My brother says I have t get my diploma or he won't hire me. But otherwise I could care less. *[Bell rings.]*

FRED   Oh, boy, there's the bell. We're not through talking about this, Bart. I want to challenge you all to think about how this material applies to today's world. Maybe will make that part of your next exam.

It is the next class meeting. Fred is determined to focus the students on how t history of ancient Rome relates to today's events.

FRED   OK, folks, settle down. Now, at the end of the last class meeting, I challenged yo to think about how this material on ancient Rome applies to things happening today. Now, how many of you took me seriously and tried to do that? *[No hands g up.]* OK, that's what I thought. We're not going to see these connections if we don look for them. So, with that in mind, I'm going to change the kind of test that I gi you on this material about ancient Rome from all objective-type items to part objective and part essay. The essay questions are going to focus on your making connections—drawing lessons, if you will—between events that happened then and events happening today. Yes, Marie?

MARIE   How are we going to do that? Can you give us an example of a question?

FRED   I gave this lot of thought last night. I'm going to have you pretend that you are news reporters like the people who prepare stories for the newspapers or TV. For each chapter we study, I want you to prepare headlines that describe the major events going on. Then you'll describe people who made the news, like say Julius Caesar or Nero or Cleopatra. Next comes major events that take place, like the assassination of Caesar or the fighting of the Punic Wars. Or you could even do a story on a day in the life of a Roman legionnaire. Then there are key words that you'll want to explain to your readers, like *patrician* or *gladiator* or *Pax Romana*. Finally, there are important places that you'll need to locate and describe, like the Tiber River or Sicily or Carthage. But the main thing I want you to do each time, and the thing I'm going to ask you test questions about, is what that person, event, or place is like today. Make constant comparisons. For example, I saw a movie on TV the other day about America's Caesar. Can you guess who that person is, and why he would be compared to Caesar? Yes, Bart.

BART   Probably JFK. He was assassinated like Caesar.

FRED   OK, that's good, Bart, but you based your choice on one similarity. Can anybody think of anyone in current American history, say after World War I, who would have been like Caesar in other ways? *[No hands go up.]* Well, Caesar was a soldier, wasn't he? He finally became a general and was supreme commander of Roman legions. He was a brilliant general and conquered Rome's enemies. As a result he rose to a position of power in Rome. His enemies were afraid that he was going to become a dictator, and that's why they assassinated him. But I guess that he was also a bit of an egotist and did things in a big way so people would notice him. Now, does that remind you of any American general you've heard of, say, after World War I? *[No hands are raised.]* OK, I'll give you a hint. Who were big American generals in World War II? Yes, Bart?

BART   I know who it is. It's General Patton. My grandfather said that he was our smartest general but was always making mistakes because he showed off a lot. Grandpa said that Patton was always putting his foot in his mouth.

FRED   That's an excellent guess, Bart, but Patton wasn't a big enough general to equal Caesar's position in Rome. Who were the biggest generals in World War II? Yes, Eric?

ERIC   It had to be either Eisenhower or MacArthur. I'll bet it was Eisenhower because he became president.

FRED   *[Frowning]* No, it was MacArthur. He was a brilliant general and an egotist like Caesar, and there are a number of other comparisons. Yes, Marie.

MARIE   I would have said Eisenhower and would have gotten it wrong.

FRED   Maybe I picked a poor example. If we had spent more time making comparisons by talking about the characteristics of Caesar, maybe it would have been easier. *[Pause]* Well, let's take another example. Take the Roman Republic. Suppose I asked you in what ways the Roman Republic is like our republic today. In other words, asked you to compare and contrast Rome's Republic with ours. Yes, Naomi?

NAOMI   But don't we have a democracy like Greece had? You told us that Greece ha the first real democracy and that we got the idea from them.

FRED   That was Athens, Naomi, not Greece. Don't you remember that they didn't reall have a nation but a bunch of city-states? Yes, Eric?

ERIC   You said they called themselves Hellas instead of Greece. But wasn't that a natio

FRED   *[Frowning]* Don't you remember that I said that a united nation called Hellas wa their ideal, but they didn't achieve it. Each city-state had an independent government. That's why they had trouble uniting to try to stop the Persians when they invaded. Yes, Marie?

MARIE   But wasn't Rome a city-state too?

FRED   Yes, it was. But it eventually conquered all of its neighbors and had to incorpor: them and govern them, so it became more than just a city-state. It eventually gre into a republic. Yes, Naomi?

NAOMI   I know one way they were like us.

FRED   What's that, Naomi?

NAOMI   They had a Senate. It says so on page 87 in the book.

FRED   *[Eagerly]* That's right! But did they have a House of Representatives?

NAOMI   *[Without raising her hand]* A what?

FRED   Our Congress has two houses: the Senate and the House of Representatives. Di the Romans have a two-house legislature? Yes, Marie?

MARIE   I think they just had a Senate, didn't they?

FRED   That's right! Well, I'm sure that we could think of other differences if we tried. Bart, did you think of a difference?

BART   No, well, yes. Don't we have a democracy? They only had a republic.

FRED   *[Eagerly]* Good thinking, Bart. Now tell me. What is a republic? What is a democracy? Yes, Marie?

MARIE   Don't the people run the government in a democracy? And I think a republic run by the big people.

FRED   What do you mean by big people, Marie?

MARIE   Well, you know, like people who are rich and powerful. People like the Kennedys.

FRED   Well let me ask you a question. Don't we have a republic? Like it says in the Pledge of Allegiance, "and to the Republic for which it stands." *[Pause]* Look guy in a pure democracy all the citizens would vote on everything. Since that's impractical in a nation of 250 million people, we elect representatives who do th actual voting. So we have a republic, as did Rome. But what I want you to learn do is be able to make comparisons the way we have been doing. *[Pause]* Now, di you notice that the Roman Republic fell and the Romans replaced it with an emp and an emperor? Suppose I asked you why and how that happened, and then as you if the same thing could happen in the United States today. You'll notice that they went through periods of having a dictator, and that was first used by a man named Sulla and later by Caesar as a stepping-stone to becoming emperor. Dicta was a temporary position that Sulla got the Roman Senate to change to a lifetime

FIGURE 15 A Sample of Items From Fred Myers' Exam on Ancient Greece

---

I. Matching. Match the names of the people in the right-hand column with the important roles they played in ancient Greece. Write the letter identifying the person's name in the blank to the left of the role played. Some people's names will not be used.

_____ 1. The Father of History who wrote the   A. Pericles
history of the Persian War.   B. Leonidas

_____ 2. The leader of Athens during its Golden   C. Phidias
Age (460–429 B.C.).   D. Praxiteles

_____ 3. Spartan king and commander of the troops   E. Alexander the Great
at the Battle of Thermopylae.   F. Herodotus

_____ 4. Macedonian king who conquered the then-   G. Socrates
known world.   H. Philip of Macedon

_____ 5. Sculptor who carved the statue of Athena   I. Solon
in the Parthenon.   J. Lycurgus

II. Multiple Choice. For each question select the one best answer and write the letter preceding your choice in the blank to the left of the question.

_____ 1. Which of the following Greek philosophers stressed the importance of getting to "Know thyself" to his students?
A. Archimedes   B. Socrates   C. Aristotle   D. Plato

_____ 2. At which of the following battles did the combined Greek city-states deal the Persians their final defeat in 479 B.C.?
A. Thermopylae   B. Marathon   C. Plataea   D. Sicily

_____ 3. Geographically Greece is about the size of which American state?
A. Florida   B. Maine   C. Texas   D. Delaware

_____ 4. In which Greek city-state did democracy first develop?
A. Athens   B. Sparta   C. Thebes   D. Corinth

_____ 5. Which of the following types of columns found on Greek buildings is plainest and simplest in design?
A. Delian   B. Corinthian   C. Ionic   D. Doric

III. Completion. Fill in the blank by writing in the correct answer as required.

_____ 1. The famous temple dedicated to Athena that was located atop the Acropolis is called the _____.

_____ 2. What city-state was the strongest in Greece as a result of winning the Peloponnesian War from 431–404 B.C.? _____.

_____ 3. What group of people did not have the right to vote in Athens?
_____

_____ 4. At the same time that the Persians invaded Greece, what city-state attempted to conquer the Greek cities of Sicily? _____.

_____ 5. What is the 300-year period after Alexander the Great called?
_____.

position. The men who assassinated Caesar thought he was going to become emperor and end the Republic. And I might add, that is exactly what happened a short time later when Caesar's nephew, Octavian, actually became emperor. That was the end of the Republic. Now, could that happen today in America? *[Silence]* Yes, Marie.

MARIE   Mr. Myers, I wouldn't know how to go about answering that question if you asked us to write about it on a test. How do you go about trying to figure that kir of thing out?

QUESTIONS

1. What kinds of test items are actually on the SAT? Does the SAT cover specific su jects such as social studies? Is the essay portion of the test used for college entrance de sions? Is it a good policy, given the importance of SAT scores, for school districts to teachers to teach to the test by covering the content and using the same type of items are used on the SAT?

2. What instructional objectives is Fred trying to pursue in his class? What levels Bloom's Cognitive Taxonomy is Fred aiming for? What kinds of test items and classro questions relate to those levels of Bloom's taxonomy?

3. What is transfer of learning? What is it that transfers? Can transfer be either po tive or negative? Can it be forwards or backwards? What is the formal discipline the and what does it assume transfers? How does transfer of learning apply to this case? W kinds of connections is Fred aiming for? How does a teacher teach for transfer? Wo Fred's idea of getting the students to write headlines for major historical events help learning to transfer?

4. Examine this case from the perspective of information processing theory. H do the sensory register, short-term memory, and long-term memory constructs h explain the students' retention problems? How is information moved to long-te memory?

5. What is meaningful learning? How would cognitive psychologists like Brur Ausubel, Piaget, and Vygotsky explain the processes and mechanisms by which mate becomes meaningful to a student?

6. What are mediators? Could mediators be used in this case to help students m connections?

7. What are mnemonic devices? How effective are such procedures as the keyword peg word methods or the method of loci in helping students remember material? Is s learning meaningful?

8. What are metacognitive strategies? What metacognitive strategies might work t for Fred's students?

9. What role does motivation play in this case? For example, how might Ames' m tery versus performance goal orientations help explain student behavior in this ca What kinds of teaching procedures foster mastery learning? How might Fred use s teaching procedures with Bart, who wishes to become a mechanic?

10. What are the strengths and weaknesses of objective and essay test items? Which makes more sense given Fred's instructional objectives?

11. From an operant conditioning framework, what kinds of student behaviors is Fred trying to shape? What are the effective reinforcers? What contingencies have been established? What changes should Fred make?

12. Given Fred's desire to help his students learn to make connections between past and present events, what would be the best teaching methods and evaluation procedures for him to use? What kinds of questions might he ask in class to stimulate that kind of student thinking? What might a typical test question look like?

13. What answers should Fred give Marie? What changes should he make in his teaching methods to accomplish his instructional goals?

C A S E **15**

THE PROBLEM
WITH PROBLEM-SOLVING

Key Content to Consider for Analyzing This Case:
(1) problem-solving; (2) classroom management
(especially Teacher Effectiveness Training); (3) physica
development; (4) Bloom's Cognitive Taxonomy.

ori Hart and Ann Todd are good friends who both teach sixth grade at Beach E
mentary School. The school, which is ten years old, is located in an upscale su
urban area of a large city on the West Coast and enrolls approximately 800 pup
in grades K–6. Approximately 65% of the pupils come from white middle- to uppe
middle-income families, 20% are from lower-middle- to middle-income African-Americ:
families, 10% are from lower-middle- to middle-income Hispanic families, and t
remaining 5% are from middle- to upper-middle-income Asian-American families.

Lori joined the faculty at Beach four years ago after graduating with a B.S. in ed
cation from a major downstate university. Ann was employed the following year after s
graduated with a B.S. in education from the nearby state teachers college. At that tir
Lori helped Ann find a place to live and to become established in the school and cor
munity. They became very close friends.

Just before summer school ended, Norma Workman, the principal, asked Lori ai
Ann to come to her office after school. When they arrived, Norma showed them a fl
announcing a two-week workshop on "Problem-Solving Skills in the Classroom," to
taught in the local high school auditorium by Dr. Joseph Sligo, professor of education
Ann's alma mater. Norma told the teachers that there was sufficient money in the sch
budget to send the two of them to the workshop if they would like to go. Ann becar
very excited because she had taken an educational psychology course from Dr. Sligo a
thought it was the best class she had in college. Ann's enthusiasm was contagious, a
Lori agreed to attend the workshop with her.

On the day the workshop was scheduled to begin, Lori and Ann arrived early a
sat in the front row of the auditorium. When Dr. Sligo arrived, he recognized Ann a
came over to greet her and find out where she was teaching. Ann introduced him to L
and both teachers were quite pleased that he acknowledged them. Then Dr. Sligo wen
the speaker's dais on the stage and introduced himself.

JOE   I appreciate all of you coming to this workshop. I'll do my best to ensure that
        you're not disappointed that you came. My name is Joseph Sligo. I'm a professor of
        educational psychology at State Teachers College. I'd like all of you to call me Joe.
              The title of this workshop is "Problem-Solving Skills in the Classroom." I
        believe that problem-solving is such an important factor in pupils' academic success
        that the teaching of problem-solving should be a major academic goal. *[Surveying
        the audience]* Are you all familiar with Bloom's Cognitive Taxonomy? *[Most teachers
        respond by saying "Yes" or nodding in the affirmative.]* Good. Then I'll use that as a
        starting point to get us thinking about higher-order learning. Our schools today
        focus primarily on the first three levels of Bloom's taxonomy. *[Addressing the
        audience]* Who can tell me what those three levels are? *[Nods toward Sue, who had
        immediately raised her hand]*

SUE   The first three levels are knowledge, comprehension, and application.

JOE   *[Enthusiastically]* Right! And, basically, those are the things we teach in our schools
        today.

LUKE *[Speaking out]* But aren't those things we *should* teach our pupils to do?

JOE   *[Emphatically]* Absolutely! We must teach those cognitive skills. But those skills
        represent just half of the cognitive skills we should teach our students. Who can
        name the other half of the cognitive skills that we should teach our pupils
        according to Bloom? *[Teachers yell out "analysis," "synthesis," and "evaluation" in
        various orders and degrees of loudness. Everybody laughs.]* It's obvious that not only
        have you studied Bloom's taxonomy, but you've learned it well. But I'll give you a
        copy of Bloom's taxonomy anyway. *[Passes out handout]*

JOY   Is it just the schools in this area that you think are failing to teach higher-order
        thinking skills, or is it all of our nation's schools?

JOE   It's a problem that's nationwide. And this isn't just what I think. There are many
        studies comparing the academic performance of students in terms of problem-
        solving skills in most of the industrialized nations of the world. Students in the U.S.
        are near the bottom in nearly every one of these studies. And the gap between our
        students and those of other nations is increasing, not decreasing. *[Teachers express
        disbelief and distress at this information.]*

ANN   But why is this? How come students from other countries learn more about
        problem-solving than our students? Our students can't be intellectually inferior.

JOE   Well, for one thing, our school year of approximately 180 days is the shortest
        school year of the group. Students from other nations attend school 280 days per
        year and attend school at least eight hours a day. We're also the only nation that
        sponsors school athletic teams, feeds students at school, and transports students to
        school. And, to make it worse, our students are the most undisciplined students in
        the world.
              Another reason is that schools in other countries really stress problem-
        solving as well as the higher-level thinking skills as represented by Bloom's levels
        4, 5, and 6. Also, we lack standardized tests to measure student gains in both the
        higher levels of Bloom's taxonomy and problem-solving skills. *[Abe raises his
        hand.]* Abe?

ABE   It that what we're going to study in this workshop—Bloom's levels 4, 5, and 6?

JOE   No, Abe, it's not. This workshop will be based on a five-step problem-solving mod that I derived from the literature and have found to be very successful in working with students in upper elementary grades, junior high, and senior high school.

JOY   Is it based on Bloom's upper levels?

JOE   Well, it involves a problem-solving model intended to help pupils learn to solve a type of problem they meet. However, in doing so they usually use the upper three levels of Bloom's Cognitive Taxonomy. Here are some handouts [distributes them] that you might find useful in helping your students learn the problem-solving model we'll be using. [Ty raises his hand.] Yes?

TY   Are you going to explain your model today?

JOE   Absolutely, I'm beginning right this minute. The first step in my model is to ident or recognize that a problem exists. This may seem obvious, but pupils are often given an assignment that contains no apparent problem. Students like to solve problems. And when students are given a problem to solve, they usually employ the levels of Bloom's taxonomy.

Let me give you the remaining four steps. Step 2 is to clarify and define the problem. Step 3 is to generate possible solutions to the problem. Step 4 is to test each possible solution by examining its advantages and disadvantages. And step is to choose the best solution and implement it. A step 6 might also be added, namely, to look back at the solution and assess how well it worked.

Now, for the remainder of the workshop you'll practice using at least the fi five steps on some typical problems so that you'll have some experience that will enable you to help your students in their problem-solving activities. First, let's begin with a math problem. And, by the way, before we begin let me give you so handouts on problem-solving curriculum materials. These are copies of the COR Program and Feuerstein's Instrumental Enrichment Program.

On Monday of the week following the workshop, Lori explained the five-s problem-solving model she learned in the workshop to her sixth-grade class.

MONA   [Speaking out] That sounds neat. Are we going to get to study that way? [Other students express interest in the problem-solving approach.]

LORI   [Pleased] Yes, in fact, we're going to use the problem-solving process right now. [Passes out handout entitled Problem-Solving Exercise #1.] Listen carefully now. [Pau As you can see, your problem is to plan your family's vacation for this coming summer. Begin to work at your desks right now.

MONA   [After a long pause, speaks out] Well, what do I put down as the problem?

LORI   What did I just tell the class. The problem is . . . ?

MONA   [Questioning] Our family's summer vacation?

LORI   [Encouraging] That's right, Mona. That's your first step already done. You've identified the problem—planning your family's vacation.

MONA   But, I don't know where my family plans to go on our vacation. I don't know how much money they'd have to spend, or how they'd want to travel—

LORI   [Interrupting] Those are all good questions, Mona. You have moved to step 2 in problem-solving process—clarifying and defining the problem. How can you fin out where your family would like to go? What things do the members of your family like to do together? How does your family generally travel on your vacations? What are the things your family usually spends money on, and how much do they usually spend?

MONA   Do you mean I have to plan transportation, the activities that we will do, where we're going to stay, how much money it will cost, and all those other things you asked? *[Lori nods her head in the affirmative.]* Gosh! That's really a lot of work!

LORI   But those are things that most families do when they plan a vacation. It's part of problem-solving. When you learn problem-solving skills, you learn to plan things very effectively. *[To Mona]* Do you think you can take it from here and start to plan your vacation now?

MONA   *[Hesitantly]* Yes, I guess I can do that. But it's a lot more work than I thought it would be when you first explained problem-solving.

LORI   But after you practice solving problems on your own, you'll learn to do it faster and eventually it'll become automatic. *[Approaches another student]* LeRoy, how are you doing?

LEROY   *[Shaking his head despondently]* Not too good, Ms. Hart.

LORI   What seems to be the trouble?

LEROY   Well, Dad's been talking about all of us goin' to visit my uncle in Detroit this summer, so can that be identifying the problem?

LORI   *[Smiling]* Yes, LeRoy. That's what you need to plan for. Now what questions do you need to ask to clarify and define the problem?

LEROY   I don't know. Do you mean like are we going in our car?

LORI   Yes. How you're going to get there is an important question to answer. What are some other questions you need to answer?

LEROY   *[Thinks for a while]* I guess when we'll go and how long we'll stay. And what special things we'll do while we're there. I want to see a baseball game.

LORI   *[Pleased]* See, you did have some questions to ask, and those are important questions, LeRoy. You're breaking your big problem down into sub-problems. I think you're going to be a good problem-solver. *[Sees Dot raise her hand and walks over to her desk]*

DOT   Ms. Hart. My Mom and I go to visit Mom's college roommate every summer. She's nice, but her son Mike's a real brat. He's my age and he teases me the whole time I'm there. And that can really be a problem.

LORI   *[Chuckling]* Yes, Dot. I agree that could be a problem.

DOT   But what questions could I put down about that?

LORI   Well, there are lots of questions you could ask. Maybe you should ask what you can plan to do or say to Mike to help the two of you get along better. But, I have a feeling that since you're both a year older, you'll get along better this year.

DOT   Maybe so. I hope so. *[Blushing]* Mike's really cute. Thanks, Ms. Hart.

After school on Friday afternoon, Lori sees Ann walking toward the parking lot. She calls out to her, and Ann stops and waits for her.

ANN   How's your class doing with the problem-solving?

LORI   Not bad. The problem I gave them is to plan a summer vacation for their family.

ANN   That's a good problem. It's something they all can relate to and will involve subjec matter from several areas.

LORI   Yes, but most of them had trouble getting started. They wanted me to give them the questions to ask. But I refused to do that. Instead I asked them what they needed to know in order to plan their vacation. All of them could think of a few things they needed to know, so that got them started. Most of them are doing well now. How about your students?

ANN   An interesting situation has developed. On Monday following our workshop with Joe Sligo, I'd planned to present them with a problem which basically involved math skills. I reviewed the steps in the problem-solving model and was just ready to introduce the math problem when Julie Oxley raised her hand and asked me if used the five steps when I have to make decisions or plan something. I explained that I didn't really learn the model on the handout I gave the class until I went to the problem-solving workshop, but that after I attended the workshop I realized that I've been using that technique on many problems I face. As an example, I explained to them that I'm in charge of the sixth grade end-of-the-year party in mid-December this year.

LORI   Yes, I read that in last week's newsletter. *[Smiling]* Aren't you the lucky one? I'll help you plan it. That'll really require a lot of work.

ANN   Thanks. I'll need all the help I can get! There are so many problems I have to sol before I can organize that party that I plan to begin work on it right away. In fact, told my students that I planned to use the problem-solving model to begin my planning for the party. At that point Julie said, "Why don't you assign the plannin of the party to our class as a problem-solving project?" The other members of the class thought that was a wonderful idea.

LORI   Well, I agree with them. But that might be too difficult a problem for them to tackle!

ANN   I agree. But they wanted to try anyhow.

LORI   That's fascinating. What happened?

ANN   We devoted an entire class period to asking questions that they thought were pertinent to identifying the problems involved in putting on the party. Amy Head copied down the questions.

LORI   There must have been a lot of them.

ANN   Yes. After they got started there were. But at first the students kept asking me to give them questions. And if they did have a question, they wanted me to answer

LORI   That's interesting. The very same thing happened in my class. But when I insiste that they ask the questions, they slowly began to get the idea. Then they went wi asking questions.

ANN   *[Smiling]* The very same thing happened in my class. For about ten minutes we didn't have a question. But in the next thirty minutes, Amy had copied eighty-sev questions.

LORI   That's fascinating! What did you do with eighty-seven questions?

ANN   We used them to break the problem down into sub-problems. Amy and Julie agreed to combine the questions into categories and present them in class the next day.

LORI   And?

ANN   They ended up with seven general categories: entertainment, refreshments, gift exchange, room arrangements, decorations, publicity, and cleanup.

LORI   Well, those categories seem to cover most of the problem areas that I can think of. How are you going to use the categories?

ANN   Again the students came up with a plan. All the students in the class will select the category group they'd like to work with. Then the members of each category will go through the problem-solving process again and generate more questions that need to be answered in their specific category.

LORI   *[Interrupting]* And then each member will be responsible for one or maybe more of the individual categories. Neat! You've not only taught them the first two steps in the problem-solving model, but you've also taught them how to break a comprehensive problem down into sub-problems. Since I'll be helping you with the party, I'll be able to see how it works out. I have a feeling it'll really be effective.

The next day, students in Lori's class are working on their problem-solving project at their desks. Lori notices four boys in the back of the room obviously making comments about a rather physically well-developed girl in the class.

TOM   I'd say that Corinne definitely has the biggest ones in class.

BARRY   Yes she does. I dare you to tell her that.

TOM   Tell her what?

JIM   Man, just tell her she has a great body!

TOM   She'd tell on me and I'd get into trouble.

BARRY   No she wouldn't. She'd love it. You want to go out with her, don't you?

TOM   You know it, man. I think she's definitely foxy!

BARRY   Then tell her you like her body and ask her to go out with you. I tell you, man, she'll think you're cool. She'll know you're interested in her.

Before Lori can walk to the back of the room, Tom goes over to Corinne's desk. He leans down, smiles, and whispers into her ear. Corinne shakes her head "No," tears up, buries her head on her desk, and begins to cry.

LORI   *[Walks over to Corinne]* What's wrong, Corinne?

CORINNE It's OK, Ms. Hart. I just don't feel very good. My stomach's upset. *[Brightens up]* I'll be all right.

LORI   OK, but if there's anything I can do to make you feel better, just let me know. *[Lori notices the boy and his friends smiling conspiratorially.]*

Lori stops by Ann's class after school.

LORI   Hi, Ann.

FIGURE 16   Problem-Solving Handout to Lori Hart's Sixth-Grade Class

PROBLEM-SOLVING EXERCISES #1

When you solve a problem, there are five, and sometimes six, steps involved: (1) identify or recognize that a problem exists; (2) clarify and define the problem; (3) generate possible solutions to the problem; (4) test each possible solution by examining its advantages and disadvantages; and (5) choose the best solution and carry it out. A sixth step, if possible, would be to look back at the solution later and see how well it worked.

Your first assignment is for you to plan a vacation for your family next summer. You must: (1) decide where to go so that everyone in your family will have a good time; (2) decide what things to do while you are there; (3) decide what dates are involved and what you plan to do each day; (4) decide where you are going to stay and eat; (5) decide how you are going to travel to all the places involved; (6) give all the information on making all reservations needed for travel, housing, and admissions to planned activities; (7) give a complete budget of all expenses involved.

Since this assignment will call for you to obtain information from your family members and various travel agencies, you will have one month from today to complete it. (Due in class on Monday the 15th) Some time will be given in class to work on this project, including working with other students in small groups and sharing information.

ANN   Hi, Lori. Thanks for stopping by. What's up?

LORI   I have a problem I want you to help me with.

ANN   Well, you've come to the right place. I recently attended a workshop on problem solving, you know. What's the problem?

LORI   *[Describes the incident involving Corinne in great detail]* So, Dr. Ann, I'm not sure what to do. Should I just ignore the situation? Corinne didn't ask for help, and I guess boys will be boys. On the other hand, I think they believe they've put one over on me, and they really did upset Corinne. They might do something worse i just let this go. What should I do?

QUESTIONS

1. What is problem-solving? Is Dr. Sligo's six-step problem-solving model a curr view of the problem-solving process or a historical one? How can it be updated in ter of current literature?

2. How do experts and novices differ in the way they approach and solve proble• How can Ann and Lori take this into consideration in teaching problem-solving skills sixth graders?

3. What is Bloom's Cognitive Taxonomy? How do the six levels of the taxonomy re• to problem-solving?

4. What instructional objectives is Lori pursuing with her vacation-planning activity? What levels of Bloom's taxonomy are involved? How do these levels relate to the six steps in Dr. Sligo's problem-solving model?

5. What did Dr. Sligo mean when he said that tests weren't available to measure either the upper levels of Bloom's taxonomy or problem-solving skills? Is this true? If so, what are the implications for educational goals, instructional objectives, and the measurement of teacher effectiveness?

6. What is academic learning time, and how important is it? Do students in other nations, such as Japan, have longer school days and school years? What are the implications of this for the amount of academic learning time? What are the implications of Dr. Sligo's statement about the lack of discipline in American students for academic learning time?

7. What is an early developer? How can early physical development in a girl like Corinne affect her self-concept and school achievement? Why did the four boys behave the way they did toward Corinne?

8. What classroom management models work best with sixth graders? How effective would a technique like Teacher Effectiveness Training be in Lori's class? How well would Method III, the six-step problem-solving conflict-resolution process, fit in with the problem-solving learning activities?

9. Dr. Sligo gave the teachers in his workshop copies of the CORT and Feuerstein problem-solving materials. What are they, and how well would they work with Lori's sixth-grade class?

10. What advice should Ann give Lori about handling the situation between the four boys and Corinne? Can Lori apply the six-step problem-solving model to this situation? What solutions might Lori try? To what extent does the job of teaching involve effective problem-solving?

WHICH IS HIGHER?

Key Content to Consider for Analyzing This Case
(1) Bloom's Cognitive Taxonomy; (2) problem-solvir
(3) cognitive theory (information processing, Ausub
Bruner, constructivism); (4) motivation (intrinsic vs.
extrinsic); (5) creativity; (6) measurement and
evaluation (objective vs. essay tests).

T he Queen's Island School District is located in a large urban area in the No
eastern part of the United States. Approximately one-third of the student po
lation served by the school district is comprised of minority racial and/or etl
groups. There are six senior high schools (grades 10–12) in the district, and each has c
sen a social studies teacher to represent it on the school district's committee to revise
secondary history curriculum.

Dr. Tom Blakely, the social studies curriculum director for the school district,
the task of chairing the committee. He has arranged for it to meet in a comfortable c
ference room in the downtown and centrally located school board and administra
offices complex. After the usual handshaking, greetings, and backslapping has died do
each teacher takes a seat in a comfortable leather chair around a long, rectangular woc
table. Tom stands at one end of the table in front of his chair and gently taps the t
with his knuckles to call the meeting to order.

TOM   *[Smiling]* As you all know, each of you has been selected by your school to assi
the revision of our social studies curriculum. This year we'll focus on our histor
courses. All of your schools require world history the sophomore year, U.S. hist
the junior year, and offer elective courses like Non-Western Cultures the senior
year. We'll begin our work by considering revisions for our world history course
Perhaps we should begin by introducing ourselves. I'll start, and we'll go arounc
the table beginning on my left. *[Sits down in his chair]* I'm Tom Blakely, the social
studies curriculum director, or should I say coordinator, for our district. I can ne
remember which title is correct. This is my third year in the job. I used to be a
social studies teacher at Central High. *[Applause from Eric, the Central High
representative, while others smile and laugh]*

ERIC   *[Smiling]* See what high-quality people we hire at Central?

TOM   Thank you, Eric. I can truthfully say that I really enjoyed my years at Central.
[Nods to Luis on his left]

Lᴜɪs   I'm Luis Garcia from Garfield High. My favorite course is U.S. history.

Eʀɪᴄ   Well, I'm Eric Tannenbaum from Central High, the home of the Fighting Cougars, state champions in basketball. *[Good-natured cheers and jeers]*

Loɪs   I'm Lois Blakely from Van Buren High, and no, Dr. Blakely and I are neither married nor relatives. We just happen to have the same last name.

Lᴇᴇ   I'm Lee Cheng from Kennedy High, and let me add that Central was lucky to beat Kennedy with a last-minute field goal in the tournament. *[All laugh.]*

Dᴇʟɪᴄɪᴀ   *[With reserve]* I'm Delicia Jackson from South Point High.

Mɪᴄʜᴇʟʟᴇ   *[With enthusiasm]* I'm Michelle McMurray from Westside High. We don't win many athletic championships, but we do have more National Merit Finalists than any other high school in the district. Now let me hear you top that, Eric! *[Everyone laughs.]*

Toᴍ   *[Stands back up and passes out packets of material to the teachers to his left and right to pass on down.]* Let me hand out these packets on our world history course and give you the assignment of studying them carefully and meeting back here next week at the same time and place to begin our consideration of revisions. We'll need to agree on textbooks, objectives, teaching methods, evaluation procedures, and so forth. I'll adjourn the meeting now so we can all go to the back of the room and enjoy the refreshments provided for us by Ms. Wiggins, the superintendent's secretary, and get to know one another better! *[Polite applause]*

It is two weeks later. Tom had to postpone the previous week's meeting due to requests for more time to read the curriculum materials handed out at the first meeting.

Toᴍ   *[Smiling]* Good morning. I trust that everyone has had a chance to look over the world history curriculum materials. Any comments?

Mɪᴄʜᴇʟʟᴇ   Yes. I for one was very surprised at how, what shall I say, factually oriented the whole thing was. The emphasis seems to be on getting the students to memorize people, places, dates, battles, and so forth. No wonder I hear some students say they can't stand history. I hope this committee is going to make some serious changes in our world history program! *[Delicia and Lois voice their agreement.]*

Eʀɪᴄ   *[Agitated]* What are you talking about, Michelle?! The committee that developed these curriculum materials spent many long hours and a lot of hard work in the process. I know because I was on it! What's wrong with asking our students to learn a few facts?

Mɪᴄʜᴇʟʟᴇ   No offense, Eric, and I'm sure that all of you worked very hard. But memorized facts don't stick with students very long. Now, principles learned in a context that students can relate to can stick with them for life.

Eʀɪᴄ   I suppose that you're going to tell us that historical facts don't matter! A lot of our students would have done a lot better on standardized tests and had college scholarships today if their teachers had insisted on a bit more rigor in their learning. Fun and games are motivating enough at the time, but later on the student wonders why he's never heard of Charles Martel or the Battle of Tours, much less its significance in determining whether Europe became Christian or Moslem.

MICHELLE   Eric, I'm not saying that who Charles Martel was or what the significance of the Battle of Tours was is not important. I'm saying that there's more than one way of getting students to learn and remember such information. Just telling them to memorize facts because they're going to be tested over them is no guarantee that they'll remember them later on when they take a standardized test.

ERIC   Are you advocating discovery learning? Do you want us to waste our time finding ways to help kids discover the facts of history?

MICHELLE   No, I'm not, Eric. I guess I probably use more of a problem-solving approach in my classes. Perhaps it does involve some discovery, but not in the sense that I think you mean. No, I guess that I'm talking about higher-order rather than lower-order learning. That certainly involves presenting facts in a larger context so that they're more likely to be remembered and applied.

TOM   Let me jump in here. Michelle, when you say higher-order learning are you referring to Bloom's Cognitive Taxonomy?

MICHELLE   Why, yes, that would certainly be involved.

TOM   *[Passing out handout]* Then let me pass out this handout on Bloom's taxonomy. Perhaps it will help provide a framework for some of our discussion.

ERIC   *[Looking at handout]* Yes, I remember this. And the upper levels are important, but the problem is that students have to learn the lower-level stuff before they can do the higher-order type of thinking.

MICHELLE   I beg to disagree. The real problem is that we have always just taught history at the first two or three levels. We never get to the upper levels. Teachers always say that they're important and then go back to having their students memorize facts.

ERIC   Everything I've ever read on creative thinking, your level 5 or synthesis level here, says that for a person to think creatively he must have a knowledge base of information to draw from. In other words, level 5 isn't possible without levels 1 and 2.

MICHELLE   You're not hearing what I'm saying, Eric. I'm not saying levels 1 and 2 aren't important. I'm saying that levels 1 and 2 are all that we teach. We don't even try levels 4, 5, and 6. Sometimes I'm not even sure of level 3.

ERIC   Who says I don't teach anything beyond level 2? Speak for yourself, Michelle!

MICHELLE   I never said anything about your teaching, Eric! Don't put words in my mouth! But since you brought it up, give me an example of higher-order learning one of your world history classes.

ERIC   *[Puzzled]* Yeah, well, I guess I'd have to think about that for a minute. *[Angrily]* Well, tell us what you do at the higher levels, Michelle.

MICHELLE   I'd be glad to, but I'll bet that you and I don't use the same types of teaching methods, and I'll bet we give different types of tests. You see, I think problem-solving and creativity are important and are the real instructional objectives that aiming for and trying to teach toward. Other teachers aren't really aiming toward them, and you can tell it in their teaching methods and testing procedures. For example—

TOM   *[Interrupting]* Let me jump in at this point and stop you, Michelle, as important and fascinating as this discussion is. Our time is up, but perhaps we could all look at our own instructional objectives, teaching methods, and evaluation procedures, as well as those of our fellow teachers, and see if we can't begin to come to some resolutions of our differences next time. See you next week.

It is one week later. In the meantime, all six teachers have informally surveyed fellow teachers in their building regarding the issues discussed at the last meeting.

TOM   OK, I understand that some of you took me seriously and polled your fellow teachers about some of the issues raised by Eric and Michelle at our last meeting. Perhaps we should begin by sharing the results.

MICHELLE   I have the results for Lois, Delicia, and I, and I must admit that I was somewhat surprised. Roughly two-thirds of the history teachers agree with what Eric said.

ERIC   And the other third teach like you. That's about what Luis, Lee, and I found, only it's more like one-fourth and three-fourths. So that ought to tell you what the majority of our history teachers feel is important. I strongly urge us to yield to their wisdom and their collective majority by following their wishes in designing our program.

MICHELLE   The majority isn't automatically always right, and it's often a minority that brings needed change to institutions in our society. Might I point out to my fellow history teachers that those who favored independence were in the minority in American society before the Revolutionary War began. [Pause] In any case, Eric, let me ask you a question or two about the best way to teach history. What teaching method do you use mostly in your classes?

ERIC   Oh, lecture-discussion without question. And I make no apology for that. It's the best and most efficient way to present information. I try to organize my lectures and discussions so that I go from the general to the particular and from the simple to the complex. I might add that I do have my students do reports in small groups, and we do bring in and discuss current events. But lecture-discussion is the most common way I teach.

MICHELLE   Do you give mostly objective tests?

ERIC   Yes, I do. Multiple choice, matching, fill-in-the-blank, and usually, but not always, one essay. I hardly ever give true-false.

MICHELLE   Do you give quizzes?

ERIC   Yes, usually ten objective questions each Friday.

MICHELLE   What would be an example of one of your essay questions?

ERIC   One that I gave on my last test was: "Give and explain three reasons why Rome defeated Carthage in the Punic Wars."

MICHELLE   Did you go over and discuss three reasons in class?

ERIC   Yes, of course. In great detail. I considered it to be important material.

MICHELLE   Would you say that most of your test questions are like that one?

ERIC   Yes, pretty much.

MICHELLE   And how would you grade a question like that?

ERIC   By how close the answer comes to covering all the important points that we went over in class.

MICHELLE   Then even your essay questions are at the first level of Bloom's taxonomy. T
kids don't have to look anything up independently or discover anything on their
own. They just memorize and repeat back what you stress as important.

ERIC   But Michelle, I don't have time to go over material that isn't important and let
them fool around trying to discover stuff on their own. I present or discuss the
material in the most understandable way I can, and then I test them over it to se
if they got it. Why should I let them fumble around trying to grasp material tha
can explain to them so that they can understand it? Why should I waste their
time and my time. After all, there's only so much learning time in a school day.
Why waste it?

MICHELLE   Maybe so that what you're teaching the students will be remembered after
the exam is over. If what you're teaching them isn't meaningful to them and isn't
understood by them in a form they can relate to and remember, it's forgotten with
forty-eight hours after the test is over.

ERIC   I don't believe that is so, but pray tell us poor misguided teachers the right way t
teach. I suppose that you let your students discover the answers for themselves.

TOM   Let me break in here, Eric and Michelle. I feel that this, shall I call it a debate, is
right on target as far as our task as a committee is concerned. Do the rest of you
agree? *[All teachers nod or voice agreement.]* If we can settle these issues, we can get
down to the job of writing. Please proceed, Michelle, and tell us how you teach
world history.

MICHELLE   I make the assumption that what students learn in my class won't stay with
them very long unless they see its relevance to their lives and are able to connect
to what they already know. So I use a problem-solving approach in my world
history classes. I ask my students individually and in small groups to focus on
problem areas that interest them about each unit we study. As we discuss a unit o
say, ancient Egypt or ancient Greece, students give their reports as their problem
areas come up, and the rest of the students ask them as well as me questions as w
discuss the material. I do very little lecturing and really don't take center stage
during the discussions.

TOM   Like what kinds of problems, Michelle?

MICHELLE   Like I said, students choose problem areas that interest them. One of the
most popular ones with boys is: "How has the art of warfare changed?" The girls
like: "How has the role of women in society changed?" Other problems focus on
things like the best form of government, the nature of communications, the form
that the arts take, or religion, the family, education, recreation and sports, why
people become famous, and so forth.

ERIC   What do you do about the areas that the students need to know about but don't
choose as problems?

MICHELLE   I try to fill those in myself by bringing them up. Hardly anyone ever choose
business and commerce or transportation, for example. But even if we leave some
gaps by not covering material thoroughly, the material that we do cover sticks wit
them longer than just until the next test. For one thing, I notice that the students
consistently choose the same problem areas. Boys interested in the art of warfare i
ancient Egypt become intrigued with how the Greeks changed it and then the

Romans. This often encourages them to read books in the library on their topics, so they go beyond the text.

ERIC   And I suppose that you're going to tell us that you primarily test them on the material that the students present.

MICHELLE   Not only that, I have each student or problem-solving group write test questions over the material that they present in class at the end of their presentation, and I often use some of their questions in my own tests.

TOM   What kinds of test questions, Michelle?

MICHELLE   Oh, most of my questions are essay that I deliberately focus at all six levels of Bloom's taxonomy. I also try to make sure that the questions I ask in class during our discussions focus on all six levels. It's one thing to ask students a level 1 question like "Who was the Spartan king who commanded the Greek troops at the Battle of Thermopylae?" and quite another to ask a level 5 question like "Create a battle plan that Xerxes, the Persian King, could have used to defeat the Greek troops in one day at Thermopylae."

TOM   So the students usually write essay questions to go with their reports?

MICHELLE   *[Pondering]* Both essay and objective. To tell you the truth, I'd say they write more multiple choice than any other type.

ERIC   And I suppose their questions cover all six levels of Bloom's taxonomy.

MICHELLE   No, of course not. I think it's just easier for them to write and ask the other students objective-type questions.

ERIC   In all honesty I can see why your students would enjoy your classes, Michelle, but it would really bother me to teach that way. First, I don't buy your assumptions that what your students learn would stay with them longer. I'll bet my students do better on the SAT than yours, or if not the SAT, any standardized test that covers social studies that you want to name. But also, your coverage can't be as thorough and as in-depth as mine. I think that focusing on problem areas like that would leave a number of content gaps either not covered or just barely covered. Finally, just using those problem-solving types of projects and all the reporting and discussing would take up tremendous amounts of class time. Your approach is interesting, but a more traditional approach makes more sense for most teachers.

MICHELLE   *[Angrily]* Again I ask, what good is coverage if the kids forget most of what you teach because they're bored out of their skulls or are half asleep? We've been teaching history that way for too many years! It's time our school district made some changes!

TOM   OK, let me jump in here. We appreciate very much the two of you sharing what you do. But what about the rest of you? What direction do you feel we should move in, or should we attempt some compromise?

LUIS   I agree with Eric. His approach makes sense for most of the teachers in this school district.

LEE   And I agree with Eric as well. That's how I teach as well.

TOM   Are you going to make it unanimous, Lois?

LOIS   Absolutely not! What I do isn't exactly the same as Michelle, but close to it. Only if students are allowed to get themselves into what they're learning is it going to stick with them.

BLOOM'S COGNITIVE TAXONOMY

1.00 KNOWLEDGE

The ability to remember, recall, or recognize. Often rote memory. Student responds without necessarily understanding the material.

Objective: Students will be able to orally spell correctly 80% of the words dictated to them by the teacher.

2.00 COMPREHENSION

The ability to respond with understanding. Student is able to translate or restate information in other words. Student not only receives the information but is able to use it.

Objective: Students will be able to define correctly in his or her own words 70% of a list of 50 words presented on a teacher-made written test.

3.00 APPLICATION

The ability to use rules, principles, and abstractions in problem-solving.

Objective: Given ten rectangles on a teacher-made written test, the student will be able to write correctly with 90% accuracy the area of each rectangle by applying the formula $A = L \times W$.

4.00 ANALYSIS

The ability to break down a problem into its elements and to identify the relevant elements in a problem. Emphasis is on breaking down a whole into its elements and then correctly applying a principle to solve the problem.

Objective: After reading at least five books from the reading list, students will be able to write, in not more than two sentences each, at least four major causes of World War II with 75% accuracy as judged by the teacher.

5.00 SYNTHESIS

The capability to work with elements of a problem and to combine these elements into a new whole. The student must express his or her own ideas, and the product is typically a "new" or "creative" statement.

Objective: Given copies of examples of cubism in Picasso's paintings and pointillism in Renoir's paintings, the student will combine at least three elements of each of these two techniques by creating a painting that expresses at least three of the following feelings: happiness, surprise, sadness, anger, love.

6.00 EVALUATION

The ability to make qualitative and quantitative judgments about the adequacy of materials. These judgments must be supported by reasons which draw upon principles, rules, facts, and modes of analysis.

Objective: Given a video tape of the president's two most recent public addresses, the student will in written form rate the speeches on a seven-point scale in terms of eye contact, persuasiveness, clarity of expression, voice modulation, and physical gesturing.

DELICIA   I agree with Lois. I got a lot of good ideas just listening to Michelle, and I hope you don't mind, Michelle, if I use some of them in my classes.

MICHELLE   *[Smiling]* Not at all, Delicia. I've certainly borrowed enough from teachers I have known.

TOM   Well, it sounds like we're divided right down the middle on this. We don't seem to agree on instructional objectives, teaching methods, or evaluation procedures! Can any of you creative individuals see any way that we can synthesize or combine these two different approaches? *[No response. Three women and one man shake their heads negatively.]* No creativity here?

MICHELLE   Maybe none of our education professors let us think at the upper levels of Bloom's taxonomy when we took our course work. Where are students going to learn to think creatively if we don't ever give them a chance to do so in their classes?

TOM   I hear what you're saying, Michelle, but this committee is hopelessly divided. Don't any of you have any ideas on how to help us get off dead center? Do both sides have to be 100% right? Can anybody give a little here?

QUESTIONS

1. Michelle argues that students are more likely to forget factual material than principles. Is that true? In what forms can facts and principles be presented to increase their retention? What research has been done on "forgetting curves"?

2. Eric argues that Michelle's approach wastes learning time in the classroom. What is academic learning time in the classroom? What differences have been found between American and Japanese students with regard to academic learning time?

3. Examine this case from the perspective of information processing theory. Explain Eric's and Michelle's positions from the standpoint of sensory register, short-term memory, and long-term memory. What is forgetting from a the standpoint of retrieval theory?

4. What is meaningful learning? What are derivative and correlative subsumers from Ausubel's cognitive theory, and how might they be used to explain meaningfulness? What is reception learning, and does it come closest to what Eric or Michelle is doing in the classroom?

5. Examine this case from the perspective of Jerome Bruner's cognitive theory. What are coding systems and categories, and how are they different from Ausubel's organizers? What are discovery learning and the spiral curriculum according to Bruner, and whose method of teaching would they best relate to—Eric's or Michelle's?

6. What is constructivism? Would viewing the learner as acting upon his or her environment be more compatible with what Eric or Michelle is doing? What is the zone of proximal development? What are instructional scaffolds? How could these constructs help either teacher?

7. What instructional objectives do Eric and Michelle seem to be pursuing in world history? Does the distinction between process and product objectives help explain the differences in their teaching methods?

8. What differences exist between Michelle and Eric with regard to their orientatic toward Bloom's Cognitive Taxonomy? How do their teaching and evaluation procedu differ with regard to Bloom's taxonomy?

9. Michelle argues that her approach to teaching is more intrinsically motivating students and will therefore result in greater content retention. What is motivation? Wl is the relationship between motivation and retention?

10. Michelle favors a problem-solving approach to teaching. What is problem-solvi and how is it best taught? Do problem-solving approaches increase transfer of learnin

11. What are mnemonic devices? What are the keyword, peg word, and loci methoc Can such devices increase content retention? Would they be useful to either Eric Michelle?

12. Eric and Michelle seem to differ on the value of objective and essay tests. Wl are the strengths and weaknesses of each? Which is most useful in measuring the typ of cognitive productions at the different levels of Bloom's taxonomy?

13. What is creativity? Is Eric correct in asserting that creativity depends on a defin knowledge base? How does Bloom's taxonomy define creativity? Whose approach teaching—Eric's or Michelle's—would best foster creativity?

14. What advice would you give Tom and the committee about resolving the diff ences that have emerged? Which position do you favor, and why?

TEAMWORK

Key Content to Consider for Analyzing This Case:
(1) cooperative learning; (2) motivation (intrinsic vs. extrinsic); (3) cultural diversity.

For three years, Dr. Howard Deeble has been principal of Fort Henry Middle School, which is located on the eastern border of a state in the Midwest. He applied for the position and was accepted the year after he completed his Ed.D. in school administration at the state's major university. Prior to earning his doctorate, Howard had taught science for five years at Winters Middle School, which served an upper-middle-class population in the northern part of the state.

Fort Henry Middle School was built thirty years ago in what was, at that time, a white middle-class suburb of a relatively small city. Since then, the city has quadrupled in area and the population has increased from 25,000 to 150,000. The student population of Fort Henry has increased from approximately 200 to 500, and changed from predominately upper middle class to lower middle class, with a sizable low-income component. The racial/ethnic distribution of the school population is approximately 60% white, 30% African-American, 5% Hispanic, and 5% other.

Howard conducted his doctoral dissertation study—"The Administration and Evaluation of a Cooperative Learning Program in a Middle School"—while he was teaching in his previous position. One of the significant findings of the study was that the use of cooperative learning significantly increased the number of science concepts learned by the students in the cooperative learning program.

This morning he recalled his dissertation study when he read in the local newspaper that one of his former professors from State University is conducting a workshop on cooperative learning the following Friday evening and all day Saturday at the local high school. Although he realizes that the student population at Fort Henry is substantially different from the pupil population at Winters, he wonders whether the cooperative learning approach might improve the performance of his students at Fort Henry. Eventually, he makes up his mind to see if some of his teachers would be willing to give it a try. Since school has been in session for less than a month, he believes that there is ample time to make the necessary arrangements to implement a new program. He decides to talk it over

with Paul Mobley, a teacher he had taught with at his last position and had brought wit
him to Fort Henry.

The following morning before classes started, Howard went to Paul's homeroom
and asked if the two of them could meet in Paul's office during the second period, which
is Paul's free period. Paul agreed to do so and arrived at Howard's office at the appointe
time.

HOWARD   Thanks for meeting with me on such short notice, Paul. I need to get your
advice on something I'm considering.

PAUL   I'm glad you asked. We haven't had much time to visit since classes started.
What's up?

HOWARD   We've talked before about how poorly some of our students perform
academically, and I've been trying to think of ways we could improve their
performance.

PAUL   Well, I'm with you so far. Have you come up with any ideas?

HOWARD   Yes, I have. This morning I read in the paper that one of the professors I
studied with at the university is conducting a workshop on cooperative learning
next weekend at the high school. The article caused me to reminisce about the
cooperative learning program we started at Winters five years ago.

PAUL   *[Pleased]* That was a good program. It worked really well with those students. But
the students here at Fort Henry are a far cry from those at Winters. We have so
many slow pupils. Do you think they could work cooperatively with other
students?

HOWARD   I really don't know, but it might be worth trying. What do you think?

PAUL   Well, you know me well enough to know I'm a skeptic. But it might be worth
running a pilot study with one class in several subject areas rather than
implementing it throughout the entire school. That way you could handpick the
teachers who seem to have good potential for coordinating that type of program.

HOWARD   *[Smiling]* I knew there was a reason I thought I should talk with you about thi
before I made any great plans. That's an excellent suggestion! Do you have any
teachers you'd like to recommend for the pilot group?

PAUL   Yes, I do. I think we should begin the program in the sixth grade. That way if it's
successful the pupils in the program can continue it in seventh and eighth grade. I
you choose to expand the program, the other classes can begin the following year.
It would also give you an opportunity to select the teachers who could best handle
that type of program.

HOWARD   Great suggestions! Would you be willing to be one of those teachers?

PAUL   Yes, I'd like to try cooperative learning with my fourth-period social studies class.
And if I could pick three teachers I'd like to work with, I'd recommend Cindy Baza
for English, Kim Tease for math, and Tanya Justin for science. They're far and away
the best teachers in the school to help start a program like this. They like each
other and work together well. And I can work well with all of them.

HOWARD   They're all excellent choices. Would you be willing to talk with them about th
program and see if they're interested? If they are, all four of you will need to attend

that workshop next weekend. The school will pay the registration fees and any other expenses you incur.

PAUL   Sure, I'll check with them. If there's a problem, I'll get back to you. If there's no problem, we'll just plan to attend the workshop and begin planning to implement the program.

HOWARD   Thanks, Paul. I knew I could count on you.

The four teachers attended the cooperative learning workshop, and have since met together several times as a team. After reviewing the various programs presented, the teachers selected the STAD (Student Teams—Achievement Divisions) approach. Each teacher selected one sixth-grade class to teach by forming the class into student teams consisting of one high performer, one low performer, and two average performers. Teams will also be heterogeneous with regard to socioeconomic status (SES), gender, and ethnicity. The teams are organized in this manner to encourage cooperation and reduce competition. The teachers will present a lesson and then the students work within their teams to make sure that all team members learn the material presented. Peer tutoring is used within the teams to help students who have trouble completing an assignment. In that way the students learn to cooperate on the overall project. Finally, the students take individual quizzes over the materials. Each student's quiz scores are compared with his or her own past averages. Points are then awarded based on the extent to which students meet or exceed their earlier performance.

Tanya Justin's science class is beginning a unit on "The Plant Kingdom." Today, Tanya distributes a copy of the first lesson to each student in the class (see lesson plan on page 172).

TANYA   Now, I want you to get together with the members of your group. Use this lesson plan as a study guide. Remember that this is a group project. It's the responsibility of the group members to make sure that every member of the group completes the assignments and is able to pass the test I'll give at the end of the lesson.

FU   *[Raising his hand] [Tanya nods to him.]* Ms. Justin, I have a problem with this project.

TANYA   *[In an understanding tone]* What's the problem, Fu?

FU   Do we have to work in our groups? I'd much rather work alone. I do a lot better when I'm able to work on my own.

SUSAN   *[Speaking out]* Yes, I agree with Fu, Ms. Justin. I think groups waste too much time talking about other things and messing around, especially if you get in a group with people who aren't interested in learning anything.

EMILIO   *[Laughing]* Are you talking about me, Susie?

WILL   *[Interrupting]* I agree with Susan. Every time I've been in a class where they've worked in groups it's turned out to be a big waste of time.

SUSAN   That's right. The lazy or dumb people slow everything down. Those of us who want to work hard have to do all the work!

ANGEL   *[Laughing]* Yeah. People like me slow down all you smart guys, and you don't like that.

WILL   You're right, Angel. I don't like it. I don't come here to waste time.

TANYA   *[Jumping quickly into the discussion]* Well, I'm in sort of a bind about the cooperative groups. Dr. Deeble asked four of us teachers to participate in an experiment with cooperative learning groups in our classes. I went to a workshop last weekend and learned how to do it, and I feel that I must keep my word and have you work in groups.

FU   Maybe you could let some of us work alone if we want to and then see how we do compared with people who worked in groups.

TANYA   There are other classes in the research project. Dr. Deeble is comparing the performance of our class and the other three experimental classes to that of all the other classes that aren't using cooperative learning. So, it isn't possible to let any o you work alone, because it would affect the results of the experiment.

SUSAN   Aren't people who do studies supposed to get some kind of permission from th people in the study?

TANYA   *[Cautiously]* I think that's true only when the experimental group is not doing tl same thing as the other groups. In this study all the classes are studying the same topics.

SUSAN   But we're doing it a different way.

TANYA   Probably every class in Fort Henry is different from every other class just because each teacher teaches differently from every other teacher.

SUSAN   Well, it somehow doesn't seem right to be forced into working in a group wher you don't know whether or not you'll learn that way.

Paul's cooperative learning students are reviewing map and globe skills prior their study of the world's earliest people. He has already divided the class into six stude teams of five pupils each. He has given every student a lesson plan that they're expecte to follow.

NAVADO   *[Shouts out]* Mr. Mobley. I'm supposed to explain what a map legend is and make one for this map I'm drawing. I don't know what a map legend is.

CRYSTAL   *[Sarcastically]* Unfold your sample map and look at the legend on the bottom dummy!

PAUL   OK, Crystal. That's enough of that kind of talk.

CRYSTAL   *[Offended]* Well, Navado's dumber than a box of hair. *[To Navado]* Unfold the map Mr. Mobley gave you. *[Navado unfolds it.]* Now, look at the bottom of your map, Navado. Do you see where it says "Legend" in big letters? That's the legend.

PAUL   *[Walks over to Ting, whose hand is raised and looks at his map]* That's really a great vegetation map, Ting.

TING   Thanks. My question is, should I put the color key of the different vegetation areas on the map directly on the map or on a separate page, which I'd put next to the map?

PAUL   Good question. Usually the map keys are shown directly on the map. Put them i a place where they won't cover important information. *[Pointing]* On your map, yo could put them over that part of the ocean.

TING   *[Nodding]* Thanks. I wasn't sure what to do.

MOLLY   [*Loudly*] Stop that, Carlos! Mr. Mobley, I'm trying to make these diagrams showing the rotation of the earth around the sun during the different seasons, and Carlos keeps moving the poster paper! He's doing it on purpose.

PAUL   Carlos, you're supposed to be helping Molly, not annoying her.

CARLOS   Molly's always annoyed, Mr. Mobley. She thinks she's better than the rest of us. But it's OK with me to be out of the group. I don't like the way Molly bosses everybody around.

MOLLY   I'm not bossing you around, Carlos. I'm trying to help you learn something, but you don't even understand that, so I'm giving up. Mr. Mobley, can't those of us who want to learn something in this class either work with each other or work by ourselves? Carlos and some of his friends either can't or don't want to learn anything in here. And that's their own business. But they don't have any right to keep everybody else from learning. I'd rather work by myself and learn something!

PAUL   The purpose of working in groups is so students who know some of the information we're studying can help students who need some help.

MOLLY   That's a good idea, but what happens when you get grouped with students like Carlos who don't know anything about the topic and don't want to know anything about it?

PAUL   It'd be nice if you were able to help Carlos find something he could and would like to learn that's related to your project.

MOLLY   I don't think I could do that when no teacher's been able to do it in six years of school!

The cooperative learning teachers meet in Paul's room after school on Thursday afternoons. They have gathered for their third meeting today. This meeting is different from the others because, during the current week, eleven complaints from parents have been received by the four teachers of the cooperative classes.

PAUL   Thanks for coming so promptly. As you all know, we have a new agenda item for our meeting this afternoon.

KIM   Yes, this seems to have been the week for parent complaints. I had two.

CINDY   I think all of us had at least that many.

PAUL   We did better than that, Cindy. You, Tanya, and I all beat Kim. Each of us had three.

TANYA   I wonder why they all came this week. Do you think it was some kind of group planning?

PAUL   I doubt it. It's probably because students have a very difficult time writing reports for the first time. They have trouble selecting a topic, they don't know how to organize or write it, and they're very frustrated. So they tell their parents how terrible cooperative learning is.

KIM   What disturbs me is that my complaints were from the parents of my very best students.

TANYA   [*In chorus with Cindy and Paul*] Mine, too. [*Laughter*]

PAUL   Who were your parents who complained, Kim?

KIM   The Ryersons and the Stines—Mel's and June's parents.

PAUL   Who were those in your class, Tanya?

TANYA   Fu Kai's dad, Susan Cory's mother, and Will Picardo's dad.

PAUL   Cindy?

CINDY   Mine were the Bartlos, the Havers, and the Mazios.

PAUL   And mine were all fathers: Dr. Fang, Mr. Moses, and Mr. Mason.

KIM   It looks like a pattern, doesn't it? I could've picked all of those parents. There are three or four others who, I think, might also have complained.

PAUL   Yes, it does seem to be a pattern of the parents of our best students, Kim. And we might well hear from those other three or four parents yet.

TANYA   Mr. Kai and Ms. Cory asked if they could talk with someone about the cooperative program.

PAUL   What did you tell them?

TANYA   I told them that we were having this meeting today, and that I'd share their complaints with the teachers in the other cooperative classes. I told them I'd get back to them.

KIM   *[Laughing]* I did the same thing. Passing the buck is what its called, I think.

CINDY   None of mine asked for a meeting, but they all asked that their children be take out of the cooperative program. I told them that I'd have to check with the principal before I could make such a decision.

PAUL   That's good. We do need to reach some kind of agreement with the parents. Since I'm the team leader of the program and the one who got you all into this, why don't I check with Dr. Deeble and see what he'd think about my scheduling an evening meeting here at school for the parents who are upset. Maybe we coul come to some sort of agreement. I'm sure you'd like to come and talk with the parents of the students in your classes. So I'll get some times that you'd be available to meet and coordinate the whole thing with Dr. Deeble. In fact *[takes out a pad of paper]*, why don't you write all the evenings and times those evening that you could meet with the parents. The meeting shouldn't take more than an hour and a half.

The following Thursday evening, Paul approaches the school library at approx mately 7:15. Kim has already arrived and is waiting at the door.

PAUL   *[Unlocking the door]* Hi, Kim. You're really an early bird.

KIM   Yes, I can hardly wait to see how you're going to handle all those angry parents.

PAUL   *[Smiling]* They don't call me "Slick Paul" for nothing.

KIM   *[Retorting]* Your optimism is exceeded only by your audacity.

PAUL   *[Looking through the door]* Aha! Here come the rest of our group now, with some parents close behind! *[Walks to the door and greets Tanya, Cindy, the Ryersons, Mr. Ka and Dr. Fang. He and Dr. Fang then move three tables together and put ten chairs on eac side of the table. They wait until the remaining parents arrive.]*

PAUL   *[Raps on the table to get everyone's attention]* Welcome to Fort Henry Middle Schoo I'm Paul Mobley, and I teach social studies. *[Nodding toward each teacher, in turn]* This is Tanya Justin, science, Kim Tease, mathematics, and Cindy Bazar, English. You're all here this evening because you've expressed misunderstanding or dissatisfaction or both regarding our experimental cooperative education approach in the classes your children attend.

I'd like to give you some background information on this program and why we're using it, which might help answer some of your questions. Then, you can either meet with your child's teacher to ask further questions, or you can ask your questions to all of us and we can respond, whichever you choose.

When Dr. Deeble came to Fort Henry three years ago, he brought me with him because we'd worked well together at Winters Middle School and the idea of continuing our work relationship appealed to both of us. At Winters, we implemented this same cooperative learning program that we're using in your children's classes, and it was very successful. However, although the student body at Winters is a little different from the one here, we still thought that the program might be just as successful. And it still might prove to be. It's just in the very beginning stages at this time.

The basic concept of our cooperative learning program, which is called STAD, is to reduce competition between individual students by dividing the class into teams of four or five pupils who represent a cross-section of the class with regard to academic performance, gender, and race. All the competition is between the teams. The overall goal of each team is to prepare its members to do well on the weekly quizzes so they can score more points than the other teams. The teacher first makes a presentation of each lesson and provides worksheets and other materials for the students. Then, team members work together, quiz each other, help members who are unable to understand certain concepts, and so on. At the scheduled time the teacher tests the students over the work. Each student earns points for his or her team in relation to a base score which is an average of all previous scores. So, student scores are based on improvement rather than an arbitrary standard. That way, each student has an equal opportunity to succeed in the class and help his or her team. The whole process recycles this way every three to five days. *[Pause]*

Since the program hasn't really been in operation that long, we don't really have much real evidence on which to evaluate it yet. So, at this point I'll stop. Now, you can either ask questions to all of us, or if you prefer, you can meet individually with your child's teacher. *[Sees Ms. Ryerson raise her hand]* Ms. Ryerson.

MS. RYERSON   My son, Mel, wants to attend the International Baccalaureate Program at Central High School and attend an Ivy League school. It's very important to him and us that he acquire as strong a background as possible in middle school. I'm sure that the students he's required to help don't have as strong a need to learn as Mel does. I don't think it's fair for middle school students to use their own learning time to tutor other students. That's the teacher's job.

DR. FANG   *[Speaking out]* And a related problem is that some of the members of my son's group not only fail to do their own work, but they also create disruptions that interrupt the learning of the other students. To have such a situation makes no sense at all. I would like Ting to have an opportunity to work alone on his own studies.

MS. STINE   I'm offended that one of the students in June's group consistently uses language so vulgar that it could make your ears burn! I don't think there's any place for that kind of talk anywhere in school!

MS. RYERSON I know exactly who you mean, and I agree with you about the inappropriateness of such language.

KIM I'm June and Mel's teacher, Ms. Stine and Ryerson. Until now, I haven't been aware of the situation you've described. If you'll talk with me after this meeting, I can guarantee you that this situation will stop. I fully agree with you, and I'll put an end to it first thing tomorrow!

PAUL I fully agree that students shouldn't be interrupted in their work by other students, but I'd like to point out that such interruptions typically diminish after those students who have been unable to succeed in school learn that they have an equal chance with everyone else in the class to succeed. *[Looking to the other teachers]* Would any of you other teachers care to address this issue?

TANYA You beat me to the punch. I was just about to make that comment. I think the interruptions are already becoming less frequent in my cooperative learning class. But, I also find that there are differences in the interruptions in my cooperative learning class and my other classes.

MR. MOSES I'd be interested in what the differences in the interruptions are.

CINDY I think that in the regular classes, more of the interruptions are pupils trying to get attention by making irrelevant statements. In the STAD class the pupils seem to be talking all the time, which we often think of as interruptions, but in those classes the talking is usually focused on problem-solving—students helping each other, talking about how to write something, and so forth.

MR. MAZIO I'm probably old-fashioned, but I think it's the teacher's job to teach and the students' job to learn. It's hard for me to think that sixth-grade students are capable of learning to their full capacity at the same time they're teaching the weaker students in their class.

PAUL There's quite a bit of research concluding that both the brighter and slower students improve their learning in STAD classes. And I don't think we've really given this program a fair chance. I'd like to urge you to bear with us on this program until your children have had an opportunity to participate in it for at least a full semester. Since we've really just begun the STAD program, the students have been working hard to adapt to it and to learn how to work with each other. After all, it takes a while to get used to any team approach. Just think how long it takes to get used to a team sport. Also, the students' scores on the tests they've taken so far indicate that motivation and learning are both at high levels. But I'm confident that after they're organized, they'll feel proud that they've taken charge of their own learning and, indeed, have learned efficiently. I think at this point, I'll sit down and invite you to talk with each other or your child's teacher. You may stay until all your questions are answered.

Two weeks after the parent meeting, Howard's secretary visits each of the STAD teachers and finds that each of them can meet at the end of classes the following day. They are all waiting outside his office at the appointed time. Howard walks out of his office and greets them. He motions them in, and they all take seats.

HOWARD *[Smiling]* Thank you all for coming on such short notice. I'm afraid that I've called this meeting to share some bad news.

PAUL *[Speaking out]* No doubt it has to do with the cooperative learning program.

HOWARD Yes, it does. I'm afraid we have a number of parents upset with our cooperative learning program.

CINDY *[Shocked]* Oh, no! I thought they'd seemed pretty well satisfied at the end of our meeting.

KIM Yes, I did, too. I haven't heard from any of my parents who were at the meeting, so I just assumed they're happy now. I think the class is going much better than it was before they came to that meeting.

TANYA Well, I must express surprise, too. I haven't heard from any of my parents who came to the meeting, either.

PAUL Well, I guess maybe the parents who were there got the idea from my pitch that we were sold on the program and that it wouldn't do any good to complain anymore.

HOWARD Regardless of why you've not heard from any of the parents, we've had the situation go from bad to worse.

PAUL *[Surprised]* How is that, Howard?

HOWARD For the remainder of the week during which you held the parents' meeting and the following week, I had no calls from any of those parents. But beginning the first day of last week, I've had a constant barrage of telephone calls from the parents who attended the meeting and from others who did not attend the meeting. *[Pause]*

KIM *[Concerned]* What are they saying about the program?

HOWARD In an nutshell, they don't like it. Some of them want me to move their children to other sixth-grade classes here. But, even more threatening are those who are planning to remove their children from Fort Henry and send them to private schools if I don't comply with their wishes. And to make matters worse, their children seem to be our best students!

TANYA *[Almost in tears]* Isn't there anything that we can do about it?

HOWARD I've decided to grant the requests of the parents who attended your meeting and have requested that their children be transferred within the school. There aren't enough of them to have a great effect on your classes. But now other parents are complaining. I offered to set up a meeting, just like we did with the other parents, but they have their minds made up—either I move their kids to regular classes or they'll move them to a private school. It's just a horrible situation, and I'm embarrassed about the entire situation!

But, I asked you here today not only to let you know what has happened, but also to ask you to help me examine our options. Let me ask all of you this: Is there anything we can do at this point to salvage the pupils whose parents are unhappy with the program? Why are the students and their parents unhappy with the program? Could you have restructured the cooperative learning program any differently? Did you use the correct STAD procedures? What can you tell me that might help me sort all of this out?

FIGURE 18   Tanya Justin's Lesson Plan on the Plant Kingdom

Teacher: Tanya Justin   Course: Science
Period: Fourth   Date: September 27

Goal: At the end of this lesson, students will be able to describe and make a
    passing grade on the functions plants must perform to stay alive.

Specific objectives:
Students will be able to:

1. Describe the basic needs that all living things must satisfy to stay alive.
2. Learn that the life processes, which are the activities that keep living things
   alive, are: getting food, releasing energy, removing wastes, growing, and
   reproducing.
3. Describe how green plants obtain the three things they need to make food:
   water, carbon dioxide, and light energy.
4. Explain how green plants transport these things to the food-making parts
   of the plants.

Materials:

1. Science text: Chapter 1
2. Several different kinds of plants.
3. Pastel pencils and drawing paper.
4. Six microscopes. (One for each group)
5. Photocopied worksheets for evaluation.

Procedures:

1. Introduce lesson by asking students to bring one or two plants to class.
2. Carefully shake the soil off the roots of the plant, and make a drawing of
   the plant.
3. Tell which plants have fibrous roots and tap roots. Label roots on your
   drawings.
4. Tell which plants have root hairs. Write an explanation of what root
   hairs do.
5. Cut a one-inch section of the root of your plants. Identify the two kinds of
   tubes within the stem. Write a description of how water is transported
   through these tubes.
6. Identify the veins and stomata on leaves. Explain the functions of these
   parts.
7. Pass a written test on the information you have collected.

QUESTIONS

1. How do cooperation and competition affect student learning and motivation?
what extent do cooperative learning methods address the problems created by compe
tion? Do all cooperative learning methods shortchange high-ability students?

2. Is there a conflict between the homogeneous grouping of students by ability (e.g., advanced-placement classes) and cooperative learning methods? Can the two approaches be combined?

3. Paul and the other teachers are using the STAD cooperative learning method. How well have they implemented it? How effective is STAD compared to other cooperative leaning methods, such as TGT, TAI, and CIRC? What are the advantages and disadvantages of each?

4. Do cooperative learning methods encourage intrinsic or extrinsic motivational patterns among participating students? Do students in such programs seem to value learning for its own sake or for more extrinsic reasons, like earning points for the team? Does the age or grade level of the child matter in this regard?

5. What is cultural diversity? How effectively does STAD take student differences into consideration? How might students and parents from different social classes and racial/ethnic backgrounds react differently to cooperative learning methods?

6. Do any of the teachers have biases toward some students? Do some students and parents express biases toward other students? How can such biases result in self-fulfilling prophecies and discourage the performance of some students while encouraging that of others?

7. What concerns do the students express about STAD? How effectively do the teachers handle such concerns? What could have been done at the beginning of the program to prevent such problems from developing?

8. How well did Paul handle the meeting with the parents? How well does Paul communicate? What should he have done differently?

9. How could Howard and Paul have evaluated the effectiveness of the STAD program? What formative and summative types of evaluation data should be gathered? What types of process and product variables should be examined?

10. Since certain parents played a critical role in rejecting the program, could anything have been done from the very beginning to involve all the parents? Did Susan have a valid point about getting permission from participants in experimental programs like this one? What procedures are usually involved?

11. A major problem with some parents was peer tutoring. How valid was their concern that it was preventing their children from maximizing their own learning? Is there any value in peer tutoring for the high-ability student?

12. Do some students function and learn better in cooperative learning situations? For example, is cooperative learning equally effective with African-American, Hispanic, Native American, and non-Hispanic white students? How well does it work with field-dependent and field-independent learners?

13. What is parent involvement, and what parent involvement procedures might have been effective in this situation? For example, could parents have been involved as classroom volunteers or as tutors of their own children at home? Could parent advisory groups, such as PTA or the school advisory committee, have been involved in setting up and monitoring the project?

14. What can be done at this point to salvage the cooperative learning experiment? Should the program be scrapped for this school year and attempted later on? What mistakes were made? What should have been done differently?

C A S E **18**

THE LITTLE ENGINE
THAT COULDN'T

Key Content to Consider for Analyzing This Case:
(1) motivation (mastery vs. performance goal
orientations, attribution theory, learned helplessness,
sense of efficacy); (2) cultural diversity; (3) information
processing theory; (4) home environment/parent
involvement.

R ussell Esky is a beginning teacher in his fifth day of teaching a sixth-grade cla
in Sparta Elementary school. He is plagued with mixed emotions regarding bo
his reaction to his pupils and his perception of his own ability as a teacher.

Russ recently graduated from a private college in a southern state which offers a program th
enables students to qualify for a B.A. degree plus a teaching certificate in elementary educatio
awarded by the state. During his final month at college, Russ interviewed for an elementary teachi
position at Sparta Elementary school, which is located in a large city in the southern part of the sai
state. Of the more than 900 pupils enrolled in the school, approximately 30% come from midd
income homes, while 70% come from low-income homes. Approximately 50% of the pupils a
white, 40% African-American, 9% Hispanic, and 1% Asian-American.

It is Friday morning before the lunch period has begun. Russ has asked his twent
eight class members to work on individual assignments until lunchtime.

RUSS *[Seeing three girls with no work on their desks giggling and talking]* Are you girls
working on your science report?

SARA We don't know how to start it.

RUSS Have you decided how to divide up the work?

PAT No, we've never worked on a group project before. We don't know how to divide
up the work.

RUSS Surely you've been asked to write reports in classes before.

SARA *[Giggling]* Yes, we've been told to do reports, but none of us has ever done muc
on them. We were always in a group and the other people knew what to do.

RUSS *[Sternly]* Well, in this class you're going to learn to do your own work, and I
expect each of you to give me an outline of your part of the report before you lea
school today. The report must have something to do with plants. You can find a l
of information in the first chapter of your science text. *[The girls appear to be
confused.]*

RUSS   [*Notices Kevin looking out the window*] Kevin, how are you doing on your multiplication of decimals problems?

KEVIN   [*Embarrassed*] Not so good, Mr. Esky. I can't figure out how to do them.

RUSS   But Kevin, I just worked the first three problems with you less than ten minutes ago. Tell me how to figure out where the decimal point goes. Don't you remember?

KEVIN   No. I forgot. It has something to do with how many numbers come after the decimal points.

RUSS   But you worked the examples correctly when I was explaining how to multiply decimals early in the week.

KEVIN   Yeah, I know. But I guess I just got lucky. I don't even remember how I worked those problems.

RUSS   You really can do math, Kevin. If you could do them a few days ago, you can do them today. You just have to apply the right formula, which you did. [*Taking a paper and pencil*] Here, let's work some problems together. [*Writing some examples*] Notice in this problem there are two numbers after the decimal point in the top number and one in the bottom number. So, in the answer there are three numbers after the decimal. [*Writes another problem*] Now, you solve this one.

KEVIN   [*Looks at the problem for a long time*] I don't get it. I just can't get math. My parents couldn't do math either. They can't help me with my homework.

RUSS   [*Patiently*] OK, Kevin. It's not really hard. Let's try it again. Do you remember what you need to look for to find out how many numbers are after the decimal in the answer?

KEVIN   How many numbers are after the decimal in the top and bottom numbers?

RUSS   Right! I think you'll be able to do it now. [*Writes three more examples*] Now, let me see you work these problems.

KEVIN   [*Looks at examples for a long time, then turns to Russ*] Will you help me get started?

RUSS   First, do the multiplication. [*Kevin does it.*] OK. Now tell me how many numbers are after the decimal in the top number.

KEVIN   There are two. And there's only one in the bottom number.

RUSS   Great! Now put the decimal point in the answer. [*Kevin puts it in the right place.*] [*Really excited*] That's terrific, Kevin! Now do the rest of the problems that same way!

KEVIN   OK. I'll try. But I probably won't get them right.

RUSS   [*Optimistically*] Sure you will. Think positive. You can do it! [*Walks over to Paula*] You did a good job on your geography test yesterday. I'm proud of you!

PAULA   Thanks, but I was just lucky.

RUSS   Why do you say that? You answered all but three of the questions correctly. If you can answer short-answer questions correctly, I'd say you know the material.

PAULA   I don't know the material. I just made lucky guesses. I have trouble understanding school stuff. And I can't remember things very long, even when I learn them.

RUSS   Paula, I want you to do something for me.

PAULA   What?

Russ   I want you to take credit for knowing things. When you make correct answers, want you to take credit for them. I want you to say, "I know that information." W you do that?

Paula   I guess so. But I'm not sure I'll believe it.

Russ continues to work closely with Paula and becomes increasingly concern about her lack of confidence. During the two weeks following the test incident, Pa continued to forget procedures Russ has taught in class. So, one evening, he called Pau home. A woman answered.

Russ   This is Russell Esky, Paula's teacher. Is this Paula's mother?

Pat   Oh, hello, Mr. Esky. I recognize your name. Paula's talked a lot about you. She sa you're nice to her and try to help her at school.

Russ   I certainly try, and that's why I'm calling you this evening. I've told Paula that I think she could be a really good student, but she doesn't seem to have any confidence in herself as a student.

Pat   Well, I don't know about that. Paula's never done very good in school. Her broth Paul, hasn't either.

Russ   I've never met Paul, but I think that if Paula could get some help with her homework, she'd be a good student.

Pat   Well, my husband and me would like her to do better, but, to tell you the truth, was really a poor student at school myself and so was my husband. But he at leas graduated and we got married that summer. I never went back to school. I didn't want to.

Russ   But I think it's more important to graduate from school today than it was even when you were in school. Many employers won't even interview applicants who aren't high school graduates. Some employers require a college degree.

Pat   I'm afraid Paula'll be out of luck for those kinds of jobs. We aren't college people No one in our family ever went to college. In fact, most kids in our neighborhoo drop out of school, get married, and then go to work.

Russ   What kinds of jobs do they get?

Pat   Laboring jobs mostly—working on road crews, lawn service, construction, custodial work, night watchmen. My husband got a job as night custodian in the battery plant before we got married, and he's still there. Before we had the kids, l was a cocktail waitress and made good money. But neither of us would be able to get a job where you have to take tests and go through training programs. We ain' good enough at those things.

Russ   But that's exactly why I'm calling, Ms. Espinoza. I think Paula is smart enough go to a training program. She could even go to college. All she needs is encouragement and support. I'm willing to spend extra time with her at school, you and Mr. Espinoza will need to help her, too. I'd like you to encourage her to work hard at school to get good grades and start her thinking about going to college. I'm sure she could get a college scholarship if she tries. Then she could a really good job.

PAT   Well, we'd like for her to, but like I said, we're not college people. We don't have that kind of money. And we don't even know anybody who graduated from college. We just don't live at that level. I appreciate your taking an interest in Paula, Mr. Esky, but I just don't see how she'll ever be able to do that.

RUSS   *[Frustrated]* But can't you see that going to college could change Paula's life for the better?

PAT   Like I said, no one in our family has ever gone to college. We're laboring people and Paula'll have to settle for the kind of jobs people in our neighborhood get. She'll likely live here, get married, and have children right here in the neighborhood. It might not be doing her a favor, Mr. Esky, to put foolish ideas in her head. But, I do sincerely thank you for your taking an interest in her.

It is after school the following day. Russ sits in the classroom of fellow sixth-grade teacher Sid Willis, who has taught at Sparta for seven years. Russ and Sid sit in chairs in front of Sid's desk.

SID   What do you mean, Russ, when you say you're having problems with some of your students? What kinds of problems?

RUSS   Well, I guess I'd have to say that the problems are more in the area of academic performance than in the area of discipline.

SID   That's good. It's my experience that discipline problems and academic performance problems go hand-in-hand. So your problems are cut in half if discipline's not a problem. Give me some examples of the kinds of problems you're having.

RUSS   OK. *[Spends some time in thought]* I was planning to tell you about some specific incidents that have happened in class. But as I reviewed them in my mind, it occurred to me that they're basically variations on the same theme.

SID   Which is what?

RUSS   It seems that a large percentage of the pupils in my class are unable to cope with independent learning activities. They just aren't able to work on their own.

SID   How many of your pupils fit into this category?

RUSS   More than half of them. And they're generally the pupils who come from low-income homes. And, what to me is really sad is that so many of them have the ability to do the assignments. But they just don't seem to be able to get their act together.

SID   Why do you think they're like that?

RUSS   I think it's their home environment. Some of them have no learning strategies. Others know how to do the work but aren't really interested in learning. And I'm sure that in most of their homes, no one ever suggests the possibility of attending college.

SID   Can you give me a specific example of what you're talking about?

RUSS   Yes. A good example is Paula Espinoza. I think she has the ability to succeed in college. Her mother essentially told me not to encourage her daughter to think about going to college.

SID   Did she give you any reasons why?

RUSS   Oh yes, she gave me several. Her family's not what she calls "college people." No one from their neighborhood ever goes to college, nor do they ever encourage thei children to go. They don't have enough money to send her to college. And they expect her to get some kind of unskilled job like the rest of the people in their neighborhood.

SID   That kind of feedback doesn't do much to motivate children to perform well in school, does it?

RUSS   No, it doesn't. Paula doesn't come close to performing at her potential. And I'd be willing to bet that I'd hear the same story from the majority of the parents of the students who perform poorly. Can you think of anything I could do to change this situation?

SID   While you were telling me about Paula, I thought about the many times I've gone out to catch crabs. I always take a bucket to put the crabs into when I catch them. never worry about their getting out of the bucket, because if one of the crabs gets close to the top of the bucket, the others pull him back down. [Smiles] It seems th maybe your classroom groups function similarly. When a group member makes ar effort to get the group on track, another member pulls him or her back down. Do that seem like a fair analogy to you also?

RUSS   Unfortunately, it does. But what can I do to change this?

SID   You told me you think Paula is college material, right?

RUSS   Yes, I think she is.

SID   Approximately how many of your low-income pupils do you think would fall into that same category?

RUSS   [After a long pause] I'd guess there are probably ten.

SID   What would you think of forming your class into groups of four or five pupils based on their ability and SES? Divide them into ability levels, but mix them up b SES. That way the low-SES pupils with high ability could interact with other students of high ability and maybe raise their sights toward college. And low-SES pupils with low ability can interact with other pupils with low ability and see that they're just as good as they are.

RUSS   [Enthusiastically] That sounds like a great idea! It certainly wouldn't be a difficult strategy to use. They would be grouped homogeneously by ability, but heterogeneously by SES. I like that idea. Thanks for suggesting it.

SID   I'm anxious to see what happens. Let me know if I can help you in any way.

Russ used school cumulative records to assign his pupils to seven groups of fo members each. There were two groups of average and above, two groups of average low average, and three groups of below average. Work assignments for each of the thr groups were different, but each was on an appropriate level of difficulty for the pupils that group. Russ approaches one of the above-average groups.

RUSS   What project is your group working on, Lo?

LO   We're studying the conservation of natural resources, Mr. Esky. Each of us has selected a resource and will prepare a report about what our country's doing to conserve that resource.

RUSS   That's a good topic, Lo. What's your report about?

LO   I'm describing efforts that are being made to conserve our water supply.

RUSS   That's an interesting topic, and certainly an important one. *[Turning to another pupil]* What's your topic, Gail?

GAIL   I'm writing about what we're doing to stop air pollution.

RUSS   Another good topic. *[Looking at Art]* How about you, Art?

ART   Paula and I are working together on the conservation of natural resources. Paula's report will focus on plants, and mine will focus on animals.

RUSS   Your group has certainly chosen critical issues to report on. I'm looking forward to hearing your reports. *[Turns his attention to pupils in one of the below-average groups who don't appear to be doing any work]* Sara, what topic is your group working on?

SARA   *[Giggling]* We don't have one yet. We just can't decide on one.

RUSS   Well, tell me some of the topics you're considering. *[No response from any group member]* Sara, what topics are you considering? *[No response]* Raul, what topic would you like your group to study? *[No response]* Pat, how about you? *[Pat looks at the floor.]* Mose? *[No response]* All right, since you don't seem able to select a topic for yourselves, I'll give you one. Your group will prepare a report on the oceans. Sara, you'll report on the oceans, their names, and their characteristics. Raul, you'll report on the movement of the ocean: waves, tides, and currents. Tell how they're caused and how they affect the earth. Pat, you'll report on the composition of ocean water and tell how the various gases and chemicals get into the water. Mose, you'll report on how the oceans affect our weather. I want to see all of you outlining your reports right now. If I see you fooling around, I'll have you stay in the room during activity periods for the rest of the week.

PAT   But, I don't even have a clue about where to start a report on ocean water.

RUSS   That's easy. You can find lots of clues on pages 24–30 of your science book. Those pages are all about that topic. I suggest you start by reading those pages. *[Looking at each of the pupils]* Before the end of the period, I expect all of you to have your outline started. *[The students moan and complain, but Russ walks on to another group.]*

On the following Thursday after school, Russ met with Rita Gonzalez, the school principal. She was in the process of having a short meeting with each of her teachers just to see how things were going and to see if they had any suggestions for improving the education program of the school. Russ shared his concerns about his class with her. Rita suggested that he make an appointment with the elementary curriculum supervisor, Sharon Maris. She said that Sharon is excellent in helping teachers apply appropriate teaching methodology in situations like those that Russ described.

Russ followed Rita's suggestion and made an appointment with Sharon for the following week. He has just arrived at the waiting area outside Sharon's office at the appointed time.

SHARON   *[Seeing Russ enter the waiting area]* Hi, Russ. Come on in and have a seat. *[Motions to a chair facing her]*

RUSS   Hi, Sharon. *[Sits in the designated chair]*

SHARON   I understand that you have some concerns about your sixth-grade class. Wha
are they?

RUSS   There are so many different things that concern me about my class that I'm not
sure where to begin. I guess the first thing would be that the majority of the pupi
are apathetic about school. They truly seem not to care whether they learn or not.
Nor do their families.

SHARON   Can you cite some specific behaviors that led you to this conclusion?

RUSS   Sure. They don't do either classroom or homework assignments. When I try to
help them, they just don't seem to understand what the assignment is all about or
how to do it. But the most frustrating aspect of the whole situation is that they tru
don't believe they can do the work. And I believe that many of their parents don't
care whether they learn or not.

SHARON   Why do you say that?

RUSS   Well, for example, I called the mother of one of my students to tell her that I thi
her daughter is capable of doing much better work in school, but doesn't seem
interested in doing so. I asked her to support me in encouraging her daughter to
her classwork and homework.

SHARON   And?

RUSS   And her mother essentially told me that she doesn't think her daughter can do l
work either. She said that they're not "college people," that she expects her to get
married and do some kind of service or laboring job in the neighborhood. She le
me to believe that most of her neighbors feel the same way.

SHARON   I'm sorry not to be able to say that this surprises me, but it doesn't. A large
proportion of our parents have this attitude. What other concerns do you have
about your class?

RUSS   Probably my main concern is the work attitudes of some of my kids. They seem
believe that they're predestined to just drift along completely at the mercy of thei
environment. They don't seem to have any goals, ambitions, or aspirations in life
They just seem to live for the day.

SHARON   Have you tried any strategies to motivate them?

RUSS   Yes, several weeks ago I talked with a fellow teacher, Sid Willis, about the
situation. He suggested that I group my pupils by ability, but mix them up by SE
That way I could adapt the assignments to the various ability levels so each group
could work at its own level.

SHARON   And how did that work out?

RUSS   It seemed to work out much better for the high-ability white and Asian-Americ
middle-class students. But it had no effect at all on the low-ability, disadvantage
African-American and Hispanic pupils. They didn't do any worse, but they didn'
do any better.

SHARON   So where are you now?

RUSS   I'm very frustrated and concerned. This is my first year of teaching, and I
expected to be a much better teacher than I seem to be. I don't know what to d
Are there other teaching strategies I could use that would work better with the
students? Would I be more effective teaching at another grade level or at anoth

type of school? Or am I just an ineffective teacher that would be better off preparing for another career? To tell you the truth, Sharon, I'm not sure I know how to motivate my students to learn. Their home environments seem to work against their staying in school, much less becoming even average students. What can a teacher do when the home and the parents seem to be working against him? Can you help me?

IGURE 19 Student Information Assembled by Russell Esky on His Sixth-Grade Class

Name	Eligible for School Lunch	Achievement Scores[1]	Ethnic/Racial Origin[2]	IQ[3]
1. Adams, Sara	Yes	6.1	AA	102
2. Brown, Gail	No	7.0	W	111
3. Butler, Latisha	Yes	5.8	AA	87
4. Castillo, Raul	Yes	5.3	H	90
5. Clark, Patricia	Yes	5.6	AA	92
6. Davis, Wayne	No	6.5	W	100
7. Deleo, Tammy	No	6.2	W	96
8. Eisner, Kevin	Yes	5.7	W	89
9. Espinoza, Paula	Yes	6.5	W	105
. Felton, George	Yes	5.7	AA	89
. Gully, Isaac	Yes	5.3	AA	82
2. Ho, Wan	No	7.4	A	130
3. Min, Lo	No	7.2	A	123
. Nazario, Rita	Yes	5.0	H	84
5. Okabe, Elsa	Yes	5.2	AA	86
. Pace, Natasha	Yes	4.9	AA	80
. Petty, Arthur	No	7.2	W	120
. Ramond, Hosea	Yes	4.9	AA	79
. Sanchez, Elena	Yes	4.5	H	84
. Sanders, Rose	Yes	4.8	AA	81
. Thompson, Harry	No	7.3	W	129
. Thomas, Melany	Yes	5.2	AA	89
. Voit, Thomas	No	5.8	AA	87
. Vincent, Carl	No	6.2	W	94
. Watson, Mose	Yes	4.8	AA	79
. Williams, Patti	Yes	5.3	AA	88
. Yates, James	No	6.1	W	98
. Zebo, Loretta	Yes	6.4	W	95

tal grade-level equivalent score from the Metropolitan Achievement Test, Intermediate Level Battery (grades
6). Decimal scores refer to months, e.g., 6.5 = 6th grade, 5th month.
= Non-Hispanic white; AA = African-American; H = Hispanic; A = Asian-American.
tal IQ score on California Test of Mental Maturity.

QUESTIONS

1. What is cultural diversity? What kinds of student diversity are represented in Rus class? How can a teacher take such diversity into consideration in terms of choosing instruc tional objectives, teaching methods, evaluation procedures, and methods of classroom mar agement?

2. What is attribution or locus of control theory? Are there examples of external attr butions in Russ' class? How can attribution training procedures be used to change studer attributions?

3. Weiner adds the dimensions of stability and controllability to internal and externa locus of control to explain student beliefs. How do these three dimensions help to explai student academic problems in this case?

4. What is learned helplessness? How does it relate to student academic behavior pa terns in this case?

5. What is sense of efficacy? What student efficacy patterns exist in this case wit regard to academic achievement? How is student sense of efficacy formed, and how ca it be changed?

6. Examine student academic behavior in this case from the standpoint of Ames' ma tery versus performance goal orientations. How are such motivational patterns forme and under what conditions can they be changed?

7. Russ refers to a lack of academic self-confidence on the part of students like Pau and Kevin. What is a lack of self-confidence, and how does it relate to the self-conce from the perspective of Shavelson's model, for example? How is the self-concept—esp cially the academic self-concept—formed, and under what conditions does it change?

8. Analyze this case from the viewpoint of information processing theory. What exan ples can you find of students forgetting information in short-term memory? How do retrieval theory explain such forgetting? How can retention of mathematical procedures the case of Kevin be increased?

9. What are metacognitive strategies, and how do they help students learn materia What metacognitive strategies would be helpful to Kevin?

10. What are rehearsal, organization, and elaboration in cognitive learning theor How they might be used to assist student learning in this case?

11. What role does the home environment play in forming student learning and mo vational patterns? How do the observational learning constructs of modeling and imit tion explain how students learn such patterns from their parents? What patterns do y see in Paula's home, and how do they help explain her academic learning patterns school? What parent involvement procedures can teachers and schools employ to he change such patterns?

12. How good was Sid's recommendation that Russ group his students by SES a ability? Why was this grouping ineffective with the low-ability students? How else mig Russ have grouped his students? How well might cooperative learning methods ha worked in Russ' class? How effectively did Russ work with his groups (e.g., Sara's grou which was having trouble getting started)?

13. What are teacher locus of control and teacher efficacy? How well do they expla Russ' beliefs as a teacher? What advice would you give Russ if you were Sharon?

A S E **19**

THE INS AND OUTS OF DISCIPLINE

Key Content to Consider for Analyzing This Case:
(1) classroom management; (2) operant conditioning;
(3) Teacher Effectiveness Training; (4) parent
involvement; (5) motivation (intrinsic vs. extrinsic).

Sugar Creek Elementary School is located in the New England town of Mapleton, which has a population of approximately 30,000. Its attendance district is approximately 80% white and 20% African-American.

Marti Weldon and Maria Del Rio are about to begin their second year of teaching third grade at Sugar Creek. They have been close friends since their freshman year of college, having pledged the same sorority, served as officers of the sorority their senior year, lived together as roommates, taken many of the same classes together, and obtained a teaching position at the same elementary school and grade level. Their friends often refer to them as the M&M girls.

Since they had some discipline problems their first year of teaching, Marti and Maria signed up to take a workshop on classroom management during teacher pre-planning prior to the beginning of the new school year. The workshop is being conducted by an educational psychology professor from a nearby state university, Dr. Wilson Busby. Having attended the morning session, they go to the school cafeteria, where a lunch break has been set up by the school for all teachers. Marti and Maria get their trays and sit down at one end of a table by themselves. They are soon joined by Alice White, a veteran teacher with fourteen years of teaching experience.

ALICE *[Standing with a tray in her hands]* May I sit with you two?

MARTI *[Eagerly]* Please do, Alice. You're just the person we need to talk to.

ALICE *[Smiling]* Oh, oh! Sounds like I'm in trouble! What are you two up to?

MARIA We're attending Dr. Busby's workshop on classroom management. Our job is to decide what model of classroom management we'll be most comfortable using this year. He gave us a survey form to fill out on what we believe about discipline, and then we're going to talk about our choices this afternoon and select the classroom management model we're going to learn to use.

MARTI Yes, and Maria and I filled our forms out separately. We usually see eye to eye on most things, but not this time! Help us out, Alice. You're considered an excellent

183

teacher here. How do you handle discipline in your classes? Which classroom management model do you like best?

ALICE   Oh, there are lots of good ones, I know. But I guess I do like most teachers and use my own based on my own experience.

MARIA   Well, like what? Tell us, Alice!

ALICE   Well, I don't think the method you use is as important as your having one and being consistent. I guess the first thing is to care for the children and let them knc that you care so that they trust you. Second, you have to be firm and let the children know what you expect of them. At the beginning of school I usually writ down the rules and discuss them with the children. It's important to praise them when they do well and, of course, punish them when they get out of line. The punishments you use should be in order of increasing severity. Also, and I'm sure you've heard it many times, never make a threat that you don't intend to carry ou Consistency is the key. [Pause] I might add that an old teacher told me when I firs started teaching that it's best to be strict at the beginning with a new group of students, and then you can gradually ease up a bit as you go along! I've found tha to be very good advice.

MARIA   Wow! You sure make it sound easy! I wish somebody had told me those things before I began teaching last year!

MARTI   Then you don't really follow any particular model like we're going to learn in t workshop?

ALICE   No. But if I were where you two are now, I might very well want to take a workshop like that. Discipline isn't a problem for me, so I see no real reason to change what I do. What models are they teaching you?

MARTI   We'll only learn one. Dr. Busby gave us an overview of several different ones ar then this instrument to fill out. We'll go back this afternoon and discuss our belie and choose which one model we want to learn and try out this school year.

ALICE   Which ones did Dr. Busby talk about?

MARTI   [Looking at her notes from the morning session] Let's see. There's behavior modification and one called Reality Therapy. Then there's Assertive Discipline and—what did I forget, Maria?

MARIA   Teacher Effectiveness Training. I think I like that one best.

MARTI   Yes, he called that TET. And then there's that other one named after a man—

MARIA   Kounin. That's his name. The one about the teacher knowing about everything going on in the classroom.

ALICE   [Laughing] The old eyes in the back of the head business! Yes, I've known quite few teachers like that. In fact, some of my students say that about me. [All three laugh. Alice points to the paper in Maria's hand.] Is this the survey that you have to out on your beliefs? Can I see it? [Takes the form and reads it] Now, this first one is interesting about whether the child or the curriculum is more important.

MARTI   Yes, isn't that a terrible question? Of course both are important, but it asks wh should be shaped to which, and I think that the curriculum exists before the chil gets to school. The child has to conform to the curriculum. Why else is he attending school? It isn't up to the child to decide what and when he's ready to learn. The child is there for the teacher to lead him to learn.

MARIA   But Marti, kids aren't empty vessels waiting to be filled! They're not going to learn anything if they're not motivated to learn. So you've got to motivate the child first, and that means adjusting things to him so he'll be interested and understand them.

ALICE   This is all very interesting, but what does it have to with discipline?

MARTI   That's what we're going to talk about this afternoon. Apparently, different beliefs about these issues lead you to prefer different classroom management models. This is just the first instrument he's giving us to fill out. I think he said he'll be giving us two more like this.

MARIA   Yes, I wrote down what he said about his one. *[Looks at notes]* He said that "this will separate the behaviorists from the humanists," so I guess that's what it measures.

ALICE   Which models are those?

MARTI   I'm not sure. I guess behavior modification is one and I'm not sure which is the other.

ALICE   *[Smiling]* Well, it sure sounds like a fun workshop to me! I'm sure you'll both get a lot out of it.

It is the end of pre-planning and the classroom management workshops. Classes begin Monday. After discussing their beliefs about students, the purpose of education, and classroom management in the workshop, Marti and Maria made different choices regarding classroom management models and attended different workshops. Marti attended the one on behavior modification, and Maria chose one on TET. They sit at student desks facing one another in Maria's classroom talking about their workshops at the end of the workday on a Friday afternoon.

MARTI   *[Enthusiastically]* It was wonderful, Maria! I've never had a workshop—or a college class, for that matter—that was that good! I know exactly what to do and how to do it.

MARIA   *[In a serious tone]* What I don't understand, Marti, is why you didn't take the TET workshop with me. Even though Dr. Reed taught it instead of Dr. Busby, it was wonderful too! Dr. Reed—or Suzie, she made us call her—is one of the warmest, most honest, most positive people I've ever met! You would've loved her!

MARTI   Yeah, maybe! But Dr. Busby was so knowledgeable and well organized. He seemed to have an answer for every problem we brought up. He said that teachers who prefer behavior modification are usually people who prefer structure and business-like organization. He said that people who prefer TET often are more feeling people who believe that human relations are at least as important as teaching content. He said that behavior mod people are often a bit more on the intellectual side than the TET people.

MARIA   *[With a touch of anger]* I don't think that's true! TET is a definite system too, but you have to be your genuine self when you use it. I think any classroom management system can become artificial very fast if you just follow the procedures without putting you heart into it! And, yes, we do care about the whole child, not just their learning subject matter!

MARTI   Whoa! Don't get angry just because we're different! You do your thing and I'll
mine. Isn't that what you humanists say?

MARIA   *[Smiling]* You're right, of course. I guess the truth is that it bothered me that w
weren't in the same class together just like old times!

MARTI   Yes, me too. Give me a hug. *[They stand up and embrace.]*

It is one month later. Marti has implemented a token economy using "Sugar Cr
Dollars" as tokens and utilizing the Premack Principle as a basis for determining re
forcers. Also, she uses contingency contracts with particularly difficult students. In ad
tion, Marti has contacted the volunteer coordinator for the school system and develo
a system for involving as many of the parents of her students in the classroom as po
ble. This is based on Dr. Busby's theory that if parents are brought into the classroom a
learn to work with operant techniques, then those techniques will find their way into
home and result in home and school working together in the area of discipline. Marti
four parents work in the classroom as volunteers for one grading period (six weeks) a
then rotates in four new parents.

Marti's four parent volunteers for the first grading period—Rose, Shirley, Mak
and Tekha—meet with her after school for a planning session. They sit at movable s
dent desks which they have arranged in a circle so that they face one another as they t

MARTI   I just wanted to meet with you for an hour this afternoon without the childre
around to see how everything is going from your point of view. You all seem to b
doing such a good job during the day that I'm not aware of any problems. But th
I'm so busy too that it may be that I'm not noticing problems you're experiencin

SHIRLEY   Oh, Marti, this is just the best experience I've have in a long time! It took me
while to catch on to giving reinforcers for competing good behavior and ignoring
bad behavior, but once I saw how marvelously it works I've even started doing it
home with Jimmy. I use Jimmy's allowance as a reinforcer and a big chart with g
stars as tokens.

MARTI   That's wonderful, Shirley! Just what I want to hear. But are there any problem:

ROSE   Well, yes. Jerry Rozelle. He is so hyper that getting him to stop running and
keeping his hands to himself is almost impossible. I don't think the Sugar Creek
Dollars are enough. I have to sit down with him one-on-one to get him to do his
work. He takes so much time and attention!

MARTI   Yes, Jerry can be a handful. Do you think we need to identify some new
reinforcers for him?

ROSE   Yes, I do. All he seems to like are sports. We let him watch videotapes and play
handheld computer sports games during reinforcement time, but that doesn't se
to reduce his energy any. He probably needs to go to the gym and do some real
physical rough-and-tumble to take some of the steam out of him.

MARTI   Maybe that can be arranged. Let me talk to Mr. Oeffler, the phys ed teacher. D
he do anything bad enough for us to go to time-out?!

TEKHA   What's time-out?

ROSE   Oh, you know, Tekha. What we did with Michael the second week when he wa
hitting other children. We took him to that empty office next door for fifteen

minutes, and then he'd sit in the back of the room when we brought him back. Don't you remember? Marti would say "time out" when Michael hit another child, and I would go over calmly to him and take him to that office. He'd just sit in there and be bored for fifteen minutes.

TEKHA   Oh, yeah. That's right. Will we do that with Jerry too? It straightened Michael right out in no time.

MARTI   *[Frowning]* Maybe. If so, we have to take Jerry aside and explain it all to him. You're right, Rose, it's been two weeks since we've had to resort to time-out. But you know, I wonder. *[Pause]*

SHIRLEY   You wonder what, Marti?

MARTI   I need to check to see if Jerry is hyperactive. I wonder if he's supposed to be on Ritalin or something to calm him down. Well, let me check. *[Writes note on pad of paper]* OK, then we'd better focus in a bit more on Jerry's behavior. Maketa, do you remember how to chart baseline data?

MAKETA   You mean like I did for Roger?

MARTI   Yes. Except this time you'll be focusing in on Jerry's hitting behavior.

MAKETA   You mean actual hits? Not just threats or near misses?

MARTI   Yes. Rose, do you think we should have Maketa record threats too?

ROSE   I don't know. He's always threatening someone. He doesn't hit that often, but when he does all heck breaks loose.

MARTI   OK. For now, Maketa, just chart his hits.

MAKETA   The whole school day?

MARTI   No, no! Rose, when does he usually do the hitting? What's usually going on in class?

ROSE   It's usually when he's supposed to be doing seatwork. I think he gets bored and just hauls off and hits someone, usually little David.

MARTI   OK, just keep track of his hitting during seatwork for ten minutes, Maketa.

MAKETA   You want the number of times per minute, like with Roger?

MARTI   Yes. Of course, that was for speaking out without raising his hand, but use the same recording procedure.

MAKETA   OK. I'll start tomorrow and go for a week.

MARTI   Excellent. Thank you, Maketa, and I think maybe we should begin class tomorrow by going over the rules again. We'll involve the class in reevaluating our rules and especially emphasize not hitting other students. Later on in the day we'll pull Jerry out from one of the group activities and explain the time-out procedures. How does that sound?

SHIRLEY   *[Smiling]* That's wonderful, Marti! I'm just amazed at how easily you handle problems like this! You always seem to know just what to do without any hesitation! I just wish I always knew what to do at home like that!

MARTI   *[With exaggeration]* Just stick with me, kid! You'll soon be able to modify behavior with the best of them! *[All laugh.]*

Meanwhile, Maria has implemented TET procedures in her classroom. Inspired by Marti's example of using parent volunteers in her classroom, Maria decided to involve two

parent volunteers each grading period in her classroom. Currently these two parents a
Christy Lang and Latesha Jackson. Maria stands in front of her twenty-four students, w
are seated in a semicircle on the floor. Christy and Latesha stand in back of the childi
on different sides of the room.

MARIA   Boys and girls, I'm calling a class meeting because I have a problem that I need
help with. There's too much talking going on in the room, and Ms. Lang, Ms.
Jackson, and I are having to spend too much time getting people to quiet down.
have to keep repeating directions and going over material with people who are
talking instead of listening. Still, I know that people need to talk sometimes. Let
write down here on the blackboard any ideas that you have that might help. Yes,
Ann?

ANN   I think you should change the seats around.

MARIA   Thank you, Ann. *[Writes "change seating" on blackboard]*

BARRY   Maybe everyone should whisper instead of talking loud.

MARK   If they talk you should punish them.

MARIA   Punish them how, Mark?

MARK   I don't know. Make them leave the room. Make them go with Ms. Lang or Ms.
Jackson someplace else.

MARIA   OK. Any other ideas?

ROGER   Maybe it would be OK to talk at certain times. Like you could set times when
we could talk but not all the time.

MARK   Maybe some of us could talk while the others work.

MARIA   Explain that one for us more, Mark.

MARK   Like you divide the class in two and let one half talk while you teach the other
half. Then change around.

MARIA   So you're saying teach half the class while the other half talks, then change
around.

MARK   Yeah. That would be cool!

MARIA   Any others? *[No response]* OK, I have five ideas on the blackboard: change the
seating, let students whisper, punish by making persons leave the room, have tim
when class can talk, and teach half the class while the other half talks. Now let's
cross off the ideas we don't like. I don't like the last one about teaching half the
class. Also number three about making people leave the room when they talk.
What about the first one: change seating.

BARRY   You already did that, and it didn't work.

MARIA   OK, what about whispering? *[No objections]* What about having times when it's
OK to talk? *[No objections]* All right, it will be OK to whisper, and we'll need to
decide what times it's OK and not OK to talk. Let Ms. Lang, Ms. Jackson, and I gi
that some thought, and we'll bring our ideas on that back to you at the beginning
of class in the morning so we can all decide on the best times together. OK?

It is March and the school year begins to wind down. Dorene Lantz, the buildi
principal, has asked both Marti and Maria to come to her office after school on a Frid
Dorene sits behind her desk as the two teachers sit in chairs facing her.

DORENE   I'm sure you're both curious as to why I asked to meet with you. Let me begin by saying that I think that you both have grown more this year than any two beginning—or maybe I should say second-year—teachers I've known! Your students are learning, your parents are involved, and you handle your discipline problems so well that I'm not real sure you've had any this year.

MARTI   Thanks, Dorene. That's real nice of you!

MARIA   Yes, thank you very much!

DORENE   My problem is that Dr. Scoggins [superintendent of schools] has asked me to nominate one of you as "Teacher of the Year." You both are doing such a good job that I don't know what to do! Whichever one of you I nominate, the other will be disappointed. I've observed both of you three times this year, and you both made the highest possible scores on our rating instrument. Is there any way you can help me with this decision?

MARIA   Wow! This really comes as a pleasant surprise! I wasn't expecting anything like this at all!

MARTI   I'm blown away! [Pause] What can we tell you that would be helpful, Dorene? Frankly, I think you should give it to Maria. She's done a super job!

MARIA   Oh, come on, Marti! You know that you've been my mentor, especially about involving parents in the classroom!

DORENE   Now, now! That's not helpful! [Pause] I'll tell you what. Why don't each of you tell me why you think the other person is doing the better job—and stick to the facts.

MARIA   OK. Let me go first. Marti has involved more parents in the classroom than I have, for one thing. Another is that she's so well organized and structured. She spends more time planning with her parents, she has to run off those Sugar Creek Dollars, and she's very clear about the student behaviors she's aiming for, both academically and discipline-wise, and what rewards—I mean reinforcers, I guess— to use to motivate the students. Things just run like clockwork in her room. I've observed her too!

DORENE   Marti?

MARTI   I hate to say it, but when I've visited Maria's room I came away with the feeling that her kids and parents love her more than mine do. Oh, mine admire me, and I'm very efficient like Maria says, but she's so positive and outgoing that she gets both her students and parents more enthused and excited than I do. It's like she convinced them that they're doing what they want to do and that they have a say in changing things at any time. I guess you could say that her class is more child-centered, while mine is more teacher-centered. [Pause] Maybe there is something to the business about there being a difference between getting people to do stuff that's self-rewarding rather than using rewards to get them to accomplish the teacher's objectives. Maria is a master at convincing students that what she wants them to learn is their idea.

DORENE   Wow! You two are good friends! What a hard decision! But I've got to make one and make it today.

MARTI   Well, go ahead and tell us Dorene. We're big girls. Which one of us are you going to recommend?

CLASSROOM DISCIPLINE SURVEY

FORM A

Check whether you agree or disagree with the following statements. Make no mark if you neither generally agree or disagree with a statement.

Agree   Disagree   I believe that:

_____   _____   1. it is more important to shape the child to the curriculum than to shape the curriculum to the child.

_____   _____   2. if a child is a behavior problem, the teacher must look for the cause of the misbehavior inside the child rather than in the classroom environment.

_____   _____   3. it is possible for a teacher to motivate students to learn by using rewards and punishments.

_____   _____   4. motivation comes from within the student and the student must choose to be motivated.

_____   _____   5. many things taught in classrooms can't be sugarcoated. It is OK for the teacher to use rewards external to the learning activity, such as grades and gold stars, to help the student learn.

_____   _____   6. the most important job of the teacher is to help students develop positive relations with other students and a more positive self-concept.

_____   _____   7. the teacher has to gain control of student behavior before student learning is possible.

_____   _____   8. if the teacher teaches in ways that are motivating to the students, discipline will not be a problem.

_____   _____   9. an excellent strategy is to find out what students like to do and use those as rewards for getting them to do things they don't like to do (such as reading, math, and behaving well in class).

_____   _____   10. the teacher's job is to understand what the student sees as interesting and relevant, then try to figure out ways of adjusting what is being taught to each student's interests.

_____   _____   11. while students' opinions should be sought by the teachers about appropriate classroom behavior, it is ultimately the teacher's job to establish rules of student conduct and enforcement procedures.

_____   _____   12. teachers and students should treat one another with respect as equals and not try to "overpower" one another.

Continued

_____ _____ 13. it is OK, as a last resort, for teachers to use corporal punishment in the case of clear rules violations.

_____ _____ 14. the teacher should view his or her job as one of teaching children to become better human beings, not as one of teaching subject matter.

_____ _____ 15. the teacher's job is to take the student where he or she is and move the student in small steps as far as possible toward learning goals (both academic and behavioral) set by the teacher (with or without student input).

_____ _____ 16. motivation and discipline are opposite sides of the same coin, but if one has to make a choice, motivation comes first.

QUESTIONS

1. What is the difference between classroom management and classroom discipline? Where do teachers learn classroom management skills? Is classroom management part of most teacher education programs?

2. One position on classroom discipline is that the goal is for each student to learn self-discipline. What is self-discipline, and how can it be fostered in students?

3. One position regarding discipline problems is that motivation techniques are more important than methods of classroom management, since discipline problems are minimal in a motivated class. The opposing position is that the teacher has to gain control of student behavior before learning can take place. Which position do you agree with most, and why?

4. What role should punishment play in classroom management? Under what conditions, if any, can punishment be effective in fostering student learning? What forms does punishment take, and what role should corporal punishment play in the classroom as well as at home?

5. What method of discipline do most teachers use? What beliefs does the average teacher hold about good discipline? What is the origin of such beliefs? How do they get passed on from teacher to teacher?

6. What are the most widely used classroom management models? How often are behavior modification, TET, Reality Therapy, Assertive Discipline, and Kounin's model used by teachers? Is there any research evidence as to which model is most effective? Is one just as good as the other?

7. How do the intrinsic and extrinsic views of motivation differ? Does the behavior modification method used by Marti better fit intrinsic or extrinsic assumptions? How about the TET methods used by Maria? Which has the most positive impact on student learning?

8. What are the strengths and weaknesses of behavior modification techniques? Which techniques does Marti use? How effective is behavior modification in motivating students to learn?

9. What are the strengths and weaknesses of TET? How effectively did Maria use Method III in the classroom? What assumptions, methods, and applications underlie humanistic psychology and educational practices?

10. Both Marti and Maria involved parents as classroom volunteers partly to help influence discipline in the home. How effective are such programs? Do teacher education programs prepare teachers to involve parents and provide them with the necessary skills of classroom planning and management necessary to produce successful parent involvement?

11. What decision should Dorene make? Which model of classroom management do you prefer, and why? What information should Dorene gather to help her make a decision?

THE COMEDIENNE

Key Content to Consider for Analyzing This Case:
(1) classroom management; (2) observational learning;
(3) operant conditioning.

L akeview Middle School, located in a predominately middle-class city of approximately 50,000 in the Northeast, was constructed in 1988 to accommodate the student population of a rapidly growing, upscale population in this section of the city of Landsford. The school now serves approximately 1,800 pupils from the surrounding area, with approximately 600 pupils in the sixth, seventh, and eighth grades. Approximately 87% of the students are white, 12% African-American, and 1% other ethnic groups. The student population by SES level is approximately 10% upper, 60% middle, and 30% lower.

Tom Tolbert has been teaching seventh-grade science at Lakeview since he graduated five years ago from the state's major university with a master's degree in education and a major in science. It is a brisk, sunny October day as Tom begins to review some information his second-period class of thirty-two students discussed yesterday related to their unit on matter.

TOM What's one of the characteristics of matter? *[Daniqua raises her hand.]* Daniqua?
DANIQUA It takes up space.
TOM How do you know that?
DANIQUA We blew up balloons yesterday, and we could see the air taking up space inside the balloon.
TOM Good, Daniqua. Tell me the other characteristic of matter, Marge.
MARGE *[Seriously]* It's very religious, because it has mass. *[Class members groan.]* Well, it tells us that right on page 15 of our science book. *[Holds up open book for class to see]*
DON *[Speaking out]* What a dork you are, Marge.
TOM OK, let's get on with our lesson. We know that the two characteristics of matter are that it has mass and takes up space. Who can give us an example of matter? *[No response]* How about you, Si?
SI *[Long pause]* Is it air?

TOM   Good, Si. But air's part of a larger category. Who knows what it is? *[Lori raises her hand immediately.]* Lori, tell us what it is.

LORI   Air's a mixture of gases.

ROSE   *[Speaking out]* I always thought gases were sort of bad for you to breathe. Like the gas in your stove or furnace.

TOM   Good point, Rose. There are all kinds of gases, and some of them are poisonous.

MARGE   *[Without raising her hand]* And some gases aren't poisonous, but they smell bad *[Tom sends her a warning look.]* I mean like sewer gas and gases like that.

TOM   Who can tell us another characteristic of gases? *[A long pause. Finally Chu raises hi hand.]* Chu.

CHU   Gases can be compressed.

TOM   That's good, Chu. And yesterday we prepared some experiments that should demonstrate this, and some other characteristics of gases. If you remember, we blew up two balloons. We put one in the refrigerator and tied the other outside the window where the morning sun shines. Jeff, would you go to the refrigerator and take out the balloon? *[Jeff gets the balloon out and puts it on the table in the front of the room. Then he walks toward his seat.]* Now, let's measure the balloon and see if it's th same size it was when we put it in the refrigerator yesterday. *[Just then, a loud, obnoxious sound filled the room as Jeff sat in his seat.]*

DAVE   Hey, nice one, Jeff!

MARGE   *[Who sits immediately behind Jeff]* Goodness, Jeff. You should excuse yourself. *[The class explodes with laughter.]*

JEFF   *[Embarrassed and angry]* You put that whoopee cushion on my seat as I was sitting down, Marge. That's not even funny, it's crude!

MARGE   *[Smiling innocently]* It seems that some of us thought it was funny, Jeff.

TOM   You know better than to do something like that in class, Marge.

MARGE   *[Innocently]* But Mr. Tolbert, I was just doing an experiment to help us find out if air is matter.

TOM   Oh, really. Please tell us about it.

MARGE   Well, I got the idea from our class yesterday. And it worked. When Jeff sat on the cushion it mashed the air molecules inside together. That forced the air out of the opening, which it wouldn't go through without the molecules being mashed together.

TOM   *[Not knowing whether to be angry or amused]* That unexpected demonstration wasn really necessary. We'd already planned enough experiments to demonstrate this principle. And Marge, "mashed together" is called "compressed" by scientists.

MARGE   *[Apologetically]* I was just trying to apply a principle we're studying on my own

TOM   *[Tongue in cheek]* Well, we all appreciate your efforts. Probably Jeff more than anyone.

JEFF   *[Sarcastically]* Yeah, right.

The remainder of the class was spent discussing the fact that cold air compresse the molecules of the balloon in the refrigerator, and the warmth from the sun expande the molecules of the balloon hanging in direct sunlight.

Since the third period is Tom's planning period, after the bell rang and the students left the room, Tom went to the teachers' lounge. When he arrived, he found Martha, a sixth-grade English teacher, Paul, a sixth-grade math teacher, and Angie, an eighth-grade social studies teacher.

TOM   *[Smiling]* Well, I see that I was lucky enough to have my planning period with the beautiful people of the school.

MARTHA   *[To Angie]* Tom's Irish, you know, and it's evident that he's kissed the Blarney stone.

ANGIE   Yes, I can see that. But I like what he said anyway.

PAUL   Nice to see you, Tom. How're your classes going this year?

TOM   Based on what I've seen so far, I think all of them will be interesting to work with.

MARTHA   When I passed your room on my way here at the end of last period, I saw Marge Green in the hall. Did she come out of your second-period class?

TOM   Yes, she's in that class.

MARTHA   I had her in my English class last year. She was really entertaining. She seems to have a terrific sense of humor.

TOM   *[Somewhat sarcastically]* Yes, she demonstrated her sense of humor in my class this very morning.

MARTHA   *[Smiling]* You sound as if you didn't appreciate her effort. Can you tell us what she did?

TOM   Just as the student who sits in the seat in front of her was sitting down, she slipped a whoopee cushion under him.

MARTHA   *[Laughing out loud]* Oh! That sounds just like Marge. She's so funny!

TOM   Well, the student who was the victim of her attempt at humor didn't think it was so funny. He seemed to think that Martha entertained the class at his expense.

ANGIE   And he's right! Sometimes the class clowns don't realize that fact when they do their entertaining.

MARTHA   That's true. I never thought of it that way when she was in my class last year. Her entertaining was always at someone else's expense.

PAUL   I think Marge comes by her desire to entertain naturally. I'm in a service club with her dad, and he's quite a clown himself.

TOM   What type of clowning does he do, Paul?

PAUL   Well, he seems to have the standard repertory of annoying equipment: rings that buzz when you shake hands with someone, whoopee cushions, artificial dog poop, vomit, and other replicas of gross things. And he has a repertory of dirty jokes that allows him to go on forever.

MARTHA   Do people seem to resent him?

PAUL   No, I don't think they do. He seems to be pretty well liked, and people act as if they enjoy having him around.

TOM   I wonder if Marge enjoys being the class clown, or if she feels somehow obligated to carry on the family tradition?

ANGIE   That's really an interesting question, Tom. Maybe by the end of the school year you'll find the answer to that question. *[A bell rings.]* Well, back to the old grind. See you all later. *[The teachers leave the lounge.]*

By the end of the second week of school, Tom's second-period students had com
pleted their study of matter and had taken a unit test over the material. At the beginnin
of the third week of class, the students began a study of atomic theory, and Tom ha
asked the students to read the chapter dealing with this topic over the weekend.

TOM   I think you'll enjoy working with the information in this chapter. The study of
atomic theory is still in its beginning stages. Everyone in your class may eventually
drive atomic-powered cars, fly in atomic-powered spaceships, live in atomic-
powered homes, and work with atomic-powered tools. Who can tell us what the
ancient Greeks discovered about atomic theory? *[Jeff raises his hand immediately.]* Jeff

JEFF   They were the first to think that matter was made up of little particles that were
hooked together. They called these particles atoms. But they thought that
everything was made up of air, water, earth, and fire.

TOM   That's good, Jeff. Now, who can tell us when this idea was changed? *[Chu raises his
hand.]* Chu.

CHU   It wasn't changed until the 1800s when John Dalton changed it.

MARGE   *[Shouting out]* I know him! He and his brothers were outlaws! They called them
the Dalton Brothers!

DAN   Oh, God! That's great! The Dalton Boys!

MARGE   *[Pointing her fingers like guns]* Bam! Bam! Pow! *[Other class members join in the
shoot-out.]*

TOM   *[Angrily]* Class! Stop! Cut it out immediately! *[The ruckus continues. Tom finally
takes his wooden meter stick and slams it across the top of his desk. Startled by the sharp
report, the students gradually quiet down. Those who were out of their seats quietly sit
back down.]* Quiet down! Now I want all of you to listen carefully. *[Students sit
motionless.]* We're not going to have any more incidents like the one we just
witnessed here today. I know which of you participated, and I've already put a
check by your names in my grade book. Any more demonstrations like this and
you'll find yourselves in a situation that you don't want to be in! Now, Chu *[who
didn't participate in the shoot-out]*, you were telling us about how the Greek model of
matter was changed. Will you please continue?

CHU   Yes, Sir. John Dalton was an English chemist and physicist. He accepted the Greek
idea of small particles, but he believed that the small particles or atoms in each
element were alike and that those from different elements were different. Dalton's
called the father of atomic theory because of his work.

TOM   That's great, Chu. Now who can tell us about J. J. Thompson's model? *[Matt raises
his hand.]* Matt. Go ahead.

MATT   Thompson said that all matter is electrified and has positive and negative charges
His model was like a bowl of pudding with raisins stuck in it. He called positive
charges protons and negative charges electrons. When you run a plastic comb
through your hair, you transfer electrons from your hair to your comb. That gives
your comb a negative charge, and it will attract small pieces of paper. *[As Matt
explains about the comb and the paper, Marge runs a comb through her hair with great
fanfare, then picks up small pieces of paper with it to the amusement of students sitting
near her. They get the attention of other students and point to Marge.]*

TOM   *[Shouting angrily]* Marge!

MARGE   *[Startled]* Yes, Sir.

TOM   I'd like you to come to my room immediately after your last class!

MARGE   *[Obviously upset]* What for?

TOM   You'll find out this afternoon.

MARGE   But—

TOM   *[Interrupting her]* We're not going to discuss it now! Be here immediately after school!

MARGE   *[Quietly submissive]* Yes, Sir.

Shortly after the last class has been dismissed, Marge comes to Tom's classroom as instructed. When she enters, Tom is working at his desk. Marge sits in a chair at one of the front tables and waits quietly.

TOM   *[Walks over to the table at which Marge is sitting and sits in the chair beside her]* Hello, Marge. Do you know why I asked you to come here after school?

MARGE   I think you're angry with me because of the things I did in class today.

TOM   Do you think it would be unfair for me to be angry with you?

MARGE   No, Sir.

TOM   If you think it's fair for me to be angry with you for acting the way you did, you must think that the ways you acted in class were inappropriate. Is that right?

MARGE   I guess so.

TOM   Aren't you sure?

MARGE   *[Looking down at the floor]* I'm sure. I shouldn't do some of the things I do in class.

TOM   Then why do you do them? *[Marge continues to stare at the floor and does not respond to the question.]* I'm referring to your speaking out in class with statements that have nothing to do with the lesson that you think are funny. Do you feel a strong need to make the other students laugh?

MARGE   I guess I do. I don't know why! Maybe I got it from my dad. He's always making people laugh, and everyone likes him.

TOM   Do you see any differences between making people laugh in social situations and in a school classroom?

MARGE   *[After a long pause]* I guess so.

TOM   Tell me what the difference is.

MARGE   *[Another long pause]* Well, in a social situation people usually are just visiting and not working on an important project or anything thing like that.

TOM   So making funny remarks or playing practical jokes doesn't really harm an informal social situation. Is that true? *[Marge nods her head.]* But in school, this kind of behavior can totally destroy the effort of the teacher or students to concentrate on learning. *[Again Marge nods her head.]* So when you do what you've been doing, you're basically disrupting the learning of your entire class, right?

MARGE   I guess so.

TOM   Don't you know for sure?

MARGE Yes, I do disrupt the class. I know I shouldn't do that, but I just can't seem to help myself.

TOM You're going to have to help yourself, Marge. I think I've been quite patient with you since school started, but you're getting more and more disruptive, and now other students are beginning to imitate you. And I'm not going to tolerate that! So I'm asking you to be a help to the class rather than a distraction. And I'm sure you can. But if you choose not to, I'll have to take strong disciplinary action. Do you understand that?

MARGE Yes, Sir. I'll try my hardest not to disrupt the class.

TOM You'll have to do more than try, Marge. You'll have to do it.

MARGE Yes, Sir.

It is Friday, a week after Tom and Marge had their conference after school. Tom h shared the results of his conference with Marge in the teachers' lounge on Monday. He h not gone to the lounge since then. This morning he decided to go there. As he is wal ing down the hall, Angie walks out of her room.

ANGIE Tom. Hi, are you on your way to the lounge?

TOM Yes, are you?

ANGIE Yes. I've been hoping to see you. Ever since you told us Monday about your Friday conference with Marge, all we third-period planners have been curious to hear how your plan has worked. But don't tell me now. Let's wait until we get to th lounge—I know the others will be interested, too.

TOM It's nice to know that my classroom management problems have generated such widespread interest.

ANGIE Well, you know why, don't you? *[Without waiting for a reply]* We all know that any of us could have the same problem, and we want to see how you handle it.

TOM I appreciate your interest regardless of your motives. It's nice to have colleagues who are willing to listen to my problems. It's quite therapeutic to know that someone else cares. *[They arrive at the lounge. Martha and Paul are already there.]* Speaking of our colleagues, they're already here. Hello, Martha; hello, Paul.

MARTHA We're glad you came today, Tom. We've been curious about Marge's behavior this week.

PAUL Yes, it's been the main topic of lounge conversation this week.

TOM *[Smiles]* I just told Angie that it's really comforting to have colleagues who are as supportive as you three are.

PAUL Enough of the accolades. Let's cut to the chase. Has Marge shaped up?

TOM All right. I'll give you a very direct yes and no answer.

ANGIE What kind of answer is that?

TOM I'll explain. Marge and I had our conference Friday after school. On Monday, as I told you, she was perfect. She paid attention to everything that went on in class. She participated fully and was very helpful.

MARTHA That's good to hear! So what's happened since then?

TOM Marge was delightful on Tuesday, Wednesday, and yesterday—just like a Girl Scout: helpful, courteous, kind, obedient, and so forth. But then this morning, it seemed as if the clown penned up inside her could no longer be contained. *[Pause*

PAUL   *[Eagerly]* Don't keep us in suspense. What did she do?

TOM   This is a suspenseful situation, Paul. I think I should draw it out so that you fully appreciate the intrigue of the situation.

ANGIE   *[Pleading]* Oh, come on, Tom! Tell us what happened.

TOM   OK. You talked me into it. At the beginning of class this morning, Marge was as cooperative as she'd been all week. But about halfway through the class, she raised her hand during a written exercise and asked if she could sharpen her pencil. I nodded yes and she got up out of her seat and started toward the pencil sharpener, which was clear across the room from her seat. Before I knew what had happened, Marge paused behind shy Johnny Roth's desk, put her arms around him, and kissed him on the neck. Johnny jumped out of his seat as if he'd been shot. The class went wild. I couldn't really tell whether Johnny was in agony or ecstasy.

PAUL   *[Smiling]* So much for class decorum.

TOM   Exactly. The class went wild, but I quickly reined them back under control. By then, Marge had finished sharpening her pencil and was sitting demurely in her seat.

MARTHA   *[Sounding disappointed]* Was that it?

TOM   Unfortunately, that was only the tip of the iceberg. *[Immediately the other teachers became attentive as Tom continues.]* She worked quietly at her seat for a short time until Rachel Goodman raised her hand. I motioned her to come over to me. Unfortunately, Rachel walked down the aisle past Marge's seat, and Marge stuck her foot into the aisle and tripped Rachel. Fortunately, Rachel wasn't hurt, but she was quite embarrassed.

PAUL   *[Enjoying the intrigue]* What did you do then?

TOM   I immediately moved Marge into a seat back in the corner of the room near the AV equipment and told her that if she did anything more to disturb the class I'd take her directly to the office. I then assigned the students to write the answers to the questions on the board in their science journals. As they were working, the librarian came to my doorway and motioned me to the door. When I went to the door, she told me that a new science book I'd asked her to order had arrived. I walked down the hall with her, and she gave me the book to examine. I took the book and immediately started back to my room.

ANGIE   *[In a stage whisper]* I can hardly wait to hear what you found.

TOM   I won't keep you in suspense. As I neared my room I heard music playing. I ran the rest of the way up the hall. As I approached my room, the first sight that greeted me was Marge dancing the Charleston in the front of the room with the entire class clapping in accompaniment. She was at the part in the dance where she was moving her hands back and forth over her knees. And I must say she was good at it. She looked like a professional dancer.

MARTHA   *[With obvious interest]* What did you do then?

TOM   I lost my cool and told her to go straight to the dean's office. Now my problem is that I definitely need to punish her. And I should tell her what her punishment will be when the dean finishes with her. But I can't decide what would be the most effective thing to do. She needs a relatively severe punishment for her disruptions of the class. I can't teach effectively with all the disruptions she causes.

FIGURE 21 Portion of Marge Green's Cumulative Record

LAKEVIEW MIDDLE SCHOOL

Cumulative Record

Name: Margaret Green Home Phone: 391-2874 Former School: Oak Elementary
Address: 537 Walnut Lane
Father: Henry Green Occupation: Salesman Health: Excellent
Mother: Rebecca Green Occupation: Homemaker Health: Excellent
Siblings: None Date of Birth: 8/20/86

INTELLIGENCE TESTS:

	Form	IQ	Date	Grade
Otis-Lennon School Ability Tests	Elementary 1	116	10/10/94	3
	Intermediate	111	10/15/98	7

ACADEMIC RECORD

Grades 1–5 (Year Averages)

	1	2	3	4	5
Reading	B	A	A	A	A
Mathematics	A	B	A	A	A
Science/Health	A	A	A	A	A
Social Studies	A	A	A	A	A
Language	A	A	A	A	A
Spelling	A	A	A	A	A
Music/Art	A	B	B	B	A
Citizenship	A	B	B	B	B

Grades 6–8 (Year Average)

	6	7	8
English	A	A	
Geography	A	A	
Mathematics	A	A	
Science	A	A	
Physical Ed.	A	A	

Personal Development (Grades 1–5)

	1	2	3	4	5
Conduct	B	B	C	C	C
Effort	A	A	A	A	A
Follows Directions	A	A	A	A	A
Initiative	A	A	A	A	A
Attitude	B	B	B	C	C
Work Habits	A	A	A	A	A
Participation	A	A	A	A	A

PAUL   Well, there are certainly many options. You could visit her parents, talk with the
administration about suspending her from school for a few days, or give her
detention for several days or weeks.

ANGIE   You could also send her to the guidance counselor or give her a failing grade for
the day each time she does something outrageous.

MARTHA   I sometimes give students extra assignments to complete for each disruption
when they begin to misbehave frequently.

TOM   *[Gratefully]* I really appreciate your suggestions. I'd thought of many of them
myself, but you've mentioned others that hadn't occurred to me. And some of them
seem as if they'd be effective. But that's my big problem. At this point, I just don't
know how to handle her. I want to take an approach that'll motivate her to change
her behavior, but I just don't know what strategy would be the best.

QUESTIONS

1. From an operant conditioning perspective, what kinds of undesirable behaviors are
being emitted by Marge? What reinforcers are maintaining her behavior? What role are
the teachers and other students playing in this process? What operant techniques could
be used to change Marge's behavior?

2. In terms of observational learning, what models does Marge seem to be imitating?
What is vicarious reward, and how does it apply to Marge? What is disinhibition, and
how does it explain the interactions between Marge and the other students in the classroom? What is cognitive behavior modification, and how can students like Marge be
taught to use it to change their behavior? What are self-regulation techniques, and how
can they be used to change behavior?

3. What role does Marge's home, especially her parents, play in encouraging Marge's
clowning behavior? How could the teacher involve Marge's parents in resolving this situation? What methods of parent involvement do schools use, and which ones would be
most helpful in this situation?

4. What classroom management models would be most helpful to Tom in this case?
Could Tom use Assertive Discipline, Teacher Effectiveness Training, or Reality Therapy in
this situation? What classroom management beliefs does Tom have, and how effective are
they?

5. Tom and his fellow teachers seem to think of various methods of punishment as the
best way to handle Marge. What is punishment, and how effective is it in promoting student learning? Under what conditions is the use of punishment most effective? What
types of punishment are the best to use?

6. To what extent do teachers learn from other teachers? To what extent does teacher
education influence the classroom management and motivational methods that teachers
use? To what extent is the teacher's behavior influenced by his or her own family background in terms of SES and racial/ethnic values, especially in the area of discipline?

7. Marge's peers seem to be a source of social reinforcement for her behavior in the
classroom. What group social reinforcement techniques can a teacher like Tom use to deal

with such situations? How can the behavior of a student like Marge serve as a model fo other students to imitate?

8. What are Kounin's principles of classroom management? Which ones are relevan to this case? What are "withitness" and the "ripple effect"? What techniques of Kounin can Tom use in the situation?

9. If Tom decides to refer Marge for help, should he send her to a dean, a guidanc counselor, a school psychologist, or an educational psychologist? What differences exi between these different professionals? What methods do they typically use?

10. At what level of Maslow's need hierarchy is Marge primarily operating? How ca Tom use this information to deal with Marge? What humanistic techniques are most use ful in dealing with students like Marge?

11. Examine Marge's cumulative record (see figure on page 200). What does it tell yo about Marge? What is the best interpretation of her intelligence and academic data? D her chronological age and the fact that she has no siblings suggest possible explanatior for her behavior?

12. How appropriate would it be for Tom to use a classroom meeting approach (base on William Glasser's Reality Therapy) for dealing with Marge's behavior? What might th results of such a classroom meeting be?

13. If you were advising Tom, what would you tell him to do in dealing with Marge What strategy would be best? How can Tom motivate her to change her behavior?

CASE **21**

FAMILY VALUES

Key Content to Consider for Analyzing This Case:
(1) observational learning; (2) cultural diversity;
(3) home learning environment; (4) teacher biases/self-fulfilling prophecy.

Matt Howe is a white middle-class teacher who teaches seventh-grade English at Walt Whitman Middle School. Whitman is located in the inner city of a large metropolitan city in the Northeast. Matt's second-period class of thirty-two students is representative of the school population generally with twelve African-Americans, two Asian-Americans, seven Hispanics, and eleven whites. With disproportionately high numbers of African-American and Hispanic students, Whitman is truly a multicultural school. The majority (59%) of the students are from low-income families.

Matt graduated with a B.S. in education with a major in English from a nearby state university and immediately accepted a teaching position at Whitman. This school year Matt begins his sixth year of teaching seventh grade at Whitman, and this year's classes are typical of his classes from previous years. Of the thirty-two pupils in his second-period English class, three of the African-American pupils are middle income and nine are low income; five of the white pupils are middle income and six are low income; three of the Hispanic students are middle income and four are low income; and both Asian-American students are from middle-income families.

Since Matt was assigned bus duty during the first week of classes, he arrived at school twenty minutes before the buses arrived and the school doors were unlocked. His responsibility was to observe the interaction among students while they were outside the school and relatively unsupervised, and to intercede in any behavior that was inappropriate.

As the first school bus arrived and students began to exit the bus, Mark, a white middle-income student, was carrying several books and a trumpet case. As he was trying to get down the steps of the bus, some of his books started to fall. He stopped on the steps and tried to get them under control. Alphonso, a large, low-income African-American, was behind Mark.

ALPHONSO   C'mon man, I ain't got all day!

MARK *[Smiling]* Sorry, I'm having trouble with all my gear. I don't seem to have enough hands. *[Some of his books slip out of his arms and fall on the steps.]*

ALPHONSO *[Angrily]* Get outta the way, stupid! You're holding me up! *[Shoves Mark off the stairs onto the ground. Mark's books are scattered and his trumpet case has come open.]* You're really a lost cause!

MARK *[Rubbing his shoulder as he gets up off the ground while trying hard not to cry]* What's wrong with you, Al? You could've broken one of my bones. Why're you in such a hurry to get off the bus? You're surely not excited to get to school, are you?

ALPHONSO I just like to mess up you little rich white kids once in a while. *[Smiling and sticking out his chest]* It makes me feel good.

MARK Well, I'm glad you feel good now. In a few years, you'll be in jail, and you won't feel good there!

ALPHONSO *[Grabbing Mark and pulling him to his feet roughly]* You little jerk, I'll make you feel bad right now. *[Pulls back his fist to hit Mark. Matt rushes to Mark's aid, grabs Al's arm forcefully, and tells him to stop.]*

ALPHONSO *[Angrily]* That's right. Go ahead and take this little worm's part. Last year my brother Len hit a white kid who was really giving him a lot of grief. The teacher who saw the fight took the white kid's part, just like you're doing!

MATT I don't know what happened with your brother last year, but I saw what happened here, Al, and you're out of line on this one. I want you and Mark to come to my classroom for a few minutes right after school ends. We'll talk about this some more. *[Al gives a dirty look to both Matt and Mark and then walks away. Matt watches Alphonso walk toward the school and sees him approach a white middle-income boy, Carl, conversing with an African-American girl.]*

ALPHONSO Yo, Kenora.

KENORA Hey, Alphonso. What's happening?

ALPHONSO Al's upset that his honey's rappin' with this wimpy honky, that's what's happenin'! *[Turns to Carl]* Take off, honky. I'm Kenora's main man.

CARL That's OK, Al. I know you're her main man. Kenora and I are just friends.

ALPHONSO *[Approaches Carl and grabs him by the arm]* No, it ain't OK, man. I don't want Kenora to have honky friends. Now move away now, or I'll move you away!

KENORA Alphonso, what's wrong with you? You're my main man, but you don't run my whole life. You can't tell me who I can and can't talk to!

ALPHONSO Yes I can, and I will! *[Looking at Carl]* If you ain't walkin' away by the time I count three, you're in trouble, man!

KENORA Al, you're ridiculous! I can talk to anyone I want to.

CARL It's OK, Kenora. I don't want to cause you any trouble. I'll see you later. *[Walks away]*

ALPHONSO *[To Kenora]* See, that white boy ain't got no guts. I don't want you talking to him anymore. If you're with me, you don't have no other boys as friends, especially honkies. In my neighborhood, we don't let honkies mess wit' our women. *[Takes Kenora by the arm, and they walk in the other direction from Carl. Luis Aguillo sees them and walks over to them and puts his arm around Kenora's shoulders.]*

LUIS Hi there, Kenora! You look beautiful this morning.

ALPHONSO *[Angrily]* Back off, spick! She's with me!

LUIS   That's OK, Alphonso. She'll soon see the light. She must already be getting tired of hanging around with a crude ugly dude like you when she could have a cool Latin lover like me. My uncle Alfredo is a great lover, and I take after him. He must have thirty women in love with him. *[Smiling at Kenora]* I'm going to replace him soon. And you will be my number one squeeze.

ALPHONSO   *[Scowling]* I tole you to back off, Luis.

LUIS   *[Laughing]* *[To Kenora]* See there, he's worried to death already! See you later, Kenora. *[To Al]* You, too, Tiger. *[Walks casually toward the school]*

ALPHONSO   *[To Kenora]* That Luis is really a mess, isn't he? [They walk slowly toward the school.]

At the end of the school day, Mark and Alphonso have both come to Matt's classroom, as he requested.

MATT   I asked you to meet with me this afternoon because I think it's important for us to talk about the incident this morning. I believe that one of the jobs of teachers is to help people settle problems through discussion instead of violence.

ALPHONSO   Man, if you think like that, you wouldn't get out of my neighborhood alive! My brother Len taught me long ago that you can't take any crap off'a anybody or they'll think you're weak. If somebody starts messin' with you, knock 'em flat before they do it to you.

MARK   It's not that way where I live. My parents have taught me that you should treat everybody the way you would like to be treated.

ALPHONSO   Neither one of you would get out of my neighborhood alive.

MATT   But you seem to go beyond what Len has taught you, Al. Mark wasn't doing anything to you. He was just having trouble carrying all his gear off the bus. If I'd been behind him, I would have offered to carry his trumpet for him. That would have solved the problem a lot better than your violent approach.

ALPHONSO   I guess how you act depends a lot on what the people you grow up with tell you is right.

MATT   That's a very wise statement, Al. If you'd been in Mark's place and the roles were reversed, how would you have wanted Mark to treat you?

ALPHONSO   *[After several seconds of thought]* I don't know. But he'd better not push me!

It is the second week of school. Matt's second-period English class has been studying a unit on cultural diversity. As a part of the study, Matt has been reading each day from *The Great American Shame*, a classic story about a young Cherokee, Little Hawk, who was left with his grandparents when the government forced all Indians in North Carolina to move to Oklahoma. Matt chose this story because many problems of the Cherokee, a minority group, are similar to those of most minority groups in the United States today. Since there are no Native Americans in Matt's class, the problems of discrimination represented in the book can be discussed in class objectively, even though they pertain to many of the students in the class.

MATT   Who can review for us the plot and setting of this story? *[Lei immediately raises her hand.]* OK, Lei. You tell us.

LEI   The setting of the story is in North Carolina in the late 1830s. White settlers moving into the area don't like the Cherokee, so they talked the members of Congress into passing a law requiring the Cherokee to move to the Indian Territor in Oklahoma. The Cherokee have chosen to walk rather than ride their horses. Little Hawk's grandparents, who live in the mountains far from the reservation, think many of their people will die or be killed on their march. So they asked Litt Hawk's parents if he can stay with them until they become settled in Oklahoma. The parents agreed to let Little Hawk stay with them.

MATT   That's good, Lei. Thank you. *[To the class]* Now, who can tell us why the settlers don't like the Cherokee? How about you, Ahmed? *[A long pause]* Ahmed. Do you know?

AHMED   No, man. I don't remember.

MATT   How can you not know? We talked about this just yesterday. Didn't you hear th answer to that question when I read the story?

AHMED   *[Unenthusiastically]* No, man. I wasn't listenin' for no answers.

MATT   *[Concerned]* I can't understand why you didn't hear it when I read it in class.

AHMED   I didn't listen to the story, man. I don't like stories! I don't like school! I don't even like bein' here now! There's nothin' here for me! Black guys don't get no breaks in school!

ALPHONSO   That's right, man! The people in the stories we read ain't real. They don't li like we do.

DUN   I don't agree, Al. This story is true. The Cherokee were a minority group. That's why the settlers drove them away. There was plenty of space for the settlers to far and ranch and for the Cherokee to live in their villages. The white people drove them away just because they were different . . . just like some of us are different.

AHMED   *[Shouting]* You're full of it, Dun! Stories ain't nothing like real life. The guy wh wrote this just made it all up.

DUN   *[Quietly]* You're wrong, Ahmed. This whole story we're reading is about things tl people do to you and me every day. And that's prejudice. The Cherokee didn't do anything bad to the settlers. The settlers just didn't like the Cherokee because the were different, and they didn't understand them. They called them savages and redskins, just like people call me a Chink.

ALPHONSO   People call me worse than that, Dun!

MATT   What do they call you?

ALPHONSO   Nigger, spade, spook—Lots of things.

MATT   Why do you think those names are bad?

ALPHONSO   They put us black people down! That's why I don't like 'em! I pound peop down for calling me those things.

MATT   What would you like to be called?

ALPHONSO   An African-American, I guess.

LUIS   *[Shouting out]* You call me a spick all the time, Al!

MATT   What would you like to be called, Luis?

LUIS   A Hispanic, I guess.

MATT   Alphonso, if Luis calls you an African-American, would you be willing to call him a Hispanic?

ALPHONSO   I guess so.

MATT   That's great. Each ethnic group seems to have a particular name they prefer to be called.

DUN   Well, that takes care of everybody except us Asians. We like to be called Asian-Americans.

MATT   That's good, Dun. Thanks.

On Friday morning Matt decided to go to the teachers' lounge during his free period. Three other teachers were there when he arrived, and they greeted him enthusiastically.

CHRIS   Well, look whose here! Is third period your planning period, Matt?

MATT   *[Nodding to all]* What are you all talking about?

MARY   Nothing important. Any problems you'd like to discuss?

MATT   Yes. I have just one. I'd like this group of professionals to explain to me how I can arrange for my low- and middle-income students and all the different ethnic and racial students in my classes to work cooperatively and to like each other.

SAM   Well, that's easy. All you have to do is to put each student in a separate cage.

CHRIS   I doubt whether that would work, Sam. After a few days, they'd probably bring slingshots and shoot marbles at each other. *[The other teachers smile and agree with Chris.]*

MATT   I really meant for that to be a serious question. It seems to me that my classes this year have more friction along the lines of socioeconomic, ethnic, and racial differences than those I've had in the previous four years.

MARY   I'm having a lot of trouble in those areas, too. Yesterday a low-income African-American boy, Keno, snatched a dollar from a middle-income white kid. When the white kid tried to snatch it back, Keno hit him in the face and blackened his eye. I sent them both to the principal, and she gave Keno detention. Then he threatened to beat up the white boy for getting him into trouble. It seems that you just can't win with low-income kids!

CHRIS   I know what you mean. I had Keno in class last year. He beat up his father so badly that he had to spend several days in the hospital.

SAM   Yes, I remember that incident. It seems that his father is one of the big drug pushers in the neighborhood. He makes a lot of money. I remember this because I had the older brother in class. He was really smart and was a tremendous athlete in both football and basketball. Several college coaches tried to recruit him because his grades were good enough to get him admitted to college, and he's an outstanding athlete. But, unfortunately, I think he decided that he could make big money quicker by working for Dad.

MATT   It's too bad that one of the main characteristics of the low-income kids is that they aren't able to control themselves. They have to get everything they want right now. The middle-income kids seem to develop self-control. Both groups seem to develop these characteristics very young. There are some low-income kids who are

in athletics or other activities that help them develop self-control, but the majorit
of them don't seem to learn it ever.

CHRIS *[Looking at her watch]* Well, I'm afraid our big discussion's about to end. The
fourth period's coming to an end. There's the bell. *[The other teachers get their boo*
and papers and prepare to leave.]

It is several weeks later. Matt has finished reading *The Great American Shame* to
class. This morning he has written the following test questions on the board for the s
dents to answer.

Test Questions on *The Great American Shame*

Write answers to each of the following questions. Answer each question fully, 1
make your answers brief and concise.

1. Describe in detail at least three issues of disagreement that existed between t
   Cherokee and the white settlers in North Carolina. Present both sides of eac
   issue.
2. Tell how the settlers were able to convince government officials that they
   should force the Cherokee to move to Oklahoma. Do you think this was a fa
   decision for the government to make? Explain why.
3. Explain why the journey of the Cherokee from North Carolina to Oklahoma
   became known as the "Trail of Tears." Describe some of the hardships they s
   fered during the journey.
4. List and describe the arrangements that the government made to help the
   Cherokee get settled in Oklahoma.
5. Describe another situation in which our government selected a group of min
   ity citizens and confined them in a segregated community. Tell whether you
   approve of this decision and explain why.

Some students take out a sheet of paper and begin to write immediately. Oth
begin to complain.

JULIO Man, you didn't cover all that stuff in class.

LOMA Yea, I don't remember ever hearing nothin' called the Trail of Tears.

ALPHONSO Me, neither.

HELEN *[Disgusted]* We talked about all those things in class this week. We went over t
answer to the fifth question yesterday.

LOMA Who asked you, Miss Know-It-All?

HELEN Nobody asked me, I just volunteered the information because I get tired of
hearing you three complaining all the time.

LOTTIE It's not the work that bothers me. I don't understand why we haf'ta take a test
on a book about something that happened a hundred years ago. That doesn't ma
sense!

MATT Now, all of you. Stop talking and answer the questions on the board! You're
wasting time!

The following morning as Matt walks toward the school, he sees a low-income white male student approach Mark, a middle-income white male in Matt's second-period class.

SAM Hey, Mark, my man.

MARK *[Suspiciously]* Whaddya want, Sam?

SAM Gimme a dolla. I need some lunch money.

MARK Why don't you get it from somebody else? You're always asking me.

SAM *[Grabbing Mark's arm]* Let's not have big trouble about this, Mark. Just give me the money and we'll both be happy. If you don't, we'll both be sad. But you'll be sadder than I am, 'cause your body'll be hurtin'.

MARK *[Handing Sam a dollar]* OK, I'll give it to you this time, but don't ask me for money anymore or I'll report you.

MATT *[Approaching the boys from behind]* OK. Time to give the dollar back, Sam.

SAM It's OK, Mr. Howe. Mark just lent me this dollar until tomorrow.

MATT Nice try, Sam, but I saw and heard what happened. Now, do you want to return Mark's dollar, or do you want us all to go to Mr. Dennis' office and explain what we all know about this situation?

SAM *[Disgusted, reaches into his pocket and returns the dollar to Mark]* Here you go, wimp. I'll deal with you later. *[Mark takes the dollar and walks away.]*

MATT Do you need money so badly that you have to shake down other students to get it, Sam?

SAM *[Frowning]* Things are so bad at home that you wouldn't believe it! My dad's gone all the time. He deals drugs, gambles, and keeps girlfriends all the time. My older brother Dan's about the same way. If I tell 'em that stuff is stupid, they rough me up and tell me what to do.

MATT I can understand how that puts you under a lot of pressure. But you're smart enough to make good grades, and you're an excellent athlete. I'd like to see you go to college on an athletic scholarship.

SAM I'd like to do that, but I'm not sure I could. People in my family don't go to college. I know I'm good at most sports, but making grades in school's really hard for me. And nobody at home thinks school's very important anyhow. They probably wouldn't want me to go to college even if I got a scholarship. Dad'll probably make me work with him and Dan.

MATT I think you'd be much better off in the long run if you went to college. I'm willing to help you get an athletic scholarship and get admitted to college, but you'll have to buckle down on your academics and your behavior in class. No more shaking down kids for money. Think about it. You have good leadership potential. Going to college could change your life for the better. Let's work toward that goal.

SAM *[Pleased but not convinced]* I'm glad you're interested in helping me, but I think the deck's stacked against me going to college. I'll quit shakin' down Mark, Mr. Howe.

The following morning, Mark asked Matt if they could meet sometime soon. He said it was very important. Matt asked him to come to his classroom immediately after school was out. Mark arrived promptly.

Mark   I really appreciate your talking with me, Mr. Howe, and I also appreciate your helping me with Sam. I'm really ashamed that you had to do that, but I'm scared t death of Sam and his gang. That's part of the reason I want to see you. Those guys take money from me, steal my clothes, make me give them my homework, embarrass me in front of my friends, and generally make my life miserable. I'm so stressed out all the time that it's beginning to affect my grades. I want to go to college, and my parents want me to go too, but if this keeps up I might not be abl to make it.

Matt   I understand the situation you're in. Have you discussed all this with your parent:

Mark   Yes, and they're really upset about the situation, too. Dad's been to school and talked to the principal and even looked into private high schools, but they're so expensive that if he sent me to one of them, he couldn't afford to send me to college. He wants me to stay away from the gang and do my own thing, but I don seem to be able to do that. Those guys in the gang always find me and steal my things and rough me up. I could hold my own with any one of them, but if I beat one of them up, they'd all gang up on me. I'm half scared to death all the time, an the principal can't help me. What can I do, Mr. Howe?

The following morning, Matt asks Sam if he can come to his room for a few mi utes after school that afternoon. Sam agrees to come. When Sam arrives, Matt is waiti for him.

Matt   Thanks for coming, Sam. I need some information that I think you might be abl to give me.

Sam   I will if I can. What do you want to know?

Matt   Well, I know that you and some of your friends give Mark Inman a bad time. I' like to know if there's some special reason that you're so hard on him. Has he don something to one of you? Or is there something he should be doing that he's not? [Pause] I guess I'm really asking what it would take to make you stop bothering him

Sam   [A long pause] I really don't know. He's not a bad guy, and he hasn't really done anything to us. I guess he just stands for everything that makes us angry. He's rich smart, good-looking, has everything he wants, and plans to go to college. I guess when we shake him down or beat him up, it makes us feel like we're getting even with all the people who have the things that we want to have, but can't.

Matt   But it's not his fault that he has those things.

Sam   I know, but it's not our fault that we don't.

Matt   You told me the other day that you'd let Mark alone. Did you talk to your gang about that?

Sam   [In a panic] Whoa, man. I can't do that. I've got to stay in the gang to survive. If I took his part against my friends, I'd end up worse off than he is. I just told you th I personally would leave him alone, and I will.

Matt   What if I talked to them about this?

Sam   What could you say that would change anything? What can anybody do to chan anything around here?

FIGURE 22   Student Information Assembled by Matt Howe on His Second-Period English Class

NAME	ELIGIBLE FOR FREE LUNCH	IQ[1]	GPA[2]	NO. OF SIBLINGS	MOTHER'S OCCUPATION	FATHER'S OCCUPATION
. Aguillo, Luis	yes	78	1.5	4	maid	prison guard
. Aquino, Vanessa	yes	89	2.0	2	homemaker	truck driver
. Baker, Alphonso	yes	76	1.0	3	waitress	road crew
. Banks, Lottie	yes	86	2.4	6	homemaker	janitor
. Corrales, Julio	yes	72	1.2	5	homemaker	laborer
. Daniels, Nathan	no	78	2.6	1	homemaker	mechanic
. Delacruz, Edwardo	yes	90	2.1	2	cook	sales clerk
. Epps, Carl	no	102	2.0	0	homemaker	mechanic
. Ford, Kenora	yes	103	2.2	1	secretary	sales rep
. Gunter, Darryl	no	110	2.7	0	teacher	musician
. Habgood, Samuel	yes	105	2.1	2	nurse	painter
. Hughes, Dana	yes	90	2.1	1	childcare	musician
. Inman, Mark	no	110	3.0	0	homemaker	landscaper
. Jones, Moses	yes	70	1.2	2	clerk	unemployed
. Kahn, Ahmed	yes	75	1.4	4	homemaker	carpenter
. Ling, Dun	no	112	3.7	1	secretary	chemist
. Linton, Ellis	no	106	2.9	2	homemaker	taxi driver
. Masquida, Carlos	yes	86	1.6	4	babysitter	prison guard
. McCool, Loma	yes	90	1.8	2	homemaker	paper hanger
. Soo, Lei	no	115	3.6	1	homemaker	chef
. Oehler, Paul	no	110	3.5	1	homemaker	teacher
. Pardo, Vicki	yes	94	2.2	2	seamstress	army sergeant
. Ponce, Rachael	yes	95	2.0	1	clerk	musician
. Poppe, Oscar	no	98	2.8	2	cook	paperhanger
. Ramirez, Alina	yes	87	1.7	5	homemaker	mill laborer
. Scott, Helen	no	112	3.3	1	teacher	salesman
. Subak, Eleanor	yes	102	2.7	2	clerk	lawn care
. Tanner, Roscoe	no	110	2.8	2	secretary	boat repair
. Tracy, Daniel	no	111	3.2	1	homemaker	policeman
. Vogler, Carolyn	no	113	3.4	1	homemaker	plumber
. Wasula, Angie	yes	100	2.2	2	homemaker	cook
. Wright, Otis	yes	94	1.9	3	maid	laborer

[1] tal IQ on Otis Lennon Mental Ability Test given in sixth grade.
[2] PA at end of sixth grade based on A = 4, B = 3, C = 2, D = 1, and F = 0.

QUESTIONS

1. What is cultural diversity? What forms has diversity taken at Whitman Middle School? How can teachers be educated to deal with such diversity? What is the diversity picture in the future for the United States?

2. What role does a common language, such as standard English, play in unifying "melting pot" culture like that of the United States? Could a common culture exist wit out a common language? How should a classroom teacher handle language differences the classroom?

3. What is social class and how is it measured? How does social class differ fro socioeconomic status (SES)? Why are compensatory education programs in schools (e.g school lunch programs, Head Start, Title I) based on SES?

4. What role does the home environment play in shaping student attitudes towa school, school achievement, and self-discipline? What kinds of techniques can the scho use to involve parents in their children's education? What barriers can prevent such met ods from working?

5. Why do students from different backgrounds, such as those due to socioeconom ethnic, and racial differences, acquire different values about physical aggressiveness, ga membership, self-discipline, delay of gratification, and the value of academic achiev ment? What values do schools and teachers typically hold regarding these matters? Wh can be done about this clash in values?

6. From the standpoint of observational learning, what models are the students in th case learning to imitate? For example, what models are operating in the lives of Alphon and Sam? How do we choose the models we imitate? What can a teacher do to prese alternative models?

7. What is sense of efficacy in observational learning? What sense of efficacy do Alphonso have about academics? Sam about group membership? Mark about his abili to deal with Sam's gang and physical aggression?

8. What is a juvenile delinquent? Is Sam a juvenile delinquent? How can juven delinquents be identified, and what role can teachers play in this regard? What can done to help such a child?

9. How are gangs formed, and why? What can teachers do about gangs, and how c they help students like Mark who are terrorized by gangs?

10. What is a school dropout? What is an at-risk student? What can be done to he such students when identified? Are there any at-risk students in this case?

11. What are prejudice and stereotyping? What biases do teachers have that influen their behavior toward different students? What can be done about such biases?

12. What is cooperative learning? Would cooperative learning methods be helpful dealing with the socioeconomic, racial, and ethnic differences in this case?

13. What is life stress, and how is it measured? How much stress is there in Mar life, and how is it likely to affect his school performance? What techniques can peop learn to help them deal with stress?

14. At the end of the case, Sam asks Matt, "What can anybody do to change anythi around here?" What kinds of things can a teacher like Matt do? What can Matt do to he Mark or Alphonso, or Sam?

PARENTS AS PARTNERS

Key Content to Consider for Analyzing This Case:
(1) observational learning; (2) parent involvement;
(3) cultural diversity; (4) home environment.

Matt Howe is a white middle-class teacher who teaches seventh-grade English at Walt Whitman Middle School. Whitman, built in 1960, is located in an area that has depreciated from a middle-class suburban area to the inner city of a large metropolitan city in the Northeast. Matt's second-period class of thirty-two students is generally representative of the school population with twelve African-Americans, two Asian-Americans, seven Hispanics, and eleven whites. With disproportionately high numbers of African-American and Hispanic students, Whitman is truly a multicultural school. The majority (59%) of the students are from low-income families.

Matt graduated from a nearby state university with a B.S. in education with a major in English and immediately accepted a teaching position at Whitman. This school year Matt begins his sixth year of teaching seventh grade at Whitman, and this year's classes are typical of his classes from previous years. Of the thirty-two pupils in his second-period English class, three of the African-American pupils are middle income and nine are low income; five of the white pupils are middle income and six are low income; three of the Hispanic students are middle income and four are low income; and both Asian-American students are from middle-income families.

It is Monday, the beginning of the second semester of classes. Last Tuesday, Matt stopped in the principal's office and asked the secretary to make an appointment for him to see Dr. Sam Dawson, the principal. He made the appointment for today as soon as the last class was over. Matt is sitting in the outer office as Sam opens the door to his office.

SAM   *[Sees Matt in the office and immediately greets him and shakes his hand]* Matt, it's nice to see you. I noticed last week that you'd made an appointment to see me. Come into the office, and you can tell me how things are going with your English classes.

MATT   *[Rises, smiles, and returns Sam's handshake]* It's nice to see you, too, Sam. We both seem to be too busy to have much time to visit each other.

SAM   *[Motioning Matt to a chair]* Unfortunately, that seems to be the case. But I don't think it's limited to schools. I think it's just a sign of the times. Everybody's too busy. *[Smiles]* And we are, too. So we probably ought to get to the purpose for your visit.

Matt   *[Returns Sam's smile]* I agree. And I'll get right to it. *[Pauses to collect his thoughts]* Basically, it boils down to the fact that I'm in my sixth year of teaching here, and I haven't been able to do a good job of teaching. This year, I'm so concerned about a situation that I wanted to talk with you about it.

Sam   *[Completely taken by surprise]* But—the other teachers consider you to be one of our best teachers. Your evaluations are excellent.

Matt   Maybe I'm good relative to some of the teachers at Whitman, but my concern is that the nature of our school population keeps any of us from teaching the way we were taught to teach in our teacher education classes.

Sam   Such as?

Matt   Probably the most obvious difference is that there's such a wide diversity of ethnic groups, many of whom strongly dislike each other, that a fight can and frequently does break out at any time of day. The students tell me that their parents have negative attitudes toward other ethnic groups. So the situation involves more than what goes on in the classroom. Some African-American students are essentially running a protection racket and demanding money from middle-class white kids— pay up or get beat up. I've heard these students talk about their older brothers doing the same thing. My students probably learned the racket from them. There's also a disproportionately large representation of low-SES *[socioeconomic status]* students who have little or no interest in the traditional school curriculum. And from conversations with them, their parents felt the same way about school when they were students. This results in an unusually high truancy rate as well as a real problem in maintaining any type of classroom discipline. What they learn in school has no relevance to the lives they lead. The wide range of ability levels in the class makes it virtually impossible to meet the needs of most of the students. Many days I feel like I'm refereeing a free-for-all instead of teaching a class. I do the best that I can, but I'm starting to get burned out. I feel that I'm cheating my students.

Sam   *[Overwhelmed]* Whew! I didn't realize you were so frustrated with your job!

Matt   Please don't misinterpret what I'm saying, Sam. I love my job, and I love these kids. My discontentment springs from my feeling that they have so many needs that I'm not able to deal with. They develop a negative attitude about school from their parents and siblings before they even have a chance to judge school for themselves. They arrive at kindergarten expecting to find a hostile environment—and they do.

Sam   *[Seriously]* Have you thought of anything I could do to enable you to meet more of your students' needs? I've certainly been aware of these same problems, but I haven't been able to think of any reasonable solutions.

Matt   I've been trying to think of solutions to these problems for about five years now, but I haven't found any surefire formula. But I keep coming back to one idea.

Sam   Well, don't keep me in suspense. Tell me what it is!

Matt   When I was in college, one of our professors received a federal grant that provided money for the local school district to hire parents to work as aides in classrooms. They chose mothers of low-income minority students. As I recall, everybody involved thought that the program was quite effective.

SAM   Yes, I remember some school districts that hired parent aides. As I recall, most people involved in these programs were generally pleased with the results.

MATT   *[Encouraged]* Is there any possibility that we could try this program here at Whitman?

SAM   *[Walks to a filing cabinet, removes a folder, and studies it briefly]* I have enough teacher aide money in the budget to employ two mothers for one class as an experimental program. But this would put an extra burden on the classroom teacher they work with. That teacher would have to plan what the mothers would do, teach them how to do it, and supervise their efforts. This could involve a significant amount of time and effort.

MATT   *[Enthusiastically]* I'd really like to have the mothers in my room, Sam, and I'd be willing to do whatever I need to do to make the program a success. And I've even thought of the mothers I'd like to have if they're interested.

SAM   *[Smiling]* My, you've really given this a lot of thought! Tell me their names, and your reasons for picking them.

MATT   I'd like to work with the mothers of Alphonso Baker and Luis Aguillo.

SAM   Interesting choices. Why those two?

MATT   Mainly because I have the most trouble with those two boys. But in addition to that, Al and Luis are leaders of the members of their ethnic groups in the class. They're also discipline problems in the class. But from conversations with both of them I get the idea that they pretty much do what their mothers tell them to do at home.

SAM   Well, those are reasonable criteria. Why don't you go ahead and offer them the job. I'll have the secretary bring me the budget, and then you and I can talk about salaries, benefits, job descriptions, and other information you'll need for the interviews.

After school the following Thursday, Matt met with Martha Baker and Maria Aguillo in his room. In attempting to arrange a meeting with them, he found that neither was interested in meeting him in their home, but they were willing to come to the classroom. Martha arrived first and spent some time getting acquainted. When Maria arrived, the three of them socialized for a few minutes. Matt had told both women that he wanted to talk with them about a job at the school, but said that he would explain the job more fully when they met. So, after they had become acquainted, Matt began to talk about the position.

MATT   The duties of the position I'm offering you is what the title suggests. As my aides, your job is to help me teach the class. At the beginning I'll tell you what to do at the start of each day, but after you've been here a week you'll probably know what needs to be done each day and do it on your own.

MARTHA   *[Sighs]* Oh, that's good. I was worried about how I'd know what to do.

MARIA   Me, too.

MATT   Classes begin at 8:30. Teachers are supposed to be here at 8:00. Classes end at 3:30 and teachers stay until 4:00. The half hours at the beginning and end of the day are used for planning. The aide position pays $5.00 an hour, so you'd each

make $40.00 a day. Unfortunately, hourly positions don't pay any benefits, such
health care and retirement. That generally covers the job requirements and salar
Do either of you have any questions?

Martha   I think I'd like that job, but why do you ask me? I know Alphonso skips
school a lot, gets into fights, and doesn't do his homework. Why do you want th
mother of a boy like that in your class?

Maria   That's my question, too. Luis does the same things. I scold him for it, but I kn
he skips school because I saw his absences on his report card last week. I think r
son believes I live in another world. He embarrasses me with the things he does.
raise him better than that.

Matt   [Smiling] Actually, the two of you were my first selections for two reasons. The
first is that your sons are leaders of their cliques, and the second is that your son
respect you.

Maria   Luis doesn't respect me. He does things that he knows I don't want him to do

Martha   That's the same with my Alphonso.

Matt   [Smiling] No, I don't think that's true. Do you know why I say that? [Both moth
shake their heads.] Because when I've tried everything else to make your sons stoj
doing something I don't want them to do, I can usually make them stop by sayir
"If you do that again, I'll have to talk to your mother." And they stop doing it—a
least for a while. [Both mothers laugh with delight.]

Martha   I'd really like to have this job if you think I could do it. I've got a waitress jc
that's OK, but it's at night and Al's got to sit with the younger kids. [Laughing] I'n
not sure he does a good job. And I don't like going to bed at 1:30 or 2:00 in the
morning and getting up at 6:30 to get the kids ready for school. But, can I do thi
job? I didn't even finish high school.

Maria   I worry about that, too. I didn't finish high school either, but I really made go
grades the three years that I went. I baby-sat my neighbor's children for money l.
year, but this year they sent their kids to the free day-care center in our
neighborhood. We really need money because of our four children, and my
husband doesn't make much money as a prison guard. I'll try hard to learn the j

Matt   I think you'll both do fine. Here's a list of the duties you'll have. [Hands both a
sheet of paper] And I'll be in the class with you if you need help. And I hope Al a
Luis will behave better with their mothers in the class. [Martha and Maria laugh
seem pleased.]

During the first couple of days, Matt assigned Martha and Maria to specific stud
whom the aides helped with completing individual assignments. Gradually, as
became more confident and began to take more active roles, Matt had them work
students who raised their hands for help. It is now Wednesday of their second wee
school. The students are having a reading workshop which involves each student rea
a library book of his or her own choice. Martha and Maria are monitoring the pu
reading efforts.

Al's and Kenora's chairs are next to each other. Al reaches over and puts his
around Kenora's waist just as Martha walks up their aisle.

Martha   Alphonso! You take your arm from around that girl's waist, right now! Read your book. You need practice readin' more than you need to paw over girls. *[Al, obviously embarrassed, moves his arm and stares at the book.]*

Luis   *[Laughing]* Be careful, there, Al. Mama's watching.

Maria   *[Aggressively]* You be careful yourself, Luis! Read that book on your desk. You don't need to be worrying about what Al's doing. *[Luis immediately open his book and begins to read. Maria looks at Martha and winks.]*

Martha   *[Sees Sam attempting to take a paper away from Mark. Walks over to their desks]* What's going on here, boys?

Sam   Nothing.

Martha   I saw you trying to take that paper, Sam. Don't tell me that nothing's going on! Mark, what's on that paper? *[Mark remains silent. Martha takes the paper from Mark.]* That looks like the class work you're supposed to be doing now. Is that what it is, Sam? *[No response]* *[Sternly]* I asked you a question, young man! Were you trying to take Mark's classwork to copy?

Sam   *[Very softly]* Yes.

Martha   *[Loudly]* So you were trying to take Mark's classwork and copy it! *[No response]* OK, young man. You come to the table at the back of the classroom with me. You're going to do the class assignment. And I'm going to see that you do it right! It embarrasses me to see you trying to copy another person's work, like you're not smart enough to do it yourself. You're just lazy, that's all. Don't you think you could do the classwork here if you tried?

Sam   *[Submissively]* Yes, Ma'am.

Several days later, after the second-period class leaves, Matt and the two aides remain in the room to plan for the remainder of the day's classes. Matt compliments the aides on how well they have functioned in the class.

Matt   I think I need to tell you how much you've improved as teachers since you've been here, and how proud I am of you. Martha, you've brought about such a change in Al's attitude that if you didn't ever do anything else in this class, that would be enough. But, you're making a change in the attitudes of all the African-American students. The same's true of you, Maria. Luis is a different boy since you've been here. Both Al and Luis have great potential, but I haven't been able to convince them of that. And the other African-American and Hispanic pupils are working much harder than they've ever worked. You two are really great role models, and the students all respect you. I can't tell you how glad I am that you're here.

Maria   I've scolded Luis about his attitude. He's been terrible in all his classes, not just this one. And all the teachers he has care about him and do their best to help him learn. The problem's his. And he was trying to make me think that his teachers don't like Hispanics. Now I know that's not true. And I've told some of my friends that and they're clamping down on their kids. Do you think it might be that they see their parents and older kids being suspicious of white people, and so they think there must be some reason for it?

MARTHA   *[Nodding in agreement]* Yes, I think that's true. I've been talking with Al about how the minority students have such a hard time relating to white teachers. They even seem to be suspicious of you. And it can't be because of anything bad you've done to them. You make a special effort to treat all the kids alike and you're really nice to all of them. I've been embarrassed at the way Al has acted in your class and in school generally. He's been taught to behave better than that. So, we've had several serious conversations. I appreciate his teachers more than ever now.

MATT   *[Pleased]* I'm pleased that you're working with your sons at home as well as in the class. That may be the best answer to the problem. I'm convinced that many kids, both minority and non-minority, are brought up in segregated neighborhoods. I was brought up in a segregated white neighborhood. Martha, your kids live in a segregated African-American neighborhood. Maria, your neighborhood is a Hispan neighborhood. In neighborhoods like we grew up in, it's easy to blame other group for your problems. I live in a multi-ethnic neighborhood now. I play tennis with an African-American man across the street. My wife and I alternate Saturday dinners with the Ramirez family next door. So we don't think of these friends as African-Americans or Hispanics. We think of them as neighbors and friends.

MARTHA   Couldn't it be the same in schools? If all ethnic groups could start out togeth in kindergarten, by the time they get to seventh grade they'll probably think of th classmates as people, not Jews, Hispanics, African-Americans, or whites.

MATT   Yes, they would. And, I must say that having you two in this class has made an unbelievable difference in the way pupils view the class and each other. Some of t greatest admirers of you and Maria are white students, and the white teacher you working with.

It is the last week of the second six-week grading period. Matt leaves his room the end of the second period to get a cup of coffee at the teachers' lounge. When returns to his classroom about fifteen minutes later, he overhears his aides discussing incident at the PTA meeting.

MARIA   *[Laughing]* I thought that PTA president was gonna faint away when you told l you thought white teachers and kids're afraid of minority kids.

MARTHA   Yes, and what's really funny is how she acts like she's scared to death of us.

MATT   *[Interrupting]* What are you two talking about?

MARIA   We went to the Whitman PTA meeting last night. When the president lady as for new business, Martha asked why so many teachers made the white kids beha and study, but let the African-American and Hispanic kids act up and not do thei homework and school assignments. *[Giggling]* Martha told her that's a form of prejudice.

MARTHA   Yeah! I thought the president lady, that Ms. Watson, was gonna faint. She sa that teachers tried to make minority students do their homework, but that many them refused to do it. They tell people they aren't interested in learning and don like school. *[Laughing]* I tole her that Mr. Howe's seventh-grade English class, wh we work, has minority students who work hard doin' their homework and say th like school.

Matt   *[Taken aback]* I didn't know you were planning to attend the PTA meeting.

Maria   Oh, yes. We met Dr. Dawson, and he told us one day that we should go. He's nice. We also went to the SAC *[school advisory committee]* meeting last week.

Matt   Did you speak there also?

Martha   Yes, I told that group that they should tell the principal to hire more of us mothers of minority students to work as aides in our school.

Matt   What was the reaction of the members of the group?

Maria   They asked us a lot of questions about how we learned to work in a classroom, what we did, and how the children responded to us. What they wanted to know was, were we able to keep the children under control.

Matt   *[Smiling]* What did you tell them?

Maria   They'd been talking about in-service training for teachers. So Martha told them that you'd given us in-service training to work as aides. Then she said that because we're members of minority groups, we know how to keep our children under control. I told them that you said that the kids were much better behaved since we were coming to the class.

Matt   And that's definitely true. How did the SAC group respond to your suggestions?

Martha   They seemed to have a hard time believing that we could be of any help in a class. They asked a lot about our education and training and things like that.

Matt   How did they respond to your suggestion that they recommend that the principal employ minority mothers as teacher aides?

Martha   I think one or two of them thought it was an interesting idea. *[Smiling]* It seemed to turn off most of them right away. But that doesn't matter, Maria and I are going to the meeting of the school board next week. I'm going to recommend the same thing there. But I'm going to prepare better for that meeting. At the SAC I just decided to bring it up on the spur of the moment. Why don't you come to the board meeting with us? You teachers should go to meetings like that. That'd be a good way for you to get the things that you want. It's hard for people to say no when you're sittin' there lookin' at 'em.

Matt   Well, I certainly agree with you about that. *[Smiling]* But I don't know about going to a meeting with you two. You're liable to get me into trouble.

After the last class two weeks later, the aides have gone home and Matt is preparing materials for the following day. As he is writing lesson plans in his book, Sam Dawson appears in his doorway.

Sam   Got a minute?

Matt   *[Knowing why he is there, smiles]* Sure, Sam. Come in and have a seat. To what do I owe the honor of this visit?

Sam   *[Sits in a student chair beside the desk]* Did you know that those mothers working with you were taking an active role in the school PTA, the SAC, and even the school board meetings?

Matt   Yes, I just found out this morning that they'd been to the meetings you mentioned.

Sam   *[Abruptly]* What do you think of all this?

FIGURE 23   Teacher Aide Job Description Developed by Matt Howe for His Sevent▮ grade English Class

---

WALT WHITMAN MIDDLE SCHOOL

Description of Duties of Teacher Aides

Goal: The responsibility of the teacher aide is to provide instructional support in assisting the classroom teacher in the following ways:

1. To set up classrooms and prepare materials for specialized instructional units
2. To handle attendance reports and related clerical functions for the teacher
3. To assist in assembling and putting materials on bulletin boards and to keep such displays current
4. To administer and score objective tests and mark errors
5. To obtain all required equipment
6. To operate audiovisual equipment
7. To prepare room for special activities
8. To obtain the required equipment
9. To return all equipment to storage
10. To assemble, adjust, and maintain equipment used in the instructional program
11. To assist in small-group instruction
12. To tutor pupils at teacher's request
13. To work with students to assist them in completing various assignments and projects
14. To record pupil status and improvements
15. To assist teacher in maintaining discipline and other instructional and non-instructional functions

---

MATT   Well, I don't know what you mean by "all this." I thought we encouraged all of our parents to attend school meetings. Is there something you know about their attendance of the meetings that I don't?

SAM   *[Becoming defensive]* I understand that not only did they attend the meetings, bu▮ they also had quite a bit to say about teacher aides being made up of minority group members, and how white middle-class teachers don't understand minority students and minority students don't understand white middle-class teachers.

MATT   Yes, they told me that they'd discussed those issues at the meeting.

SAM   *[Angrily]* Well, do you want classroom aides who you recommended to work wi▮ you in your classroom going to educational meetings and making inflammatory statements like that?

MATT   *[Calmly]* I must be missing something here, Sam. We have two newly employe▮ teacher aides who, on their own time, are attending school-related meetings that you urge all your teachers to attend, who are reporting quite positively about a n▮ program that we've implemented in our school. And you're asking me how we c▮ stop them from doing this?

SAM   They're telling parents and school board members that white middle-class teachers
      don't understand low-income minority students, and that schools should employ
      more mothers of low-income ethnic students to work as aides in the schools.
MATT Yes. They've already told me that they made those recommendations.
SAM   *[Loudly]* Well, I don't like that one bit! Here we have two women who haven't even
      graduated from high school, working in our school with our students, and telling
      everyone who'll listen that they can relate better to low-income minority students
      than our trained and certified teachers can. And they're saying that schools should
      employ more aides like them instead of college graduates who are certified. Since
      you hired them, I want you to put a stop to all this.

QUESTIONS

1. Analyze this case from the standpoint of observational learning. What kind of modeling and imitation is taking place? Are there examples of vicarious reward and punishment? How has being a teacher aide affected Martha's and Maria's sense of efficacy as parents? From an observational learning perspective, how does behavioral change occur?

2. How do schools involve parents as volunteers, aides, supporters of school activities, in parent advisory groups, as adult learners, through and as home visitors, and as tutors of their own child at home? How does parent involvement affect the achievement of the involved parent's child in school?

3. Examine the teacher aide role description in the figure on page 220. Should parents without high school diplomas be allowed to engage in such activities? Should the role description be expanded? For example, should Martha and Maria be trained to make visits to the homes of the other children in the class, especially those of the same ethnic/racial backgrounds as Martha and Maria? Should Matt consider rotating other parents of his students in as teacher aides—with each new grading period, perhaps?

4. Are teachers like Matt trained in their teacher education programs to function as a team leader who regularly plans with and monitors the activities of teacher aides? Is such training desirable and essential?

5. Are such variables as the availability of reading material, educational games, parent expectations and pressures, parent modeling of reading and language behavior, and clear-cut discipline patterns related to student achievement in school? Are such home environment differences more strongly related to SES, to racial/ethnic differences, or both? How do such variables as family income, family size, and single parenting relate to school achievement?

6. What is cultural diversity? What different forms of cultural diversity does this case illustrate? What kind of teacher is most effective in highly diverse schools, and why? What programs for involving parents from diverse populations are most effective?

7. What is social class, and how does it differ from SES? What social class differences are illustrated in this case, and how do these differences relate to ethnic/racial differences? What social class background do teachers like Matt come from? How do the biases of teachers, administrators, parents, and students originate, and how can they be overcome?

8. How do discipline patterns differ between social classes and racial/ethnic grou
Do children tend to imitate the discipline patterns they experience in the home wh
they become parents? If so, why? How can teachers adjust the classroom managem
procedures they use in the classroom to take into consideration the different discipl
patterns their students have experienced at home? How do discipline patterns chan
Could serving as a teacher aide in the classroom affect a parent's discipline patterns
home?

9. From the standpoint of Maslow's need hierarchy, at what need levels are Sam a
Matt primarily operating? How do these differences help explain their reactions
Martha's and Maria's behavior in the PTA and SAC meetings?

10. How do the different parenting styles described by Baumrind (authoritari
authoritative, and permissive) affect student performance in school? How do such p
enting styles differ in terms of SES and racial/ethnic family patterns?

11. Why is Sam upset with Martha and Maria? Would he be as upset with them if th
were white middle-class mothers? Why do the activities of parent groups like PTAs a
SACs threaten some principals like Sam? What kinds of things do such principals oft
do to keep such parent groups from becoming too strong and active? Is active par
involvement a good or a bad thing?

12. What should Matt do? How should he respond to Sam? Should he say anythi
to Martha and Maria?

DELISHA THE DISRUPTER

Key Content to Consider for Analyzing This Case:
(1) operant conditioning; (2) teacher biases/self-fulfilling prophecy; (3) classroom management; (4) observational learning; (5) intelligence.

Judy Bowers is beginning her second year of teaching at Lincoln Elementary School, which is located in a large urban area in the Northeastern part of the United States. Lincoln's student body is 53% non-Hispanic white, 35% African-American, 10% Hispanic, and 2% other. Its physical plant is old but well maintained. The twenty-eight students in Judy's third-grade class rather closely approximates the typical student body composition at Lincoln.

It is the second week of the new school year, and Judy finds her students to be bright, eager, and reasonably well mannered except for one rather average-sized African-American girl named Delisha Davis. From the first day of school, Judy noticed that Delisha didn't seem to be able to stay in her seat, was constantly talking to her neighbors, and was frequently making noises and disrupting the class. After talking to some of her fellow teachers about the situation, one of whom had Delisha in class last year, Judy decided to do something about Delisha's behavior.

JUDY *[Motioning with her hands]* Boys and girls, I want you to make a circle so we can have a talk about our class.

DELISHA Are you going to read to us?

JUDY No, Delisha, and remember that I asked you to raise your hand instead of speaking out like that. *[Students sit in a semicircle while Judy stands. She holds a piece of chalk in her hands so she can write on the blackboard.]* Boys and girls, we are going to be together all this school year, and I know that we all want to learn a lot and have a lot of fun as we learn.

DELISHA *[Smiling]* Yeah, a lot of fun!

JUDY *[Frowning]* Let's all be quiet now, Delisha, while I talk. *[Pauses as Delisha smiles]* We can have a good time in this class learning this year if we all try to do our best getting along with one another. *[Pause]* Now boys and girls, I want to talk about being a good class member. This class belongs to all of you. What do you want this class to be like this year? I'm going to write your ideas up here on the blackboard.

[Most students raise their hands. Delisha stands up and begins a slow dancing movement as she stands in place.] Yes, Marie? Let's start with you.

MARIE   *[Timidly]* Everyone likes one another.

JUDY   *[Smiling]* You mean that everyone likes one another and will be nice to one another? *[Marie nods her head affirmatively while Judy writes "Everyone is nice and gets along."]* Maria?

MARIA   We get to do things.

JUDY   Do you mean we get to learn new and interesting things so class won't be boring? *[Maria nods her head affirmatively.]* Scott, you had your hand up. *[Scott sits next to Delisha, who begins to dance more vigorously.]* What do you think a good class should be like?

SCOTT   I think people should leave other people alone and not bother them.

JUDY   Tell us a little more about that, Scott. Can you give us an example? *[Judy writes "Do interesting things" on the blackboard.]*

SCOTT   I mean like Lisa here. She's always making trouble and bothering people. You aren't supposed to be doing that.

DELISHA   *[Brings her right fist down hard on Scott's head]* You're stupid! My name's Delisha, not Lisa, and I can dance if I want to! Dancing is good. I see it on TV all the time. *[Scott yells upon being hit and remains seated as he begins to rub his head and cry.]*

JUDY   *[Runs toward Scott and Delisha]* Delisha, that's a terrible thing for you to do to Scott! *[She kneels down and comforts Scott.]* Are you OK, Scott? *[In a few minutes she helps Scott up and takes both Scott's and Delisha's hands.]* Children, I want you to go to your desks and read the story about the Alaskan bears on page 29. Please read to yourselves quietly, and we'll discuss what you've read when I come back. I need to take Delisha and Scott to Ms. Rannum's *[building principal]* office so that the school nurse can look at Scott and make sure he's OK. I'm sure that Ms. Rannum will want to talk to Delisha about hitting Scott and call her parents. *[The children all scramble to begin to read their books. Judy waits until she is satisfied that everyone is working and, still holding each child by the hand, leads Scott and Delisha to the principal's office.]*

It is the next day. School is over and all the children have left. Judy goes to the office of Meg Ryerson, the school guidance counselor.

MEG   *[Smiling]* Hi, Judy. How are you?

JUDY   *[Smiling back wanly]* OK, I guess. Did you hear about Delisha Davis hitting Scott Grimes in my room yesterday?

MEG   *[Frowning]* Yes, I did. Betty *[the building principal]* told me about it. I gather that the nurse examined Scott and he's going to be OK.

JUDY   Yes. She really hit him on the head hard, Meg. I was afraid he might have a concussion or something. I wasn't sure at first whether I should move him or not. But then the idea of having him lie on the floor while the school nurse checked him out with all the kids watching was just too much. So I got him to stand up, took him and Delisha by the hand, and walked him to Betty's office. Fortunately, she was there and called the school nurse right away. I guess I took a chance getting him up on his feet, didn't I?

MEG   I guess so, but I certainly understand why you did it. You'd had enough disruption as it was.

JUDY   *[Angrily]* Disruption is Delisha's middle name, I think! This is the first time she's hit another child, but she's constantly disrupting the class!

MEG   Talking when she's not supposed to? Interrupting other children? Constantly getting out of her seat without permission?

JUDY   *[With surprise]* Why, yes! It sounds like you were watching her, Meg.

MEG   *[Smiling]* Not really, but I'm real familiar with her record. She's had problems like these going back to her days in the Head Start program.

JUDY   She was a discipline problem back in Head Start?

MEG   Yes, it started back then. *[Pulls a cumulative folder out of a large stack of such folders on her desk and opens it up]* This is Delisha's cumulative record. Believe it or not, when they gave her a group intelligence test in the first grade—the California, I think—her non-language IQ was 111. Her language IQ was only 98, however. She comes from a large family of six siblings headed by her mother, who works on the assembly line making electric motors at International Motors. I'm not sure where the father is, but he doesn't live with the family. From what little bit I've learned, mainly from the eighty-year-old grandmother who lives with them, the mother uses corporal punishment at home a lot to keep the kids in line. I've never been able to get the mother to talk to me though, so I really don't know her. The grandmother just says that her daughter works real hard to keep the family from going under financially and doesn't have much time to spend with them. Betty asked me to contact Delisha's mother yesterday after that incident in your class, but, of course, I couldn't. The grandmother said she'd give her the message when she came home from work, but I wouldn't hold my breath. My guess is that we won't hear from her.

JUDY   *[Frowning]* You've certainly given me a different slant on Delisha. I had no idea that she comes from that kind of situation.

MEG   I suspect that you have to fight for attention in Delisha's family, and I also suspect that hitting is a normal way of relating to others in her family.

JUDY   You may well be right, Meg. But what am I going to do? She can't be hitting other children in my classroom! And even if she never hits anyone again, I can't have her continually disrupting the class!

MEG   Judy, my suggestion would be for you to call Tony Garcia, the director of psychological services for the school system. Maybe he'd be willing to have one of his people do a workup on her and make some recommendations. Would you like me to write down Tony's number for you? He'd want to ask you some questions about what she's been doing in class.

JUDY   *[Smiling]* Why, yes, I would! I knew you'd think of a way to help me! I really appreciate this, Meg!

MEG   *[Smiling]* My pleasure! Always glad to help, Judy.

It is about 10:00 the next morning. Judy and her class have reviewed the multiplication tables, and Judy handed out a worksheet for the twos through the tens and told each student to complete the worksheet at his or her desk. About fifteen minutes into the deskwork, Delisha begins to make sounds with her mouth like she is "passing air." Se eral of the children laugh and then look guiltily toward Judy.

JUDY   Delisha, please stop making those noises! *[Delisha stops for six seconds, then gets up and starts walking toward the pencil sharpener.]* Delisha where are you going?

DELISHA   To sharpen my pencil.

JUDY   Don't you remember that you are supposed to ask permission first? You don't just get up and go whenever you feel like it. What if everybody in the class did that?

DELISHA   *[Pouting]* I can't do my sheet if I don't sharpen my pencil!

JUDY   OK, go on ahead. But next time I want you to ask permission first, OK?

DELISHA   OK. *[As she walks by Scott's desk she thumps him hard behind his left ear.]*

SCOTT   Ow! That really hurt. Ms. Bowers! Lisa hit me!

JUDY   All right, Delisha, take your seat right now!

DELISHA   But I got to sharpen my pencil or I can't do my paper!

JUDY   Never mind, Delisha. You're not going to do your paper! Your picking on Scott ha to stop! *[Judy walks over to Delisha's desk, picks up the multiplication worksheet, and tears it up.]* I'm afraid I'm going to have to give you an F on this work. Now sit down and don't move, or I'll send you to Ms. Rannum's office.

Delisha sits down and becomes bored doing nothing, so she tries to talk to Mari who tells her to leave her alone so she can do her work. In a couple of minutes, Delish stands up and begins to dance standing in place as though she hears music.

JUDY   *[Looking up and seeing Delisha when a couple of students laugh]* OK, Delisha, that's it. Let's you and I walk down to the principal's office. Keep doing your problems, children, and I'll collect your papers when I come back. *[Judy motions for Delisha to follow her out the door. Delisha has a big grin on her face as they leave the classroom. As the walk down the hallway side by side, Judy talks to Delisha.]* Delisha, why do you do these things?

DELISHA   Don't know. Just wanted to.

JUDY   You knew you'd get into trouble if you kept it up, didn't you?!

DELISHA   *[Smiling]* I don't care! I can do what I want to!

It is after school that same day, and all the children have left. Judy goes to the prin cipal's office and calls Tony Garcia. He is in his office as Judy calls.

TONY   Garcia here.

JUDY   Dr. Garcia, this is Judy Bowers over at Lincoln Elementary. I need to ask you for your professional help with one of my students.

TONY   Oh, yes, Judy. Meg Ryerson said you might be calling. What's the name of the child who's giving you a problem?

JUDY   Delisha Davis, an eight-year-old African-American girl who is constantly disrupting my class. She causes more trouble than all my other twenty-seven students combined.

TONY   *[Laughing]* She certainly sounds like a handful! I'll tell you what, Judy. I'd like to assign one of my school psychologists, Brad Barber, to collect some in-class observation data on Delisha. Then he'll sit down and go over the data with you and make some recommendations for working with her.

JUDY   You mean he'll come into the room and observe her while I teach?

TONY   Yes. He knows how to observe unobtrusively so Delisha won't know that she's the one he's collecting data on. The kids will get used to him being there rather quickly. He'll be busy recording data and will tell the children that he has to work if they try to talk to him.

JUDY   I guess that'll be OK. Shouldn't I tell the students not to bother him?

TONY   That would be excellent.

JUDY   Dr. Garcia, do you think Delisha will be moved to another classroom? She's become a serious discipline problem, and I've been told that this goes back to her days in Head Start.

TONY   We'll just have to take it a step at a time, and please call me Tony, not Dr. Garcia. That makes me feel like a college professor or something.

JUDY   *[Laughing]* OK, Tony. When will Brad come?

TONY   He'll start Monday. Now could you give me a little information that will help Brad?

JUDY   Yes, of course. What do you want to know?

TONY   Brad will be using behavioral recording techniques. I understand that Delisha is disruptive, but what kinds of behaviors is she engaging in, specifically?

JUDY   Well, for one thing she won't be quiet. She makes inappropriate noises at inappropriate times. Like today when she was supposed to be working she made noises like she was "passing air." Then she began to bother the other children while they were trying to do their seatwork.

TONY   By trying to talk to them?

JUDY   Yes, it seems like she has trouble doing seatwork very long, and before long she's doing something to bother the other children. *[Pause]* I guess the thing that bothers me most, though, is her getting up out of her seat without permission to dance or to go to the pencil sharpener.

TONY   Dance?

JUDY   Yes, she stays in one place and dances like she hears music.

TONY   OK. Let me summarize. What I'm trying to do is come up with categories of behavior for Brad to use when he comes to your room to observe. I've got three categories or types of behaviors that I've heard you describe. First, we've got inappropriate "getting out of seat" behavior. Second, inappropriate talking to her peers. And third, I guess I would just call it off-task behavior.

JUDY   Off-task behavior?

TONY   Yes. Inappropriate behavior she engages in when she's supposed to be doing seatwork. Things like making noises, daydreaming, doodling, and so forth. Anything that's not on-task or doing her work. Do those three about cover it?

JUDY   Yes, I guess so. Her dancing would be part of inappropriate getting out of seat?

TONY   Yes. Also, I believe Meg said that Delisha hits other children.

JUDY   Only once, and only one child, Scott. Well, she thumped him on the head with a pencil today. I guess that's the second time, but I don't think you'd observe much hitting.

TONY   OK. We'll omit that, although I'll mention it to Brad.

JUDY   Will Brad be there observing all day, Tony?

TONY   No, I'd say maybe forty minutes a day for a couple of weeks. He'll work out whe
he should observe with you by asking you when Delisha usually engages in her
problem behaviors.

JUDY   When? You mean like what time of day?

TONY   What is usually going on in the classroom when she does these things? Seatworl
When you have group activities? When you're reading to them?

JUDY   Oh, I see. He'll want to observe her at those times.

TONY   Exactly. Let him come in and observe for a couple of weeks, and then we'll
discuss what we should do.

JUDY   That sounds great, Tony! Thanks so much for your help.

It is Friday after school a little over two weeks later. Judy, Dr. Garcia, and Brad Ba
ber sit around a small table in the office of the principal, Betty Rannum.

BETTY   So, Brad, you've been collecting observational data on Delisha Davis in Judy's
classroom?

BRAD   I actually observed forty minutes per day for nine days, a total of six hours. I
broke the forty minutes per day down into four ten-minute observation periods
during those times that Judy said Delisha would be most likely to display disrupti
behavior. [Passes out sheet of paper with data summary] This is a summary of what I
observed.

BETTY   Could you explain what this chart means and how you did it?

BRAD   This is what we call a function analysis in that I not only record each behavior
that Delisha emits but also the consequence, or what happens immediately after th
behavior is emitted. As you can see, we placed her undesirable classroom behavio
in three categories. We then generated competing opposite categories of desirable
behavior to see if any such behaviors were being emitted and, if so, what
consequences followed each. Of course, these desirable kinds of behaviors will be
the new target that Judy should use to shape the child toward.

BETTY   [Frowning] I'm not really completely following what you're saying, Brad. Can yc
give an example?

BRAD   [Smiling] Of course.

JUDY   [Interrupting] Then you're going to recommend that Delisha stay in my class?

TONY   Yes, we are. We'll talk about that when Brad explains the data a bit more, but we
think you can definitely change Delisha's behavior.

BRAD   Well, for example, when Delisha would get out of her seat without permission,
say, to dance, and Judy yells at her to sit down, I would categorize that as a "Gettir
out of seat" behavior followed by a negative consequence.

BETTY   Oh, I get it! Then POS means positive reinforcer, NEG means negative reinforce
and IGN means ignore.

BRAD   No, not really. It just means that the consequence appeared to me, the observer,
as a positive or negative or ignoring one. Appearance is one thing. How it affects
the behavior as observed is another.

FIGURE 24   Baseline Data Collected by Brad Barber, School Psychologist, on Delisha Davis, Third Grader

	FUNCTIONAL ANALYSIS						
	TIME: 6 HOURS (9 DAYS—40 MINUTES PER DAY)						
	Consequences						
Behaviors	**Teacher**				**Peers**		
Desirable	**POS**	**NEG**	**IGN**		**POS**	**NEG**	**IGN**
Staying in seat	1	0	73		0	0	74
Being quiet	1	0	61		0	0	62
On-task	12	0	67		3	1	75
Undesirable							
Getting out of seat	0	3	11		4	0	10
Talking to peers	0	3	28		16	0	15
Off-task	0	4	26		4	0	26

BETTY   What do you mean?

BRAD   I mean that what appears to be a negative consequence, such as a verbal reprimand for dancing, may actually be serving as a positive reinforcer, since it doesn't decrease the behavior it follows. Calling one child a good student in front of the class may be positively reinforcing to that child and cause her to work harder. Saying the same thing to another child might cause her to quit working because she doesn't want to be seen as a teacher's pet.

BETTY   So it's the actual effects of the consequences that you observed that counts?

BRAD   Right.

JUDY   The "Teacher" and "Peers" columns bother me. It's like you're saying that the other students in the class and I are responsible for Delisha's behavior. What about Delisha? Isn't she responsible for her own behavior? Why am I made the bad guy?

TONY   This behavior modification procedure is based on the work of B. F. Skinner, years ago. Skinner believed that the cause of an individual's behavior is in the environment that the individual is operating in. That's why the same child will behave one way at school and another at home. Two different environments.

BETTY   Then Skinner didn't see the cause of bad behavior as coming from inside the child?

TONY   That's right!

BETTY   Then why do we have counselors and other mental health professionals who a
supposed to work with individuals one-on-one or in small therapy groups? They
pull them out of the environment—the classroom—to do that.

TONY   That's very true. They are working from the standpoint of a different set of
psychological theories altogether. They would disagree with Skinner's position.

JUDY   [Looking intently at data handout] Brad, if I read this chart right, there were seven
four times that I could have delivered a positive consequence to Delisha for stayi
in her seat, and I only did it once.

BRAD   That's right. There were seventy-four occasions when you were close enough to
her or in a position to deliver some kind of positive consequence such as praise,
but only on one occasion did you do so.

BETTY   This is fascinating data, Tony and Brad, but let's get down to the practical part.
What does it really tell us about Delisha? What are you recommending to Judy th
she do differently in her classroom? How can she go about changing Delisha's
behavior?

QUESTIONS

1. With regard to school law, what should Judy have done when Delisha hit Scott
the head? Should she have moved him, or should she have had him lie still while she
one of the students went for help? Could she be legally liable if one of her students •
injured while she took the two students to the principal's office?

2. Which of the following classroom management models would have been m
effective in Judy's classroom: behavior modification, Teacher Effectiveness Training, Re
ity Therapy, Assertive Discipline, or Kounin's Model? How effective was Judy with
attempt at teacher-pupil planning?

3. Delisha had attended a Head Start program. What is the nature and purpose of
program? How effective is it?

4. To what extent have Judy, Meg, and other teachers developed a self-fulfill
prophecy with regard to Delisha? How do teacher expectations and biases operate so t
teachers' and administrators' behaviors change toward certain students and, in tu
result in changes in student beliefs and behaviors that confirm the original expectatio
of the teachers?

5. Meg tells Judy that Delisha's language IQ was 98 and her non-language IQ was 1
on a group intelligence test. What does this information mean? How could such a difi
ence in the two kinds of IQ scores develop? How does a group intelligence test differ fr
an individual test? How well do IQ scores predict student achievement?

6. How would modeling and imitation from observational learning explain Delish
classroom behavior? How might the models in her home environment explain her cla
room behavior, especially in relation to Scott? What are cognitive behavior modificat
and self-regulation techniques, and how could they be used to change the behavior c
student like Delisha?

7. Meg indicates that she is unable to contact Delisha's mother. What parent involvement techniques have been found to be effective, especially with low-income parents? What might be some effective ways of involving Delisha's mother?

8. Tony and Brad are school psychologists. What is a school psychologist, and how does the work of a school psychologist differ from that of a guidance counselor or an educational psychologist? How often do school psychologists get to do consultation work like that of Brad?

9. Brad collected baseline data on Delisha from a behavior modification perspective. What is the purpose of such data collection? Critique the data-collection procedure that Brad used.

10. There are many pros and cons surrounding the techniques derived from the operant conditioning research of B. F. Skinner. What are the strengths and weaknesses of these behavior modification methods?

11. Tony explains to Judy and Betty that Skinner sees the cause of behavior as the environment, a position known as environmental determinism. Contrast this view with the reciprocal determinism of Bandura and the social construction view of constructivist theory.

12. What recommendations should Tony and Brad make to Judy and Betty about what Judy should do next? What does the baseline data tell you? What reinforcers seem to be maintaining Delisha's behavior? What techniques (e.g., behavior modification methods) can Judy use to begin changing Delisha's behavior? Should the techniques used involve the other students in her classroom? How can Judy determine if the techniques she decides to use are effective in changing Delisha's behavior?

INVOLVING PARENTS

Key Content to Consider for Analyzing This Case:
(1) classroom management (teacher as team leader);
(2) parent involvement; (3) cultural diversity;
(4) observational learning; (5) measurement and
evaluation (formative vs. summative evaluation).

A s Doris Larken drives her new car along the state route that takes her to Wiley Elementary School, where she recently accepted a position as principal, she experiences a wave of elation. It has taken six years of effort after graduating from a large state university in the north-central United States with a B.S. in elementary education to arrive at this point in her life.

After graduation she immediately accepted a position as a fifth-grade teacher in the same state and taught quite successfully for four years. She was a high-energy teacher who encouraged parent involvement in the schools and believed that such participation was of great value both to the parents and students. During these years of teaching, she formulated a definite idea of the practices that were necessary for an elementary school to prepare pupils successfully.

At the end of her fourth year of teaching, Doris enrolled full-time in the graduate school of her alma mater. After earning an M.Ed. degree in school administration, she immediately applied for and was awarded her current position as principal of Wiley Elementary. The school has a population of approximately 625 pupils in four sections each of grades K–5. It is located in a community of approximately 85,000 which is approximately 68% white, 20% African-American, 5% Hispanic, and 2% Asian-American.

As soon as she was employed as principal, Doris spent the entire summer becoming oriented to her school, the school district, and the community. She read in a state education newsletter a request for proposals for a grant to fund the recruiting and training of parents of low-income students to work as teacher aides in the classroom and as home visitors. Besides working in the classroom, the parents would be trained to make visits to the homes of parents from similar racial, ethnic, and socioeconomic backgrounds. Although many of Wiley's teachers were not in town when she tried to reach them, she was able to talk with some teachers about the grant. They encouraged her to apply, and she devoted much time and effort to the preparation of a proposal. Then, with the help of school system staff, she submitted the proposal to the funding agency. Several weeks later, she was thrilled to receive notice that her proposal had been funded.

Doris arranged to have a three-day workshop for her teachers on Monday, Tuesday, and Wednesday the week before fall classes were to begin. After the workshop, teachers would be free to work in their classrooms on Thursday and Friday. The first day of the workshop, Doris has told the teachers about how she came to receive the grant and now begins to describe its provisions:

DORIS   The grant makes provisions for each of you to have two teacher aides in your classroom. The focus of the grant is to involve low-income parents in the schools. I'd like to invite you to participate in the recruitment of these workers. I'm sure that all of you know—

DALE   *[Interrupting]* Are we required to have aides in our classroom even if we don't want to?

MARTIN   I was wondering about that too. I'm not at all excited about having other adults interfering in my classroom, especially parents!

DORIS   *[Somewhat taken aback]* Oh, my! It never occurred to me that anyone wouldn't want to have two aides. One of the provisions of the grant is that all classes in the school must have aides. *[Pause]* I can't see how having other adults in the class to help you with your students would be undesirable.

MARTIN   If you could've seen the aide I had in my classroom three years ago you'd understand why it would be undesirable to me. Keeping her from undoing all the things I was trying to do with my pupils took up more of my time than five additional pupils would have required. Everything she did seemed to be wrong!

DORIS   Well, it sounds like that was a special case, though, Martin. We plan to recruit and train our aides very carefully.

DALE   I think having another adult in my class ostensibly to help me *is* a bad thing. I like to teach my pupils without depending on other people. I have a reputation for running a tight ship. The thought of having an untrained layperson in my classroom every day makes me shudder. Having a formerly unemployed adult knocking around in the classroom distracting the pupils isn't my idea of helpful. *[Raising her voice]* And imposing aides on us without even asking whether or not we want one seems a bit dictatorial to me!

DORIS   *[Distraught]* I just don't know what to say. I'm stunned that some of you don't want additional help in your classes. Let me emphasize that the purpose of the grant is to increase student achievement, especially among low-income students, and to boost low-income parents' involvement as volunteers and in parent advisory groups like the PTA and SAC *[school advisory committee]*. These are all goals that I thought all of you would consider important. I'm sorry that some of you aren't excited about having aides in your room, but I hope you'll at least be willing to give the program a try for this year.

SUE   What kinds of things would our aides be able to do in the classroom?

DORIS   They can do many different kinds of things, depending on their own interests and abilities as well as your needs. *[Distributes a handout entitled "Teacher Aide Activities"]* As you can see, some of the classroom tasks they can perform are housekeeping, clerical functions, preparing materials, instructing, and evaluating. In addition, they could make home visits. The main reason for home visits will be to take class assignments to the parents of your students and encourage them to work on them with their child at home. Part of our evaluation would be to see how many of you will get your aides to move from level 1 to level 6 on the handout.

SUE   *[Enthusiastically]* Wow! That sounds good to me. I can always use help in my classroom. I do a lot of committee work, and I have independent projects I could use someone to supervise. Just sitting here realizing that I'll have two aides makes me think of dozens of ways of using them in the classroom. *[The majority of teachers chime in and agree with Sue.]*

DORIS   *[Obviously relieved]* Whew! I was beginning to think I'd have to send all the grant money back! But, as I've already explained, it was one of those opportunities that had to be seized at the moment.

MARTIN   *[Speaking out]* I'm still deeply concerned about this program, Doris. How much additional work will it require from all of us? For instance, the collection and analysis of hard data to see whether our pupils have increased their achievement, in itself, will require quite a bit of data collecting, analyzing, and evaluating. And even more time-consuming will be our work in planning with and monitoring the activities of our aides. I realize that the grant calls for the use of low-income parents, but how much time will it take to prepare people to do these tasks when they've had no education or experience in these areas? *[Emphatically]* I think our responsibilities as teachers have been at least doubled by this grant!

DORIS   I understand your concern, Martin. And I don't think anyone can answer your questions at this point. Yes, it will take time and effort to plan and work with the aides. But, after they're trained by some consultants, they'll hopefully be able to fulfill all of the tasks listed on the handout. It's conceivable that they might even reduce the amount of work you have to do. We just don't know yet. But I know you'll all try your hardest to make it work. And that's all any of us can do. We'll have answers to all these questions at the end of the year. Then we'll be able to decide whether we want to try to extend the grant so that we can have the aides again next year.

Five weeks have passed since the pre-school workshop. Applicants for the teacher aide positions have been interviewed and employed after the selection committee evaluated them. Two aides were employed for each of four class sections in grades K–5, a total of forty-eight. All applicants were female, and usually mothers of pupils in the classrooms. The breakdown of the aides by race and income is as follows: of the twenty-nine white aides, nine are middle income and twenty are low income; of the fifteen African American aides, four are middle income and eleven are low income; all three Hispanic aides are low income; and the single Asian-American aide is from a middle-income home.

The aides have had several all-day sessions familiarizing them with the school philosophy, what is expected of them, and general guidelines for the position they hold. They have been working in their assigned classroom or visiting parents for the past two weeks.

Dale is walking to the parking lot after school and meets Ann, a third-grade teacher on her way to the lot.

DALE   Hi, Ann. I haven't seen you for a while. How are your classes going?

ANN   *[Smiling]* Hi, Dale. My classes are going great. Lana, one of my aides, is the white
        low-income mother of Lisa Reynolds, who's in my class. Lana's really getting into
        classroom routine. She's learned the pupils' names and is beginning to be more of
        an asset than a liability.

DALE   *[Skeptically]* Really? What kinds of things do you have her doing?

ANN   Well, I'm starting her out on low-level housekeeping tasks, such as making
        bulletin boards, taking attendance, photocopying handouts, and administering
        tests. If she learns as quickly as I think she will, I may eventually move her up
        toward higher-level tasks like making materials, giving instruction, evaluating
        student work, and making home visits. But I'm going very slowly. I want to make
        sure she feels confident with the tasks she's doing before I move her on to more
        difficult tasks.

DALE   Well, that makes sense. But do you think it's taken more time for you to teach her
        to do the tasks than she spends doing them?

SUE   *[Considers the question carefully]* No, I think she's saving me more time than it's
        costing me to work with her. And she and I get along well. She has a nice way with
        the kids. I'd say the same thing is true with my other aide, Tywanda Jackson, too.

DALE   I'm not sure I can work with my aides the way you have.

SUE   Why? What's bothering you about it?

DALE   *[Long pause]* Giving an aide professional tasks to perform. I'm having my aides do
        simple things—distribute paper, take up assignments, sweep the floor—stuff like
        that. I'd really rather they weren't even in the room, but I don't want to get on the
        wrong side of Doris.

SUE   Oh, I'm really beginning to enjoy working with my aides! It's nice having partners.
        For one thing, Lana, Tywanda, and I together seem to accomplish more than three
        times what I could accomplish alone in the same time period. What is it that
        bothers you about working with aides? You're easy to get along with, and you're a
        great teacher!

DALE   Well, I think the main reason is that I consider teaching to be a profession. And I
        resent the fact that we're now bringing in people with no educational background
        or training—and in some cases without even a high school diploma—to function as
        teachers, and everybody seems to think it's a great thing. I feel like this trivializes all
        my university work and years of teaching experience.

SUE   But aides don't really do what teachers do. For one thing, Lana and Tywanda do
        only the tasks I ask them to do. I teach them how to do them and monitor what
        they do. They only get paid minimum wages, do only the tasks I think they can
        handle, and no one really views them as teachers—although some of the children
        call them "teacher." But that doesn't really bother me. I'm glad the students respect
        them as authority figures and do what they ask them to do.

DALE   That would bother me, but I guess I've already said that. While you were talking,
        I realized what really bothers me most about the use of laypeople in the classroom.

SUE   What's that?

DALE   I'm just not willing to have an untrained person try to teach children things I'm
        responsible for teaching them. Maybe I'm arrogant, but I really think I'm good at
        what I do. I work hard preparing for my classes every day, I know what all my

pupils are capable of doing, and I'm able to evaluate whether or not they've achieved to the level of their capacity. I don't think an aide can do that. In fact, I've worked with teachers who can't do that. Maybe my problem is that I'm an elitist. But I'd feel very uncomfortable using an aide in any kind of teaching capacity. I don't even feel right using the aide to do housekeeping duties, because I think children should learn responsibility in that area. I ask the students to be responsible for doing some of the things your aides are doing.

SUE   Based on the things you've told me, I can understand why you don't want to use aides. But I have a different point of view about my pupils and classroom, and it doesn't really bother me to have someone else in the classroom to help me.

Emma Mobley is an African-American low-income mother who, as one of the aides in a fifth-grade class at Wiley, has moved to the level of making home visits. After spending several weeks in the classroom and careful planning with the teacher, she has gone on her first home visit. She arrives at the appropriate house in the same area in which she resides and knocks on the door. An African-American woman of approximately Emma's age opens the door.

EMMA   Hello. My name's Emma Mobley, and I'm the home visitor from Wiley Elementary School. Do you remember that I called you Friday about visiting you today?

RUTH   I'm Ruth Coss, and I do remember you calling. But I think I already know you. Don't you live over on Delaware Street?

EMMA   [Laughing] Yes, I knew you looked familiar. I seen you in Richards' grocery store before.

RUTH   [Smiling] That's right. I seen you there, too. You're not a teacher, are you?

EMMA   No, I'm not a teacher. I'm a home visitor. They call me a teacher aide. I just started being it this year.

RUTH   What does a teacher aide do?

EMMA   Well, I've been working in the classroom helping the teacher, but now I'm starting to visit the homes of half the children in the room once a week. The other aide will visit the other children's homes. I'm supposed to meet with each mother and show her how to help her child with homework assignments.

RUTH   How much money a job like that pay?

EMMA   It pay five dollars an hour. And I start at 9:00 and work 'til 3:00, although I sometimes have to make my home visits after school.

RUTH   That a good job! How you get a job like that? I'd like that kind of job!

EMMA   My girl tole me they was advertizin' for people to do the job, so I went to the school office and wrote on a form. Couple of days later they tole my girl to ask me to come to the school and talk to the principal lady. I did and she tole me I was hired. I went to school for a week and a lady from the university came and showed me what to do in the classroom and how to make home visits. Before I make home visits I sits down with the teacher and we plan what I'm to bring in and show to the mother.

RUTH   I'm gonna go to that school and try to get me a job like that. That sound like good work.

EMMA   Yeah, it is good work. It's a fun job, too. I hope you get one.

RUTH   *[Abruptly changing the subject]* What'd it say on the paper about why you're s'posed to visit me? What bad things has Ross been doin' at school?

EMMA   He hasn't been doin' bad things. When he there he don't bring any homework with him. But I have to be honest with you, he just hasn't been there very much. Do you know where he been?

RUTH   No. I don't know. I thought he been at school. I guess he just been playin' hookey. I've tole him he need to be in school every day.

EMMA   You gotta do something about him missing school. That's breakin' the law. The principal will report him to the truant officer if he don't start coming every day.

RUTH   I don't know what to do about his playin' hookey, Emma! He don't pass no tests or none of his courses anyway. I 'spect he'll drop out of school as soon as he's sixteen anyway.

EMMA   What'll he do then? A boy that age has a hard time gettin' a job. He'll probably just hang around with the wrong people and get in trouble.

RUTH   I hope he'll get work and bring in some money to us. Last summer he work at the racetrack on the west side and made pretty good money for a boy his age. He good at getting work. He not good at schoolwork. You probably know that already. Are you gonna get him in trouble for not bein' in school?

EMMA   I'm not gonna get him in trouble. My job's to work with you to get him to come to school and to study while he's there. I even brought some of the work his class is doing so that you could help him here at home. I'll come here every week to show you how to help him with his homework if you want me to. My job's to help parents help their children do good in school, not give 'em trouble. Don't you care that he misses school? He could get a better job later if he stay in school.

RUTH   I want him to go to school, but it's easier for me just to quit yellin' at him and let him miss school and work. He always get jobs and make money, and he brings a lot of it home. We need money. I try to get him to go to school every year, but the older he gets the more he seem to stay away from school. His daddy won't help me none 'cause he drop out of school when he was little. And he think Ross should be bringin' money into the house. It just doesn't do me no good to care about him missing school.

EMMA   Why don't you come to the PTA meeting next Tuesday night? They have a time after the meeting for parents to talk with their child's teacher. Ms. Rogers is a really nice teacher. She tries to help Ross when he's in school. I'll help him, too. He's smart enough to learn whatever we study. Have you met Ms. Rogers?

RUTH   No, I never met any of his teachers. I ought to come and meet her. It's a good idea. But I can't come then. I'm busy Tuesday night.

EMMA   Would you like me to talk with his teacher to see if she has any ideas about getting Ross to stay in school? I know she'd work to try to keep him in school.

RUTH   No, that's OK. It'll all work out.

Reba Green is one of the aides assigned to Rae Phillips, an African-American fourth-grade teacher. Reba is forty years old, divorced, and lives in public housing in a low-income area of the city. Her twenty-two-year old unmarried daughter and four-year-old grandchild live with Reba.

It is the last period of the day, and Rae is at her desk grading papers. The other teacher aide is out making home visits. The pupils in the class are writing answers to questions at the end of the chapter on verbs that they have just discussed in class. Rae is monitoring this assignment. Tim, an African-American pupil, is seated with his head resting on his arms on the top of his desk.

REBA   [Grabbing Tim roughly by the back of his shirt collar and jerking him upright] [Loudly] You sit up straight in your chair, boy. You're s'posed to be circling verbs in those sentences! [Points to the book]

TIM   I don't feel good, Ms. Green. My stomach hurts.

REBA   Well, you get to work findin' those verbs and you'll forget all about that stomach hurt! Go on now!

TIM   Oh, OK. [He begins to work on the assignment.] [Maria, a white student, raises her hand. Reba walks toward her desk.]

MARIA   I've finished the lesson. I was looking ahead in the book, and it talks about contractions. What are they?

REBA   [After a long pause] Don't you worry none about what's later on in the book. You just worry about if you did your lesson right.

MARIA   But contractions are the next thing we study. I just wanted to go on in the book.

REBA   [Angrily] I told you not to worry about the next lesson. We'll all go to it together. Now find something else to do and don't bother me again! [Reba stomps away, leaving Maria on the verge of tears.]

HAL   [Raises his hand and speaks out] Can I go and sharpen my pencil, Ms. Green? [Reba nods] [Hal walks toward the pencil sharpener, and Mike shoves an empty desk into his path with his foot. Hal walks into the desk.] What's wrong with you, Mike? [Holding his thigh] You really hurt my leg! You're a jerk!

Reba charges angrily across the room to Mike's seat. She jerks him roughly out of his seat, shakes him hard, and slams him back into his seat, still holding him with both hands.

REBA   Hurting people in this class is not allowed! I've told you that before! [Lifts him up and slams him back down hard] How do you like to be shoved around? Ms. Phillips and I will decide what to do about you later! [The bell rings, signaling the end of class. The pupils quietly file out of the room.]

RAE   Reba, would you come over here and sit for a minute? There are some things we need to talk about.

REBA   [Walking toward Rae] It seemed like some of the kids were peskier than usual today. Some of those little rich kids never learned how to behave.

RAE   [Motioning Reba to sit beside her] That's what I want to talk with you about. [Pause] You know, Reba, when adults work with children in churches, clubs, and schools, there are certain things that we need to be very careful about.

REBA   I know that, Rae. And I work really hard to make them behave.

RAE   That's true, and you do a good job. But the things I was thinking we should be careful about have to do with the way we treat the pupils.

REBA   Well, I try to make them act the way they ought to.

RAE   You do. But as a teacher and aide, we're both state employees. And that means we have to follow the rules the state has for schools.

REBA   *[Smiling]* I never thought of that before. Me—a state employee. That's cool! What kind of rules you talking about?

RAE   Well, the ones that come to mind first are how we work with the children.

REBA   I think I work with them pretty good, don't you? I make them mind just like my daddy made me mind.

RAE   Yes, you do. But one of the things I'm concerned about is the way you grab them, push them, slam them down in their seats. Some people might consider those things to be abuse. Do you know what abuse is?

REBA   I sure do . . . that's when you beat somebody up. You abuse them.

RAE   That's right! And what are things that people do to children to abuse them?

REBA   You have to hit them!

RAE   Yes, that's abuse. How about picking them up by the shirt or slamming them down on a chair?

REBA   *[Long silence]* No, I don't think that's abuse. *[Another long silence]* Is it?

RAE   The state says it is. We have to be careful about touching children—where we touch them and how we touch them. But jerking them out of their seats or slamming them into their seats could be considered child abuse.

REBA   Oh no, Rae. That can't be abuse. That's how my daddy raised me and how I raised Rose, my daughter. That's not abuse. It shows you care for children when you make them do what they ought to do. *[Pause]* Do you think Mike'll cause trouble?

RAE   *[Smiling]* I doubt he'll want his parents to know he was in trouble at school. But I've noticed that you're really rough on the pupils. You yell and scream, say unkind things to them, and jerk them around physically. I want you to try to explain things and reason with them more, but don't yell at them so much, and above all, don't put your hands on them.

REBA   OK, Rae. I'll try. But I was raised that way. I raised Rosie that way. I'm just trying to raise these pupils to do the right thing. I'm glad you told me what you did. I'll try hard to do things right. I hope you'll help me.

It's approximately the middle of the spring semester, and Doris Larken is presiding over the third and final teachers' faculty meeting of the school year for Wiley Elementary School. The last agenda item under the heading of old business has just been voted on and passed. Dale raises her hand and is recognized by the chair.

DALE   There's no item on the agenda about having teacher aides again. Is the grant money available again next year?

DORIS   Yes, Dale. I was planning to add that item to the agenda. I just received a request for a proposal that's just the same as last year's. But this time I'm sure there will be more schools submitting proposals than there were last year. However, I've looked

at the data we've collected on student achievement and parent involvement, and
indicates that we've had significant increases in both of these areas! Our student
achievement is about one stanine higher compared to the norms. Parent
participation in advisory groups and as classroom volunteers is up 20%. I was a
little discouraged by the fact that only 56% of you are using your aides for
instruction, evaluation, or home-visit types of activities. Overall, however, our
chances of having the grant renewed are excellent.

DALE   Will we have an opportunity to express our views on whether or not we want
aides this year?

DORIS   *[A bit miffed]* Of course! The only reason you weren't able to participate last ye
is that some of you were on vacation and couldn't be reached. And those of you
that I was able to talk with encouraged me to submit the proposal.

ANN   I'm all in favor of the teachers having input, but I think we need some ground
rules for making the decision.

DORIS   What kind of ground rules?

ANN   Well, for instance, should a simple majority vote determine whether or not we
apply for the grant? Or should we require a two-thirds majority?

TOM   That's a good suggestion. I have another suggestion relating to the selection of
volunteers. We need to establish some selection criteria other than the fact that t
applicant is low-income. We have some aides this year who are not only useless,
but actually have a negative influence. Perhaps requiring a high school diploma
evidence of social skills would be a good idea.

SUE   Yes. We did have some aides who weren't very effective. But we also had some v
were outstanding. We need to see what characteristics the outstanding ones have
and see if we can build them into our qualifications.

RAE   I agree with what you've said. But I'd like to point out that I spent quite a bit of
time and effort to stop one of my aides from yelling insults at and physically
punishing pupils in my class. After we'd talked about it and I showed her some
alternatives, she turned out to be an outstanding aide. In fact, I'd love to have h
for an aide again next year. I guess what I'm saying is that probably most of our
disadvantaged aides are educable.

DORIS   *[Speaking out]* It sounds as if some of us have concerns about whether we sho
apply for the grant, and, if we do, what changes we should make to enable our
aides to be more effective. And I'm sure there are many other questions we'd lik
have discussed. If we try to do it all in this meeting, we'll be here until midnigh
think we need to appoint a committee to provide some alternatives to resolve th
issues that have been brought up, as well as the dozens of other issues that have
been brought up. In my role as principal of this school, I'd like to ask Martin if
be willing to chair such a committee.

MARTIN   *[Surprised]* Doris, you know that I'm opposed to requiring teachers to have
aides in their classes.

DORIS   *[Laughing]* Yes. I know that, Martin. How could I not know it? *[Pauses]* But
also know that you're objective and fair in dealing with issues that affect the
school. I feel comfortable having you as committee chair if you would feel
comfortable.

FIGURE 25   A Taxonomy of Teacher Aide Activities Distributed by Doris Larken, Building Principal, to Wiley Elementary Teachers

TEACHER AIDE ACTIVITIES

1.0 HOUSEKEEPING

1. Dusts, cleans, straightens up the room
2. Helps children with clothing
3. Arranges classroom furnishings
4. Helps maintain order
5. Decorates bulletin board

2.0 CLERICAL

1. Collects monies
2. Takes up papers
3. Fills out routine reports and records
4. Duplicates and distributes materials
5. Administers tests

3.0 MATERIALS

1. Locates materials
2. Compiles bibliographies
3. Sets up displays
4. Prepares demonstration materials

4.0 INSTRUCTION

1. Tutors children
2. Organizes play activities
3. Selects or develops materials
4. Teaches individuals and/or groups
5. Maintains discipline

5.0 EVALUATION

1. Grades papers
2. Makes anecdotal records
3. Organizes case study
4. Evaluates materials
5. Makes tests
6. Interprets test results

6.0 HOME VISITS

1. Helps teacher develop home-learning activities
2. Plans with teacher for home visit
3. Demonstrates home-learning activity to parent
4. Monitors parent teaching home-learning activity to child
5. Encourages parent(s) to participate in parent involvement activities
6. Evaluates home visits by completing home-visit report form.

MARTIN   Well, I'm flattered, but I'm also interested in seeing that we all have an opportunity to have input regarding whether or not we continue the program, an if we do continue it that it be structured to be as successful as we can make it. So, I'll accept your appointment.

The remainder of new business is discussed quickly and the meeting is adjourne After the meeting, two faculty members approach Martin.

SUE   I'd like to be on your committee, Martin. I enjoyed having aides this year, but I think we can establish guidelines that will make the program more effective if we' funded.

MARTIN   Great, Sue. I'd like to have you on the committee. We've been on enough committees together that we're almost a team.

PAM   That's why I'm here. I'd feel left out if you two were on a committee and I didn't get to play with you. *[Laughter]*

MARTIN   I really appreciate both of you agreeing to work with me. Our job may not be as complicated as it seems. I think the most efficient first move we can make is to list all the issues that we'll have to deal with. But let me ask both of you a questio right now. Even if we're able to make some improvements in the program in bette selecting and training the aides, do you really think this program is worth keepin Are we doing a better job of teaching? Are the kids learning more? Is this kind of parent involvement worth the cost?

QUESTIONS

1. What is parent involvement, and what forms can it take? What evidence is th that parent involvement increases student success in school? At what grade levels is p ent involvement most frequent? What kinds of parents most often participate? What f tors determine whether or not parent involvement programs are successful?

2. What are teacher aides? How do they usually participate in schools, and how they differ from parent volunteers? How many teacher aides operate at levels 4, 5, an on the "Teacher Aide Activities" form? What qualifications should a teacher aide have

3. What is social class, and how does it differ from socioeconomic status (SES)? W are compensatory education programs, and how effective are they in increasing the s dent achievement and parent involvement of low-income families? How does SES v between different ethnic and racial groups? What values do low SES parents and stud typically hold toward education, school personnel, and discipline?

4. How do discipline patterns differ in the homes of various ethnic and racial grou For example, how do different racial and ethnic groups differ in their attitudes toward desirability of using corporal punishment? Toward the use of reasoning with a child v misbehaves?

5. How well prepared are classroom teachers for the role of team leader, in which t have to plan with and monitor the activities of other adults in the classroom (e.g., teac aides and parent volunteers)? Where should teachers learn such skills?

6. Would a middle-class white teacher or a low-income African-American teacher aide make the best home visitor to a low-income African-American home? In other words, are the best home visitors ones from the same or similar ethnic/racial/SES background as the parent being visited? How important would it be for such a home visitor to be at least a high school graduate? What kind of training would such a home visitor need?

7. What relationships exist between different parenting styles identified by Baumrind (authoritarian, authoritative, and permissive) and different ethnic/racial/SES groups? To what parenting style has Reba Green been exposed? What relationships exist between parenting style and school achievement?

8. From an observational learning perspective, how could physically aggressive behavior like that of Reba Green serve as a model for students in a class or children in a family? If Rae could get Reba to change the way she relates to students and thus model a different pattern of disciplinary behaviors, how might this affect Reba's children as well as the students in the classroom?

9. Dale clearly doesn't want other adults working in her classroom. How do you explain her attitude? At what level of Maslow's need hierarchy might she primarily be operating?

10. What was the purpose of having aides make home visits in the Wiley program? What are the strengths and weaknesses of such a home visit program?

11. Dale is upset because her aides are not trained professionals. What are the characteristics of a profession? Are teachers professionals in the same sense as physicians and attorneys? What would it take for teacher aides to become professionals?

12. What is the purpose of evaluating a program like the one in this case? What does Doris' summary of the summative evaluation of the teacher aide program tell you about how well it is doing? Based on that information, should the program be kept or dropped? What other kinds of information would you like to have in order to make a decision?

13. What should the teachers do? Should they vote to keep the teacher aide program? If they keep it, how should it be changed? What are the program's strong and weak points?

CASE **25**

MOTIVATION OR CONTROL?

Key Content to Consider for Analyzing This Case:
(1) classroom management (especially punishment);
(2) motivation (mastery vs. performance goal-orientations).

S aguaro Senior High School is located in a large city in a state in the Southwest. the more than three thousand students attending Saguaro, approximately 10% from upper-income homes, 50% from middle-income homes, and 40% from low income homes. The ethnic distribution of the student body is approximately 65% wh 20% African-American, 13% Hispanic, and 2% Asian-American. Of the 120 teachers, are white, 8 are African-American, 10 are Hispanic, and 2 are Asian-American.

Because the teachers and staff have been experiencing a considerably larger num of discipline problems than ever before, the principal arranged to employ Dr. Karen Ch a classroom management specialist from a nearby state university, to conduct a worksh with the Saguaro teachers for the purpose of helping them to devise and implemer common classroom management model throughout the school. It is the first day of workshop, and Dr. Howard Peake, the principal of Saguaro, has introduced Dr. Chee the teachers. Dr. Chee then addresses the audience.

KAREN Good morning, fellow teachers. As Dr. Peake has told you, my name is Karen Chee. Dr. Peake has asked me to work with you on classroom management, whie is one of my specialties. There are many different approaches to classroom management, and all of them are effective in certain situations. The main objecti of this workshop, as I see it, is to find the approach to classroom management th will be most comfortable for you teachers to use and, at the same time, the most effective one for your pupils. *[A teacher raises his hand, and Karen nods in his direction.]*

PAUL My name's Paul, and I was wondering how you're going to decide what the bes approach is.

KAREN Good question, Paul. But you might not want to hear my answer.

PAUL Why's that?

KAREN *[Smiling]* Because my answer is that I'm not going to make that determination *[Emphatically]* You are!

MARTHA   [Speaking out] But I thought that's why you're here—to tell us which management system would be best for us.

KAREN   But I can't make that decision—only you teachers can do that.

PAUL   Then what are you going to do?

KAREN   I'm going to help you find the answer to the question. As you know, there are many classroom management models. After we explore the major ones, you'll be able to narrow them down to the one or two that you, as a faculty, feel comfortable with and that you believe will be appropriate for the student body at this school.

EDNA   [Speaking out] But I wonder if we'll be able to agree with one another on the best approach to classroom management. We may have different views on how to handle discipline problems.

KAREN   Such as?

CARL   [Jumping into the discussion] Well, I'll be glad to share my position with you. We have to learn how to control the pupils. We can't teach them anything until they learn to behave themselves and pay attention to what we're trying to teach them. If they're out of their seats running around the room, there's no way learning can take place. We have to get their attention before we can teach them anything. Without discipline, there's no learning.

EDNA   [Responding] See, that's what I mean. I don't agree with that at all. That's the old-fashioned philosophy that discipline comes before learning. [Looking at Carl] You have it backwards, Carl. Without motivation, there's neither discipline nor learning. Preschool children learn effortlessly because they're motivated to learn. They don't become discipline problems until we try to regiment them and treat them like army recruits. If we motivate them to learn, the discipline problems disappear and learning occurs naturally.

CARL   That's all very nice in theory, Edna, but you can't sugarcoat everything you teach and make it interesting to all your students. The fact is, a lot of the students simply aren't going to be motivated by what you're teaching.

PAUL   [Speaking out] Which of these approaches do you think is the right one, Karen?

KAREN   It doesn't matter so much what I think, Paul, as it does what you think. And that's what I intend to find out this morning. [Holds up a questionnaire] This instrument is designed to assess your core beliefs on classroom management. [Hands copies of the questionnaire entitled "Classroom Management Beliefs" to several teachers in the front row to distribute] I'd like each of you to fill out one of these questionnaires right now. I'll tabulate them before our next meeting. Perhaps the results will enable us to work toward a common model of classroom management.

It is the first period on Monday following the workshop, and Carl is introducing the concept of sets and relations to his ninth-grade algebra class.

CARL   All of us talk about groups of objects in our everyday conversation. We talk about a deck of cards, a book of matches, a football team, or many other kinds of teams. Who can think of another group of objects?

MAX   [Yelling out] A team of horses!

CARL   That's right, Max. But what's our rule that tells us what to do when we want to give an answer?

MAX   We're supposed to raise our hand and wait for you to call on us.

CARL   [Walks to chalkboard and writes Max's name] That's right. So you get your name on the board. [Max waves his hand, but Carl ignores him.] We've identified several collections of objects. Who can tell us what these groups of objects are called in algebra? [Carman raises her hand.] Carman?

CARMAN   They're called sets. [Pause] And I don't think it's fair that you put Max's name on the board. He wasn't talking to another pupil and disturbing the class. He was participating in the lesson.

CARL   [Not pleased with the comment] What rule did Max violate, Carman?

CARMAN   He talked out without permission.

CARL   That's right. The rule doesn't mention any exceptions. If several of you decided to call out to me during a class discussion, it would be just as disruptive as if you were talking to each other. Besides, you must get your name on the board with two mark: after it before you must leave the class and get an F for the day's work. So Max is OK unless he talks out two more times. If he does, he'll go to the principal's office.

CARMAN   I still don't think it's fair when he was trying to be cooperative! [Carl walks to the board and writes Carman's name under Max's. Members of the class seem upset.]

CARL   I will not tolerate talking out in this class. [Looks around the classroom] I explaine: my system of discipline to you quite thoroughly the first day of class. At your age it's very important for you to learn self-discipline. People with self-discipline are more successful in life. When a class is out of control, none of the students learn a: much as they should learn. And that's why you're here—to learn.

So I'll explain the procedure again. For the first offense, I write your name c the board. For the second offense, I put a mark after your name. For the third offense, I send you to the principal's office and fail you for the day's work. The thi: time a student is sent to the principal's office, the principal schedules a meeting with the pupil's parents. [Sue raises her hand.] Sue?

SUE   What happens then?

CARL   Good question. But it's hard to answer. It always depends on the student's past behavior. It can result in anything from the student's being put on probation to being expelled from school. Now, who can think of some other examples of sets? [Latisha raises her hand.] Latisha?

LATISHA   There are lots of them—days of the week, weeks in a month, months in a yea

CARL   That's right, Latisha. Good. Now who can tell me what a subset is? [Ned raises h hand.] Ned?

NED   A subset is a set that's part of a bigger set.

CARL   Right. [Addressing the class] Now I want you to open your books to page 12. Complete exercises 1.2 and 1.3 on that page and then complete exercises 2.4 and 2.5 on page 13. These exercises will help you learn about sets, subsets, proper subsets, and equivalent sets.

LEROY   [Whispers to Latisha] You got a pencil I can borrow? [Carl walks to the board and writes Leroy's name below Carman's.] Hey, man, why'd you write my name up there just borrowed a pencil.

CARL   You didn't raise your hand. You talked out.

LEROY   If I'd raised my hand, how would Carman know that I want a pencil? That's dumb. *[Carl goes to the board and puts a mark beside Leroy's name. Leroy raises his hand, but Carl ignores him.]*

The same week, Edna began a unit on writing in her second-period ninth-grade English class. For the first five minutes of this morning's class, she presented a five-minute minilesson on the characteristics of sentence fragments and run-on sentences because she had noticed examples of both kinds of sentences in some of the pupils' writings from last week.

EDNA   All right, students. I hope you'll all be able to avoid the writing of these kinds of sentences. Now we'll have a state-of-the-class conference. Rita, what are you doing this period?

RITA   I'm still selecting a topic.

EDNA   OK, but I want you to have one by the end of the period. You were selecting a topic on Friday. Two days is too much time to spend selecting a topic.

RITA   I've narrowed it down to two topics.

EDNA   That's great. Come and tell me when you make the choice. *[Looks at Raul]* Raul, what are you doing?

RAUL   I'm writing.

EDNA   Good, Raul. Take it to the editors when you finish your first draft. *[Looks at three girls talking among themselves]* Paula, Anita, Jamaica. What are you doing?

ANITA   We're conferencing. We're reading each other's introductions and making suggestions.

EDNA   Good idea. You should be able to do that in about fifteen minutes. *[At the end of five minutes, Edna finishes polling the class on what they are doing. She makes notes on a form made for that purpose.]*

   All right, class. It sounds as if you're all making pretty good progress on your writing. Now, you'll have thirty-five minutes to write or conference on your projects. *[Some students form into groups of two or three and share and revise their writing. Others sit by themselves and write. And some hold up their hands for Edna to help them. Edna approaches one of these students.]* How can I help you, Isaac?

ISAAC   I finished writing this story on Friday, but I don't like the ending.

EDNA   *[Reads the story carefully and looks at Isaac.]* That's a good story, Isaac. I like the introduction. And you have the events in a logical sequence. But, I agree that the ending could be stronger. Can you think of some other ways that you could end the story?

ISAAC   Well, I could have John tell his problems to his dad instead of his friend Paul.

EDNA   *[Ponders briefly]* Yes. That'd work.

ISAAC   Or I could have Paul ask John if there's something bothering him.

EDNA   Yes. I like that too.

ISAAC   Which ending should I use?

EDNA   You're the author, Isaac. You have to make decisions like that. But I do think that both of the endings you're considering could improve the story if you handle them well. *[She sees three girls who seem to be visiting and walks over to their seats.]* Are you girls doing all right?

ROXY   *[Smiling]* Yes. Mandy just read her story to us, and it's really funny! Do you want to hear it?

EDNA   *[Smiling]* Yes, I do. But since our write and conference time is up, I think it might be nice for the whole class to hear it. *[Looking at Mandy]* Mandy, would you be willing to read your story to the class?

MANDY   *[Obviously pleased]* Yes. I'd like to.

EDNA   That's great, Mandy. *[Walks to the front of the class]* Class. May I have your attention? *[The hum of conversation stops.]* It's time for the sharing period. Today, I've asked Mandy to share her story with you. *[Turns to Mandy and announces with great fanfare]* Mandy, you're on!

The following Saturday morning, the classroom management workshop group meets again in the high school auditorium. Karen Chee presides over the meeting.

KAREN   Welcome to the second session of our classroom management workshop. Our first item on the agenda this morning is to report the results of the questionnaire that you all filled out on your core beliefs on discipline. *[Pauses]* Overall, 67% of you indicated that you subscribe to the discipline-oriented view, and 33% subscribe to the motivation-oriented view. *[Carl raises his hand.]* Carl?

CARL   Does that mean that the school classroom management program will be based on a control-first view?

EDNA   *[Speaking out]* It doesn't seem reasonable to impose a program that more than a third of the faculty voted against.

CARL   If it were a presidential election, the control-first candidate would be elected.

PAUL   That analogy seems to compare apples and oranges. We're not electing a candidate. We're talking about strategies to use to educate students. I really don't feel comfortable using a control-first approach to classroom management. So why should I be required to use that approach when I'm so much more comfortable and effective as a teacher using the motivation-oriented approach? And I know that Carl is most effective using the discipline approach. Why should he have to use the motivation approach? We teachers talk a lot about accommodating the different learning styles of students. Why can't we accommodate the teaching styles of teachers?

MARK   Hear! Hear! Well stated!

KAREN   Yes, it's obvious that we don't have unanimity. *[Martha raises her hand. Karen points to her.]*

MARTHA   I thought the purpose of the questionnaire was to enable us to select one management system that all of us would use. Maybe our vote was analogous to a presidential election. The one with the most votes wins. *[Edna raises her hand and is acknowledged.]*

EDNA   If our purpose is to be consistent in classroom management, why can't all the control-oriented teachers meet and devise a consistent management system that they can all subscribe to? The motivation group could go through the same process

FIGURE 26 Classroom Management Questionnaire Disbributed by Dr. Karen Chee to Teachers Attending Classroom Management Workshop

CLASSROOM MANAGEMENT BELIEFS

Directions: Please answer the following questions as fully as possible. Their purpose is for you to state your core beliefs about these issues so that we can compare and contrast our beliefs during the workshop and, hopefully, end up agreeing on a model of classroom management to implement in our classrooms. Write your answers on separate sheets of paper as needed.

1. What causes students to behave the way they do? Is the cause of student misbehavior in the environment (e.g., classroom), inside the student, or some combination of the two?
2. What is student learning, and how can you tell when it is taking place? What must teachers do in the classroom to promote learning? How is learning related to classroom management?
3. What is a classroom discipline problem? At what point does a student become a discipline problem?
4. To what extent should teachers be concerned with student growth and learning of a non-academic nature? Where does the teacher's responsibility begin and end?
5. Is it the teacher's job to shape the curriculum to the child or to shape the child to the curriculum? To what extent should the teacher use rewards (and punishments) to motivate students to learn material they don't enjoy learning?
6. Which is it most important for the teacher to do first? (1) gain control of student behavior so learning can take place, or (2) figure out how to teach material in a motivating way so that learning occurs and discipline doesn't become a problem.
7. Is it possible for teachers to treat students as equals? When necessary, is it OK for the teacher to use the "power" of his or her position to promote student learning and discipline?
8. Is the goal of classroom management for students to develop self-discipline? If so, how can such a goal be accomplished?
9. What forms of punishment are OK for a teacher to use in the classroom? Is corporal punishment acceptable under some circumstances? How do you differentiate between major and minor rules violations?
10. Should classroom management procedures be adapted to student differences (e.g., age, stage of development, socioeconomic status, gender, race, ethnic background), or should all students be treated exactly alike?
11. To what extent should students be involved in establishing the rules and procedures for classroom management?
12. Is it possible for a teacher to be a warm, caring, facilitative person and still be a good disciplinarian?
13. Can parents of your students be involved in your classroom management procedures? If so, how?
14. Suppose you had to describe your classroom management procedures to a beginning teacher. What would you tell him or her?
15. List and briefly describe as many models of classroom management as you can. Then indicate which one comes closest to matching your beliefs about classroom management.

That way we could have two management systems consistent within the group
using each one, and we all could manage our classes the way we feel most
comfortable.

KAREN   Obviously, our task now is to decide whether to have one management system
that approximately one-third of the teachers don't subscribe to, or to have two
management programs which will enable all the teachers to use the one with which
they feel most comfortable. *[Nods toward Elaine, who is waving her hand]*

ELAINE   What's the best way for us to go here? And what classroom management models
fit the two classroom management orientations? And why should we limit ourselves
to two approaches? Aren't we professionals? Why can't each of us choose our own
individual approach to use in our classrooms?

QUESTIONS

1. What is the difference between classroom management and classroom discipline?
Which is the preferred term, and why? What role does the use of punishment play in dis-
tinguishing the two terms?

2. The goal of classroom management is student self-discipline. What is self-discipline
and how can it be accomplished?

3. What are the different assumptions underlying the motivation-oriented and control-
oriented approaches to the role of classroom management? Which is the most valid
and why?

4. What is motivation, and what role does it play in human learning? What differences
exist between the mastery and performance goal orientations of students (as described by
Ames), and how do they relate to the method of classroom management used?

5. What is the difference between a teacher-centered classroom and a student-centered
classroom? Which is most desirable, and why? How does each relate to the method of
classroom management used?

6. What is the cause of student behavior problems in the classroom? Is the problem
inside the student or in the classroom environment, or perhaps both? How does the
answer to this question relate to the classroom management procedure chosen?

7. Should a teacher consistently use the same methods of classroom management with
all students, or adapt methods or even use different methods according to varying student
characteristics? For example, should different methods of classroom management be used
with diverse student populations (e.g., those which vary in socioeconomic status, gender,
racial and ethnic background, and/or academic ability)?

8. Compare and contrast the classroom management procedures used by Carl and
Edna. Which one is more control-oriented? Which is more motivation-oriented? Is one
more likely to foster student learning than the other? Which do you prefer, and why?

9. Answer the fifteen questions on the "Classroom Management Beliefs" questionnaire given to the teachers by Dr. Chee. What do your answers tell you about your
classroom management orientation? For example, are you more oriented toward control
or motivation? What model of classroom management comes closest to fitting your
belief system?

10. Should the school adopt only one method of classroom management for all teachers to use, or should two approaches be allowed? Or should each teacher be permitted to develop his or her own individual approach?

11. What classroom management models (e.g., behavior modification, Assertive Discipline, Reality Therapy, Teacher Effectiveness Training, and Kounin's approach) come closest to fitting the control and motivation orientations of the teachers? Where would parent involvement methods fit in?

C A S E 26

TEACHING TO THE TEST

Key Content to Consider for Analyzing This Case:
(1) measurement and evaluation (standardized tests, objective vs. essay tests, norm- vs. criterion-referenced evaluation); (2) Bloom's Cognitive Taxonomy; (3) home learning environment/parent involvement.

In 1948, Tecumseh High School was built in a middle- to upper-middle-income suburban neighborhood. For several years it was the most elegant school in the large West Coast city in which it is located. However, beginning in the 1960s the more upwardly mobile families, both African-American and white, began to move out of this neighborhood into the newer suburban areas springing up in the outer perimeters of the city. Today, the families that remain in the T.H.S. district are largely low income. Of the slightly more than two thousand pupils enrolled in the school today, approximately 40% are African-American, 20% Hispanic, 10% Asian-American, and 30% non-Hispanic white.

The gradual shift in the socioeconomic level of the T.H.S. student body has taken a toll on its scores on the state-mandated eleventh-grade tests given each spring. In the early 1960s the average T.H.S. student achievement scores on reading, writing, and mathematics skills were the highest of all the eleven high schools in the city. In the 1970s T.H.S. students' scores ranked fourth out of eleven. In the 1980s T.H.S. had dropped to ninth out of eleven. This year T.H.S. scores dropped to eleventh, the lowest in the city.

It is Monday of the last week of classes, and teachers are reviewing the year's work to prepare students for their final examinations. Dr. Lu Ping, the principal, called an unscheduled faculty meeting in the school auditorium to begin thirty minutes after the end of the last period. After the last class ends, teachers begin to walk toward the auditorium individually and in small groups. Tom Arena, a thirty-five-year-old mathematics teacher who is completing his eighth year at T.H.S., catches up with his friend Jed Cass, a twenty-four-year-old history teacher who joined the T.H.S. faculty at the beginning of the school year and has proved to be very popular with the students. Earlier in the year the students voted him "Teacher of the Year."

TOM I wonder what this meeting's about. I'm so busy I really don't have time to go to an unscheduled faculty meeting.

JED   I heard by way of the rumor mill that our students were at the bottom of the heap in their scores on the standardized curriculum test, and our superintendent's not at all happy with our poor academic performance.

TOM   Oh, oh! That's bad news! You can bet there'll be a change in either the curriculum or in the testing program—maybe both. *[They approach the door to the auditorium.]*

JED   *[Whispering]* It won't be long before we find out. *[They select seats near the stage.]*

After being introduced by Scott Harold, the assistant principal in charge of curriculum, Dr. Lu Ping walks to the microphone and addresses the teachers. Dr. Ping is an Asian-American female in her early fifties.

DR. PING   *[Loudly and clearly]* I know you're all very busy bringing closure to your classes and planning final examinations, but I just received word of a major change in academic accountability adopted by the school board.

TOM   *[Whispers to Jed]* Well, I'll bat at least .500 on my guess. *[Jed smiles and nods.]*

DR. PING   It seems that our eleventh graders throughout the entire school district have scored lower than they have ever scored before on the standardized test on reading, writing, and mathematics. And even more unfortunate is the fact that the scores of our students were the lowest of all eleven high schools in the city. *[Teachers react to this information by whispering various responses to those sitting near them.]* Needless to say, our superintendent, Dr. Webb, is not happy with these test results. *[She pauses for effect.]* So he has issued an edict to all the high school principals that in the coming year, the basic skills achievement scores of every eleventh-grade student will increase significantly on the state's annual assessment test. Each teacher, regardless of subject-matter specialty, will stress all the basic skills.

TOM   *[Whispering]* Bingo!

JED   You batted 1.000!

DR. PING   To improve our scores, then, I am initiating several new procedures this year. I expect all of you to do your part to increase the basic skills achievement of our students. *[She pauses and looks over her audience for several seconds.]* I want all department heads to schedule department meetings after the last class tomorrow afternoon. By that time I will have prepared a list of all the specific skills for which less than 75% of our students achieved mastery. I then want each department to develop a plan of action for raising the levels of mastery for those skills. And I'm not referring to just the skills taught by teachers in your department. I want all teachers in all departments to teach reading skills, writing skills, and math skills. *[In response to this last remark, many of the teachers in the audience squirm in their seats and whisper to one another. Dr. Ping continues with a renewed authoritative quality to her voice.]*

I know it means an effort on your parts, but it must be made if we are to raise test scores. In addition, I want you to know that I *am* serious about this! Like it or not, our school's effectiveness is judged by how well our students do on the state's test of basic skills. *[She pauses as if to give teachers an opportunity to reflect on her remarks.]*

Now let me tell you about *my* action plan. I'm asking several things of you. First, I'm asking all departments to develop weekly lesson plans that must include instruction in all the basic skills, not just those related to your discipline. Next, I'm asking each of you to give monthly practice tests in the basic skills to prepare our students for the state's test in March. I'm also asking each of you to begin immediately to initiate a schoolwide campaign to stress to students the importance of increasing test scores. And, finally, I'm lining up two in-service workshops later in the year to improve students' test-taking skills.

After Dr. Ping adjourns the meeting, Tom and Jed walk back to their classrooms.

JED   Wow! *[Pause]* I know Lu wants to increase the students' level of performance so the school will look better, and I certainly can understand the reason for this, but it really grates on me when I hear educated people express the belief that you can improve pupils' learning by drilling them on test items. The idea is absurd. Students in this school are so lacking in educational experiences that they have no background information to which they can relate isolated facts. Lu's drill on test items is a total waste of time. It will accomplish exactly the opposite of what she's trying to achieve. Students will begin to hate schoolwork, because it will be meaningless to them.

TOM   *[Nods his head in agreement]* I agree. That misses the whole point of education.

JED   *[Stopping at the door of his classroom]* Also, imposing skill-drill on all the students in the school when only the eleventh grade has to take it doesn't make any sense either. *[Pauses]* But, I guess that if you're a principal, the name of the game is to make the school look good on paper. If you can go from the seventy-third percentile to the seventy-fifth on a single skill, that makes you look good, even if you sacrifice the pupils' overall understanding of the subject so that they can memorize test items.

TOM   That's true. Objective tests don't test students' understanding of principles, concepts, and applications. *[Reflects for a moment]* I have an idea! Why don't you find out how the people in the math department feel about this testing business. If a lot of them feel the way we do, then maybe you, as a department chair, could meet with Lu and communicate their concerns to her.

JED   *[Chuckling and with sarcasm]* Thanks a lot, pal. I appreciate your endorsement of my magical powers.

TOM   *[Smiling]* And your professionalism is exceeded only by your outstanding tact. You are truly a great tactician! *[Seriously]* You're one of our most influential faculty members for both the students and teachers, Jed. No one on our faculty could articulate our position as effectively as you.

JED   I appreciate the compliments, Tom, but I'm not going to let you off the hook. I'll survey the social studies teachers if you'll survey the math teachers. Then the two of us can meet with Lu together if we decide there's a need to do so.

TOM   *[Holds his hands up in surrender]* What can I say? You social studies teachers are so democratic! *[Pause]* OK, I'll do it, but you know I'll have to work around Paula

Cato. As our department chair, she's liable to question my motives. She's a great advocate of objective testing, you know.

JED   *[Slaps Tom on the back enthusiastically]* I know you can handle it!

After school the following day, Tom is meeting in the math lab with the six other mathematics teachers in his department. At Tom's request they're reviewing the mathematics skills that fewer than 75% of the eleventh graders have mastered. Tom has written the ten skills on the board:

The student will:

1. Round a number less than 10 with more than two decimal places to the nearest whole number.
2. Round a mixed number with a whole number component less than 100 to the nearest whole number.
3. Put in order three whole numbers less than 10 million.
4. Identify an improper fraction that is equivalent to a mixed number less than 100.
5. Identify a decimal or percent that is equivalent to a proper fraction having a denominator of 2, 3, 4, 5, 20, 25, 50, or 100.
6. Multiply two three-digit numbers.
7. Divide a five-digit number by a two-digit number.
8. Divide two numbers, each having no more than two decimal places.
9. Estimate capacity in liters, cups, or quarts.
10. Solve real-world problems by finding simple interest.

Tom stands just to the left of the skills he has written on the board. The teachers are seated in a semicircle a few feet from him.

TOM   *[Gesturing toward the material on the board]* These are the ten math skills, then, that we're supposed to emphasize in our classes.

MS. WILKS   *[Pointing to what Tom has written on the board]* I can go along with those, Tom, but what I want to know is, what are we supposed to do about the reading and writing skills? *[Shaking her head]* I'm a math teacher, not an English teacher.

TOM   Remember, Dr. Ping said that *every* teacher is to be a teacher of all the basics. But let's decide what we're going to do about the math skills first. Then we'll turn to the other areas.

MR. PLATT   *[Sarcastically and with a smirk]* I want to see what the folks in physical education do about this. *[A few of the teachers chuckle.]*

MS. NEFF   *[With obvious irritation]* She wants *all* of us to emphasize these skills to *all* of our students?

TOM   That's my understanding.

MS. NEFF   Well, there's a fundamental problem here that bothers me. If we aim our teaching at the test, the kids will just master the lower-order skills those tests measure.

MS. PAYNE   *[Shaking her head and turning in her seat to face Ms. Neff]* No, the tests just measure the minimum things the kids are to learn. We don't teach *only* what's on the test.

MS. NEFF   That may be the case, but unless we're careful, the minimum will become the maximum.

TOM   *[Thoughtfully]* Yes, this is something we need to guard against. I've seen it happen before. Tests like the one in our state can pressure teachers to teach only what the test measures. And what most of these tests focus on are lower-order cognitive skills.

MR. NIXON   *[Emphatically]* He's right. The test ends up determining the curriculum. Whatever's tested is what teachers focus on. Somewhere in the process, higher-order thinking skills, problem-solving skills, and practical application get lost.

TOM   Jed Cass in the social studies department pointed out a related issue that I wasn't aware of: the writing portion of the test doesn't ask kids to write. They just bubble in answers to multiple-choice questions.

MS. NEFF   That sure isn't writing!

TOM   *[Speaking slowly and choosing his words carefully]* Let me try this out on you. There seem to be many of us who have some doubts about the influence the state assessment test is having on our curriculum. Nobody here is against testing; we just want it kept in proper perspective. *[A few teachers nod in assent; others murmur their agreement.]* How does it sound if we make a list right here on the board of our concerns, and then I meet with Dr. Lu and tell her about our reservations?

MS. NEFF   That's a good idea. We owe it to ourselves to make our views known.

MR. PLATT   *[Hesitantly]* Maybe we should find out how teachers in some of the other departments feel.

TOM   I know that Jed Cass is discussing the same thing with the social studies teachers.

MR. PLATT   Good. Maybe the two of you could go talk to Dr. Ping. It would have more of an impact if she knew that the math and social studies departments had the same concerns. Do you think you could get Jed to go with you?

TOM   *[Smiling]* I suppose I could try. But I'm not too sure Jed would want to go around Paula Cato. I know she's really in favor of testing.

MR. PLATT   Well, maybe you can convince him. It seems to me that if a lot of social studies teachers feel the same way we do, someone has a right to represent them.

Three days later, Tom and Jed enter Dr. Ping's office. She greets them at the door with a smile, then shakes hands with each of them before motioning them into the two brown leather chairs in front of her desk.

DR. PING   May I get either of you something to drink—coffee, tea, soft drink?

TOM AND JED   *[In unison]* No, thank you.

DR. PING   *[Smiling as she sits down in her chair]* Mr. Arena, you said earlier that some of the teachers in your department have concerns regarding our basic skills program.

TOM   *[Leaning forward in his chair]* That's right, Dr. Ping. None of us is against stressing basic skills or testing students' knowledge. It's just that we're concerned that too much emphasis is being placed on the tests.

JED   *[Hesitantly at first]* The social studies teachers have the same concerns. Actually the state's test covers only a fraction of our total eleventh-grade curriculum. The rest of our curriculum's totally ignored.

TOM   Our basic concern is that by placing too much emphasis on the state's assessment test, we'll restrict the curriculum that we present to the kids. What's tested will be what's taught. One of my teachers even referred to the current push to increase test scores as "teaching to the test."

DR. PING   *[Seriously]* I understand what you're saying, but you must remember that the minimum standards covered don't reflect the higher-order skills for which individual teachers may hold students accountable.

TOM   I think we understand the theory. Our concern is that many teachers and students alike believe that if it's not tested, it's not important.

JED   I agree. Minimum-competency tests like our state test really have a limiting effect on the social studies curriculum.

DR. PING   What do you mean, Mr. Cass?

JED   When we evaluate teachers according to how their pupils do on tests that require them to recall isolated facts, teachers focus their teaching and tests on the easy-to-measure bits of information that these tests usually cover. Creativity and problem-solving in the curriculum are gradually phased out. The tests don't measure the kind of growth we want our kids to achieve.

DR. PING   I think you're being overly critical of these tests. They're simply tools for us to use to see how effective we are at ensuring that all our students get the basics. These are skills that are required for everyday living, and we need to have a systematic way of guaranteeing that every student acquires them.

JED   I think Tom's math teachers are right. These tests stifle teacher and student creativity and self-direction. If students see that we place so much emphasis on discrete bits of knowledge, they're not going to be inclined to learn to solve problems, think logically, and communicate clearly.

DR. PING   *[With some irritation]* Now, Mr. Cass, you're forgetting that the discrete bits of knowledge are necessary for anyone to be able to do the things you've mentioned. In effect we have to establish the ability of pupils to engage in lower-order thinking before there can be higher-order thinking. Right?

JED   *[Tersely]* I follow what you're saying. There's another area that these tests ignore entirely, and that's the affective area. In social studies we believe it's important for students to develop appreciation for other races, nationalities, and customs. When you look at the state's test, though, it doesn't address such goals.

DR. PING   *[Sighing]* Gentlemen, I have to go back to what I've said before. Our state's test only outlines the minimum objectives for our curriculum. Each teacher is entirely free to go beyond those objectives. And I would add that they should do so.

TOM   I guess the point we're trying to make is that if we start giving monthly practice tests, working basic skills instruction into our weekly lesson plans and all the rest, there won't be much time left for the rest of the curriculum. The kids will be spending most of their time with rote learning.

FIGURE 27 List of Student Achievement Basic Skills Prepared by Dr. Lu Ping, Principal, to Be Increased to the 75% Mastery Level by all Teachers

---

TECUMSEH HIGH SCHOOL

Basic Objectives With Less Than 75% of Students Achieving Mastery

OBJECTIVES	Percentage
Reading	Mastery

1. Identify frequently used words by sight.	74
2. Determine the main idea stated in a paragraph.	69
3. Identify the order of events in a paragraph.	70
4. Identify the cause or effect stated in a paragraph.	68
5. Follow written directions.	73
6. Identify the pronoun referent in a sentence or paragraph.	69
7. Identify the main idea implied in a paragraph.	59
8. Identify the cause or effect implied in a paragraph.	60
9. Obtain appropriate information from pictures, maps, or signs.	71

Writing

1. Write the plural form of nouns correctly.	71
2. Write declarative sentences having compound subjects and/or verbs.	69
3. Make subjects and verbs agree.	65
4. Use appropriate forms of common irregular verbs in writing.	64
5. Generate headings for groups of words or phrases.	72
6. Organize information related to a single topic.	68
7. Proofread for spelling.	71
8. Spell months of the year, days of the week, and numbers from 1 to 121.	74
9. Spell commonly used "survival" words.	73
10. Use a comma between names of cities and states and between the day of the month and the year.	72
11. Use an apostrophe to form contractions.	69
12. Use an apostrophe and s to show the possessive of singular and plural nouns that do not end in s.	65
13. Capitalize appropriate words in titles.	68

Mathematics

1. Round a number less than 10 with no more than two decimal places to the nearest whole number.	74
2. Round a mixed number with a whole number component less than 100 to the nearest whole number.	72
3. Put in order three whole numbers less than 10 million.	70
4. Identify an improper fraction that is equivalent to a mixed number less than 100.	67
5. Identify a decimal or percent that is equivalent to a proper fraction having a denominator of 2, 3, 4, 5, 20, 50, or 100.	65

6. Multiply two three-digit numbers.	69
7. Divide a five-digit number by a two-digit number.	67
8. Divide two numbers, each having no more than two decimal places.	70
9. Estimate capacity in liters, cups, or quarts.	68
10. Solve real-world problems by finding simple interest.	61

Dr. Ping   I understand your concern. However, I want you to know that I feel a tremendous responsibility to the students who have failed to master certain parts of the test. *[With determination]* I truly believe that 100 percent of our students can achieve mastery on every skill covered by the test.

Tom and Jed nod in agreement with what their principal has just said. The three then sit in silence for several minutes. Tom glances at Jed as though looking for a cue on what to say next.

Dr. Ping   I have an idea. *[She pushes her swivel chair back from her desk and twirls a quarter turn to the right.]* I appreciate your willingness to be candid with me about how you and the other teachers feel. I know we all have our pupils' best interests at heart. *[She turns her chair back to the left and makes direct eye contact with Tom.]* I'd like to create a basic skills task force with the two of you as co-chairs. You'll select one teacher from each department to be on the task force. Your job would be to study the problem from all angles. Then develop a plan for increasing the scores of those students who have mastered less than 75 percent of the reading, writing, or math objectives. You should also develop plans for going beyond the basic skills. What do you think about that?

Tom   Hmm . . . I appreciate your openness to our input, Dr. Ping. Frankly, I'm not sure what to say. I wasn't expecting this.

Dr. Ping   Well, I believe both of you are truly committed to our students' learning. If you and a group of teachers can come up with a better plan for guaranteeing that all our students learn the basics, as well as go beyond them, then you've got my support. *[Turning toward Jed]* What do you think? Are you up to the challenge?

Jed   I'm like Tom, I guess. I'm not sure how to respond. Could we think about it for a day or two and then get back to you?

Dr. Ping   *[Standing up]* Sure. That's all right. Talk it over. Get back to me in a couple of days.

Dr. Ping smoothly and graciously escorts them to her doorway and, once again, shakes their hands. A few minutes later, Tom and Jed are climbing the stairs to their classrooms.

Jed   *[Excitedly]* Wow, was I surprised when she came up with the idea of us heading up a basic skills task force.

Tom   You're not the only one. *[Sighs, then continues slowly]* She's right. It's a real challenge, developing a basic skills program that won't end up weakening or watering down the rest of the curriculum.

JED   Tom, do you really think it's possible to develop a program like that? What do you think it would look like? Why do we let standardized tests get us into messes like this?

QUESTIONS

1. What indicators of school effectiveness can a school district use besides standardized achievement tests? What are the characteristics of effective schools?

2. Should every teacher become a teacher of the basic skills? What are the advantages and disadvantages of such an approach?

3. To what extent do standardized achievement tests represent the goals of education? Do they measure creativity and problem-solving? Do they measure affective goals such as those related to values, attitudes, and appreciations? Do they measure goals related to physical education, art, and music?

4. What is Bloom's Cognitive Taxonomy, and how does it relate to higher- and lower-order thinking skills? Which levels of the taxonomy do standardized achievement test items measure?

5. What does Ms. Neff mean when she talks about the danger of the minimum becoming the maximum? Why does this happen, and what can be done to prevent it? Can a program be developed that emphasizes both minimums and maximums?

6. Are most standardized achievement tests of the multiple-choice variety? If yes, why? What are the strengths and weaknesses of multiple-choice items? Could essay-type items be used in such tests? Would this help? What are the most valid and reliable standardized achievement tests in current use?

7. Does the standardized test used at T.H.S. involve norm-referenced or criterion-referenced evaluation? What are the advantages and disadvantages of each?

8. How can the school district take into consideration differences in socioeconomic status, racial and ethnic background, and academic ability of the students in its eleven high schools when it compares the standardized achievement test scores of its schools? Should such differences be taken into consideration?

9. What other approaches might Dr. Ping have tried to improve basic skills other than by emphasizing basic skills testing? Why is there such a strong emphasis in our society on the use of standardized tests, such as the SAT, for measuring school and teacher effectiveness?

10. Should teacher effectiveness be measured by pre-post (beginning of school year versus end of school year) standardized testing of student achievement gains? What are the pros and cons of using such a teacher evaluation program, for example, as a basis for merit pay?

11. How much influence can the home and parents have on student achievement in school? What kinds of parent involvement programs can be developed that might improve a school's standardized achievement test results?

12. Should Tom and Jed agree to head up a special task force? Is it possible to develop a program that goes beyond the basic skills?

IGNORING THE TEST

Key Content to Consider for Analyzing This Case:
(1) measurement and evaluation (standardized tests, objective vs. essay tests, norm- vs. criterion-referenced evaluation); (2) instructional objectives; (3) Bloom's Cognitive Taxonomy; (4) teacher effectiveness.

I t is the first day of classes at Tecumseh High School (described in the previous case) two years later. During the previous school year, T.H.S. fully implemented the schoolwide accountability program initiated by Dr. Lu Ping, the school principal. This program requires all teachers to teach all the basic skills included on the statewide standardized test of reading, writing, and mathematics and to administer monthly practice tests on these skills.

This is a critical year for Jed Cass, a social studies teacher beginning his third year of teaching at Tecumseh, since it is his "up or out" year. If, at the end of this year, Jed is rehired for the following year, he receives tenure. If the school administration decides that he should not be given a continuing contract, he will need to find another teaching position.

When Jed entered the building this morning, he went to the office to check his mailbox. There was a brief note from Dr. Ping asking him to stop by her office briefly after his last class. At the end of the school day, Jed entered the principal's outer office and was about to tell the secretary he had an appointment with the principal when Dr. Ping saw him, walked out of her office, and approached him.

DR. PING *[Extending her hand]* Jed, thank you for coming. *[Ushers Jed into her office]* I wanted to talk with you today to remind you that because this is the beginning of your third year of teaching at Tecumseh, you'll be coming up for tenure at the end of this school year. You're a fine teacher, Jed. Your students and their parents think very highly of you. In fact, I just received a call from Sarah Eoff's mother yesterday telling me how much she and Sarah appreciate you as a teacher. But, Jed, we have a problem that you must deal with this year.

JED What's that, Dr. Ping? *[Sits down in a chair. Dr. Ping sits behind her desk.]*

DR. PING The state's annual assessment test. As you know, Dr. Webb *[superintendent]* and the school board place great emphasis on increasing our students' scores on the test, especially the basic skills portion, and your students' performance has been below average.

JED   I thought my kids had done rather well on the test.

DR. PING   You mean on the social studies subtest. About average, as I recall, and that part
OK. It's the basic skills in reading, writing, and math that I'm concerned about.
Remember, Dr. Webb insists that all teachers—and that includes social studies
teachers, Jed—must teach the basic skills in their classes as well as their subject.
Frankly, Jed, if your students' basic skills scores aren't at least average when we test
the students at the end of the school year, Dr. Webb and the school board may not b
willing to grant you tenure, no matter how good of a teacher I tell them you are.

It is the third period of the first day of classes, and the thirty juniors in Jed's Ame
ican history class have just entered the room and taken their seats.

JED   Good morning, class. Welcome to American history. As you've probably guessed, I
majored in social studies in college. The reason I chose this major is that it can hel
us to learn how groups of humans have solved the problems that have confronted
them throughout history. And that's how I conduct my social studies classes.

I know that many teachers teach social studies by having students memorize
facts like names, dates, and places—you know, the better you memorize, the highe
the grade you receive—but I don't teach my classes that way. I try to teach you hov
to solve problems that face you in school, in the local community, and in the wider
community, just as the citizens we study in American history solved the problems
they faced in their own communities.

So in this class you'll be asked to identify current problems in our school or
community that you'd like to study. After studying the problems, you'll be expecte
to suggest several possible solutions for them. Of course, you'll need to learn the
history behind the problems to understand them fully. So, basically, this course wil
be a practice in problem-solving and you will choose your own problems. *[A
student raises his hand.]* Yes, tell me your name.

ROY   My name is Roy, Mr. Cass. Does this mean that we'll all be working on different
problems in this class?

JED   Yes, it does mean that. But some of you might choose to work in small groups if
you select a large problem to study.

ROY   Then that raises another question I have. How will we be graded?

JED   Well, as I said before, I don't test you on how many names, dates, and places you
can memorize. My grades are based upon the amount and quality of individual
work you do. In fact *[begins to distribute a handout]*, I was just about to explain my
grading plan. It's outlined on this sheet. *[Waits until the handouts are distributed]* OK
Do all of you have a copy? Good.

LOUISE   *[Speaking out]* Wow! Mr. Cass. This looks complicated!

JED   *[Smiling]* After I go over my contract grading plan, I think you'll like it better than
the grading plans you're used to. If you'll look over the plan, you'll see that you ca
decide what grade you want to contract for at the beginning of each of the six
grading periods of the school year. Obviously, there are not as many requirements
to earn a C as there are if you want to earn a B. And there aren't as many
requirements to earn a B as there are if you want to earn an A.

RANDY   *[Speaking out]* What if we contract for a B and make B's in some of our assignments and C's on the others?

JED   According to the notes at the end of the contract, you'll receive whatever grade your grades average.

RANDY   Oh, I see it now. Thanks. *[Pause]* The contract also mentions tests. How often will we have tests, and what kinds of tests will we have?

JED   Good questions. Sometimes I present information in class through lectures, films, guided discussions, and so forth. I sometimes check your knowledge of this information by giving a brief essay test. But I don't always give tests because I get so much feedback on the quality of your work through your reports, presentations, journals, and class discussions. *[Arlene raises her hand.]* Yes?

ARLENE   But how can you tell what our grades are when we don't have tests that have right and wrong answers? Like how do you grade a report or journal?

JED   It's quite easy for me to separate reports that are well organized, thorough, accurate, well thought out, and well written from poorly organized, sketchy, inaccurate, rambling ones. Let's face it, these factors tell me more about your knowledge and understanding of broad overall concepts than scores on multiple-choice or true-false test items. And it will also help you to be better educated because you'll learn to be thorough, accurate, and succinct in your thinking and writing, which isn't always the case. Many students graduate from high school without ever learning how to think well or to write well. *[Tanisha raises her hand.]* Yes?

TANISHA   I'm glad you're doing our class this way. I'm a junior in high school, and I've never had a class where the teacher did anything to help me learn to think or write well. If I could learn those things, this would be my best year in school.

JED   Thanks for telling us that. And I promise you that I'll work with you on your thinking and writing.

Several weeks later, two students from Jed's third-period American history class are sitting at a table in the school cafeteria with two students who are complaining bitterly about an eleventh-grade American history class taught by another teacher, Carl Shaefer, a friend of Jed's.

ANDREA   It's definitely the worst class I've ever had. Every morning I wake up dreading to go to school because I hate that class so much.

SHERRY   What's wrong with the class? Mr. Shaefer seems like a nice guy.

ANDREA   Oh, he is a nice guy. It's just that his class is so boring I can hardly stay awake!

MARK   What does he do that's so boring?

TIM   *[Speaking out]* I can tell you what he does! He spends every period reading a bunch of names, dates, and places to us out of his notes in a dull monotone voice. Then he gives us a multiple-choice, true-false test every Friday where you have to pick the right name, date, or place. I think the tests must be old, because sometimes the questions ask for stuff that he's never mentioned in class. It's boring and stresses me out!

MARK   That's definitely not cool. I'm in Mr. Cass' class, and I've learned more there than I've learned in any class in school.

Tim   [Smiling] Well, that wouldn't have to be very much, would it, Mark?

Mark   I know I'm not a great student, Tim, but I really do like Mr. Cass' class. And I really am learning a lot!

Andrea   [Looking at Mark] Mr. Cass must really be spectacular if you're learning a lot i his class! What in the world does he do that you like so much?

Sherry   [Jumping into the conversation] I can tell you one thing all of us in his class rea like. [Pauses] He uses a contract grading plan. That means we can choose whethe we want to work for an A, B, or C. Each grade has specific types of assignments y have to complete to earn it. The A has the most requirements and the C has the fewest. And we can pick our own assignments as long as they're the right type.

Tim   Like, what kinds of requirements do you have?

Mark   [Smirking] As you would probably guess, I contracted for a C. To earn a C, I'm writing a ten-page report on the historical significance of the Meriwether Lewis Building, and I'm making an oral report on it in class. I'm also writing a report o two books from the classroom library and giving an oral report on them in class. get credit for writing in a social studies journal every day and for participating in class every day. If I make a C in all these things, and on a test if we have one, I'll a C for the six weeks. Next six weeks I'll have to sign another contract. And I can sign up for an A, B, or C, just like this six weeks.

Tim   Do you mean you might not even have tests?

Mark   We might have tests, but if we do they'll be essay-type tests, not the multiple-choice, true-false type you guys take.

Andrea   Killer! What are your classes like? What do you do?

Sherry   They're fun. Each day's different, but Mr. Cass doesn't lecture much. Usually different students give book reviews or historical reports, or he leads a discussion on some important historical event. His reports are really interesting, but he also gets us to participate a lot in the discussion. I've learned more in his class than in any other class I've had in school, but it doesn't seem like a school class at all. He sort of treats us like adults, if you know what I mean.

Tim   Boy! You guys are lucky. That sounds like a really cool class! I wish I'd gotten int your history class instead of mine. I wonder if there's some way I could get move to that class. [Pause] But I guess it's too late. If the principal lets one of us move, then I suppose she'd have to let other students move too. So I don't suppose they let us.

Several days later, Jed is reading student book reports in his classroom after sch has dismissed for the day. Carl Shaefer walks past his classroom. He sees Jed and con back to his doorway.

Carl   Knock, knock.

Jed   [Looks up and sees Carl] Carl, come in and visit for a while. [Carl walks into the roo and takes a seat in front of Jed's desk.] I haven't seen you for a while. How are your classes going?

Carl   [Smiling] Well, according to some of my students, they're not as much fun as yo classes.

JED   You're kidding, aren't you? I make my students sign contracts that involve more work than a lot of them want to do.

CARL   That's interesting. My students tell me I should teach American history the way you do. But there's no way I'm going to do that.

JED   *[Curious]* Why's that?

CARL   Because I want to survive in this system.

JED   Meaning what?

CARL   Well, think about it for a minute. Dr. Webb has issued an edict that our school will give monthly practice tests on the basic skills. Dr. Ping is making sure that every teacher does just that. Our students are at the bottom of the barrel on the state tests, and there'll be hell to pay if they're in the same position next spring. Therefore, the name of the game is teach to the test.

JED   But we both know that pupils don't really improve their knowledge of basic skills through practicing for the kinds of items that are on the state test.

CARL   Sure, I know that. But I also know what's important for survival in this school system, and that, my friend, is to get your kids ready to take the state test. And, Jed, I recommend that you take the game seriously also. Because, for you, winning the game means tenure. You're coming up for tenure at the end of the year, aren't you?

JED   Yes, I am. But you and I both know that the kinds of things that the state tests measure don't constitute real learning.

CARL   There you go again. *[Emphatically]* You still don't get it. The issue isn't what you think is real learning. The name of the game is having our students score high on the test, especially the basic skills part. Don't you see all the signs around you? All teachers—even those like us who don't teach reading, writing, and math—are required to have weekly drill on those subjects!

 I know my students don't like my drilling them on names, dates, and places, but those are the kinds of items that appear on both the social studies and the basic skills portions of the state test. So I drill them every day on American history names, dates, and places, and every Friday on the three R's. If I were in your position, I'd be drilling my students every day, too. Otherwise you'll end up on the wrong side of the school administration.

JED   I know you're looking out for my best interests, Carl, and I really do appreciate it. You're a good friend! But I just can't prostitute myself by teaching history that way! The reason I'm a history teacher now is that I had several teachers who made history come alive for me when I was in school. And I think I'm making history come alive for several of the students in my classes. I just can't risk destroying my pupils' interest in history so that I can get tenure.

CARL   I know you're making history come alive for many of your students, Jed, because I hear them talking about your classes in glowing terms. But the reason I'm here is that I want you to continue being a member of our faculty. Just think, once you get tenure, you can continue on here as long as you choose, and you'll be able to teach history any way you want to. *[Stands up and prepares to leave the room]*

JED   *[Sincerely]* Thanks Carl. I know you mean well, and I really appreciate your trying to give me your best advice.

FIGURE 28 Contract Grading Plan for Mr. Cass' Eleventh-Grade American History Class

---

C GRADE

1. Select a historical site in town (monument, dedication plaque, building). Write a ten-page report describing the historical significance of the site. Make an oral presentation of your findings to the class.
2. Read and write a report on two books from the classroom social studies library. Present a fifteen-minute report on these books to the class.
3. Keep a social studies journal in which you write out your class assignments and reports.
4. Attend class every day and participate actively in class discussions.
5. Average a C grade on all assignments and tests.

B GRADE

1. Select a significant event in American history. Write a scholarly paper on this event in which you describe the factors, such as occurrences in other countries, desires of political leaders, and natural phenomena leading up to this event. Describe effects caused by the event.
2. Read and write a report on four books from the classroom social studies library. Present a fifteen-minute report on these books to the class.
3. Keep a social studies journal in which you write out all your class assignments and reports.
4. Average a B grade on all assignments and tests.
5. Attend class every day and participate actively in class discussion.

A GRADE

1. Select a significant event in American history. Write a scholarly paper on this event in which you describe the factors, such as occurrences in other countries, desires of political leaders, and natural phenomena leading up to this event. Describe effects caused by the event.
2. Either compare and contrast the effects caused by this event described in assignment 1 to those caused by a different significant event in American history, or read and write a report on six books from the classroom social studies library. Present a fifteen-minute report on each of these books to the class.
3. Keep a social studies journal in which you write out all your class assignments and reports.
4. Average an A grade on all assignments and tests.
5. Attend class every day and participate actively in class discussions.

NOTES:

1. Exams and quizzes will be essay in format.
2. Partial completion of a contract may result in a plus (+) being added to the next lower grade (teacher's choice).
3. Failure to complete the C contract will result in a D or F at the teacher's discretion. Exam and test scores will be the primary consideration in this situation.

It's the beginning of the last month of the school year, and Jed is seated in the principal's office having a conference with Dr. Ping at her request.

DR. PING   Thanks for meeting with me on such short notice, Jed. The reason I wanted to meet with you as soon as possible is that I've just received the results of Tecumseh's scores on the state's standardized test. *[Pauses]*

JED   And?

DR. PING   Well, I'm afraid I have bad news. Your students' basic skills scores were below average again. I'm both disappointed and concerned. I know you could have worked with them on the basic skills, and I asked you to do that. But I also know that you're truly a good teacher and a conscientious teacher and are philosophically opposed to teaching to the test.

JED   That's true. In fact, I'm convinced that it demeans our entire school system to participate in a practice that's counterproductive to real student learning. The memorization of isolated facts cannot in any way be considered learning, and is, in fact, replacing practices that generate real learning.

DR. PING   You've made your position on teaching to the test clear to me, Jed. And I've tried to make clear to you the fact that Dr. Webb is determined that our students will not continue to be the lowest in the city on the state test of basic skills. The bottom line is that your students are below average! What arguments can I use to convince Dr. Webb and the school board that you should be given tenure?

QUESTIONS

1. Should every teacher become a teacher of the basic skills? What are the advantages and disadvantages of such an approach?

2. To what extent do standardized achievement tests represent the goals of education? Do they measure creativity and problem-solving? Do they measure affective goals, such as those related to values, attitudes, and appreciations? Do they measure goals related to physical education, art, and music?

3. What levels of Blooms' Cognitive Taxonomy do standardized achievement tests typically measure? At what levels of Bloom's taxonomy is Jed aiming his teaching? What about Carl?

4. Should students' performance on standardized achievement tests be a consideration in evaluating teacher effectiveness (e.g., as data for making tenure decisions)? What evidence should be used for such decisions?

5. Are most standardized achievement test items of the multiple-choice type? What are the strengths and weaknesses of such items compared to essay-type items? Do some standardized achievement tests use essay items?

6. What are the differences between norm-referenced and criterion-referenced evaluation systems? Which would work best in the school system described in this case?

7. How might Jed have involved the parents of his American history students? For example, could parents have been involved as classroom volunteers, as tutors of their

own children at home, or as participants in a parent advisory groups such as PTA? Wh
effect might such parent involvement have had on Jed's being granted tenure?

8. What are the strengths and weaknesses of contract grading plans like Jed's? Ho
could Jed's evaluation procedures be improved?

9. What are Jed's instructional objectives in his American history class? How do th
differ from those of the school system? Should the school system or the classroom teach
set the instructional objectives for a particular course like Jed's?

10. Jed tells his students that the focus of his class is on problem-solving and the rel
ing of historical material to current issues. How appropriate a goal is this for an Ame
can history class? How well has Jed designed his class to accomplish his problem-solvi
goals?

11. At what level of Maslow's motivational need hierarchy are Jed, Carl, and Dr. Pi
primarily operating? How can Jed use this information to deal with this situation?

12. What are the differences between mastery and performance goal orientations
described by Ames and others? Which goal orientation does the school system's testi
program promote?

13. Jed criticizes Carl for focusing on the memorization of facts in his class. Does t
research on the retention of facts versus principles support Jed's position? What cogniti
processing techniques can students use to increase their long-term retention of inforn
tion? What kinds of information are remembered longest?

14. Analyze the standardized achievement testing system that the school district h
set up in terms of contingency management theory (operant conditioning). What cont
gencies have been established with the teachers? How does this explain Carl's behavi
Does Carl's "I know how to play the game" attitude precede or follow his behav
changes?

15. Bronfenbrenner analyzes human interactions in terms of the dimensions of cc
text. Analyze this case in terms of his microsystem, mesosystem, exosystem, macrosyst
model. How are all the external environmental forces impinging on Jed's classroom a
career?

16. What should Jed do next? What should he say to Dr. Ping? Should he meet w
the superintendent and school board? Should he get a job in another school system? Ev
if he is granted tenure, should he stay?

GRADING THE TEACHER

Key Content to Consider for Analyzing This Case:
(1) measurement and evaluation (grading policies and procedures, norm- vs. criterion-referenced evaluation, objective vs. essay tests, standardized tests);
(2) instructional objectives; (3) teacher stress;
(4) teacher effectiveness; (5) motivation (intrinsic vs. extrinsic); (6) Bloom's Cognitive Taxonomy.

Montcalm is a city of approximately 75,000 located in the Midwest. Its leading industries are steel, coal mining, and agriculture. Its school district is approximately 79% non-Hispanic white, 20% African-American, and 1% other. Montcalm's secondary school program is comprised of three high schools: North, Central, and South. Its school board is 100% white and may be described as very conservative in its orientation toward most educational issues.

Tanya Hardy graduated last spring at a nearby teachers college and is beginning her first year as a social studies teacher at South High School. She is at the high school for an appointment with the principal, Christine Brinkman, and on her way to the office she passes a large trophy case full of a variety of trophies ranging from football to basketball. She stops for a second to admire a long sign over the top of the case which reads: "Mighty Spartans Go for a Three-Peat in Football." When Tanya reaches the principal's office, Christine walks out of her office past the secretaries' desks, greets Tanya, and invites her into her office. Tanya sits down in a comfortable chair in front of Christine's desk.

TANYA I'm really excited to be here, Ms. Brinkman. I noticed that they're expecting another good football season this year.

CHRISTINE *[Smiles]* Please call me Christine, Tanya. We don't stand on ceremony around here. Yes, Coach Jenkins has done quite a job the last two seasons, and, as I understand it, has most of his players back who won the Division 4A state championship last year. So that makes everyone happy, including the school board. *[Pause]* So, Tanya, are you all finished with the personnel office? Since teacher preservice begins Monday, I thought it might help for us to talk today. *[Hands Tanya a sheet of paper]* You'll notice that you'll be in Room 311 upstairs. As you can see, you'll be teaching three sections of world history and two of U.S. history. I've been told by Chayne Sanders, the social studies department chair, that all the textbooks you'll need are in the closet in the back of your classroom.

TANYA   *[With surprise]* Oh, the school district furnishes the textbooks? The students don't buy their own?

CHRISTINE   That's right, although some parents do buy their children their own copies. Talk to Chayne about the procedures for checking out the books to your students *[Pause]* Now, do you have any questions I can help you with?

TANYA   I really love history and I can't wait to start teaching, but I was wondering abou grading. Does the school district have any policies for teachers and grading?

CHRISTINE   You really need to talk to Chayne about the social studies area, but when y see our report cards you'll notice that we use a common set of grading standards f the school district. It's the usual one that you'll find in most school districts in this state, where 95 to 100 is an A, 88 to 94 is a B, 77 to 87 is a C, and 70 to 76 is a D However, our English department has decided to be a bit more liberal. They use 9 to 100 as an A, 80 to 89 as a B, and so forth. They make 60 a passing score instea of 70. I forget exactly why they made the change, but as I recall it had to do with the fact that they do more subjective grading, like scoring compositions, than you folks in social studies and other areas do. So they wanted a little more flexibility i grading to allow for scoring errors.

TANYA   Then social studies teachers generally give objective tests?

CHRISTINE   Well—again now, I know I'm beginning to sound like a broken record—yc need to ask Chayne, but as I recall from talking with him and other social studies teachers, they almost all use objective tests. You know, multiple choice, matching fill-in-the-blank, and so forth. I don't think they do much essay-type testing.

TANYA   Why is that?

CHRISTINE   Well, we're very proud of the high percentage of our student body that graduate and go to college, more than either Central or North. We also have more National Merit Finalists than the other two schools. *[Laughing]* We're good at academics as well as sports, I guess I'm trying to say!

TANYA   But why do they use objective tests instead of essay?

CHRISTINE   Because those are the kinds of items on the standardized tests that our kid take, and because those are the kinds of tests the kids will have to take when they enter college. Why, Tanya? Do you have some concerns about objective tests?

TANYA   I think some objective tests are fine, but I think essay tests are equally importa I'd like to give both kinds. Essay items challenge the kids to think, analyze, organize, create, evaluate, and write in ways that objective test items never can. T me there's a big difference between asking a student to learn *who* discovered America and asking him to explain *why* the discovery of America took place.

CHRISTINE   I think a combination of objective and essay will be all right. Ask Chayne.

TANYA   Well, let me ask this. Suppose I give a test and it turns out to be a hard test an the top grade is say 85?

CHRISTINE   Well, I think what most of our teachers do is add points onto every studer score until the scores conform to the 95 to 100 is an A scoring scheme.

TANYA   I see. Well, let me ask this. What teaching methods do most of the social studi teachers use?

CHRISTINE   *[Smiling]* You've really got to ask Chayne about this one. But I'd say that most of them use a combination of lecture and discussion.

TANYA   Do any of them do much with small-group work, especially small-group problem-solving projects?

CHRISTINE   [Smiling] Not that I know of. Sounds to me like you want to try some things out in your classes, Tanya. Perhaps you'd better tell me what you have in mind.

TANYA   Well, mainly I want my students to be able to do more than just memorize facts. I want them to be able to really understand what went on in the past and to see how it relates to today's and tomorrow's events. The way I'd like for them to learn to do that is by doing individual and small-group problem-solving and current events projects in which they try to solve different problems of interest and compare past events with current ones. For example, boys might be interested in warfare and how it is conducted or in how police matters were handled. Girls might be interested in such things as fashions or in women's rights. Of course, I think that both objective and essay tests should be given over the material in the text as well.

CHRISTINE   That sounds just fine to me, Tanya. You'd be giving objective tests over the regular material, and you'd be using teaching methods that sound like they'd be motivating to the students in that they'd be learning problem-solving skills and making tie-ins with current events. How would you grade the students?

TANYA   I'd like to use a point system that I learned about in one of my college courses.

CHRISTINE   Will your point system conform to the 95 to 100 is an A grading system that the other social studies teachers use?

TANYA   I don't see why not.

CHRISTINE   Well, Tanya, it sounds to me like you're going to be a breath of fresh air around here! Please keep me informed as to how things are going. Don't hesitate to call me if I can help in any way.

It is the first day of classes, and Tanya meets with thirty-four sophomores in her fifth-period world history class as the bell rings.

TANYA   OK, people, settle down. Please raise your hand as I call the roll. [Tanya calls the roll and marks two students absent. Then she has two students help her distribute textbooks to all students present.] Now, people, let's talk about what we're going to be doing in this class this year. Your assignment for tomorrow is to read the introductory material entitled "You and World History." We'll begin a discussion tomorrow about the reasons why we study history. [Pause] However, right now let's get down to the business of talking about what you really want to know: what do you have to do in this class to make a good grade. [Several students laugh, and Tanya passes out a copy of her grading plan to all students.]

Do you all have a copy of this? [Holds up a copy of the grading plan. No one raises his hand.] OK. First you'll notice that each grading period I plan to have two exams. They will have both objective and essay items on them and will be worth 100 points each. We'll also have five quizzes worth 10 points each. They'll be multiple choice. Yes, Jennifer?

JENNIFER   Will they be surprise quizzes?

TANYA   No, they'll be announced at least a day in advance and will most likely be on Fridays. If you're absent, however, you might not know that one is coming up unless you check. You'll notice that participation is worth 50 points. That involves not only being here but participating in what we do, especially class discussion. *[Pause]* You'll notice that each grading period I expect you to participate in a problem-solving activity and a current events report. You can do this individually or in small groups of four or less. Yes, John?

JOHN   What do you mean problem-solving? How can you solve problems that are already over?

TANYA   What I'm trying to do with both the problem-solving and current events activities is get you to do more than just memorize facts about people, dates, battles, and places. I want you to think about why events happened and how they relate to events happening today. We can learn a lot from the lessons of the past an apply what we learn to the problems of today. That's what I want you to learn to d in these activities. Yes, John?

JOHN   Well what kind of problems?

TANYA   I'm glad you asked that, John. Let's all turn to page 24 in the text. You'll need t read this material for tomorrow anyhow. Now look at the section entitled "The Basic Human Activities." What that section is saying is that we can take the basic human activities and see them as falling into ten areas. First is protecting and conserving life, clearly the work of our police, fire departments, hospitals, and military. Second is producing and distributing goods, the work of the world of business, commerce, and agriculture. Then we have transportation, communicatio government, religion, the arts, the home and family, education, and recreation an sports. Now, I'll bet that you can give me examples of problems that fit under ever one of these. Yes, Jennifer?

JENNIFER   Do you mean problems like why does a woman have to work on the job an at home too, while a man only has to work at a job?

TANYA   Right. That problem would fit under both the home and family and the world business. But let me ask you, Jennifer, while that's a problem in America today, ha it always been a problem? What was life like for the prehistoric woman, the Egyptian woman, the Greek woman, and so forth? How did things get to be the way they are today? Do you see what I mean?

JENNIFER   Yes.

TANYA   Yes, Barry?

BARRY   If Jennifer did one on women like that, would she be doing a current events report or a problem-solving activity?

TANYA   In the example she would be using history to explain how things became the way they are today. That's a current events report. If, however, she studies, say, ho life was for Egyptian women and tried to figure out ways that Egyptian women could have changed their situation, that would be a problem-solving paper. The key is whether you're trying to solve a problem that existed in the past or explain how a current problem came to be. Yes, John?

JOHN   How long do these have to be, and do they have to be written?

TANYA   We'll go into all that step by step as we go along. There won't be any doubt in your mind about what you're supposed to do. *[Class laughs.]* Yes, Jennifer?

JENNIFER   I don't understand. Are you going to grade us on a curve?

TANYA   No, if what you mean is am I going to arrange your scores from highest to
lowest, figure out the average score, and then draw lines separating the A's from the
B's and so forth. Instead we're going to use this point system.

JOHN   How is that any different?

TANYA   The difference is that if everyone in this class made 475 points or more,
everyone would get an A. That can't happen if you grade on a curve. Now you'll
notice that the point system conforms to the grading standards on your report
cards. On your report card it says that 95 to 100 is an A. So 475 points are 95% of
the maximum number of points you can earn, which is 500. This approach may be
a little different from the way you're graded in your other classes, but I think you'll
like it because you always know how many points you need to earn a certain grade.
Plus, if you fall down on one test you can bring it up on another.

JOHN   [Frowning] Can't you do that anyway?

TANYA   If you grade on a curve and convert scores to letter grades, you end up averaging
letter grades together to figure up an average letter grade. Each letter grade represents
a range of points, so it's like compressing all the numbers down to four or five and
adding those together. With this point system you have the full range of points to
add together before deciding on a letter grade. For example, a B on a 100-point test
represents points from 88 to 94. However, I think you'd agree that getting the 94 is
better than getting the 88, since it's only one point from an A. If you get a 94 and
then get a 96 on the next test, you made a 95 average and end up getting an A. Do
you see what I mean?

JOHN   Yeah, I think so.

TANYA   Yes, Akia?

AKIA   Then you're not going to give so many A's, and so many B's, and so forth?

TANYA   I know there are teachers who grade that way. For example, 7% get A's, 24% get
B's, 38% C's, 24% D's, and the rest F's. Well, let me ask you, how are you being
graded in your other classes? Please don't name the teachers or classes. Jennifer?

JENNIFER   On projects, most of them just give so many A's and so many B's, like you said.
On tests they just move the highest score up to 95 and then add that many points
onto everybody's score.

TANYA   That's what I thought. John?

JOHN   I think the way you're going to grade us is a lot better. [Most of the students in the
class smile and nod their heads in agreement.]

It is Friday at the end of the third grading period approximately four and a half
months later. Jennifer and Akia, students from Tanya's fifth-period class, sit together eating lunch in the school cafeteria. John, Barry, and Ramos sit on the opposite side of the
table talking to the two girls while three chairs next to the two girls are empty. Two other
girls—Shanna and Tricia—carry their trays over and sit next to Jennifer and Akia.

SHANNA   Hi, Jen. Hi, Kia.

JENNIFER   Oh, hi Shanna and Tricia. [With a mischievous grin] I haven't seen you since
Saturday night.

SHANNA   [As she and Tricia sit down next to Jennifer and Akia] Oh, God! Don't even start. I've got enough trouble today.

JENNIFER   [Frowning] What's the matter?

SHANNA   Oh, it's Kelly—you know, Kelly's world history class. We got our big tests back today and I did terrible! How does he come up with those nitpicky questions? God, his test was terrible! I think I'll die! My parents will kill me! I'll never get to go out on a date again!

AKIA   It can't be that bad! What did you get?

SHANNA   I can't talk about it! But I'll tell you one thing! I've knocked myself out studying, and there's no way I'm going to get an A. I don't have a clue what he's going to ask on a test. It's all a big surprise. There was only one A in the class. The highest score was 82 out of 100! So he added 13 points on everyone's score and I still barely broke the C level! God, I'm going to die!

JENNIFER   I'm really sorry, Shanna. I know you studied hard—your mom wouldn't let me talk to you on the phone unless it was an emergency because she said you were studying for a big test.

SHANNA   He's killed me! How am I going to get admitted to any college if I make C's?

JENNIFER   I told you to have your parents get you out of Kelly's class. Everyone knows he's hard.

SHANNA   They tried. They went to see Ms. Brinkman and she wouldn't budge. She said that if she made an exception in my case that she'd have to make an exception for everyone else. [Pause] I suppose you two got A's on your tests as usual!

JENNIFER   Well, we sure didn't have any trouble in world history.

SHANNA   Oh? Why not?

JENNIFER   Ms. Hardy is a great teacher! She grades on a point system, so you always know where you stand. Her tests aren't all nitpicky like Kelly's. She asks essay questions that count as much as multiple choice. But the stuff we do is really interesting. Like Akia's group's report on the role of women in the Catholic Church today.

SHANNA   [Frowning] What's that got to do with history? I saw something about that on TV the other day. They said that those creepy old priests actually let women give communion now.

JENNIFER   Yeah, well, we do what Hardy calls current events reports, and we go back and look into the history of things like that.

SHANNA   God, that sounds cool! All old Kelly does is lecture and make us take notes. Every now and then he grills us with questions for variety. [Everyone laughs.] Gosh, Jen, you always luck out! Why did I have to get Kelly?!

It is Friday after school is out approximately one month later. Tanya catches Christine Brinkman's eye through the open door of her office. Christine smiles and motions for Tanya to have a seat in front of her desk. When Tanya is seated, Christine gets up, closes her office door, and then returns to her seat behind her desk.

CHRISTINE   I assume that you got my note to come in and see me after your last class.

TANYA   Yes, I did.

CHRISTINE   Well, Tanya, a matter has come up that I need to talk to you about.

TANYA   *[Frowning]* Yes? What is it?

CHRISTINE   Tanya, do you remember our first meeting back before school started? You told me you wanted to try out some new teaching methods and grading procedures, and I said OK as long as they stay within school district policies?

TANYA   Yes. Have I done something wrong?

CHRISTINE   Well, Chayne Sanders came to see me Wednesday after school and we had a long talk. It seems that several teachers in your department have come to him to complain about your teaching.

TANYA   I can't believe it! Chayne never said anything about that to me!

CHRISTINE   Hasn't he been around to see you several times asking about how you teach and grade in your classes? Hasn't he made suggestions to you each time?

TANYA   Well, yes. But he never said that he or anyone else had any complaints. I just took it as friendly advice.

CHRISTINE   That's Chayne's way. He tries to be positive, non-interfering, and helpful. He doesn't see his role as a heavy-handed administrator who does what I'm doing now.

TANYA   Well, what are these teachers complaining about?

CHRISTINE   Mostly that you are an easy grader and try to entertain your students instead of teaching them something of substance that will prepare them for the SAT and college.

TANYA   I don't suppose you're going to tell me who they are? I don't think anyone but Chayne really knows what I do in my classes.

CHRISTINE   Tanya, believe it or not, I didn't tell you this to upset you or to make you think that I think you're doing a poor job of teaching. Chayne's observational ratings of your teaching this year have been quite high. I don't really know what's behind their complaints. Maybe jealousy, I don't know. Several students and parents of yours have told me what a good teacher they think you are. However, I thought you needed to know what's going on.

TANYA   Well, what do you want me to do?

CHRISTINE   That's a hard one. I don't think you should make any radical changes in the way you teach and grade. That would be upsetting to your students and parents. At least I wouldn't make any changes for the rest of this school year. Perhaps you can think things over this summer and decide whether or not you want to change anything. However, there is one problem you need to think about.

TANYA   What's that?

CHRISTINE   One of the teachers complaining is Nina Neal, the superintendent's niece. You won't have tenure for two more years. He can let you go without giving you a reason or a positive recommendation no matter what I say in your behalf. I'm not trying to scare you, Tanya, or get you to change the way you teach, but you do have to think about these things for your own sake. OK? *[Pause]* Let me ask you one thing.

TANYA   What's that?

CHRISTINE   How important is the way that you teach and grade your world history classes to you? Are you convinced that the way you do it is that much better than what the other teachers do?

FIGURE 29 Grading Plan for Tanya Hardy's World History Classes

Grading Plan:

	Max	A (95%)	B (88%)	C (77%)	D (70%)	F
Exams (2)	200	190	176	154	140	less
Quizzes (5)	50	47	44	38	35	less
Problem-Solving	100	95	88	77	70	less
Current Events	100	95	88	77	70	less
Participation	50	47	44	38	35	less
Totals	500	475	440	385	350	less

NOTES:

1. Exams will be a combination of essay and objective items. Quizzes will be objective.
2. Participation includes both class attendance and active participation in class discussion. Tardiness to class will also be included.
3. The final letter grade for each grading period will be based on the total number of points accumulated. It is possible to "fall down" in one area and compensate by picking up points in another area before the final letter grade is determined.
4. Problem-solving activities can be individual or small groups (not more than four students). For example, explaining why the Roman Empire declined and fell and offering solutions that could have prevented it from happening.
5. Current events reports should make comparisons and contrasts between current events and those being studied. For example, comparing the role of women in the American workforce with those of women in ancient Greece, particularly Athens.

QUESTIONS

1. How desirable is it to have school-system-wide grading policies? How much la▮ tude should teachers be given as professionals to develop their own grading procedure How much commonality in grading procedures should exist among teachers in the sar school? Should school grading standards like those at Montcalm South be applied to subject areas and with all types of students?

2. What is the purpose of grading? How does it relate to teacher objectives? Wl instructional objectives does Tanya seem to be pursuing? The other social studies teache▮

3. What are norm-referenced and criterion-referenced evaluation? What are the strengths and weaknesses of each? Which type of evaluation is Tanya using? Which are the other social studies teachers using?

4. What does it mean to grade a test on a curve? What kind of grading standards is Tanya's point system of grading related to? How else could Tanya have graded the class?

5. What are the strengths and weaknesses of objective and essay tests? What is the best way to grade essay tests? What is test objectivity, and what are the best kinds of objective test items?

6. How important is the SAT as a measure of performance in American education? Given the importance of SAT scores, should teachers be encouraged to "teach to the test"? What educational objectives does the SAT measure? What is the danger of "minimums becoming maximums" when such standardized tests are emphasized?

7. Montcalm South's faculty take great pride in the number of graduates who enter college. How important is this as an educational objective? What can be done for the non-college-bound and at-risk students at such a high school?

8. What is item analysis, especially item difficulty and item discrimination? What is a table of specifications? How can these be used to improve teacher-made tests?

9. At what levels of Bloom's Cognitive Taxonomy is Tanya interested in testing? What about the other social studies teachers?

10. Tanya emphasizes group problem-solving in her class. What is problem-solving, and how does it differ from the "memorization of facts" approach used by the other teachers? How do such problem-solving teaching methods relate to Bloom's Cognitive Taxonomy?

11. Does Tanya's approach to teaching emphasize an intrinsic or extrinsic motivation model? What are the strengths and weaknesses of each? Would Mr. Kelly's lecture and Tanya's current events projects best exemplify intrinsic or extrinsic approaches? Why is Tanya's class so much more popular than those of the other social studies teachers?

12. Teacher stress and burnout is a serious problem in American education. What are the most serious stressors in this case? What can be done to help teachers who work in a stressful school environment?

13. What is tenure in teaching? Does Tanya's lack of tenure affect her options in this situations? How would having tenure help Tanya? What, if anything, should she do next?

CASE **29**

THE CHANGE AGENT

Key Content to Consider for Analyzing This Case:
(1) measurement and evaluation (standardized tests, essay vs. objective tests, norm vs. criterion-referenced evaluation); (2) instructional objectives; (3) teacher effectiveness; (4) Bloom's Cognitive Taxonomy.

Montcalm is a city of approximately 75,000 located in the Midwest. Its leading industries are steel, coal mining, and agriculture. Its school district is approx- mately 79% non-Hispanic white, 20% African-American, and 1% other. Mon calm's secondary school program is comprised of three high schools: North, Central, an South. Its school board is 100% white and may be described as very conservative in i orientation toward most educational issues.

Tanya Hardy is now a social studies teacher with seven years of teaching experienc at South High School. Not only was she granted tenure, but she completed her master degree in social studies education at a nearby state university and is currently working o a specialist in education degree at night and during summers. Her favorite course that sh has recently taken is one on measurement and evaluation in education.

Tanya's first year of teaching was a difficult one (see the previous case), since he teaching methods and evaluation procedures made her popular with her students an their parents but earned her considerable criticism from other teachers—one of who was the superintendent's niece—that she was not rigorous in her teaching methods an used evaluation procedures that would not help her students to pass the SAT or to ent college.

With the support of her principal, Christine Brinkman, Tanya revised her teachin methods toward more lecture-discussion and her evaluation procedures toward mo objective testing. She continued to motivate her students to learn and also, according data collected by Christine, achieved excellent results in terms of her students' SAT scor and college admissions. Armed with this data, Christine saw to it that Tanya was grante tenure at the end of her third year of teaching.

During her years at South, Tanya began to gradually get to know and win over t other social studies teachers in the school district, including Nina Neal, the superinte dent's niece. It came as no surprise to anyone that when Chester Neal, the superintende of schools, decided to form a school district-wide committee (chaired by Evan Dye, t director of evaluation and research) to make recommendations regarding grading and report card procedures, Christine chose Tanya as the teacher representative from South High. Tanya and Christine sit in Christine's office during Tanya's planning period to discuss Tanya's participation on the committee.

TANYA   How many will be on the committee, Christine?

CHRISTINE   Let's see. Evan Dye, of course, the three high school principals, three teacher representatives, and a professor from State who is acting as consultant to the committee. So that's eight regular members, although we can call in whomever we need at any time. I recommended to Chet [Dr. Neal] that he have some parent representatives on the committee, but he decided against it.

TANYA   Oh, really? I wonder why.

CHRISTINE   I think that down deep Chet really sees parent participation as a threat to the administration. He pays lip service to parent participation in the school system, but then I notice that he does this kind of thing. Also, you'll notice that none of our PTAs or SACs [school advisory committees] are really very strong. They'd have to get strong on their own, because Chet would never do anything to encourage them.

TANYA   [With a twinkle in her eye] Well, it seems to me that South has a rather active SAC!

CHRISTINE   [Smiling] Yes, you're right, of course. But you haven't been here when Chet calls me on the phone and points out the dangers of involving parents who have no college work in education—in fact, some of them don't even have high school diplomas—in the decision-making of this school. So his not appointing any parents to this committee comes as no surprise to me.

TANYA   [In resignation] OK. I get it. Christine, I want your permission to send a questionnaire to all the social studies teachers in the school district to ask them how they grade and teach history. I also want to ask them how they feel about our school district's grading policy. I'd like to present the results to the committee when we meet. [Hands Christine a copy of the questionnaire]

CHRISTINE   [Reading the questionnaire] This looks OK to me, but I'll have to run this by Chet. I'll put a note in your box after I talk to him.

Christine read Tanya's questionnaire to Chester Neal over the phone, and he approved sending it out to all social studies teachers provided Evan Dye, the director of evaluation and research, approves. Evan looked the questionnaire over in written form and one week later approved with a few changes that Tanya felt were good ones. The questionnaire was distributed to twenty-seven teachers along with a letter from Tanya which explained that Superintendent Neal had approved the project but that participation was voluntary. Twenty-one teachers completed and returned the questionnaire, a 77% return rate.

One month after the conference between Christine and Tanya, the grading and report card committee holds its first meeting downtown in a large conference room in the administration building. Nine people sit around a large oval table in comfortable leather chairs. The superintendent of schools, Chester Neal, sits at the head of the table to make his opening remarks to the committee. The seven school system people already know one another: Dr. Dye and three high school building principals (Christine Brinkman, South H.S.; Roy Moore, Central H.S.; Pritchett "Red" Monyer, North H.S.), plus three teacher representatives, including Tanya and Sharon Pohlman. Therefore, Chester only really had to introduce Dr. Ann Wiggams, professor of measurement and evaluation from State University, who has been employed as a consultant to the committee. With the introduction and pleasantries completed, Chester begins his task of giving the committee its charge.

Chester   Ladies and gentlemen, I can't emphasize enough the importance of your job. How we evaluate, grade, and report the progress of our students' learning is critical to our work in this school system. As I'm sure Dr. Wiggams would point out to you, how we evaluate and, indeed, the teaching methods we use are clearly related to our instructional goals. It's no secret what the teachers, parents, and administration of this school district value. We want all our students who are capable of doing so to go to college. Related to that is our students' performance on standardized tests that lead to college scholarships and college admission. In saying these things I just state the obvious. *[Pause]* However, let me say that we do care about our non-college-bound students also, and I think we do a good job with them and at-risk students as well. As important as those students are, however, I think that we would all agree that we don't want to let the time, resources, and personnel that we use to help them cause us to fail in our mission to help the cream of our society's future, the college-bound student. *[Pause]* As an aside, let me add that I have even considered proposing a merit pay for teachers program to the school board based on a pretest-posttest standardized testing program. My purpose would be to reward those teachers who produce the greatest amount of student achievement test gains during the school year. However, considering that proposal isn't the job of this committee, so I just mention it in passing. *[Pause]* So, what is your job? Your job is to answer these questions. First, shall we keep the school district's grading procedures, which have been in place since 1964, or shall we consider changing them? And second, shall we keep the way we report grades to our parents the same, or should we make changes there, too? Unless someone has questions of me, I'll turn the work of this committee over to Evan *[who sits at the other end of the oval table]* and let you begin your important work. Don't hesitate to call on me if you have problems. Yes, Tanya?

Tanya   Dr. Neal, do you personally feel that any changes should be made in the way that we evaluate and report grades? That is, do you know of any problems?

Chester   No, I don't, Tanya. My only motive here is for us to reexamine these important issues from time to time to be sure that we're doing the right thing. It's been ten years since we've looked at grading, so I decided it's time. In other words, there is absolutely no pressure on this committee to make any changes if you examine the situation and decide to make that recommendation. OK?

Tanya   Yes, thank you. *[At this point Chester gets up, smiles broadly, and leaves the room.]*

Evan   *[Passes out written materials]* I'm not going to keep you today. These are all the materials, historical or current, that we could gather on grading standards, reporting procedures, and the reports of previous committees, as well as school board policies. Please study them before our next meeting. Now, shall we all go have refreshments that Dr. Neal's secretary, Martha, has thoughtfully provided for us?

It is later that same evening, and Tanya calls Sharon Pohlman at her home. Tanya and Sharon have become friends over the years, and both are teacher representatives on the grading committee.

SHARON   Hello?

TANYA   Hi, Sharon. This is Tanya. Are you busy? Can you talk?

SHARON   Sure. Frank won't be home for a couple of hours yet. I'm just sitting here grading papers. You were upset at the committee meeting today, weren't you? Your face is so easy to read.

TANYA   That obvious, huh? Yes, it really upset me when Chester basically said that kids who aren't college-bound don't count! Where are these programs that we have for them that he's referring to? He's an elitist, Sharon.

SHARON   Yes, that's obvious. When he answered your questions, he also sounded like he wants to keep the status quo in grading procedures.

TANYA   That's true, and the trouble is I suspect that most of the social studies teachers in this county would go along with everything he said.

SHARON   Why do you say that, Tanya?

TANYA   Do you remember that questionnaire on grading procedures I sent out to the social studies teachers?

SHARON   Oh, yes. I remember filling that out. But you've never said what you found out.

TANYA   That's because the results upset me so badly I'm not sure if I want to make them public!

SHARON   Why? What were the results? I'll keep them confidential if you want.

TANYA   [Looking at the results] In a nutshell, of the twenty-one teachers who responded, the vast majority emphasize the memorizing of facts, use the lecture-discussion method of teaching, think we should "teach to the test" when it comes to standardized tests, think we should focus on students going to college, give their kids objective tests focusing on levels 1 and 2 of Bloom's taxonomy, think that the SAT measures all six levels of Bloom's taxonomy, and feel that we should keep the current school district grading standards.

SHARON   Wow!

TANYA   And how's this? The majority "somewhat disagree" with Chester's idea for giving merit pay for pre-post achievement gains.

SHARON   No wonder you haven't publicized those results! Aren't you going to have to sooner or later though, since both Christine and Chester know that you collected that data?

TANYA   Maybe. I hope not.

SHARON   Maybe that's exactly what you should do.

TANYA   Why do you say that?

SHARON   You and I both want a change in our grading and reporting procedures. Maybe you should present your results to the committee as an example of how our teachers think. Then we can point out where their thinking will lead the school district if it's followed to its logical conclusion. And who knows, maybe Dr. Wiggams will support our position.

TANYA   You know, you may be right. I guess I was thinking that if I shared the results with the committee, it would solidify their position. But it might force them to examine their position on some of these things and result in change. It's worth a try! What do we have to lose? Thanks, Sharon! I'm going to call Evan Dye right now and ask him to put the results of my questionnaire on the agenda for our next committee meeting.

It is two weeks later. Evan Dye was delighted to put Tanya's questionnaire result on the agenda of the next meeting, and he asks her to pass out copies of her results as th first item of business. All eight members of the committee are present.

EVAN   Tanya, would you please explain to us what you did?

TANYA   Yes, thank you, Evan. The questions really were mine and, I guess, came from a measurement and evaluation course that I took at State. My principal [smiles at Christine] and the superintendent approved the project. I got a 77% return, or twenty-one social studies teachers. I've been told that's pretty good.

DR. WIGGAMS   [Smiling] Anything over 70% is very good. Who was your instructor at State?

TANYA   Dr. Anderson.

DR. WIGGAMS   I'll let him know that you got something out of his class. He'll be delighted.

TANYA   Shall we proceed one item at a time?

EVAN   That sounds good. Go ahead, Tanya.

TANYA   The first question really had to do with instructional objectives. As you can see, most of the teachers were interested in their students' memorizing facts.

CHRISTINE   It looks like a sizable number were interested in current applications, though.

TANYA   I asked some of the teachers afterwards about that, and they said that what they meant was that they wanted their students to bring in current events material from newspapers and magazines to put on a bulletin board or to discuss.

SHARON   Then we're not talking about extended individual or group projects, just relatively brief sharing and discussion.

TANYA   Exactly.

DR. WIGGAMS   I do find it interesting, though, that a few of the teachers had problem-solving goals and wished to emphasize principles rather than facts, although I'm not really sure how they intended to do that.

TANYA   Perhaps question two helps a bit. The majority of teachers primarily prefer lecture-discussion teaching methods. I wish I had asked for more specific information on what they meant by small-group projects. The handful of teachers talked to said that those were usually just group reports on topics being discussed in class, or sometimes a construction project building some famous historical obje like Columbus' ship. However, the teachers I talked to afterwards said that those were of less importance than lecture-discussion and received far less weight grade-wise than test scores.

EVAN   That's not surprising given our SAT and college admissions emphasis in this school district.

DR. WIGGAMS   Yes, that ties in with the responses to items three through five. I can't help but ask, although I'm not sure who I'm directing this question to—given the strong emphasis on test scores and college admissions and even "teaching to the test," has anyone asked how the single-minded pursuit of such goals will affect the non-college-bound and at-risk students? Even if there are programs for such students, are they being neglected as being less important? *[Most nod their heads in agreement.]*

EVAN   *[Smiling]* I think the answer Chester Neal would give you is that we provide for both groups of students well. But the truth is that special pride is taken in students becoming National Merit Finalists and going on to college.

DR. WIGGAMS   And then question six makes sense in that those teachers who emphasize standardized test performance in their classes would be rewarded through merit pay. The emphasis seems clear, although it's interesting that most teachers disagreed "somewhat" rather than "strongly."

EVAN   Yes. I think the idea of being evaluated that way is probably a bit threatening to them.

DR. WIGGAMS   As well it should be. Teachers who teach advanced-placement and elective classes would have a definite advantage in such an evaluation plan. Teachers of required courses such as world and U.S. history would be at a disadvantage, since their students as a group are not likely to perform as well on standardized tests.

SHARON   And that's without even mentioning art, music, industrial arts, physical education, and other areas where such standardized tests don't measure the kinds of things taught in those courses.

DR. WIGGAMS   *[Smiling]* I hope you don't mind, Tanya—I know you're trying to cover these in order—but number nine really shocks me. Do those teachers really believe that the SAT covers all six levels of Bloom's taxonomy?! Don't they know how hard it is to write objective items at levels 4, 5, and 6?

EVAN   What's even more interesting is that, judging by the response to items seven and eight, they realize that their own teacher-made tests only measure the first two levels of Bloom. I guess they think that the experts who made the SAT are able to do what they can't.

DR. WIGGAMS   Yes, and the responses to question nine make me question whether the eight teachers who said they write items that measure all six levels understand Bloom's taxonomy.

TANYA   I asked a few of the teachers about that afterwards, and they said they measure the upper levels with essay questions.

DR. WIGGAMS   Oh. Well, I guess that's possible. But I wonder.

SHARON   But what about the overall picture here? Our teachers are primarily using lecture-discussion teaching methods to teach to standardized tests by getting students to memorize factual knowledge long enough to pass objective tests.

FIGURE 30   Questionnaire Results From Twenty-One Secondary Social Studies Teachers in Three Montcalm High Schools

1. What do you feel is most important for your students to learn in your history classes? (For example, facts, current applications, principles, problem-solving, etc.)

   Facts = 16; current application = 18; Principles = 5; Problem-solving = 3.

2. What teaching method(s) do you use most often in your history class? (For example, lecture, lecture-discussion, extended discussion, small-group projects, individual projects, current events activities, etc.)

   Lecture-discussion = 18; Small-group projects = 16; Current events = 20.

3. How important an objective is it to you for your students to perform well on standardized tests like the SAT?

   Very important = 16: Somewhat important = 5.

4. How important is it that teachers prepare their students for tests like the SAT by emphasizing in class the content covered by the test and the type of test items used on the test (also known as "teaching to the test")?

   Very important = 16; Somewhat important = 2; Neutral = 3.

5. How important an objective is it to you for your students to be admitted to the college level?

   Very important = 18; Somewhat important = 3.

6. Do you agree that teaching should be evaluated (perhaps even for merit pay purposes) by giving the same standardized test at the beginning and end of the school year to measure student learning gains?

   Agree = 3; Somewhat disagree = 15; Strongly disagree = 3.

7. What types of tests do you develop (teacher-made tests) to give in your history classes? (For example, objective, essay, and combination of the two, other)

   Objective only = 13; Essay only = 1; Combination of objective and essay = 7.

8. In terms of the six levels of Bloom's Cognitive Taxonomy, what levels do your teacher-made tests cover? (The levels are: 1.00 = Knowledge; 2.00 = Comprehension; 3.00 = Application; 4.00 = Analysis; 5.00 = Synthesis; 6.00 = Evaluation.)

   Levels 1.00 and 2.00 = 10; Levels 1.00, 2.00, and 3.00 = 3; All six levels = 8.

9. What levels of Bloom's Cognitive Taxonomy do standardized tests like the SAT primarily cover?

   All six levels = 18; Levels 1.00, 2.00, and 3.00 = 3.

10. Do you agree that the school district should keep its current grading standard of 95–100 = A; 88–94 = B, 77–87 = C, 70–76 = D, less than 70 = F?

Agree = 18; Strongly disagree = 3.

11. If you somewhat disagree, disagree, or strongly disagree with question 10, what type of grading procedures do you feel the school district should change to?

Criterion referenced = 2; No district grading policy—Let each school develop its own plan = 1.

DR. WIGGAMS   *[Animatedly]* And with the sincere belief that they are truly helping the students achieve goals of getting into and completing college. It makes you wonder how long the students retain factual knowledge taught that way.

EVAN   Perhaps that suggests some research we need to do here in the school district. *[Dr. Wiggams nods her head in agreement.]* Well, Tanya, I guess that gets us down to the last question. It looks like the vast majority of our social studies teachers want to keep our current grading standards. Although I guess we should note that three teachers strongly disagreed. *[Smiling]* I wonder if any of those teachers are present today on this committee? *[Tanya and Sharon smile.]* I'm sorry. I just couldn't resist that. I see that two wanted to move to a criterion-referenced approach, and one wants each school to develop its own plan. I guess we might also infer from this that most teachers want to keep the same procedures for reporting grades. *[Pause]* Any reactions?

DR. WIGGAMS   Well, although I realize that this just represents the social studies teachers, I suspect that their views are typical of what you might have gotten if you'd surveyed all the teachers in the school district. If that's true, I for one am disturbed about the educational philosophy and biases represented in these results. It's certainly a one-sided view of the world, and I have to ask what the consequences will be in the long run if the school district continues to pursue them.

MR. MONYER   Dr. Wiggams, with all due respect, what's so bad about this report? Let's not overreact. All it says is that the majority of our social studies teachers think that getting our kids to do well on the SAT and get a scholarship and go to college and get a degree is important. They also say that they're willing to teach and grade in ways that will increase the likelihood of their students' reaching those goals. Chester is even willing to give merit pay to those teachers who are especially good in helping their students do their best. Now what's wrong with that? Doesn't everybody want what's best for our kids?

DR. WIGGAMS   Is that really what's best for all of our kids? Is that kind of teaching and evaluation the best our teachers can manage? *[Tanya and Sharon look at one another and exchange a secret smile.]*

EVAN   You ask very good questions, Dr. Wiggams, but I'm afraid the position just state
by Red is the majority one in this school district. The majority of our teachers—
certainly our upper administration and the school board—seem to subscribe to it

TANYA   But does that mean that change isn't possible? Should the majority always dict
to the minority? After all, the United States wouldn't exist as a nation independer
from Great Britain today if the minority hadn't worked to bring about change—
changes that I'm sure we're all glad about now.

EVAN   *[Smiling]* As I recall, it took a war and the death of a lot of people to bring abou
those changes. While making changes in this school system isn't impossible, it isr
easy either. You've definitely got to have something that's clearly better than what
already in place. What kind of grading system would be that much better than
what we have now?

QUESTIONS

1. The superintendent didn't put parents on the grading committee. What were
reasons? Was that a wise move? What is parent involvement, especially in the decisi
making or advisory area, and what are the advantages and disadvantages of such par
involvement?

2. The Montcalm School District places great emphasis on SAT scores and coll
admissions. What groups of students are excluded through such a focus? How can
concentration of personnel, money, and time on such a concern result in the neglec
programs for other groups of students?

3. The majority of the Montcalm social studies teachers emphasized the retentior
factual types of information, such as the memorization of people, places, dates, batt
and events. How long is such information usually retained by students? What are prir
ples, and is their retention by students longer than that of factual knowledge? What is
best way to help students retain historical knowledge?

4. Most Montcalm social studies teachers use the lecture-discussion method of tea
ing history. What are the advantages and disadvantages of this method? Are other me
ods are more effective? If yes, which ones? Why?

5. The majority of the Montcalm social studies teachers had no problem "teachin;
the test" in an effort to increase SAT scores and college scholarships and admissions. 1
usually means teaching the content covered by the test and giving the same types of
items used on the exam. What are the dangers of such an approach? What does the !
actually measure, and what type of testing format does it use? While some believe
teachers can pursue other objectives in addition to "teaching to the test," what is the c
ger of "minimums becoming maximums"?

6. What are the advantages and disadvantages of objective tests? Of essay tests?
combination of the two the best way to test?

7. What levels of Bloom's Cognitive Taxonomy are usually covered on teacher-m
tests? Are essay tests better for testing at the upper three levels? What levels are cove
by most standardized tests like the SAT?

8. Superintendent Neal proposed a merit pay plan for teachers which involved pretesting at the beginning of the school year and posttesting at the end with a standardized test. What are the strengths and weaknesses of such a plan? Why are standardized tests unavailable for some subject areas? What educational objectives would be met if pre-post tests were given? What levels of Bloom's Cognitive Taxonomy would be covered? Would higher-order thinking such as problem-solving be covered?

9. What are norm-referenced, criterion-referenced, and individual standard types of evaluation? What are the advantages and disadvantages of each? Which one of these is the Montcalm School District currently using in this case?

10. Should grading standards like those at Montcalm be established throughout the school system, or should each school or each teacher be allowed to set their own grading procedures? How much commonality in grading practices should exist among teachers?

11. What is the best way to report pupil progress—a report card, a teacher-parent conference, a combination of the two? What would an ideal report card look like?

12. Given the results of the questionnaire, what biases seem to be operating among social studies teachers in the district? What types of self-fulfilling prophecies can be set in motion when such biases operate?

13. What is a change agent? Given the resistance of the Montcalm School District to change, how difficult would it be to get the grading procedures changed? What grading procedures should Tanya recommend to replace the current ones?

WHO'S THE BEST?

Key Content to Consider for Analyzing This Case:
(1) measurement and evaluation (validity and reliabilit
standardized tests, formative vs. summative evaluation
qualitative vs. quantitative research methods, classroor
observation methods); (2) teacher effectiveness;
(3) Bloom's Cognitive Taxonomy.

S tilson is a thriving southern city with a population of approximately 250,000. It
located in a state which borders the Gulf of Mexico and has an east-west expres
way near its northern border. The multiple access to national and internatior
transportation and the progressive attitude of the mayor and city council are two factc
that have enabled this city to become a center of both commerce and culture for t
northern part of the state. The home offices of many southern businesses, as well as t
regional offices of many national and international companies, are located in Stilson.

The management officials of these companies are highly supportive of the Stilse
School System and have encouraged their employees to be supportive also. Two yea
ago, Dr. Vernon Hartley, the longtime superintendent of the Stilson School Syster
retired. Representatives of the business community were instrumental in persuading
vigorous, innovative young educator from New England, Dr. Royce Ryan, to accept t
position. During the two years that Dr. Ryan has served in this position, his leadersh
resulted in a sharp increase in the quality of education provided by the schools a
enthusiastic school support from the community.

A week before classes are scheduled to begin, Dr. Ryan meets with all the buildi
principals for a pre-planning session. After the welcome back to school, the "state of t
school system" address, and a motivational presentation, Dr. Ryan announces that he n
with the members of the board of education the previous week. The school board w
interested in publicizing the high quality of the teachers in Stilson's schools. After expl
ing various courses of action, the majority of members agreed that they would like to i
tiate a program to select the "Teacher of the Year" beginning this year. Dr. Ryan explai
that he wanted to inform the principals first because, obviously, all of their schools wou
be affected by this program in some way. He then calls for questions and/or commen
Marion raises her hand immediately.

ROYCE   Marion?

MARION   *[Enthusiastically]* I like that idea, Royce. Having a "Teacher of the Year" would undoubtedly raise people's awareness of the importance of teachers, and I'm supportive of the idea. But, in a system this large, how in the world are we ever going to make the selection?

ROYCE   *[Smiling]* You've identified one of the most important decisions we have to make, Marion.

MARION   Do you have any recommendations for a procedure?

ROYCE   I've thought of a number of different procedures we could use, but I don't want to make these decisions unilaterally.

MARTIN   *[Speaking out]* It would help me if you'd list some of the procedures that are typically used in selecting a "Teacher of the Year." I've never participated in such a selection, but it seems to me that the teachers should definitely be involved. I've seen research indicating that teachers as a group can generally agree on who the best teachers in their schools are.

TYRONE   *[Speaking out]* Yes. I agree with Martin. Just last week I read an article that said teachers are best at recognizing good teaching. *[Several other principals nod their heads in agreement.]*

ELAINE   I think the pupils should be involved, too. They're the clients of our schools.

ROYCE   Those are both excellent suggestions. And since you're all so modest, I'm suggesting that you principals be involved also. You probably receive more feedback on teachers than any other group in the system. *[Principals nod their heads in agreement.]* May I assume then that those nods signify that you'll participate in the selection? *[Principals laugh and nod their heads again.]* *[Harold raises his hand.]* Harold?

HAROLD   I think it would be great public relations, as well as most appropriate, to involve the parents of our students in making the selection. They're certainly directly involved in the education process.

TYRONE   I agree. But how can we involve all these groups without creating bedlam?

ROYCE   If all of you agree, I'll ask our school system's director of evaluation and research to prepare a survey instrument listing all the teachers in the district. The instrument will include characteristics associated with good teaching and will be sent to all the administrators, teachers, parents, and students in the district. Recipients will each nominate up to three teachers in rank order to receive the "Teacher of the Year" award and return their ballots to the director of evaluation's office for tabulating.

The top three choices will be identified. Then a committee, assisted by our evaluation staff, will collect observation and achievement data to rank-order the three finalists. The winner of the award will receive a monetary stipend and move up three steps on the salary schedule. The runners-up will receive a lesser monetary stipend.

CLAY   That sounds like a lot of responsibility for the evaluation committee to have in the selection. I think they need a coordinator to work with them.

ROYCE   Thanks for mentioning that, Clay. And we do need a coordinator for this project. I've already appointed Dr. Janice Roth of the evaluation and research office to work with the committee on this project. And her assignment will be to do exactly as you

suggested—coordinate the entire data-collection process. She's already working
with the executive committee of the PTA and the local chapter of the American
Federation of Teachers.

CLAY   Great. It's much better to have these groups working with us from the beginning
than to risk their opposition halfway through the project. One more question, then
I'll be quiet. Who'll make up the committee to make the final choice, and how will
they be appointed?

ROYCE   You ask good questions, Clay. The board members suggested that we ask Dr.
Roth to use a table of random numbers to select three names from the roster of
non-finalist teachers. Since it is a teaching award, it seems appropriate that the fina
selection should be made by fellow teachers. These three, assisted by Dr. Roth and
our evaluation staff, will observe the three finalists in their classrooms and assemb
beginning- and end-of-school-year achievement data. [The group sits silently.] Do an
of you have any more questions, comments, or suggestions? [Silence] I'll take the
silence as assent and move on to other business.

Four weeks later, three teachers selected at random have agreed to serve on the fin
selection committee. They are Mark Budd, a high school science teacher, Luann Levy,
fifth-grade teacher, and Mary Weir, a first-grade teacher. They have all arrived at Luan
school, where they agreed to meet with Janice Roth from the evaluation and resear
office. After the teachers finish introducing themselves to each other and visiting for a fe
minutes, Janice hands Mark a sealed envelope.

MARK   Behold! The results of the survey. Shall I open it?

LUANN   [Enthusiastically] Yes! I can't wait any longer!

MARY   Yes, I want to see the candidates, too.

MARK   [Opening the envelope with great fanfare and removing a computer printout] Our thr
candidates for "Teacher of the Year" are Kay Ernst, a third-grade teacher, Bill Matz,
an eighth-grade science teacher, and Sandra Nix, a high school business education
teacher. [Passes the printout to the other teachers]

MARY   I'm surprised that an elementary teacher was selected.

LUANN   Why do you say that? There are more elementary teachers than high school
teachers, aren't there?

MARY   [After a pause] I'm not sure. It just seems to me that high school—or at least
junior high school—teachers are usually nominated for these awards.

MARK   [Looking at the breakdown of the survey returns] This is interesting. According to t
percentages of survey returns, 78% of the administrators, 47% of the teachers, 33
of the parents, and 28% of the pupils filled out their survey forms. I can't
understand why the percentage of teacher response is so low. I'd think that more
teachers would have completed the forms. It's for their own benefit.

MARY   I know why. The teachers union is opposed to the "Teacher of the Year" award
so they instructed their members not to vote. That's why the teacher vote was so
small.

MARK   Why'd the union oppose the award? It was established for the purpose of
honoring a teacher.

MARY   The union position is that it would be better for all the teachers if the district took the money appropriated for the "Teacher of the Year" winners and divided it among all the teachers. The union doesn't seem to like special awards initiated by the school administration.

LUANN   Well, we can't do anything about that now. Let's talk about how we're going to select the winner.

JANICE   Good idea. [Takes some sheets out of her briefcase] Here's the teacher observation form the principals use when they do classroom observations. [Hands a copy to each of the teachers] It seemed to our staff that we should use that instrument, since the teachers are familiar with it and it can be used at all grade levels.

LUANN   That sounds good. Now, the plan is for each of us to observe all three teachers three different times. Is that right? [Janice nods "yes."] So we each make a total of nine observations. Is that right?

JANICE   That's right. At the beginning, middle, and end of the school year. [Pause] Our office will collect data on the pre-post achievement gains of each teacher's students from the beginning of the year to the end of the year. [The teachers nod their heads in agreement.]

MARY   So we won't be able to do the last observation until after the grades come out at the end of the fifth six-week grading period. [Pauses] How are we going to compare the teachers' achievement gains?

MARK   [Smiling] Well, the answer to your first question is "Yes." The answer to the second question is harder. [Looking at Janice] How do you plan to measure the student achievement?

JANICE   We'll give the Metropolitan Achievement Test appropriate to the grade level taught and use the total score for comparison purposes.

MARY   We need to do one more thing before we adjourn. [Pauses] Dr. Ryan's asked our principals to make substitutes available for us for nine school days to provide us with time to collect and analyze the data we need. So I think we should notify our principals of the dates of the nine days we want off, so that they can make arrangements to get substitutes for us. I think we could decide on our days right now, couldn't we? [Luann and Mark nod their heads in agreement.] Good! Let's make our work schedules right now for selecting the candidate. [The others agree]

During the third week of the final sixth-week grading period, Luann, Mark, Mary, and Janice meet again. They have collected and analyzed all the data and now plan to rank-order the three candidates for the "Teacher of the Year" award.

MARY   I'm glad we're meeting today with all the data. It seems like we've been working on this project forever. I hope we can rank-order the candidates today and get this over with.

MARK   Yes. Working with all this information's getting frustrating for me. It's probably because we've been trying to collect and evaluate so much data. It was really hard for me to evaluate the teachers' lessons.

LUANN   I think it's been hard for all of us. After observing and rating each candidate three times, we didn't differ enough to find any real difference at all among the three candidates.

MARK   Well, that doesn't help much, does it? How close were the ratings?

JANICE   Let me get them out. *[Rummages around in her briefcase]* Oh, here they are. Whe we averaged the nine observations on each teacher you observed, the overall average score for each teacher was 176.6 for Kay Ernst, 174.6 for Bill Matz, and 175.6 for Sandra Nix.

MARK   You're right, Luann. Obviously, we can't legitimately discriminate between these three candidates on the basis of a couple of points. *[Turns to Janice]* What kind of differences did you find on student achievement, Janice?

JANICE   Well, we do have differences but, again, they're slight. We converted the total test scores to average stanines. One teacher's students showed what seems to be more significant growth than the others. Bill's students moved from a 5.2 to a 5.7 average. Sandra's students moved from a 5.1 to a 5.6 average. But Kay's students moved from a 4.7 to a 5.9, which is—

MARK   *[Interrupting]* But aren't we comparing apples and oranges?

LUANN   Why do you say that?

MARK   Well, Kay's a third-grade teacher and had the advantage of having the same students all day long and much more flexibility than the other two teachers, who have only one class period a day to teach the material. Kay's scores are based on th achievement of only 28 students, while the other two's scores are based on 151 students in Bill's classes and 183 in Sandra's.

LUANN   *[Following up Mary's remarks]* But you have to admit that Kay's pupils had the lowest test scores at the beginning of the year and ended up with the greatest improvement of any of the students in the study.

MARK   Well, I must admit that I don't know the first thing about elementary education Kay Ernst's class did make the greatest improvement. I guess my problem is that I don't think the procedures we used are valid and reliable in identifying the best teacher in our school system.

MARY   Yes, I've been thinking that same thing from the beginning, but I was afraid that I brought it up someone might ask me what I'd suggest doing instead. To begin with, I don't think that surveying administrators, parents, teachers, and pupils wa a good way to select the three finalists.

MARK   Well, I've read some research studies which conclude that teachers are in the be position to identify who the good teachers are in the school. I'm not sure that administrators even know what goes on in the classrooms in their schools. My principal's never even observed me teach. And surely most parents have no idea about the effectiveness of more than one or two teachers. Many don't even know their child's teacher. And I wouldn't have much confidence in the reliability of students' choices. *[A long pause]*

LUANN   To be honest, I'm not confident that my observation ratings of the teachers are very accurate. I really tried hard to be objective, but to watch a teacher teach and give a number evaluation to twenty different teacher behaviors was very difficult. But, I guess we did end up agreeing with one another. I'm amazed at that.

MARK   Well, we might as well shoot down the way we looked at student achievement gains also. I'm not sure that you can fairly compare the achievement of third-, eighth-, and tenth-grade students with one another.

FIGURE 31   Stilson School District Teacher Observation Form

Teacher: _____   Date: _____   Observer: _____

Ratings 1 = Poor; 2 = Below Average; 3 = Average; 4 = Above Average;
          5 = Outstanding

Observed Behaviors   **Rating**

A. Teaching Procedures

    1. Organization and planning   _____
    2. Knowledge of subject   _____
    3. Presentation of material   _____
    4. Efficient use of class time   _____
    5. Demonstrates interest in all students   _____
    6. Motivational techniques   _____
    7. Variety and flexibility in teaching   _____
    8. Involvement of students in learning   _____
    9. Evaluation procedures   _____
   10. TOTAL SCORE (10–90)   _____

B. Classroom Management

    1. Physical arrangements   _____
    2. Positive classroom climate   _____
    3. Effective monitoring   _____
    4. Clear rules and procedures   _____
    5. Encourages self-discipline   _____
    6. Constant awareness of behavior of all students   _____
    7. Rewards appropriate behavior   _____
    8. Handles misbehavior appropriately   _____
    9. Fair, impartial, and reasonable demeanor   _____
   10. TOTAL SCORE (10–90)   _____

C. Overall Score (20–180)   _____

MARK   Well, at this point I don't think we can do anything but submit Kay Ernst as our
       choice for "Teacher of the Year." Janice, do we have to rank-order the two runners-
       up? I don't think I could do that based on the data we have.

JANICE   I guess we could call it a tie and let them split the money equally.

MARK   Good! However, there is one thing that we could do that would make a
       significant contribution to next year's "Teacher of the Year" contest.

LUANN   What's that, Mark?

MARK   I think we should make a list of suggestions for selecting next year's "Teacher
       of the Year." Surely there must be a better way to do this. Anyone have any
       ideas?

QUESTIONS

1. What research has been done on teacher effectiveness? What are the best proce dures in current use for measuring teacher effectiveness?

2. What are validity and reliability in the field of measurement and evaluation? Ho valid and reliable were the survey, observation, and student achievement instrumen used by the school district?

3. What levels of Bloom's Cognitive Taxonomy does the Metropolitan Achieveme Test measure? Are the upper levels of Bloom's taxonomy measured? Does student achiev ment on this test represent an adequate measure of educational goals?

4. How comparable are the different grade-level forms of the Metropolitan Achiev ment Test? What do they measure, what scores do they yield, and how comparable a their total scores?

5. What is a stanine? What would an average stanine of total test scores represen Does converting the scores to average stanines adequately take into consideration the d ferences in the numbers of students involved (28, 151, 183)?

6. Can the achievement of third-, eighth-, and tenth-grade students be validly cor pared? How comparable are the characteristics of students at those different age levels? the elementary school experience (self-contained) comparable to the separate-subjec approach at the junior and senior high school levels?

7. Do the achievement test differences take into consideration differences in the ab ity levels in the students being compared? What data could be used to take such diffe ences into consideration?

8. Does it make sense to survey the four major stakeholder groups to determine tt three finalists? How adequate were the return rates? Do these stakeholders know the be teachers in the school district? Do teachers know the best teachers in their own school

9. How valid and reliable are classroom observation forms like the teacher observatic form? Can the form be used across grade levels? How many observations would be des able with such an instrument?

10. What are formative and summative evaluation procedures? Which was involved this case? Would it be desirable to use both if this award is to be given each school yea

11. What is the difference between qualitative and quantitative research method Which method is the most useful in studying teacher effectiveness? Which hold the grea est promise in determining the "Teacher of the Year" in a school district?

12. How would you answer Mark's question about how the procedures for selecti the "Teacher of the Year" could be improved? What would be a better way to do it?

A

THEORY GUIDE

T he purpose of this theory guide, like the starter questions at the end of each case, is to assist the student and the instructor in beginning the process of case analysis. It is organized as follows: content areas, subtopics, and specific theories are presented from the field of educational psychology. After each are the numbers of the cases that especially lend themselves to analysis using the content or theories. Needless to say, the student will need to learn more about the application of the content from such sources as the library, the course textbook, and the course instructor.

1. Educational Psychology
   a. History, 1
   b. Research Methods, 1, 2
2. Human Development
   a. Physical Development, 3, 6, 15
   b. Social Development, 3, 5, 6, 21
   c. Language Development, 3, 21
   d. Cognitive Development (incl. Piaget), 3, 4, 5, 9
   e. Moral Development, 7
   f. Personality Development (Erikson), 5, 7
   g. Child Abuse, 6
3. Learning Theory
   a. Operant Conditioning, 3, 9, 10, 13, 14, 20, 23
   b. Observational Learning, 6, 7, 9, 10, 20, 21, 22, 23, 24
4. Cognitive Theory
   a. Information Processing Theory, 5, 7, 12, 13, 16, 18, 27, 29
   b. Meaningful Verbal Learning (Ausubel), 5, 12, 13, 14, 16
   c. Bruner's Cognitive Theory, 13, 14, 16
   d. Constructivism, 5, 12, 13, 14, 16
   e. Cognitive Style, 4, 8, 13

USING CASES
IN COLLEGE TEACHING

T he *Commonwealth Center News* (Spring/Summer, 1991, p. 2), published by th
University of Virginia at Charlottesville, reported that the preliminary results of
survey of its readers' involvement with the case method of college teachin
revealed the following: (1) the case method was being used at ninety-five sites through
out the United States, Canada, and overseas; (2) although fewer than 15% of the respon
dents reported that they used cases as the sole method of teaching their courses, mon
than 80% used cases for some individual lessons; and (3) the most common reaso
respondents gave for using cases was to enhance the critical analysis and problem-solvin
skills of their students. Although such surveys might indicate a trend toward increase
use of the case method in college teaching, the lecture-discussion method predominat
in college classrooms. One reason for this may be that college professors see little valu
in using cases, but our guess is that most college instructors do not use the case metho
largely because they do not know how to do so. The purpose of this appendix is to shar
what we know about using the case method in the hopes of remedying the situation.

The senior author began to use cases as a graduate student back in 1965 under th
tutelage of Dr. David Gliessman at Indiana University. The junior author's experience go
back even further, to his undergraduate years at Ohio University in 1952, where he wa
first exposed to cases in an engineering course taught by a Harvard-trained professor.

WHY USE CASES?

Before getting into the "how" of using cases, we should first address the issue of "wh
educational psychology instructors should use the case method. Teacher education pro
grams in general—and educational psychology courses in particular—have made too li
tle provision for the application of theoretical knowledge and have all but ignored th
development of the most fundamental of all teaching skills—professional decisio
making. Learning to be systematic in decision-making and to be aware of cognitive pr

cessing during decision-making take just as much practice as acquiring relevant bodies of psychological, sociological, pedagogical, and organizational knowledge. In short, to be an effective decision-maker, one needs to practice decision-making. Moreover, this practice needs to be distributed over a variety of decision areas. Cases make excellent application vehicles for developing metacognitive decision-makers.

The case method can focus on a number of different instructional goals. In education it can provide the student with the opportunity to translate theories, principles, and methods into practice. Cases can also be used as vehicles for getting students to think at the upper levels of Bloom's Cognitive Taxonomy. Also, cases can serve as facilitators for (but not substitutes for) actual teaching experiences. Working through cases may help teachers develop metacognitive strategies for dealing with actual teaching situations. Further, case studies represent a middle step between course work and actual teaching experience, especially when the case used resembles events actually unfolding in schools. In short, we view good cases as realistic vehicles for the development of decision-making skills and effective teaching behaviors in the real world of teaching.

Finally, we agree with Broudy (1990), who argues that cases may even be used as a means of establishing a professional knowledge base in teacher education. He argues that if teaching is to become a profession comparable to law or medicine, it must reach a consensus regarding which problems teacher education should focus on. These professional core problems could be presented in teacher education in the form of cases.

USING THIS BOOK

The cases in this book have intentionally been left open-ended and unresolved. This permits their analysis using a variety of theoretical and conceptual frameworks. It is important that students understand that there is no one correct way for a problem situation to be analyzed. A theory or set of principles fits a situation if the student shows that it does. Different frames of reference may produce different courses of action in dealing with a given situation. Hence, for educational purposes, a theory is the correct one to use if the student shows that it fits the situation by citing evidence; similarly, a decision is correct if it is consistent with the frame of reference used. The goal, quite simply, is to force students into higher-order thinking regarding the knowledge base on which teaching practices rest.

This case book can be used either with another text or texts, or as the primary course text, with the library or teacher handouts serving as the students' primary source of reading materials. As for its integration into existing course syllabi, the following (all based on actual experience) are offered.

1. The cases can be used at the end of a course to provide practical application activities for the previously covered theoretical material.
2. One or more cases can be presented at the beginning of a course to help establish a practical rationale for the ensuing theoretical material.
3. Relevant cases can be mixed into units of theoretical study. For example, a certain theory or set of related principles can be studied for two weeks, followed by a week or two of application to relevant cases. Some variation of this pattern is probably the most common method of using cases.

4. Cases can be used as the basis of small-group decision-making activities. Such procedures have been employed by the senior author and are described in depth later in this appendix.

5. Cases can serve as the basis for role-playing activities in which the students act out the roles at the point where the case situation ends. Videotaping such role playing activities adds still another dimension to the learning process. Seeing themselves playing, for example, the role of a teacher on videotape can be bot illuminating and motivating for students.

6. Finally, the cases provide an excellent evaluation device for tapping the upper levels of Bloom's taxonomy, especially the application and analysis levels. The cases can be used in a pretest-posttest fashion to assess student gains in subjec matter mastery or in decision-making. This appendix offers a practical format for using the cases in this fashion.

As these points illustrate, this text can be used in many ways that will add variety an spice to educational psychology courses and strengthen student learning and decisio making.

CASE METHODS AND GOALS

How do college instructors go about using cases to help preservice and in-service teac ers become more effective decision-makers? A variety of teaching methods are availabl and the number of methodology books and national conferences on the case methc seems to be increasing. Before discussing the range of methods, we will first examine tl teacher as a decision-maker, since that rationale (which is presented in the Introductic of this book) for explaining the relationship between educational psychology as a scienc and teaching as an art is a very popular one and is usually presented in the first chapt of many educational psychology texts. The question is, how can the case method be use to help make teachers more effective decision-makers?

When presented with a case (or a real-life teaching situation, for that matter), fro what sources do teachers derive their decisions? From our perspective, DuBois, Alverso and Staley (1979) provided one of the best answers to this question when they listed s sources: (1) teaching traditions; (2) philosophical traditions; (3) social learning; (4) sc entific research on learning and development; (5) conditions existing in the school ar community; and (6) the teacher's own needs. Any or all of these may be brought to be when a teacher chooses a frame of reference to use in analyzing a case. Most education psychology instructors, of course, are interested in getting their students to learn to u theories, models, and sets of principles derived from scientific research on learning ar human development.

What steps are involved in the decision-making process? Allonache, Bewich, ar Ivey (1989), who conducted workshops on improving decision-making skills, focus c four steps: (1) clearly defining the matter to be decided; (2) listing alternative solutior to the problem; (3) weighing the pros and cons of each alternative; and (4) implemen ing the choices made.

Steps one, three, and four might be further subdivided or elaborated. To the first step might be added thinking about the problem from multiple points of view (e.g., that of the teacher, students, parents, principal, etc.); and using professional knowledge about teaching, learning, and human development as frameworks for examining and discussing the situation. Likewise, step three might be elaborated to include forecasting the probable consequences of each alternative. Finally, step four might be revised to include specifying and operationalizing courses of action involved in implementing the choices made.

The variety of case methods used in college classrooms seems to primarily revolve around a problem-solving or decision-making model like the one described above. Recent books by Colbert, Trimble, and Desberg (1996) and Anderson (1995) present a number of teaching methods used by a variety of college instructors at different institutions, and we hope that other books of this type will soon be available. Our more modest purpose in this appendix is to present how we use the case method, not the universe of case methods available to the educational psychology instructor.

With large groups (e.g., an entire class), the most widely used and demonstrated method of working with cases is undoubtedly the discussion method. After the case material is handed out and read by the students, the instructor uses a variety of techniques, many of them reminiscent of encounter group procedures used in the 1970s, to draw students into the process of analyzing and resolving the case. Knowing what questions to ask and how to draw students into the discussion are skills that can be learned by watching experts work. Getting students to examine and clarify the issues involved from multiple perspectives are definitely skills that most college instructors can acquire.

Cases have been used in a variety of ways besides large-group discussion. Our approach, which we call Small-Group Decision-Making (SGDM), involves working with students in groups of three to six members and will be described later in this appendix. One of the more unusual uses of cases involves acting out a case and its resolution using either regular acting methods by following a script or by using more spontaneous role-playing and/or sociodrama techniques. Sometimes such acting or role-playing is videotaped and critiqued in a manner resembling the microteaching methods used in the 1970s in teacher education. Some cases have been computerized so that a student can personally interact with the cases at a computer terminal. No doubt educational technology's role will become even more important in the future.

Gliessman, Grillo, and Archer (1988) have described a method of using cases called "thinking aloud triads." This technique involved students working on a case in groups of three. One member of the group thinks aloud about the case problem and its solution while a second group member listens and poses questions that seek clarification. The third member of the triad, called the observer, records the psychological concepts expressed by the first group member. The roles of the three students may then be reversed to work on a different case or to work on a different aspect of the same case. The work of such triads could be videotaped, and the students could produce a group paper which might be evaluated using criteria like those described at the end of this appendix.

STUDENT-DEVELOPED CASES

Having students develop cases—either based on their personal experience or by gather
ing case material from teachers—can be an excellent class project. Such cases can focu:
on local and regional issues that are not presented in casebooks like this one. Furthe
benefits to the student developing a case may be derived if the student is allowed to lea
the discussion of the case when it is presented in class. Such participation should encour
age students to develop their critical thinking and decision-making skills.

A number of legal and ethical issues arise when students develop cases. It is no
enough to have the student change names and places in a case developed from informa
tion provided by a teacher. Not only does the teacher need to sign informed-consent an
copyright releases, but the school district employing the teacher may need to do so a
well. If the case is developed as a class project, some, perhaps most, institutions of highe
learning may also need to approve the project through its research review board. Finall
a student-developed case belongs to the student who develops it, not to the professor, s
professors must obtain all legal permissions and copyright releases from such student
before publishing student-developed cases in a casebook like this one.

Assuming the proper observance of all legal procedures, how might an undergrad
uate or graduate student go about collecting case information and writing it up? The
instrument on pages 303–308 is one that the senior author has developed and used fo
this purpose. The reader should feel free to revise, adapt, and use it to fit the local situa
tion. The first section of the instrument is addressed to the student.

SMALL-GROUP DECISION-MAKING

The case method used by the senior author for over thirty years involves working wit
small groups of three to six students as they analyze and resolve a case, usually in th
form of a ten-page paper. All students in the group get whatever grade the paper receives
We have come to refer to this case method as Small-Group Decision-Making (SGDM)
and we will describe how we normally use it in both graduate and undergraduate educa
tional psychology classes taken by arts and sciences majors as well as education majors.

SGDM is based on a number of assumptions about the use of case methodology
First, we assume that students have to learn to analyze a case from one perspective befor
they begin to examine it from multiple perspectives. Second, we assume that the per
spective that preservice and in-service teachers should begin with is that of the teache
rather than that of the principal, parent, or student. Learning to view situations from mul
tiple perspectives is a long-term goal, not a beginning exercise.

A third assumption is that educational psychology students should use theories
models, and sets of principles that they are studying in their courses as perspectives fo
analyzing cases. The goal is one of learning to translate theory into practice. Our fourt
assumption is that, as students learn to analyze cases in terms of the course knowledg
base, they need to learn the process of defending their analysis by citing appropriate evi
dence from the case. Our fifth assumption is that the courses of action that the studen
decides the teacher in the case should follow to successfully resolve the case should b

FIGURE 32   Interview Schedule for Case Development (pp. 303–308)

Writing Up a Case

Your job is to conduct an interview with a classroom teacher and write up a case regarding either the most difficult or most frequently recurring problem situation he or she has faced as a classroom teacher. You will have to obtain signed legal approvals from all parties involved to do this project, and you should probably tape-record (with permission) the interview. Follow the interview protocol that follows. The final product should be a typed case in the format used for the cases in the casebook.

Problem Case Interview

(To the teacher/interviewee) You are asked to provide your name and other personal information in the event that your problem situation is selected for publication. If that happens, we would need to know how to contact you in order to gain the appropriate permissions. Also, be assured that if your problem is selected, the names of all persons and places will be changed to ensure confidentiality.

The time that you spend in this interview may make a valuable contribution to teacher education. It is extremely important that education majors be exposed to and be given the opportunity to grapple with real teaching problems like the one you will be describing. Your assistance is greatly appreciated. (At this point explain and obtain informed consent from the teacher.)

Current Personal Information

Date _____

Name _____ Sex _____
        (Last)   (First)   (Middle)

Years of Teaching Experience _____ Highest Degree Held _____

Current Teaching Position (Grade and/or Current Subject) _____

FIGURE 32 Interview Schedule *(continued)*

Current School _____

                  (Name of School)   (City)   (State)

Home Address _____

               (Street)   (City)   (State)   (Zip)

Home Phone No. _____ School Phone No. _____

            (Area Code)   (Area Code)

     1. Begin by looking back over your teaching career. What are the two or three most difficult problem situations you have had to face as a teacher or ones which seem to come up over and over again? The problem could have dealt with individual students (e.g., motivation or discipline), an entire class, other teachers, work with administrators, school-system-wide problems, situations involving parents, etc. All that matters is that you consider them difficult, not whether you were able to deal with them. When you have finished recalling the two or three problem situations, move on to the next step.

(The space below is provided for notes.)

FIGURE 32 Interview Schedule *(continued)*

2. Now, decide which one of the two or three problem situations was the most difficult or frequently recurring one for you. Once you have decided, provide the following background information about that situation.

Background Information

A. Where were you teaching at the time? Name of the school, school district, city, state (remember, the real names will be changed if your problem situation is used):

_____

_____

B. What type of school population was served by the school and the school district? For the school, please give:
   (1) Socioeconomic status (SES) breakdown (approx.) _____

   _____

   (2) Racial/ethnic breakdown (approx.) _____

   _____

   (3) Other relevant information _____

   _____

   For the school district, please give:

   (1) An indication of the size of the area that it served—for example, large urban, medium-sized city, small town, or small rural farm district. _____

   _____

   (2) Other relevant information _____

   _____

FIGURE 32 Interview Schedule *(continued)*

C. Give some personal data regarding yourself at the time the problem occurred.

(1) Year(s) and month(s) during which the problem occurred

_____

(2) Years of teaching experience _____

(3) Age _____

(4) Grade level and/or subject taught _____

(5) Any relevant personal factors (e.g., divorce, financial difficulties, pregnancy, etc.)

_____

_____

D. Please describe the people involved with the situation. Change their names if you wish, since they will be changed later anyway. Just present the "cast of characters"—don't describe the events that occurred here.

FIGURE 32 Interview Schedule *(continued)*

3. Now describe the events in the situation as they unfolded. The closer you can stick to exactly what people said and did, the better. Present quotes if you can. The format you use in describing the events in your problem situation is not as important as your being totally honest and as factual and complete as possible. However, if you feel like expressing your originality by describing the problem situation in the form of a play or a diary, that would be great!

(Attach additional pages as needed.)

FIGURE 32 Interview Schedule *(continued)*

4. Now that you have described the problem situation, summarize it by labeling the essence of the problem in a few words (for example, "A problem of motivating a child from a middle-class home who has overprotective parents").

_____

_____

_____

5. At the beginning of this form you were asked to think of the two or three most difficult problem situations you have faced before you narrowed them down to one. In the space provided below, please summarize the essence of the *other* one or two problem situations just as you did in #4 above for the problem you decided was the most difficult.

(1)

_____

_____

_____

(2)

_____

_____

_____

consistent with the way the student has analyzed the case, reasonable and practical to implement, and described in sufficient operational detail.

A sixth assumption is that the decision-making processes require that students engage in higher-order cognitive levels of thought. In terms of Bloom's Cognitive Taxonomy (Bloom, Engelhart, Furst, Hill, & Krathwohl, 1956), the application, analysis, synthesis, and evaluation levels are the ones most often involved. Students select a framework, apply it to the case, cite evidence to support the application, generate courses of action consistent with the analysis (some of these can be quite creative), and evaluate the possible courses of action in order to select the ones that might work best. Students who are applying a theory, model, or set of principles to a case engage in cognitive processing quite different from learning the same material to take an objective or even an ordinary essay exam.

Procedures

As we mentioned, cases are often used with the entire class using large-group discussion procedures. SGDM involves working with students in small groups of three to six members. Some instructors prefer to use only the case study method in teaching a course. We generally use the case method for a portion of the course. Normally, the course content is presented using traditional methods and is then followed by one or two case studies that involve approximately two weeks of class time each. Students typically work on a case both inside and outside class over a five-week period that involves ten fifty-minute periods of in-class time over a semester, interspersed with regular class meetings. As is true in many areas of education, distributed practice is better than massed practice for doing case studies.

Prior to beginning the first case study, we introduce the students to the process of case analysis through a brief case study that lasts two class periods. In this "mini" session, students (1) begin by stating what is going on in the case in their own words; (2) choose a theory or set of principles that best explains the way they have analyzed the case; and (3) cite evidence from the case to support their analysis. They do not generate courses of action in this warmup exercise. When groups have difficulty getting started, the questions at the end of the case and the theory guide are usually helpful. Often all it takes for a group to get started is for the instructor (of an educational psychology class, for example) to ask questions such as How could you say the same thing in psychological terms? or What do you mean when you talk about needs?

After a case has been assigned by the instructor or chosen by the students (as will be discussed later), each group might be given the following directions for dealing with the case:

1. Briefly analyze in psychological terms the problems faced by the teacher. Use only as much psychological theory as you need to fully cover the problem, and use only one theory if possible.
2. Cite behavioral evidence to support the application of each of the theories you have used. Be sure to indicate what you are supporting with each behavioral event that you cite.

3. State the courses of action the teacher should take to deal with the problem. Each course of action you suggest should be operational and feasible and should be consistent with your analysis on a point-by-point basis. The courses of action should fully cover the problem as you have analyzed it. Do not switch theories as you move from the analysis to generating courses of action.

In order to assist the students in producing the typical group product—a ten-page paper containing the analysis and resolution (or decision) regarding the case—each student is given a handout such as the following.

Characteristics of a Good Case Study Paper

Objectives. Each group or student will (1) analyze the case in psychological terms and objectively support the analysis with evidence from the case; and (2) present courses of action for the teacher to execute that are consistent with the analysis, feasible to execute, and operationally stated.

1. Begin with an overall statement of the problem in the language of the theory you are using. Cover all the main points and people in the case, and use the theory correctly and fully in applying it. This will normally be done in a paragraph or two.

2. Support each main point that you make in your overall statement at the beginning with evidence from the case. The kind of evidence that you cite will vary according to the theory you use. For example, an operant approach might involve a functional analysis employing only external, observable events. However, be sure that each main point that you have presented in your overall statement is systematically supported by whatever type of evidence you use.

3. Regardless of the theory used, the support evidence should be presented systematically and objectively. The reader should be able to relate it back to the theoretical contentions you are supporting, and, in most cases, the evidence should be quoted as it is presented in the case.

4. The analysis and decision parts should be clearly labeled and separated from one another.

5. Each main point you make in the analysis should be dealt with by one or more courses of action that you recommend in the decision section. This is a systematic, point-by-point process.

6. Each course of action you recommend in the decision part should clearly follow from and employ the ideas and language of the theory you used in the analysis. For example, do not analyze in operant terms and then shift to dealing with "self-concepts" or "internal beliefs" in the decision part.

7. Each course of action that you recommend should meet the tests of feasibility and operationality (as presented in the Introduction to this text).

8. The complete paper should consist of a title page with all group members' names on it, ten pages of analysis and decision, and references at the end on a separate page. Also, the paper should be footnoted as needed. In the case of the case text, however, you need only indicate the page number(s)

at the end of the text quoted in parenthesis, and you do not need to list it
in your references. Otherwise, use APA style. The ten-page paper limitation
is not hard and fast, but try to organize your thoughts and paper so that
you can come as close to it as possible. The title page and references do
not count as part of the ten pages.

9. Use correct grammar, punctuation, and spelling. For example, paragraphs
should have topic sentences, subjects and verbs should agree, and words
should be spelled correctly. Avoid sentence fragments and run-on sentences. Double check your typing and get the paper in on time. Remember,
one letter grade will be deducted for each day late.

Before we present the evaluative criteria used in scoring a paper, a couple of points
should be made. First, while a ten-page paper is the usual group product, the instructor
is certainly not limited to that outcome. In some cases, students have acted out the decision they have developed. In one workshop, classroom teachers acted out a case situation
while students videotaped the action, and later the students developed and acted out a
decision. The decision was then critiqued by the teachers who did the original acting.
Given enough time, equipment, and creativity, the possibilities are many, and are certainly
not confined to student papers.

Second, groups of undergraduate students are told to focus the decision on the
teacher in the case, that is, to generate courses of action for the teacher to execute that
follow from the analysis. They are further told that they do not have to concern themselves with presenting their plans to the teacher or motivating the teacher to execute
them. They just have to tell the teacher what to do. Of course, the test of any plan is to
execute it in the real world and observe the consequences. However, the students will not
be able to do that until they are in actual teaching situations.

On the other hand, if an instructor is working with graduate students or in-service
teachers, it may be important to learn how to work with the teacher as well as with the
other persons (parents, principal, etc.) in the case. For example, a school psychology
major may want to develop consultation strategies, or an educational administration
major may want to focus on how to handle the teacher in the case, rather than just
develop strategies for the teacher to use.

Evaluation Criteria

Each group (student) is usually handed the following six evaluation criteria which will be
used to score their paper.

1. *Application of appropriate psychological theory to case analysis.*

   a. The theory must fit the situation. Use only one theory if possible.
   b. All facets of the situation must be covered—hence it may be necessary to
      use more than one theory.
   c. Theories or sets of principles used must be clearly identified and used cor-
      rectly. Use the language and concepts of the theory for purposes of analysis.

2. *Objectivity of analysis.* All key contentions in the analysis must be supported
by evidence from the case that is objectively cited. Behavioral events in the case are

FIGURE 33 Case Study Evaluation Form

Case Study Evaluation

I. Application of Theory

_____ a. Theory clearly identified and used correctly

_____ b. Theory fits case

_____ c. Covers all facets of the case

II. Support for Theory

_____ a. Support is cited for all key contentions made

_____ b. Support is objectively cited (quotations, no inferences)

III. Consistency Between Analysis and Decision

_____ a. Point-by-point consistency exists

_____ b. Relationship between Analysis and Decision is stated

IV. Feasibility of Solution

_____ a. Courses of action are reasonable and practical for situation
described (teacher time, ability, cost)

V. Operationality of solution

_____ a. Easily replicable (clearly spelled out what should be done and
how)

VI. Organization of Paper

_____ a. Two parts clearly labeled (Analysis and Decision)

_____ b. Good, easy-to-follow order of key contentions and courses of
action.

_____ c. Typed, 8.5 × 11-inch paper, correct spelling and grammar,
approximately ten pages, APA style.

_____ Total Points

best reported as quotations or in terms that are as objective as possible. Do not try to paraphrase or summarize the evidence, and do not use inferences from the evidence to support your analysis unless the inferences are clearly labeled as such and are the only support available.

3. *Consistency between analysis and decision.* Divide your paper into two parts and label them "Analysis" and "Decision." There should be an almost point-by-point consistency between the two. Do not analyze a problem in humanistic terms, for example, and then suddenly shift to a stimulus-response model in arriving at a decision. The decision should logically flow from the analysis. It is best to indicate right in the paper how you see the decision flowing from the analysis rather than leaving it up to the scorer to figure out what the relationship is.

4. *Feasibility of the decision.* This criterion includes whether the decision you are suggesting is practical in the school situation described in the case. Demands on teacher time, abilities, cost, and so on must be considered.

5. *Operationality of the decision.* The decision should be operational enough that a teacher applying the decision can see the steps involved in putting it into operation. Be specific and spell out clearly how the teacher should deal with the situation. You *do not* need to worry about how to get the teacher to follow your advice. You may assume that the teacher will automatically do so.

6. *Organization of the paper.* If you use sources other than the case text, deductions will be made if the paper is not footnoted or does not have some kind of bibliography. A good paper will have the following organization:

   a. The paper will be divided into analysis and decision, and the two parts will be clearly labeled.
   b. The overall problem will be stated in psychological terms in the first paragraph or two.
   c. Each key psychological contention will then be objectively supported, one by one, with evidence from the case (the "Analysis" section).
   d. A consistent, feasible operational decision that follows on a point-by-point basis will come next under "Decision."
   e. The paper should be neatly typed, double-spaced, and the rules of spelling and grammar observed. The paper should be on 8.5-by-11-inch standard-sized typing paper and should not ordinarily be longer than ten pages, exclusive of title page and bibliography.

From the beginning, the instructor makes clear the evaluation criteria that will be used to evaluate the group product. Sometimes groups divide into subgroups. In other instances, individuals decide to leave a group and do an individual paper. Whatever grade is assigned to a group paper is shared by all the members of the group.

Each paper may be scored on a five-point scale for each of the six criteria, yielding a total of thirty points. Such scoring may be presented in a format such as that shown in the figure on page 312, which can be attached to each paper for feedback purposes.

SGDM Processes

Forming the Groups

The small groups of three to six students can be formed in a variety of ways. Student could choose with whom they want to work, or they could be assigned to groups b means of a table of random numbers. A third approach is to assign them by interes groups. The latter involves having them skim all the cases and then giving them three-by five-inch cards on which to rank-order the three cases that bother them the most whe they think about the job of teaching. Students are then assigned to groups on the basis c their choices. The choice of assignment procedure should be guided by the instructor objectives and feel for student dispositions and abilities.

Selection of Cases

Just as the small groups can be assigned in different ways, the case and theory that th group uses can be chosen either by the students or by the instructor. The instructor ma want all groups to work on the same case or on different cases. Also, the instructor ma want all the groups to use the same theory or may want the students to decide which the ory is most appropriate for the case. For example, if an educational psychology instruc tor wants the students to learn how to apply the principles of observational learning, th instructor would direct the students to use that theory on the same or different cases However, this is usually done when more than one case is used during the semester an the second case involves student choices.

Even if the instructor allows the students to decide which case to work on, it ma be wise to limit the number of cases from which they make their selection. For example some cases lend themselves to an observational learning analysis more readily than oth ers. Also, the instructor's evaluation procedure may dictate that only one or a few case be used by all the groups.

The Instructor's Role

Once the small groups are formed, the instructor begins by asking the group members t exchange names, addresses, phone numbers, and schedules (to set up outside-of-clas meetings). It is also important at the beginning for the instructor to lead a discussio about the importance of being an effective group member and to provide strategies fo dealing with nonproductive group members.

Once the groups are formed and the case chosen or assigned, each group is aske to select one of its members as group recorder. It is the recorder's job to (1) keep th instructor informed of when and where of all group meetings are to be held; (2) kee attendance at all official group meetings; (3) be sure that the group paper gets turned i on time and in the proper form; (4) make certain that the group meets with the instruc tor as needed; and (5) facilitate the collection and turning in of the evaluation form tha group members use to evaluate one another's contributions. (An example of an evalua tion form used by the students is presented on page 316.) After appointing a student a group recorder, the instructor moves from group to group, sometimes just listenin sometimes answering questions, and at other times asking questions for the group t think about.

Knowing when to engage and disengage from a group is a skill that an instructor gains only with experience. This is especially true when disagreements threaten to split a group, or when the group is deciding what to do about a member who is not contributing. The instructor's first inclination might be to step in and tell the group what to do. We have found, however, that groups often work out solutions better than the one the instructor would have suggested. The instructor should simply be available and ready to support and advise. The instructor will certainly have to serve as a resource by suggesting books and journal articles the students may need to obtain to learn more about the theory they are using.

In SGDM each group works together as a unit until it is time to crystallize the oral or written product. Members of the group usually divide up the labor in terms of gathering data (reviewing the literature, interviewing teachers, etc.), and use others (and the instructor if they desire) as sounding boards for their ideas. As mentioned earlier, a group consensus is not necessary. If, when they are at the point of preparing a product for evaluation, individuals or subgroups differ from the rest of the group in the way in which they analyze and reach a decision, they are free to prepare a separate product. In the case of a group or subgroup product, all the members of the group or subgroup receive the same evaluation.

Students are told at the beginning that the case study activity has two purposes: (1) to learn to apply the material learned in the course, and (2) to learn to work with others in small groups. The latter is something that teachers have to do throughout their professional careers (curriculum committees, textbook adoption committees, report card committees, etc.). They are asked to work with their group for at least one week. If at some later point the groups subdivide or individual students wish to do their own paper, that will be their choice. However, part of the purpose of the activity is learning to work with and relate to others.

Student Group Evaluation

Each small group will work somewhat independently of the instructor at times, and we usually ask each group member to confidentially evaluate the contributions of the other members of the group. We use that information as one measure of course participation. The instrument on page 316 may be used for that purpose.

Cycling and Extending

The entire SGDM process, from choosing the case to be analyzed to submitting a product to be evaluated, usually takes about ten one-hour class periods. Students usually have to meet outside as well as inside the class. The SGDM cycle can be repeated for the rest of the semester or combined with other procedures. As we have mentioned, it can move progressively from written materials to real-life experiences. Moving from written cases to filmed cases to videotaped real teaching situations to observing real teaching situations to actually engaging in teaching would be one such series of transitions.

The best test of a group decision would be to execute it and examine its consequences. This may be possible if the students have access to live teaching situations. For example, after working with cases like those in this book, the instructor might arrange for a real teacher to describe a case that he or she is currently facing. The students could

FIGURE 34   Student Evaluation Form

Group # _____

Rate the contributions of each member of your group during the case study by circling the appropriate rating opposite their name. Do NOT rate yourself. Also, the RECORDER ONLY in each group should put the number of absences for each group member (including the recorder) from all "official" group meetings in the space provided. Rate each group member's contributions according to the following scale:

O = Outstanding
A = Above Satisfactory
S = Satisfactory
B = Below satisfactory
U = Unsatisfactory

Name (first and Last)	Rating (circle one)					(For recorder ONLY) # Absences
_____	O	A	S	B	U	_____
_____	O	A	S	B	U	_____
_____	O	A	S	B	U	_____
_____	O	A	S	B	U	_____
_____	O	A	S	B	U	_____

gather data by interviewing the teacher, observing in the classroom, and so on. After ana-lyzing the data and mutually arriving at a decision with the teacher, they can let the teacher test the courses of action chosen. A next step would be to actually put the stu-dents in teaching situations and let them blend theory and experience themselves. The students can continue to meet in groups to receive help with whatever problems concern them or are identified by the use of videotape or some other means. Resource people (reading specialists, psychologists, special education specialists, etc.) could be invited to attend group sessions when the need arises. Such small-group activities make sense for teachers on the job as continuous in-service training activities. But whether the activities are in-service or preservice, the goal is always to help teachers develop strategies for translating theory into practice.

REFERENCES

Allonache, P., Bewich, G., & Ivey, M. (1989). Decision workshops for the improvement of decision-making skills confidence. *Journal of Counseling and Development, 67,* 478–481.

Bloom, B. S., Engelhart, M. D., Furst, E. J., Hill, W. H., & Krathwohl, D. R. (1956). *Taxonomy of educational objectives. The classification of educational goals: Handbook 1: Cognitive domain.* New York: Longmans Green.

Broudy, H. S. (1990). Case studies—why and how. *Teachers College Record, 91,* 449–459.

Colbert, J. A., Trimble, K., & Desberg, P. (Eds.). (1996). *The case for education: Contemporary approaches for using case methods.* Boston: Allyn and Bacon.

DuBois, N. F., Alverson, G. F., & Staley, R. K. (1979). *Educational psychology and instructional decisions.* Homewood, IL: Dorsey Press.

Gliessman, D. H., Grillo, D. M., & Archer, A. C. (1988). *Teaching educational psychology through a problem solving process.* Paper presented at the meeting of the Midwestern Association of Teachers of Educational Psychology. Bloomington, IN.

McAninch, A. R. (1995). Case methods in teacher education. In L. W. Anderson (Ed.), *International encyclopedia of teaching and teacher education* (pp. 583–588). New York: Pergamon.